PURCHASING AND MATERIALS MANAGEMENT

Integrative Strategies

PURCHASING
AND
MATERIALS MANAGEMENT

Integrative Strategies

Joseph L. Cavinato, C.P.M.
Pennsylvania State University

WEST PUBLISHING COMPANY

St. Paul   New York   Los Angeles   San Francisco

Copyright © 1984 by WEST PUBLISHING COMPANY
50 West Kellogg Boulevard
P.O. Box 43526
St. Paul, Minnesota   55164

Printed in the United States of America

Library of Congress Cataloging in Publication Data

Cavinato, Joseph L.
    Purchasing and materials management.

    Bibliography: p.
    Includes index.
    1. Purchasing.   2. Materials management.   I. Title.
HF5437.C38   1984   658.7   83-25972
ISBN 0-314-77869-1

To Mary, Janet, and Josh

Contents

Preface

Purchasing is a vital, prime activity of a firm. It attempts to secure materials and components in the right form, quantity, and at the time needed by the firm. Cost and quality problems can start here and ripple through the entire organization. Purchasing decisions have wide-reaching effects throughout the entire firm as well as with customers.

Purchasing has long been regarded as a distinct function to be optimized onto itself. That is, minimized purchase expense and minimized purchase operating costs have been traditional functional goals. But, a firm is an entire matrix with interaction and impacts occurring between each and every function. In this vein, purchasing has strong ties with production, distribution, customer service, finance, and marketing. A decision in any one of these areas causes cost and/or savings impacts in the others.

The distribution movement of the 1960s and 1970s brought to light the benefits of integrated outbound logistics activities in a firm. These include transportation, warehousing, order processing, finished goods inventory management, and other activities. The supply problems and the high cost of capital since the 1970s has caused a decided shift in many firms to integrate purchasing closer to the rest of the firm. *Integration* is the key to the current and future scene in purchasing. This integration will involve inbound inventories, transportation, storage, and production scheduling as well as marketing and overall corporate strategy of the firm.

This book is about integrated purchasing. It starts with an overview of the key strategic concerns of a firm and then proceeds to the traditional functional areas of purchasing, which include the evolving and growing management directions of the field. Materials management is the study of the entire inbound flow of goods into a firm in as efficient a manner as possible. This area is covered in depth, since it is an area to which purchasing is directly linked. An understanding of product management and pricing is essential to the study of purchasing. This covers both understanding the marketing role of the employing firm as well as those pricing strategies employed by firms selling directly to purchasing. Finally, effective organizations and their measurement are presented along with a look at purchasing in the future.

This text presents each chapter in terms of the study objectives to be gained and includes text material, sources used as well as those available for further reading, questions for review, and problems and cases. The book can be used as a resource in studying for Modules I, II, and III of the C.P.M. exams of the National Association of Purchasing Management.

Special thanks are extended to the reviewers of this manuscript who include Larry C. Guinipero of Florida State University, Victor H. Pooler of Carrier Corporation, and Arch G. Woodside of the University of South Carolina. A warm thanks is also extended to Lisa Jennings, Suzanne McHugh, Stephanie Szuba, LuAnn Jaworksi, Janine Andrews, and Janet Confer who helped in many ways to prepare this book. Finally, thanks go to Bill W. Osborne, CPM, Divine Providence Hospital, William F. Gibson, Sprout Waldron Division of Koppers Company, J. Bud Bell and Thomas H. Smith both of International Paper Co, Wilmer E. Burget, The Pennsylvania State University, Mary Ann Hoffman, Frito-Lay, Inc., Martin Garelick of New Jersey Transit Rail Operations, Robert Novack, Drackett Company, and Kathy P. Cornelius of Stroehmann Brothers Bakeries. And a final but not a small thanks to Bob Pashek and John Coyle who create the environment for things to develop and grow.

Section I presents the basic functions and processes of purchasing ranging from defining the step-by-step order and receiving processes to determining and obtaining optimum quality, final cost and assurance of supply, negotiations, and the legal realm of purchasing.

Section II explores advanced topics of purchasing. Many of these have become part of purchasing or have increased in importance in the past decade. These include purchase timing, capital asset acquisitions, taking advantage of the new environment in transportation, international purchasing, value analysis, and some special topics relating to supply strategies for the firm.

Section III covers the materials management aspects of the firm of which purchasing is a basic component. These topics include the role of materials management, inventory control, and the production-purchasing interface.

Section IV presents contemporary issues and opportunities in purchasing. One of these deals with product management of which purchasing is a key component. The understanding of vendor and the firm's own pricing strategies is covered in this section to give insights into how purchasing can take advantage of, or is constrained by, pricing. And, purchasing in wholesale and retail settings is covered along with government agency buying systems.

Section V concludes the book with analysis of organizational issues in purchasing. It deals with organizational design, trends in performance evaluation, and future directions in measuring and evaluating information needed for decision making. The future of purchasing is covered in a final chapter with points on further integration of departmental functions in the firm and other factors that will shape the task of purchasing in the future.

Though this book is about purchasing, the role of this function is expanding. This trend will continue as firms attempt to tighten coordination and control over all resources at their disposal. Purchasing in the future will require more and more "business decisions" and fewer "purchasing decisions."

PURCHASING AND MATERIALS MANAGEMENT

Integrative Strategies

PART 1

STRATEGIC PURCHASING:
THE BASIC CONCEPTS

Modern production and service organizations exist for a single or multiple set of purposes. They serve a public need by providing a product or service that is in demand. Determination of an organization's exact product or service offering entails defining a market or public need and designing the resources to meet that need. In many settings this is called strategy formulation. That is, the role and direction of the organization and its product, people, skills, and financial and productive resources are oriented toward a set of goals through a series of strategies.

Purchasing is a major component to a firm's fulfillment of strategic goals. Long considered by many in management as being a passive "order transmitter" on instructions from production and other user departments, purchasing today and in the future must be proactive and a major contributor to the firm's overall planning and operating scheme. Purchasing is the firm's eye on the supply resource markets it will use to meet its own strategic ends.

This section is devoted to the primary functional aspects of purchasing and materials management. Basic processes and procedures, price and cost analysis, quality, assurance of supply, negotiations and the legal realm of purchasing will be discussed. These basic factors underlie the entire purchasing function.

INTRODUCTION

WHAT IS PURCHASING?

> Early Period
> Sales Period
> Coordination and Control Period

PURCHASING IN THE EVOLUTION OF INDUSTRIAL ECONOMIES AND FIRMS

PURCHASING OBJECTIVES

IMPACT OF PURCHASING DECISIONS UPON THE FIRM

> Importance of Purchasing to the Firm
> Purchasing's Effect Upon Company Profit
> Purchasing Versus Sales Impacts Upon the Firm

STRATEGY IN THE FIRM

> The Need and Role of Strategy
> Components of Product Strategy
> Strategy Implementation
> Purchasing and Strategic Advantage of the Firm

EVOLUTION OF PURCHASING AND MATERIALS MANAGEMENT

> Traditional Organizations
> The Systems Concept
> Materials Management Concept
> A Trend Toward Logistics?

APPROACH OF THIS BOOK

CHAPTER OBJECTIVES

After reading this chapter you should:

- Understand the basic functions in purchasing.

- Appreciate the roles of corporate and product strategy and their impact upon purchasing and vice versa.

- Be able to quantify the impact of purchasing upon the profitability of the firm.

- Relate purchasing to materials management, distribution, and logistics.

Strategic Purchasing in the Firm

Introduction

Purchasing often represents a major share of the total expenditures of a firm. Raytheon, the major appliance and electrical manufacturing firm with sales of over $5.5 billion annually, has a small purchasing group of 38 persons who are responsible for buying goods and services that cost nearly half the total sales of the firm.[1] Heinz, the food processor, spends $77 million yearly just to buy glass containers for its products.[2] And PPG Inudstries, Inc. has a corporate-wide group of 155 that procures over $1.6 billion of goods each year.[3] These are just three examples of the magnitude of purchasing within a firm.

What Is Purchasing?

Purchasing in a *narrow* sense is the act of buying goods and services for a firm. In this way it is the activity of placing orders and often checking their condition upon arrival. This is a very limiting view, and the firm that considers its purchasing function in this manner is restricting itself from many opportunities. In a *broad* sense purchasing is the activity of obtaining goods and services for a firm. This concept encompasses any and all activities necessary for carrying out long- and short-term functions for acquiring goods and services.

Materials management is the term applied to the planning and management of all inbound goods and services into a firm. The term originally covered the act of raw material inventory control designed to efficiently feed a firm's production line. It now encompasses all activities necessary for the efficient flow of goods and services into a firm at the lowest total system cost and best timing possible. Materials management necessarily encompasses production scheduling, raw material and work-in-process inventory management, inbound transportation, materials handling, storage, and purchasing. Thus, in a broad sense purchasing is a part of materials management.[4]

Purchasing and materials management are very much a part of the strategy of a firm. Strategy is defined as "the science of planning and directing operations of...forces into the most advantageous position prior to actual engagement."[5] In a business or organizational setting, this means planning and directing the resources of the firm in order to capture the marketplace and achieve the corporate objectives the firm is seeking. The term "tactic" is a related concept. It is a short-term plan of action designed to achieve an immediate objective. Materials management and purchasing are very much a part of the overall strategic processes in a firm. Much of the thrust of this book is designed to present these functions within the overall role of the firm and its marketing missions.

Purchasing in the Evolution of Industrial Economies and Firms

The roles of purchasing and materials management have changed greatly in the evolutionary development of firms. They are two functions that have changed in operations, emphases, and roles as perceived by top management, since their early development in the 1800s. Their roles cannot be separated from the overall concept of the organization and its own role. A brief discussion of the evolution of industrial economies and firms will illustrate this point.

Early Period

The era from the early 1800s to about 1920 in the United States is often referred to as one production orientation. The economy was expanding, exports were growing as the U.S. enjoyed advantages in export trade, and the population of the country was becoming larger through immigration. Markets were generally larger than the capacity to supply them. The shortage of capacity in many industries provided high profits. The emphasis in firms was on production output and ways to increase it. Sales were not a problem, and the role of marketing was, in some cases, nonexistent. Obtaining the capital goods to manufacture and the raw materials to apply to these assets was the key to profitability.

Purchasing was often a clerical function designed to obtain needed goods in any way necessary. Often there was only one source available or top management had a long-term arrangement with a favored supplying firm. Purchasing meant buying and expediting goods. There were few supply choices to analyze and select, and little opportunity or need to study supply prices, since there was limited choice in the first place. Inventory was not valued as a resource the way it is today. Instead, inventories meant the ability to produce and sell. A good buyer was one who was able to keep the production line going.

Sales Period

During the 1920s production capacity in the U.S. began to catch up with the overall demand. No longer was the possession of a factory the key to financial success. Emphasis in firms turned to ways of stimulating demand to maintain sales from the production output. This began a period of sales orientation. From the 1920s into the 1970s major top-management stress in many firms was upon marketing. This was the era during which market research, customer service, market segmentation, product proliferation, and the overall marketing concept evolved. Firms often measured their overall strategic success in terms of maximized sales and sales growth. Market share was an important objective to maximize.

During this period purchasing continued to grow in responsibility and sophistication, but overall management emphasis did not recognize it as a major strategic function of the firm. Purchasing became important during periods of wartime commodity shortages, and its status was elevated in many firms as a major amount of the firm's resource dollars each year were spent in purchasing. But, still the main stress was upon sales and marketing, and most other functions in the firm were viewed as supportive to these.

Coordination and Control Period

The shock of energy, material, and capital shortages and cost fluctuations in the 1970s brought an abrupt change in the way many firms oriented themselves. Shortages caused many firms to shift toward financial emphasis through the judicious control and coordination of all resources in the firm. Since supply was no longer unlimited and materials and capital costs were no longer stable, firms sought to maximize financial performance through efficient use of all materials, capital assets, inventories, manpower, and funds. Inventory was now seen as an expensive asset that was difficult to control. Many firms found themselves with the wrong inventories at points of low demand and few goods where they were greatly needed. Top management emphasis turned to productivity, physical distribution, and materials management.

Demarketing was a concept that was born in the U.S. during this period. It is the active step of withdrawing from many of the markets and submarkets a firm traditionally has serviced. In practice this appeared as discontinued product lines, items in old product lines being dropped, geographic regions no longer served or abandonment of sales to certain segments of the marketing channel of distribution. The job of purchasing and materials management became more difficult because, for the first time in decades, firms faced supply markets in which goods were not always available, fewer suppliers and less competition existed, and forced substitutions became common practice. The impact of demarketing by suppliers forces buying firms to rethink what products and markets they should serve in the future. This put purchasing in the position of having to warn or inform its own company that long-standing products may no longer be available or might become uneconomical to use. The buyer might go so far as to suggest that the firm should possibly drop a product it produces that requires certain materials. In other words, purchasing turned from being a passive buyer of products dictated by marketing and production to an active participant in the overall product decision process of the firm.

The specter of soft economies throughout the 1980s stands to blur the distinction between the marketing and the control and coordination emphases in firms. In a soft economy supply tends to be plentiful, and prices for purchased goods are soft. This tends to spur production in a firm in an effort to maintain use of machinery and labor. Pressure then becomes great for marketing to stimulate sales. On the other hand, the tight supply situation in the 1970s brought to the fore the prospect that many commodities and minerals might be potentially scarce in the future. This will no doubt be seen again when the industrialized economies of the U.S, Western Europe, Japan, Korea, South Africa, and the USSR are on the upswing. This will turn many supply-glut markets into seller's markets, with upward pressures on prices and tightness of capacity and supply.

In either situation, it is imperative that firms plan with a long-term view of purpose and strategy. Short-term management with emphasis upon the current quarter financial performance alone will not lead to long-run survival. Instead, future opportunities and problems must be defined and charted. A strategic mission must be a part of this process, and every component of the firm must be seen as a part of the input to and attainment of corporate goals. Purchasing and materials management are very important to this process.

Purchasing Objectives

The overall objective of purchasing is to obtrain maximum value in goods and services for the firm. Maximum value means the lowest possible amount is spent to obtain the needed or desired physical or aesthetic qualities in goods and services. The cost includes the cost of the goods as well as the timing and movement costs associated with acquiring and positioning the goods for use by the firm.

Purchasing has many specific managerial objectives that are embodied within the maximum-value concept. Specifically, purchasing has the task of obtaining goods at the *right price*, for delivery at the *right time* and to the *right place*, with the *right quality* and in the *right quantity*. This requires an efficient organization that is effective in long-run planning and implementation as well as utilizing appropriate tactics to attain short-term ends. In carrying out the specific and overall objective, purchasing uses many managerial objectives, including the following:

- Buy at the lowest possible price
- Maintain a high turnover of inventory
- Assure a supply of goods for the firm
- Obtain consistent quality
- Develop reliable and competitive sources
- Maintain good supplier relations and goodwill
- Utilize vendor resources to the firm's advantage
- Cooperate with other departments
- Provide input to the firm's overall objectives
- Diminish the administrative costs of purchasing and materials management
- Maintain effective record and other information systems

■ Develop, motivate, and train materials management and
purchasing personnel and managers[6]

The roles of purchasing are varied. Some are simple, while others are
complex. Some relate to day-to-day operations in purchasing, and others
have pervasive, long-term impact upon the firm. Purchasing is no longer seen as a passive function with little more than a clerical mission in
the firm. It is now viewed by most top managements as being one component in the entire set of resources available for the attainment of corporate goals.

Impact of Purchasing Decisions Upon the Firm

Importance of Purchasing to the Firm

Purchasing has the responsibility of acquiring goods and services
needed in production, for production, or for direct resale. It converts
cash and the relatively liquid resources of the firm into physical goods
and services. Since purchasing is changing the firm's resources from
low-risk assets into those having less flexibility, it has a major responsibility to assure that its decisions are sound. The importance of purchasing decisions within the overall expenditures and uses of the firm's
sales dollar is seen in Table 1-1. This table shows how the many broad
categories of U.S. industries spend resources for materials, direct production labor, and energy. Purchasing is directly involved in the decisions to acquire the materials and energy.

Industries range widely in terms of the importance of the cost of purchase goods and materials versus the sales dollar. On the whole, the ratio ranges between forty percent and sixty percent of sales revenue and
is generally the largest single component of expenditures in industry.
Thus, the decisions made by purchasing directly impact upon the costs
and profitability of a firm.

Direct production labor is generally the responsibility of the personnel or the human resource department of a firm. Purchasing is often said
to be the manager of "outside production" for the firm.[7] That is, it acquires goods that have been produced by other firms in other factories.
In this way, the labor cost component of the industry and firm that purchasing buys from has a direct bearing upon the price paid for materials
it will use in its own factory. The cost of a vendor's labor is a component
of the price paid by the buying firm. The evaluation of prices paid in relation to the labor setting in a vendor industry is presented in Chapter 3.

Energy is another component of purchasing. This resource became
more important during the 1970s than in previous decades. Many purchasing departments are involved in analytical work designed to provide the firm with lower energy cost alternatives. These alternatives
range from investigating lower energy cost machinery to heat recovery
and the actual production of electricity at the factory site. This is a supply strategy activity that more and more purchasing managers are becoming involved with as the costs of energy continues to climb.

☐ **TABLE 1-1.** *Manufacturing Industry Costs for Materials, Labor, and Energy*

Industry	Costs as Percent of Shipment Value		
	Materials, Parts, & Containers	Production Wages	Energy
All Manufacturing	53.7%	11.6%	2.5%
Food and Kindered Products	69.5	6.1	1.3
Tobacco Products	51.5	6.2	.7
Textile Mill Products	55.9	15.3	2.8
Apparel Products	41.7	18.0	.7
Lumber and Wood Products	55.0	14.5	1.9
Furniture & Fixtures	46.4	18.8	1.2
Paper & Allied Products	51.9	12.1	5.7
Printing & Publications	27.8	14.7	.8
Chemicals & Allied Products	46.5	6.3	5.4
Petroleum & Coal Products	81.0	1.8	2.5
Rubber & Misc. Plastics	48.1	14.8	2.4
Leather & Leather Products	49.0	18.5	1.0
Stone, Clay, & Glass Products	38.4	16.3	7.3
Primary Metal Products	56.3	13.6	6.8
Fabricated Metal Products	47.2	16.0	1.5
Machinery, except Electrical	43.5	15.0	1.0
Electric & Electrical Products	42.5	14.6	1.1
Transportation Equip.	60.5	12.2	.8
Instruments & Related Products	34.7	13.0	1.0

☐ Source: *Census of Manufacturer's—1977* (Washington, D.C.: U.S. Government Printing Office, 1979).

Purchasing plays an important role in the impacts that occur from price increases or decreases for the goods and services it procures. All other things being equal, a $1 savings in purchase price results in a $1 profit increase; a cost increase by the same amount, on the other hand, harms the firm by $1 of decreased profit.

Purchasing's Effect Upon Company Profit

Purchasing has a direct bearing upon the profitability of a firm. The term profit applies to three key measures that are used to describe the periodic financial performance of a firm. The first is profit as a percent of sales. This is a rough measure of how much is left over from sales revenue after all costs of the firm have been paid. It is a general measure of the profit-generating potential of sales and operating activities. The second is asset turnover. This is a measure of how effectively the assets in the firm are being utilized. It is found by dividing total assets into the sales revenue for the year. A high asset turnover is considered generally better than a low asset turnover. The third key measure is return on assets. This is a measure of the profit-generating power of the firm based upon the assets necessary to produce the profit. This figure is akin to the interest return that people relate to savings accounts or money market fund earnings. A higher return figure is better than a low one.[8]

The interaction of all the key company financial components to the overall profit is seen in Exhibit 1–1. A hypothetical company is shown with revenue of $1.00 for the year. Purchases cost $.55, depreciation $.15, and other costs of operation are $.25, for a total cost of $.95 for the year. Profit is $1.00 less $.95, or $.05. Use of assets, cash, inventories, and other assets total $.40. Sales are $1.00, which sets asset turnover rate at 2.5 times. Profit as a percent of sales is .05 (or 5 percent) and the asset turnover rate of 2.5 times causes company return on assets to be 12.5 percent. This shows how a firm might have a low return on sales but a high turnover thereby resulting in a good overall return on assets. Another firm might have a very high return on sales but a low asset turnover to result in a low return on assets. All three indicators are viewed separately as well as in a combined manner.

Purchasing is important to the firm in many ways that are examined here.

Purchase Price Reduction
A reduction in purchase price by one cent reduces the cost of purchases from $.55 to $.54, and total company costs to $.94. Profit is now $.06, and profit as a percent of sales has increased from five percent to six percent. Return on assets is now .06 × 2.5 = 15 percent. A reduction in

■ **EXHIBIT 1–1.** *Interaction of Purchasing/Materials Management Functions upon Firm*

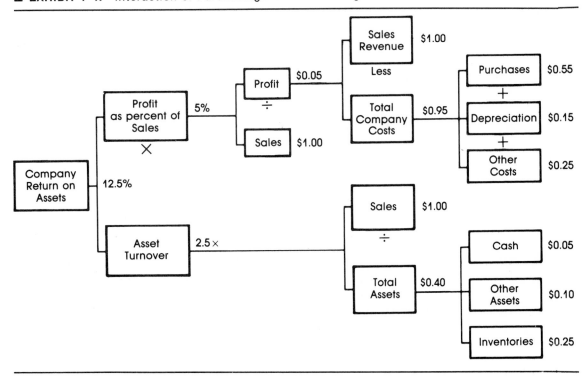

purchase price has a direct positive impact upon sales profit and return on assets.

Build Up in Inventory

Inventories likewise have a direct bearing upon the return on assets. Assume, for example, that the firm has a lax inventory control system. Over the years, its total assets are valued at $.30 instead of $.25. Annual purchases still amount to $.55. This causes profit as a percent of sales to remain at 5 percent with sales still $1.00. Total assets now are $.45 instead of $.40 and asset turnover is 2.22 times instead of 2.5 times. The return on assets is now .05 × 2.22 = 11.1 percent. Thus, any increase in assets without a corresponding change in sales or operating costs will result in a decrease in asset turnover and a drop in return on assets.

Quantity Discount Purchase at Reduction in Price

A common situation facing purchasing managers is the opportunity to buy a larger than normal lot of goods at a lower unit cost. This occurs with rate breaks offered in transportation and price breaks offered by manufacturers. As an example, a buyer may obtain goods at a price that causes the purchase cost to drop to $.53 while total inventory will rise to $.28. The question is: should the buyer take advantage of this price/quantity lot? Using Exhibit 1-1, total company costs would be $.93 and profit as a percent of sales of .07, or 7 percent. Total inventories rise to $.28 with total assets becoming $.43. Asset turnover is now down to 2.33 times. Company return on assets is 16.3 percent. Thus, it is wise to purchase the lot.

The price/quantity discount can backfire, however. Assume that a price break of $.01 could be obtained with a lot size that causes inventories to increase to $.33. In this case, profit increases to 6 percent of sales, or .06. Asset turnover drops to 2.08 times and return on assets drops to 12.48 percent.

In summary, purchasing decisions affect the firm's financial performance in many ways. Purchase price increases and decreases directly affect profits. Purchase lot-size decisions and timing of purchases affect inventories and asset turnover. Large inventories also bring up the problem of possible obsolescence, which often causes inventories to be disposed of at very low prices and harms the profits of the company. Large inventories might also require substantial storage space commitments which increase the "other costs" and thus decrease profits. On the other hand, inventories that are too small might cause inventory turnover to become high, but the lack of goods might cause production downtime and lost sales that could harm profits. Purchasing decisions have a wide impact upon the financial performance of the firm as well as that of other departments within the corporate structure.

Purchasing Versus Sales Impacts Upon the Firm

Purchasing generally has a larger profit-producing potential in a the firm than marketing does. This is seen with the profit impact of $1 savings in the purchasing area versus a $1 additional sales made by the marketing

☐ **TABLE 1–2.**

Purchasing Impact upon Profit

	Current Situation	$100 Savings in Purchases	$100 Increase in Sales
Sales	$1,000	$1,000	$1,100
Purcahses	550	450	605*
Other costs	400	400	400*
Net Profit	$ 50	$ 150	$ 95*

*At a rate of $.55 per unit on each $1 unit sold.

department. The income statement in Table 1–2 illustrates this concept using the data from Exhibit 1–1.

As in Table 1–2 indicates, each dollar of savings impacts directly upon the net profit of the firm. Additional sales, however, must be made with additional purchases each of which cost $.55 in acquisition costs. This is not to say that the firm should place its major emphasis upon purchasing and not marketing. It merely illustrates the power of dollar savings versus marketing gain when the firm might have a choice of one effort or the other.

A simple formula can be used to determine the effect of savings in purchasing versus the impact from additional sales. It is:

Profit Potential of Purchasing Versus Marketing =

$$\frac{\text{(Purchase Cost as a Percent of Revenue Dollar)}}{\text{(Profit as Percent of Revenue Dollar)}}.$$

In the example in Exhibit 1-1, purchase expenditures are $.55 on each revenue dollar or 55 percent. Profit as a percent of sales is 5 percent. It can be computed either as 55 percent/5 percent or $.55/.05, which is eleven times. Thus, a purchase savings has eleven times the profit-improvement potential as similar amounts of increases in sales revenue.

The concept of a larger profit potential in purchasing than in marketing generally carries through for most industries or firms. The relative amounts of improvement potential are different depending upon the material cost and profit-to-sales ratios. For example, Table 1-1 shows material costs comprising only 27.8 percent of the revenue dollar in printing and publishing while it is 81.0 percent in petroleum and coal industries. A comparable percent reduction in purchase costs in both industries will result in a larger total dollar impact in petroleum and coal versus printing and publishing, all other things being equal.

Analyses such as these should be conducted on before-tax bases, giving due consideration to the accounting treatment of inventories. Many tax-related opportunities exist today for finance managers to reduce corporate cash outflows through tax provisions. Firms can be inherently profitable and experience positive cash flows and yet report taxable losses. For this reason it is more precise to use before-tax profit rates for studies such as these. Similarly, inventory may be valued in any number of ways by the firm. It may be on a FIFO, LIFO or other basis. These topics are discussed in further detail in Chapter 14. For the present, it is crucial to understand that the value of the inventories sitting on the shelves inside the company might not be the same as that reported on the corporate income statement and balance sheet.

Strategy in the Firm

The Need and Role of Strategy

Strategy is the process of establishing long-run goals for the firm in order to position it advantageously in the market. It involves defining the best mission for the firm and laying out the plan necessary for achieving it. Ideally, strategy should be an on-going process that establishes the functional directions for the firm and its departmental components and operations. Strategy definition and direction is a prime element in corporate survival and health.

Corporate strategy involves setting the direction in which the firm wishes to move in the future. Examples are the development of new technology that might be used in the firm's current products as well as other products not now produced. This can be seen in the micro-chip area where long-standing firms with traditional products seek to gain future competitive advantages by developing new capabilities for their products. In other areas, some firms seek to withdraw from their traditional production technology because of lower-cost foreign competition. Instead, the firms seek to enter into other lines of business. In still other areas, some firms seek to shift from serving industrial markets to directly enter into consumer product lines. These are some examples of corporate strategy. They are long-run in nature because they involve careful analysis, capital investment, and the shifting of management and worker talents into new areas.

Firms cannot rely upon each department maximizing its own performance to assure this long-run survival. Instead, the general direction must be established by top management to guide and coordinate lower echelon planning and operations. The strategy of a firm shapes both short- and long-run decision making in each department. Without this departments could possibly conflict in actions to the detriment of the firm, with little guidance for reducing or eliminating the inherent problems. Even within one department, knowing the direction or strategy of the firm enables individual managers to make sound daily decisions that can contribute to long-term goals as well. Such is the case in one primary metal firm that is turning away from that activity and shifting toward finished goods production. The shift will take many years, but the purchasing manager has this goal in mind when hiring persons from other firms. Rather than emphasize skills in the primary metals area, she is now stressing finished metal fabrication skills in the hiring decision. This is establishing a bank of necessary skills in the firm before they are actually needed, but they will be in place when the firm begins such operations. If this was not done, the lack of necessary skills in the purchasing area for the new activity might represent a disadvantage or bottleneck to the success of the new operations.

Strategy formulation and implementation is a very necessary activity in firms. A view of the marketplace shows that most successful firms today are not producing and marketing the same product or product lines that they were a few decades ago. Some basic food brand items are exceptions, but these firms have changed by adding new products to the old lines. Products require a substantial investment to be developed and introduced; their life cycles are shorter than in the past, and strategic nonproduct operations are often the key elements that cause some of these products to be profitable for their firms. The firm must have a direction of purpose in order for it to remain in the marketplace. Firms that merely continue to produce and market the same products and/or manage them the same way as in the past will eventually be preempted by other firms or products.

The modern marketing concept is a basic component to the formulation and carrying out of a strategy in the firm. In a very basic form it states that the firm's existing and potential customers are the bases for product directions, that the firm attains growth and profitable reward by meeting the needs of these markets, and that the firm must be integrated with a corporate-wide emphasis for it to be met.[9] The orientation of this concept is toward the customer; it recognizes that the customer's needs are more important than merely viewing a physical product per se.

The implications are strong for all functions within the firm. This states that the firm is not in the prime business to produce and sell Product X. Rather, Product X might be statisfying a current need, but that need may shift and leave the firm behind if it does not recognize the fact. The firm should shift with this changed need, and it should be positioned to produce or sell anything that meets market needs and that rewards the firm with profits. The firm should not be viewed as a producer of Product X only. Rather, it is a collection of people with certain skills and a production facility that not only produces Product X buy any other product that meets market needs if Product X should become unprofitable or if other opportunities for profit arise.

Though marketing and product design and planning are primary components to corporate strategy, purchasing plays a major role in it as well. Purchasing buys the components that become the finished product for the firm. In this role, purchasing might otherwise be a weak link by acquiring poor quality items or items at a high cost that harms the final marketability of the product. In another role, purchasing is in a position to learn of new materials or components that might improve the current product. It can also suggest components not always known of by product designers and engineers. Purchasing is also in a position of being able to warn the firm of future price and material supply problems that may threaten the output or cost of the present product. In still another sense, purchasing can apply knowledge of product strategy to enhance its effectiveness as buyers of products marketed by vendors. By understanding basic strategy elements, the buyer can take advantage of opportunities in the supply market and avoid or reduce the effects of problems there as well.

Components of Product Strategy

The previous discussion centered around corporate strategy—the over-all direction the firm is seeking over a long period of time. Central to this decision is the strategy applied to the products produced and sold by the firm. This section examines the key components that make up product strategy.

Product strategy is carried out in many ways. The *product and its technology* are perhaps the main items of strategy. The product might be distinct and fulfill the needs of a certain segment. Unless the product is patented, the strategic advantage gained by product design might be short lived. Successful products are often copied or imitated by others thereby reducing the competitive edge of product design. Advantages in product distinction can be attained through differences in aesthetics. Taste, smell, color, design, and overall appeal are examples. These are important in foods, clothing, textiles, publishing, and most consumer market goods.

Process is another strategic product component and refers to how the product is actually produced. A stamped part is different from a molded one. Glass shapes can either be cut or pressed. Quality differences in many metals and chemicals exist due to the method of manufacturing.

Price is a key strategic advantage to seek in the marketplace. A lower price gains an advantage in the market. Pricing in consumer markets can also be used to seek an edge through creating a snob appeal for the product. But, in industrial and even retail purchasing, price is a key facet of the competitiveness of most any firm's products. This subject is covered in greater depth in Chapter 19.

Channels selection is another strategic decision firms must face in the market and refers to how the product is distributed from the firm to its ultimate customers. Channel options include direct producer-to-consumer links and the use of wholesalers, retailers, or other channel functionaries.

Channel margins are the differences between purchase costs and selling prices obtained by agents, wholesalers, and retailers when handling and selling the products of the manufacturing firm. A high margin encourages middlemen to promote the product to their customers. But a high margin can cause the product to be priced too high or cut into the producer's own profit. On the other hand, too low a margin will generally cause middlemen to slight the item in their marketing efforts.

Level of integration is a strategic element that defines the degree to which the firm produces all of the components needed in the product. A high level of integration means the firm owns and controls the raw material supply and all other functions through to final, finished goods sale. A low level of integration is found when the firm does not actually produce the goods, but contracts for others to produce it. Integration has implications for costs, prices, availability of supply, and control over the flow of goods from raw state to final customer.

Service on the product or in conjunction with it is another facet of strategy. This includes the repair and maintenance of an item as well as assistance in installing and using it. Service can be more global in the form of a sales and engineering staff that provides consultant services to customers having problems.

Promotion is yet another product strategy element and refers to how the product is marketed. Advertising and public relations about the firm are included here. Customers may be reached through such varied media as magazine advertisements, mailing brochures, trade show contacts, sales calls, contacts via other persons, through channel firms, etc.

Purchasing directly affects all of the above product strategy elements except perhaps channel selection, channel margins, and promotion. The product is the result of design decisions that are carried out by buyers who acquire the component parts or materials. Purchasing managers can directly influence this area by suggesting alternative materials or methods of manufacturing by suppliers. These decisions relate to the technology and quality of the final product as well as its cost. They bear directly upon the price charged by the firm, and indirectly upon the margin allowed subsequent middlemen. Level of integration is important with regard to the make-or-buy decision with which purchasing is involved. Purchasing is the buyer of "outside manufacturing."If the suppliers are not efficient or not adequate in some way, a source of last resort is often to produce the needed item in-house. Many other factors enter into this decision, but purchasing provides much information and analysis leading up to the make-or-buy decision.

Strategy Implementation

Strategy formulation is a process of determining what directions provide the best opportunities for the firm in the future. It is a top-management planning process that considers future market potentials, the role of present products, and the capabilities and weaknesses of the firm's present facilities, management, workers, and financial posture. Long-run strategies define the mission or long-run objectives of the firm. They are the ultimate goals toward which individual operations should strive. These goals may be as long as ten years into the future.

The initial implementation of corporate strategy involves interim operational plans that typically have five-year spans. It necessitates the use of policies that guide management actions toward the integration of functions necessary for bringing about the strategic goals. These are operational plans that guide work in research and development, call for new coordination between marketing and distribution in order to move toward another channel system, involve engineering and purchasing in the are of materials research, or require integrated product development work by most departments of the firm.

On the most detailed level, strategy is implemented through use of functional plans or objectives. These are departmental in scope. They are generally short run, involving no more than one year in most cases and stipulate objectives for each department to be accomplished during the year. These might be, for example, the bringing on-line of an integrated distribution-production-materials requirements planning system, the alteration of a product to include a new component, or the development of new specific skills in the personnel of a department.

The strategic process begins with an overall objective and is continuously fine-tuned into cross-functional objectives and detailed departmental goals. It is an on-going process that does not necessarily require the long-term goal to be fixed. In fact, that goal may change or be deleted as time passes.

The strategic process is important to individual managers in purchasing and all other functions. It entails the efficient daily functioning of each operation, but it requires each manager to have an eye toward shifting that department's operations in a direction needed by the firm.

Purchasing and the Strategic Advantage of the Firm

Purchasing plays a key role in the overall strategy of the firm. Many of the long-run product planning, materials modification, and long-run supply market factors were already discussed. On an operational level, purchasing plays many important roles as well.[10]

Cost advantage over others in the market is one strategic advantage that can be sought by purchasing. A cost advantage permits the firm to price its own product below others in the market. Some of the approaches that can be investigated are other sources, international suppliers, integration back into supply areas, and many others that are presented in this book.

Product features that make the firm's marketed item different from competitors is another strategic advantage to which purchasing can contribute. This might be accomplished through different materials, altered design from value analysis, or other inputs that purchasing may be in a position to suggest to the rest of the firm.

Product quality is a primary facet of strategic advantage by the firm. Purchasing plays a major role here in the sourcing decisions it makes with respect to various vendors.

Product timing is often mentioned in strategy literature as an advantage a firm might seek. This relates to the timing of products, entry into the marketplace, or the mere availability of product when competitors do not have sufficient capacity or materials to supply the marketplace. This is particularly important with the introduction of new products that are in strong demand. It is also important when the firm's product is special ordered. The customer might select a firm as its chosen vendor in a purchase because its promised lead time is the shortest of all possible vendors. The key factor might be the presence of purchased items needed for production, which the buyer was able to obtain at the time needed.

Product availability is another strategic element of the firm upon which purchasing has a direct impact and refers to the ability of purchasing to obtain goods in a tight supply market as in the commodity shortage period of 1973 to 1975. Very often the firm that obtained the raw materials was the only one able to sell in the marketplace.

Purchasing also supports corporate and product strategy by building its relative buying power in the market. That is, market force through buyer strength and firm's influence in the supply market aids in the quality, price, timing, and availability of purchased goods.[11]

Purchasing cannot be passive in its functions. It has more responsibility to the firm than simply placing orders for goods requisitioned from other departments. An active role and often aggressiveness in supply markets is required. Some of the activities that purchasing must become involved with are transportation, product materials and design, commodity price watching and analysis, and long-run planning with critical materials and minerals. In these ways it carries out and provides valuable input to the firm's strategy formulation process.

Evolution of Purchasing and Materials Management

Traditional Organizations

Management organizational structures were traditionally built upon a hierarchy of functions vertical in nature. The rationale for this type of structure was that as organizations became larger they could reap the benefits of specialization of labor and functions. The traditional disciplines tended to be manufacturing, marketing, and finance, and these three reported to top management. Other functions in the firm were either part of these three departments or were staff functions to them or to a corporate group.

The vertical organization tends to have communication flows within each department from top to bottom and vice versa. Major communications between departments cross over at the top.

The Systems Concept

The systems concept or systems approach developed in firms after World War II. It is an approach to viewing and organizing functions within a firm around the actual flow or goods and information rather than a strictly hierarchical standard. This is a recognition that activities dependent upon each other for data or goods should be located close to each other so that delays are not encountered in communications or goods flow between the two. When firms move to the systems approach greater output is achieved at the same or lesser cost. A corollary benefit arises from the fact that the organization tends to become more responsive to demands and needed changes. This has tended to diminish emphasis upon the traditional hierarchical structure.

The systems concept rests upon four basic elements. These are the total organizational view, the suboptimization of individual functions, the recognition of trade-offs and the total cost approach, and the synergy of the systems concept. These are discussed individually as follows.[12]

Total Organizational View
The basic idea behind the systems approach is that the performance of the entire organization is subject to optimization. The organization's goals should be identified and made known to each separate function. The entire organization's output and performance is the ultimate measure to optimize.

Suboptimization of Individual Components

Since the performance of the entire organization is the key to attaining corporate objectives, performance of the individual parts need not be optimal. That is, it is not necessarily imperative that each department strive for total cost reduction for the benefit of the firm. There are many instances when purchasing might pay $.05 more for an item over and above a cheaper one, only to save production $.07 in quality, scrap, and waste. When each department strives to optimize its own function, departmental conflicts arise, and the goals and performance of the entire firm are rarely met, if at all. Attaining optimal performance for the overall organization requires close links between each component.

Recognition of Trade-offs and the Total Cost Approach

The systems approach recognizes and uses trade-offs. Trade-off is a term that states that a relationship exists between two or more functions such that they either stimulate or hinder each other. There are two basic types of trade-offs. A direct trade-off is one in which an increase in one function or activity also will cause an increase in another. An inverse trade-off is one in which an increase in one is associated with a decrease in another.

Synergy of the Systems Concept

As stated above, the total performance of the organization may increase as it adapts to the systems approach, or it may meet the same total output at lesser total cost.

The basic idea behind the total-cost approach is that the organizational form should follow from the defined function or purpose which it is to serve. Firms should not necessarily adopt a traditional organization structure because that is the most basic and usual form. Rather, firms should arrange separate line and staff functions as well as entire disciplines along the lines of the mission or purpose which they are to serve. Such thinking has caused some firms to arrange managerial functions along the path of the physical flow of goods into, through, and out of the firm.

Materials Management Concept

Firms are motivated to adopt the materials management concept for many of the same reasons that they adopt the distribution concept. Materials management covers those activities involved in the flow of physical goods and their control from source to the production line. These include purchasing, inbound transportation, storage, materials handling, inventory control, and in many firms production scheduling. Some firms include all of these functions in this department while others include only purchasing and production scheduling.

Product proliferation, growth in tools available, and the need to tighten inventory control to provide production with an economic level of internal "customer service" are all reasons why firms are combining functions that handle all the inbound goods flow. In recent years, the cost of interest and capital have led many firms to accelerate the trend toward materials management functions. Raw material and work-in-process inventories represent uses for scarce corporate funds that are increasingly more expensive to obtain. Stocking lower inventories while maintaining a high level of goods necessary to support desired production activities is a balancing function that generally can be attained only through single inbound good flow control and responsibility.

A Trend Toward Logistics?

The evolution of outbound goods flow and control activities into distribution and those inbound into materials management has led many observers to state that a complete inbound and outbound coordination might be seen in the future. This is evident in moves in that direction by Whirlpool, Sandoz, and Carlisle Rubber, to name a few. The combination of materials management and distribution is called logistics. This is the control and planning of all activities involved with the inbound movement of needed goods and the outbound flow of finished products. Exhibit 1-2 shows a simplified flow of those activities needed to control and handle the physical flow of goods into and out of the firm.

The firm's logistics system consists of two primary flows, whether it is departmentally defined as such or merely a string of functions reporting to separate departments in the firm. One is the physical flow of goods from sources through the firm out to customers. The other is the control flow, which is generally established by departmental plans and operated on a daily basis from customer demand backward through the firm and out to sources. That is, the demand for goods from customers tends to stimulate action in outbound warehouses to move goods to the buyers. Low inventory levels in the warehouses will tend to cause production to produce more of the goods. Production needs place demands upon raw material warehouses and, when these are low, will cause purchasing to order goods from vendors. The firm can be described as an hour-glass shaped system through which goods come from many and varied sources to be processed in a single place only to be distributed to a widely diverse outbound market. This is the entire logistics system of a firm.

The entire logistics system controls this flow in as efficient manner as possible by taking advantage of trade-off relationships. Unlike manufacturing, which has the mission to produce the firm's goods in a minimum unit cost manner, and marketing, which is rewarded with maximized sales, materials management and distribution generally operate under the mission of attaining a certain service level for the firm and operating in as efficient cost manner as possible while meeting that service goal. This means that cost minimization is not always the key to daily operations in purchasing, transportation, warehousing, etc. It also means that materials and distribution managers will often select very expensive choices to attain a greater absolute savings elsewhere in the system. The ultimate goal is to balance the entire organization so that it attains the firm's overall mission in a low-total-cost manner. The task is

■ **EXHIBIT 1-2.** *A Simplified Materials Management and Distribution System*

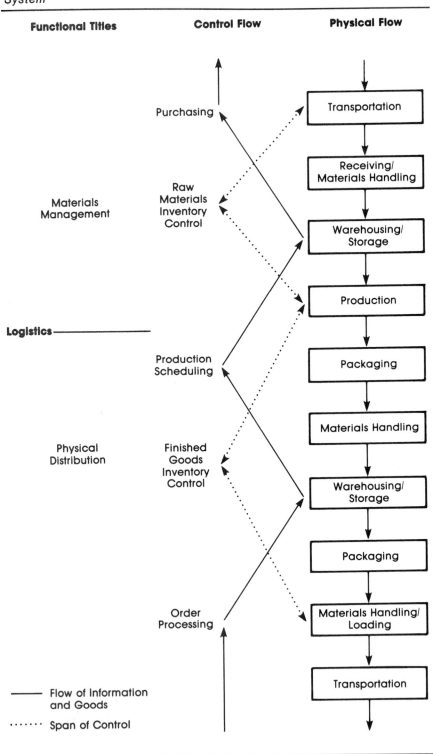

not a simple one, for it requires consideration of total firm impacts in those decisions made in materials management and distribution.

Approach of this Book

This is a book about purchasing. It covers the strategies, tactics and processes used to operate and manage an efficient purchasing department. But, purchasing is not in a corporate vacuum. It functions to obtain materials that are part of the firm's overall strategic goal and marketing mission. Decisions made in materials management affect purchasing and vice versa. Purchasing is one of the components that directly has trade-off ties with production and other physical flow activities.

FOOTNOTES

1. Somerby Dowst, "Raytheon Accents the 'Pro' in Proed., *Webster's New World Dictionary* (New York: The World Publishing Co., 1974).
2. Douglas Smock, "Make Buyers Managers of Outside Production," *Purchasing*, 5 August 1982, p. 23.
3. Somerby Dowst, "Corporate Supply: A Key to PPG's Success," *Purchasing*, 5 August 1982, p. 43.
4. David Blenkhorn and Peter M. Banting, "Broadening the Concept of Industrial Purchasing," *Industrial Marketing Management* 7 (1978):374–378.
5. David B. Guralnik, ed., *Webster's New World Dictionary* (New York: The World Publishing Co., 1974).
6. Edward J. Bierman, ed., *The New Study Guide* (Oradell, NJ: National Association of Purchasing Management, 1982), p. 6.
7. Smock, "Make Buyers Managers...".
8. Victor H. Pooler and David J. Pooler, "Purchasing's Elusive Conceptual Home,"*Journal of Purchasing and Materials Management* 17 (1981):13.
9. Donald Bowersox, *Logistical Management* (New York: Macmillan, 1977), chapter 1.
10. G. E. Kiser, "Elements of Purchasing Strategy," *Journal of Purchasing and Materials Management* 12:1 (1976).
11. Robert E. Speckman, "A Strategic Approach to Procurement Planning," *Journal of Purchasing and Materials Management* 17 (1981).
12. Bowersox, *Logistical Management*, chapter 1.

SOURCES FOR FURTHER READING

Ammer, Dean S. *Materials Management.* Homewood, IL: Richard D. Irwin, 1980., 4th edition.

England, W. B., Fearon, H. E., and Leenders, M. R. *Purchasing and Materials Management.* Homewood, IL: Richard D. Irwin, 1980, 7th ed.

Farrell, P. V. *Aljian's Purchasing Handbook.*New York: McGraw-Hill Co., 1982.

Heinritz, S. F. and Farrell, P. V. *Purchasing: Principles and Applications.* Englewood Cliffs, NJ: Prentice-Hall, 1980.

Lee, L. and Dobler, D. W. *Purchasing and Materials Management: Text and Cases.* New York, NY: McGraw-Hill, 1977.

National Association of Purchasing Management. *Guide to Purchasing.* Oradell, NJ: National Association of Purchasing Management, 1976.

Zenz, Gary J. *Purchasing and the Management of Materials* New York, NY: John Wiley & Sons, 1981.

QUESTIONS FOR REVIEW

1. What is the difference between the narrow view of purchasing and the broad view?

2. How has the orientation of firms in the U.S. changed since the 1800s?

3. What is demarketing?

4. What is the overall objective of purchasing?

5. What are the specific objectives of purchasing?

6. What managerial objectives does purchasing use to carry out its missions?

7. How does purchasing impact upon the profitability of the firm?

8. What is meant by the comment that purchasing activities have a greater impact upon company profit than marketing? How might marketing managers argue otherwise?

9. What is meant by "corporate strategy"?

10. What is product strategy, and how does it relate to corporate strategy?

11. How does purchasing fit into the systems concept?

12. Distinguish between a) materials management and b) logistics.

Problem 1-1

You have just started working in the purchasing department of Sani-Tech Products, Inc., a producer of food and medical equipment. In order to become more familiar with the firm, your boss gave you the following accounting records of the division to review. These are the income statement and balance sheet for the latest period for the food and beverage division.

Income Statement—Year 198X		($ in thousands)
Revenue		$200
Less: cost of goods sold		
Beginning inventory	$140	
Purchases	100	
Total available	240	
Ending inventory	(140)	
= cost of goods sold		$100
Gross margin		$100
Less: operating expenses		60
depreciation		30
Net income before taxes		$ 10
Taxes		4
Net income after taxes		$ 6

Balance Sheet—as of December 31, 198X

Assets		Liabilities & Equities	
Cash	$ 10	Accounts Payables	$ 35
Accounts Rec.	20	Long Term Debt	30
Inventories	100	Stock Outstanding	50
Plant & Equip.	20	Retained Earnings	35
Total assets	$150	Total Liab. & Eq's	$150

Question:
What would be the effect of shifting into another product line that would require $50 less total inventories with sales, cost of goods sold, and profit to remain the same?

Problem 1-2

You are in the purchasing department of a firm in the electric and electrical products industry. Your company cost structure is similar to that presented in Table 1-1—that is, the cost of materials, parts, and containers average 42.5 percent of the company sales dollar. Your company's net profit is 3 percent of sales.

Question:
What is the profit potential of saving a dollar of purchasing costs versus an additional dollar of sales for the firm?

INTRODUCTION

MACRO-PURCHASING PROCESSES

Need Detection
Make-or-Buy Decision
Vendor Selection
Buying Method Selection
Experience Stage

COMMUNICATIONS AND DOCUMENTATION IN PURCHASING: MICRO-PURCHASING PROCESSES

Information Systems
The Basic Purchasing Cycle
Communication and Documentation in the
Purchase Transaction

PURCHASING SUPPORT RECORD SYSTEMS

PURCHASING RESPONSIBILITIES AND ACTIVITIES

CONCLUSION

CHAPTER OBJECTIVES

After reading this chapter you should:

- Understand the overall process of purchasing.

- Appreciate the need for documentation and communication in purchasing.

- Be able to evaluate the various means of payment.

- Understand the primary responsibilities of purchasing.

Basic Purchasing Processes

Introduction

An examination of the purchasing operation at a small specialty chemical firm in New Jersey, a metropolitan hospital in Houston, and a manufacturing firm in Illinois would reveal that though there are differences in products, size of firm, and number of people employed the objectives and basic purchasing processes are the same for all. An overview of these key descriptive aspects of purchasing is basic to understanding the specific and strategic roles of this field.

This chapter presents the overall line processes of purchasing, including detection of the need for items, the make-or-buy decision, the selection of sources, and alternative methods of buying products. The second section of the chapter presents the micro-aspects of purchasing, including the forms and documentation used in the overall communications flows. Finally, with this background, the responsibilities and activities of purchasing are covered as they relate to daily operations and long-term planning in the firm.

Macro-Purchasing Processes

The macro-purchasing role in the firm consists of five basic activities. These are need detection, make-or-buy decision, selection and evaluation of vendors, buying methods, and experience. This can be viewed as a line system with a closed loop as is shown in Exhibit 2–1.

Need Detection

Need detection is the process of determining and communicating the desire to obtain certain goods or services. Purchasing is linked with other departments of the firm through various communications methods so that buyers may determine the need for goods and services. Generally speaking, the items purchasing obtains for these other departments fall into six basic groups. One is raw materials. Two is semifinished, work-in-process, or semifabricated items. Three is finished items that are bought and sold without major change or conversion by the firm. Four is maintenance, repair, and operating supplies, often referred to as MRO items. Five is services of all types. And six is capital goods for

■ **EXHIBIT 2-1.** *The Macro-Line Processes of Purchasing*

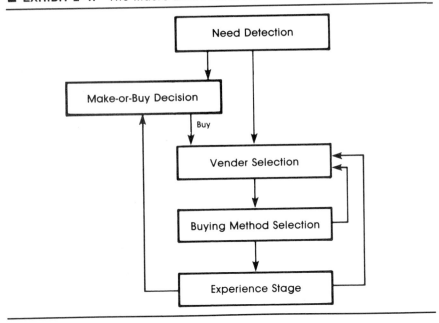

long-term use in the firm. All of these distinct products and services are sought by other departments of the firm, and purchasing is generally responsible for obtaining them using the processes presented in the macro process of Exhibit 2–1.

The need-detection system is both formal and nonformal. In manufacturing firms, materials management systems generally include systematic links between production and purchasing for routine communication of the need for raw materials, semifinished goods, and even finished goods for resale. These links consist of constant verbal communications, card files for inventory monitoring, daily production planning meetings, and materials requirements planning, or MRP systems. The majority of purchasing in activity in manufacturing firms is in this area. Supplies are goods needed to operate the firm, but they are not sold as part of the output. These include various lubricants, belts, and parts needed by production machinery, as well as janitorial goods, typing paper and ribbons, and even food items for company food systems for employees. These goods are likewise routine in nature; they vary widely in terms of types of goods. Purchasing is linked with every department of the firm with respect to supplies. Obtaining services is also a common responsibility of purchasing. This includes maintenance services for buildings and printing/copying machinery, janitorial services, periodic painting and repair, and even external production functions by other firms. Capital goods are those items used within the firm that are long-term assets in nature. These include production equipment, company autos, buildings, and office equipment, to name a few. The links here are with every department of the firm including finance/accounting, marketing, legal, and personnel.

Need detection has traditionally been the responsibility of other departments. That is, purchasing has generally played a passive role of obtaining goods once other departments advised of their needs. This condition is changing in two ways. One way is through the systematic link being built in most firms between overall distribution and materials management functions and purchasing. Purchasing is one of the on-line activities assuring the smooth flow of products into and through the firm. The second way is through proactive ties with the rest of the firm. This includes purchasing being part of the product planning and design process. Purchasing also provides an early-warning signal to the firm with regard to future problems in component supply availability or price. New material development and other improvement possibilities are also communicated from purchasing to the rest of the firm. These proactive functions are possible when purchasing is able to perform the routine buying activities with a smooth effort in order to devote time to many of these other positive aspects.

Make-or-Buy Decision

Firms have a basic choice of buying products from "outside manufacturing sources" or producing them in-house. The make-or-buy decision can be approached when a new product is being developed or at any point in product life when the firm has the capability of producing the goods itself, and the economic or strategic factors relating to the item favor that. The need to make a decision in this area often arises the first time the firm requires a new item. A second time may occur when supplies of the product are a problem.

The make-or-buy decision often is conducted with wide input from and analysis by purchasing, engineering, and production, as well as by finance, which usually analyzes the financial worth of any major project from the standpoint of the entire firm.

Vendor Selection

The next phase in the overall purchasing process is to evaluate and select a source or sources of the goods. This will occur whether or not the firm decides to make or buy. In either event, purchasing and materials management will be involved with acquiring goods. The evaluation and selection of suppliers entails three individual steps—survey, inquiry, and selection.

The survey stage in purchasing consists of determining all feasible sources for the product. Useful sources are industrial directories, catalogues, promotional literature, and any information about potential suppliers. This is where a comprehensive and up-to-date purchasing department library or filing system is of value. This topic is covered in greater depth in Chapter 5, Assurance of Supply, but the main point here is that the buyer at least initially surveys a wide range of feasible sources. The word feasible is important, and its interpretation is largely subjective. To illustrate, a standard MRO part might be available from any one of a dozen manufacturers and over one-hundred different distributors in the U.S. Most of them are not logistically or financially feasible to acquire from because of the long distances involved. Closer sources would entail less delivery cost and greater certainty in order cycle time. Similarly, an overseas source might be possible to use buy not feasible because the necessary lead time is only one month. Sourcing from the overseas supplier might take two to three months. In this instance, this source is not feasible. Therefore, the survey stage consists of obtaining a listing of all suppliers that might be feasible to acquire from within the time constraints of the initial purchase.

The inquiry stage focuses the list down to a smaller number of suppliers. In this stage the buyer is evaluating the relative qualifications and advantages of each source. This is again covered in greater depth in Chapter 5 as well as in Chapter 3, Optimum Quality, and Chapter 4, Lowest Final Cost. The key to this stage is to narrow the range of feasible suppliers to determine those with whom a possible order might be placed. Some activities found in this stage involve plant visits, evaluating samples, presentations by suppliers, and group decision processes with manufacturing, engineering, and other departments.

The selection phase involves bid evaluation or negotiations with one or more suppliers. This subject is covered in detail in Chapters 4, 5, and 6. Buyers will often place a major order with one firm and a smaller one with another. This helps to assure some degree of competition in that the main supplier is aware of another, and the smaller order firm knows that larger orders might be placed with it in the future.

Buying Method Selection

Use of the appropriate buying method is a decision that goes hand-in-hand with the selection of a vendor. Buying methods include the use of purchase orders, systems contracting, negotiated contracts or any one of the other methods possible. With some purchase decisions only one form of buying method will be feasible. But, often the use of two or more might be part of the vendor negotiation and selection process. There are several forms of buying methods available, and these are presented as follows.

Purchase Order

This system is the backbone of purchasing operations. A purchase order is a document sent from the purchasing department to a vendor. It is a document that has legal implications for both the buyer and vendor. It constitutes an offer to buy. Purchase orders require a separate process for each order. The relationship with the vendor is terminated upon delivery and payment for the goods. Purchase orders, or PO's, are used for nonroutine purchases. This often is a majority of the actual number of purchase transactions a firm makes in any time period.

Purchase Order Draft

This is similar to the purchase order in that a separate document is used for each purchase, and the relationship with the vendor is terminated upon delivery of the goods. A difference rests with the purchase order draft, or POD, in that it contains a signed bank draft that the vendor may deposit in his/her bank account upon shipment of the named goods to the buyer. This was used by Kaiser Co. for many years. It has the advantage of reducing invoicing and check-writing processes. It has the disadvantage of reduced cash holding by the buyer. That is, in a traditional purchase order setting, the buyer receives the goods and pays for them in, say, thirty days. In the POD system, the buyer's bank account often has the check cleared for payment to the vendor before delivery of the goods. This system is useful for small lot purchases. In many instances, the cost of paperwork is larger than the value or profit of the products transacted. The POD system makes even small lot sales by suppliers attractive because there is almost immediate payment for them. The buyer gains the advantage of reduced paperwork.

Contracts

Any order/buying and payment method may be arranged through negotiated contract. These range from one-shipment-one-payment to progress payments and systems contracting. Many of these are discussed below and in Chapter 4.

Standing Order

This system is usually arranged through negotiated contract. It consists of the vendor delivering goods at fixed, agreed prices covering a defined period. Standing orders are also used for machinery repair and maintenance services. This form of ordering is also referred to as open-ended ordering. Standing orders are often made with rail and motor carriers to deliver a certain number of cars or trailers per day unless contacted otherwise.

Systems Contracting

Systems ordering, systems contracting, or blanket ordering, as they are often referred to, are useful in situations involving a large volume of standardized products. MRO items are often covered with this form of contract. These are arranged with a generally agreed-to volume of purchase between the buyer and supplier over a given time period. The specific quantity is not fixed in contract. The buyer then informs his or her own plants and sites that the goods may be requisitioned directly from the vendor without paperwork through the purchasing department. The purchasing department will often publish a catalogue of products and prices for distribution to the various company demand sites. The vendor supplies the ordered goods to the individual sites, and payment is settled through purchasing and accounting. Systems contracting is often called "stockless purchasing," because the buyer does not have to maintain an inventory of the goods. Instead, the vendor holds them near the buyer's demand sites.

This form of purchasing has advantages for both buyer and seller. The seller is generally assured of a certain volume of sales throughout the time period. While this agreed-to quantity is not legally binding, it is generally sufficient assurance for the vendor to seek volume purchases from its sources. These volume purchases help reduce the final cost to the buyer. A key advantage is that a stipulated price is fixed over the period of the contract. That is, the vendor's acquisition costs are solidified in the form of stable prices for the buying firm. The arrangement simplifies the actual order process. Instead of a requisition being made between the demanding department and purchasing and purchasing making up a purchase order for transmission to the vendor, orders are made directly by the demanding department to the vendor with shipping releases or requisitions. This form is often used as a pick instruction by the vendor in his/her own warehouse.

Consignment is one form of systems contracting. This consists of the vendor actually delivering goods to the buyer firm and the goods being held by the buyer firm until they are resold or otherwise used in production. The goods are considered sold once they are moved from the initial storage shelf or site. That is, the goods are delivered by the vendor, but no bill is submitted until they are used by the buyer firm. The advantage here is that delivery is immediate, and payment is not required until used. Many consignment systems consist of fixed quantities, however. This may bind the buying firm to goods that might become obsolete over the entire time period, and a question arises often as to how to resolve the issue of poor quality units.

Bartering or Commodity Swaps

This form of goods acquisition entails the trading of goods rather than goods shipped for payment in monetary terms. This is a convenient way of acquiring goods from nations and firms who also seek goods from the buyer firm or others in the U.S. but do not possess the dollars to consummate such purchases. These arrangements require determination of comparable commodity values and swapping according to certain delivery schedules. This is discussed in more detail in Chapter 11, International Purchasing.

Each method of buying involves a different configuration of costs to the acquiring firm. Purchase orders require repeated handlings, while many of the forms of systems contracting reduce the paperwork process. But, the systems methods require some initial time, effort, and cost. The right buying method can only be determined in light of the nature of the purchase needs. If they are nonroutine, then one type is feasible. If the arrangement is for standardized items over a long period of time, then others may be investigated. Other factors entering into this decision are the size of the individual orders, the length of the relationship with the supplier, the capabilities of the supplier, and tactical considerations of the buyer in terms of developing a longer relationship with the vendor.

Experience Stage

The experience stage is the final one in the overall macro-purchasing processes. This includes evaluating the vendors, their goods and the manner in which they service the firm. Factors included in this stage include product quality and any related problems, delivery schedules, billing and payment processes, assistance with technical factors, and a host of other tangible and intangible elements noted by purchasing and other departments. Many of the elements considered here are discussed in depth in Chapter 5, Assurance of Supply.

Experience with the current vendor might later involve using another method of buying. Larger volumes over time generally call for investigating systems and other contract-type arrangements. Lesser use of a vendor might call for reverting back to the purchase order systems.

Selection of other vendors requires shifting back to the vendor evaluation and selection stage. This includes survey and inquiry of other ones on the market. If the present library of vendor information is old, then another new survey is necessary.

Communications and Documentation in Purchasing: Micro-Purchasing Processes

The core of a purchasing system is built around micro-information systems, which are a series of documents regarding methods of payment, record systems, and communications and relations with suppliers. This section explores all these of facets of purchasing as they pertain to the day-to-day operations. Later chapters discuss many of the purchasing staff and support activities.

Information Systems

Information is data arranged in a manner to be useful. It is the key working tool of purchasing. Its applications are for transactions, operational planning and control, strategy and policy planning, and scientific analysis.[1]

In the line functions, purchasing is foremost concerned with handling transactions and controlling the flow of materials into the firm. To do so they must be backed up by a strong information base so that these activities may be controlled in a desired manner. These transactions are based upon procedurally established steps or operations that require various controls for them to be timely and efficient.

Purchasing staff functions are those activities that support the line operations. These include the act of planning and establishing future goals, policies, and procedures for the function. On a day-to-day basis it includes analytical work that is designed to improve purchasing operations and their effectiveness. Many departments are understaffed or overly burdened to the extent that the daily handling of purchasing transactions are nearly the only management accomplishments. In these settings the department is so busy performing the primary line activity that it rarely has an opportunity to review, analyze, or implement improvements.

The Basic Purchasing Cycle

The basic purchasing transaction cycle consists of eight steps: 1) recognize and define the need for a good or service within the firm; 2) informs purchasing of the need; 3) investigate and select a supplier; 4) prepare an order and send to the supplier; 5) conduct a follow-up review to assure that the goods or service will be received and inspected as conformity with what was ordered; 7) audit the supplier's invoice for accuracy; and 8) close the order with accounting for payment of the invoice.[2]

This entire process contains many more individual steps. Each is designed to assure proper action and conformity as well as to establish sound legal positions for both the buyer and vendor. Each step also involves documents that become part of the control process for the transaction. These steps are outlined in the next section, which describes in detail the various documents used in the overall line-purchasing cycle.

Communication and Documentation in the Purchase Transaction

The detailed cycle of events used to place an order and receive goods is presented in Exhibit 2–2. This chart shows that, at a very minimum, eight different parties are involved in the purchasing transaction. This system utilizes up to nineteen different documents, though a few of these are sometimes used in place of others. These documents are presented and analyzed here in terms of 1) what they are, 2) what purpose they serve, 3) who prepares them, and 4) what disposition is made of them. The documents presented here are only those used in the general line activities of the purchasing cycle. Many others are used in support or ancillary roles.

The primary and ancillary documents used in purchasing systems are presented in Table 2–1. Each one is indicated by who prepares it, and the purposes and other key points are shown for each. The purchase order is one of the prime documents in the purchasing system. Its role is basic to the entire system, and it has legal significance. Special attention is devoted to it.

Purchase Order

This document is the prime communication with the vendor. It serves a legal purpose of creating an offer to buy. Upon acknowledgement from the vendor, a contract is legally created in the eyes of the law. The purchase order is the device that communicates to the vendor the goods desired, their quality, price, expected delivery terms, and any services expected in relation to the goods.

The purchase order is a preprinted form containing the following items:

1. Masthead showing buying company name, address, phone and often Telex numbers
2. Purchase order number (of buying company)
3. Order date
4. Date goods are required
5. Description of goods, and vendor company item number, if any
6. Quantity
7. Lot unit (case, ton, carton, pallet, etc.)
8. Unit price
9. Extension of unit price and number of units for total price
10. Ship-to address, if different from masthead billing address
11. Authorized buying company signature (of buyer)

■ **EXHIBIT 2-2.** *Basic Purchasing Process and Documentation Flow*

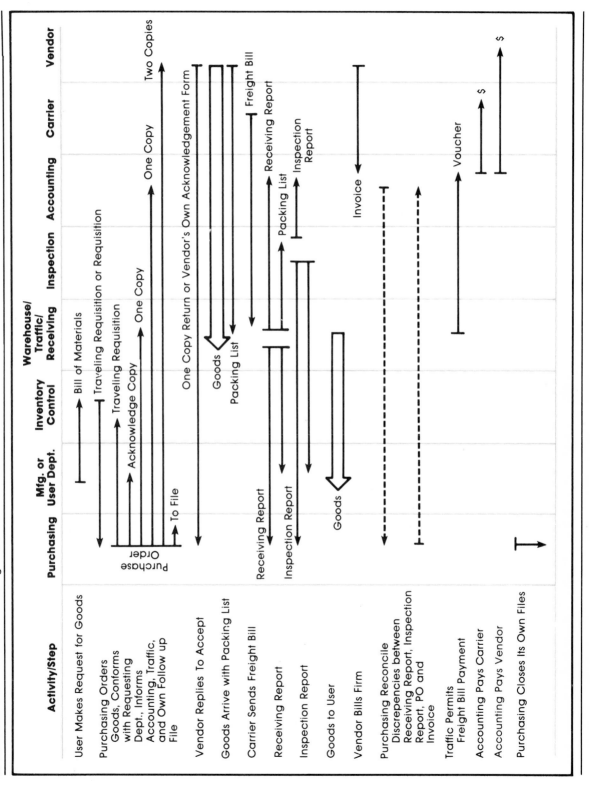

□ TABLE 2-1. *Basic Purchasing Documents*

Document	Who Prepares	Purpose and Other Points
Bill of materials	Production	Indicates all components that make up a product. Used by production to withdraw goods from raw materials inventory. Serves as pick list/instruction by personnel in raw materials inventory area. Purchasing uses in standardization and value analysis studies.
Inventory records	Department responsible for inventory	Documents that indicate current store of raw materials and other inventoried goods.
Requisition	Any department seeking items to be purchased	Used to inform purchasing of need for goods. Indicates budget from which funds are to be drawn for goods or service payment. Shows: description of goods, quantity, date needed, point of delivery desired, special instructions, material certifications (if any), department requesting goods, requisition number (for tracking) authorization/approval from requesting department, department to be charged. Purchasing to verify the validity of the authorization or approval. Serves as source document for purchasing in making up actual order. Copy returned to requesting department as confirmation.[1]
Traveling requisition	Departments that require many repeated orders	Acts in same manner as requisition. Used for routine purchases of same items. Held and prepared by user department. Contains: description of goods, several possible sources, prices, inventory records (e.g., reorder points, lot sizes), history of past usage. Purchasing acts upon as does with requisition.

Document	Source/Destination	Description
Purchase order	Purchasing	Document returned to user department upon ordering. Reduces repetitive data handling for routine purchases. Prime communication with vendor. Legal ofer to buy. Shows: firm, purchase order number, order date, date goods required, description of goods, quantity, method of delivery, lot unit, unit price, ship to address, total cost extension, authorized buying firm signature (of buyer), tax status of buyer, freight terms Multiple copies inform company treasury of future cash payment requirement, traffic of any special inbound freight or handling needs.
Shipping release	User departments	Used to communicate need for goods by user departments direct to vendors who are supplying goods under blanket order or systems contract. Contain item description, quantity, ship to address, contract identification, and budget information. Copy sent to purchasing and finance to keep records.
Confirmation or acknowledgement	Vendor	Reply to purchase order.
Purchase order change	Purchasing	Purchasing often sends to user department. Informs vendor of need to delete, alter or add to current outstanding order. Contains: original purchase order (PO) information and the desired change(s).
Bill of lading	Carrier and vendor	Serves as (1) receipt of goods shipped, (2) contract of carriage, (3) evidence of ownership, and (4) provides routing and other instructions.
Freight bill	Carrier	Invoice for freight services by carrier.

☐ **TABLE 2-1.** *Continued*

Document	Who Prepares	Purpose and Other Points
Packing list or slip	Vendor	Attached to goods, serves to inform carrier and receiving personnel as to contents of shipment.
Delivery receipt	Carrier	Carrier obtains receiving dock personnel signature as proof of delivery; carrier takes original. Serves evidence role in many loss and damage claims.
Delivery notice	Carrier	Informs receiver that goods are available for pick up from carrier terminal.
Tally or receiving report	Receiving or inspection	Document used to record quantity, description, and condition of goods actually received.
Inspection report	Inspection	Determines measures, quality, etc. of goods received. Used when firm wishes goods to be inspected prior to actual acceptance from vendor.
Invoice	Vendor	Bill for the goods purchased.
Voucher	Purchasing	Authorizes accounting to pay invoice and/or freight bill.
Ancillary Documents to the Purchasing Cycle		
Requests for quote	Purchasing	Request quotations from vendor (s). Contains: request for quote (RFQ) number, description of goods, quantity, timing, delivery point, special instructions, deadline for reply. Requests from vendors: unit cost, total cost, total time required for preparing work, how payment to be made, signature of authorizing person.[2]
Quote	Vendor	Informs the user department and purchasing of information sought in above RFQ.
Quote Acknowledgement	Purchasing	Sometimes used to acknowledge receipt of quote from vendor; tells that firm will be contacted as to decision.[3]

Award justification	Purchasing and/or user department	Document indicating reason for selecting the firm that obtained the job. Serves as record inside firm as to reasons. Helps avoid criticism of favoritism.[4]
Purchase order follow up	Purchasing, either buyer or expeditor	Follow up communication from purchasing to vendor that seeks assurance that work schedule is on-time. Used to determine status of part-shipment jobs.
Expediting request	Purchasing: either buyer or expeditor	Sent to vendor; request for speed-up of outstanding order.[5]
Price change report	Purchasing	Alerts user departments of any price changes in current orders; informs users of current market conditions. Used in budget preparation.[6]
Claim form	Traffic or purchasing	Used to file claim for loss and/or damage by carrier.

[1]Paul V. Farrell ed., *Aljian's Purchasing Handbook* (New York: McGraw-Hill, 1982), p. 5-4.
[2]Ibid, p.5-7.
[3]Somerby R. Dowst, *Basic for Buyers* (Boston: CBI Publishing Comany, 1971), p. 6.
[4]Ibid, p. 32.
[5]Ibid, p. 80.

Other items typically found on a purchase order include the tax status of the buyer and this purchase. Sales tax is generally required if the goods are to be consumed by the company. On the other hand, if they are to be resold as-is, they are often exempt from state sales tax. If there is an exception, the buying company tax exemption number will be included. Freight terms are also included on purchase order. This states who is to pay for the freight (buying company or vendor), as well as routing instructions desired by the buyer.

Many firms add terms to purchase orders that are demanded or requested of the vendor. Many of these are preprinted on the front or back of the PO, or they are typed onto the form. Some of these are as follows.[3]

- Quantity tolerance—Whether lesser or greater quantities than those shown on the order will be acceptable. In some production situations exact lot quantities are not always possible to produce.
- Inspection and Rejection by Buyer—Many food companies require on delivered goods that the title to the raw ingredients will not pass until the buying firm has an opportunity to inspect them. This is different from the normal FOB terms typically in use by most buying and selling arrangements.
- Disposition of Rejected Goods—How goods that are not accepted will be disposed of, picked up by the seller, shipped by the buyer, etc.
- Quality Alterations—Whether or not the firm will allow changes in the quality of items specified, whether notice is required.
- Price Assurance—Statement to effect that price charged by vendor is the lowest one in effect to all buyers on date of shipment, lower price than shown on purchase order is to be charged if prices dropped since placement of order.
- Payment Terms—How the goods will be paid for, one payment within number of days of receipt, early discount, etc.
- Special Services and Charges—Covers packaging and insurance for goods in-transit, etc.
- Guarantees and Warranties—Those terms the buyer seeks that may be in addition to those normally stated in the vendor's literature; can be restatement of vendor's terms to reinforce them for this purchase.
- Delivery Date Changes—Whether or not delivery date changes will be accepted; notice required if not to be met; possible penalties or liquidation.
- Order Changes by Buying Firm—The ability or inability of the buyer to change the order while in progress.
- Force Majure—A term stating that the obligations of both parties may be temporarily suspended in the event of major catastrophic events such as fire, strike, flood, etc.
- Ability or Limitation on Subcontracting—Whether or not the buyer will allow the vendor to subcontract all or part of the work; terms, if allowed.

- Disclosure of Information—Neither the buyer nor selling firms are to disclose any proprietary information to others or use it in ways not authorized by the other party.
- Patent and Copyright Infringement—Buying firm is to be held harmless in the event of patent or copyright infringement by vendor.
- Law Conformity—The vendor is to conform to the terms of the Equal Opportunity Act, Occupational Safety Hazards Administration (OSHA), and any transportation regulations pertaining to hazardous materials movement.
- On-site Responsibilities—Buyer is to be held harmless for worker liability and any other liabilities for work done by vendor on premises of buyer.

Any other terms may be placed in the order and become part of the legal relationship between the buyer and vendor for the duration of it. The matter as to whether all of these terms are accepted by the vendor is presented in the Offer and Acceptance section of Chapter 7.

Purchase orders are written by purchasing on either multiple copy forms or by computer printout. Generally, the original and one copy are sent to the vendor; other copies are sent to accounting, the user department, receiving, and traffic. Accounting is then made aware of a future cash outflow commitment. This is an important item of knowledge for the treasurer of the firm who must plan daily cash flows while maximizing the firm's cash-earning ability in overnight, weekly, and long-term securities. The user department is made aware of all the details of the purchase and receiving is authorized to accept the inbound shipment when it arrives. Some firms do not allow delivery unless previously authorized in a manner such as this. When special equipment is needed for unloading goods, this document then enables receiving to arrange for such. Traffic is also informed of the inbound shipment so that it may make arrangements with carriers or even plan to use the company's own vehicles. It is a good practice for purchasing to check with traffic before stating a specific delivery date on the purchase order so that traffic may arrange a consolidated inbound move with other shipments via for-hire carriers or in the company's own trucks. One or two purchase order copies are kept within the purchase department to act as follow-up documents until the cycle is complete.

The purchase order copies remain active in the various departments until the entire cycle is completed.

Purchasing Support Record Systems

The line and staff functions of purchasing require sound and efficient record systems. These may be informal files or loose-leaf notebooks, or they may be computerized systems that many plant sites may access on-line during the working day. Purchasing requires information in order to function. Its decisions involve large expenditures of the firm's resources. Further, many of its activities involve legal obligations. Good record systems, then, are a must in the daily operation and efficient planning activities of the purchasing function.

A *catalogue file* or library is a necessary part of purchasing. This is a file of product listings, catalogues, vendor promotional literature, and any industrial directories that contain firms and products most sought by the company. The catalogue file need not be very formal. Keys to efficient operation are that it be kept up to date, in an order or sequence logical to the users, and that it contain a check-out system. This topic is covered in more detail in Chapter 5, Assurance of Supply.

Open files are those containing all documents on outstanding orders. This is where a copy of the initial requisition, the traveling requisition, quotes, purchase order, etc. are kept until the file is closed with proper receipt of the goods and a bill from the vendor. The open file should ideally be closed out with summary notations made into a history record of the commodity and the vendor.

Vendor records are files containing background information and historical experience the firm has had with each vendor. These contain addresses, key personnel and phone numbers, history of purchases, quality and delivery experience, and any other pertinent data the firm deems important in its relations with vendors. This can be a valuable source for individual order selection and in preparing for negotiations. In many decentralized firms one plant often buys from a vendor, not knowing that another plant in the same firm has major, long-term contracts in force with that same vendor. In tight supply times, plants of the same corporate parent have unknowingly competed against each other for production capacity at the vendor's production site. Ideally, all departments of a firm should be able to determine what buying and selling experiences it has had with other firms. This high-level data system requires substantial computer programming and upkeep. The smaller the firm, the easier it is to develop such systems.

A *commodity record* is useful for repetitively purchased products. This file or record contains a description of the item, a listing of vendors, a brief history of prices, and purchase terms such as discounts, quantities, etc. While this appears to duplicate the catalogue and vendor history file, the commodity record is actually a summary of these two systems. Some buyers create a commodity record for those items typically demanded through use of traveling requisitions. These are the prime products that are repetitively acquired.

Interview records are useful for keeping a brief record of meetings with vendor representatives. Though not always necessary, such records are valuable when the details of future purchases are being discussed. Such forms can be preprinted with space for the name of the vendor and representative, time, date, items discussed and resolved or arranged. These are valuable for refreshing memories when the day-to-day activities are fastpaced.

Purchasing Responsibilities and Activities

The main activities of purchasing departments are varied. Very few activities are solely routine and unchanging. Purchasing has the task of carrying out the objectives of obtaining the maximum value of goods and services for the firm. This is done with the right price, delivery time, delivery place, and optimum quality and quantity in mind. The ways in which purchasing carries out this charge fall into two broad groupings of line and staff activities. Line activities are those involved with actually acquiring goods and services. Staff activities are those that assist and support the primary line activities.

The key line activities found in most purchasing functions are as follows:

- Provide and manage purchasing processes
- Check requisitions
- Select vendors
- Place orders
- Schedule purchases and deliveries
- Analyze bids
- Negotiate
- Follow-up orders
- Expedite
- Interview salesmen
- Handle claims with vendors
- Provide information for capital acquisitions
- Seek engineering and product improvement assistance from vendors
- Develop and train purchasing personnel and managers

Many departments include some of the following functions when purchasing is combined with materials management and/or traffic management:

- Determine quantities needed
- Establish specifications with user departments
- Determine timing of purchases
- Arrange inbound transportation
- Handle claims with carriers
- Control stores and stewardship
- Dispose of scrap and surplus
- Control inventory
- Handle inspection

These functions are the primary line activities of a purchasing department and are the core elements found in most departments. One other line activity that pervades all the above is coordination and cooperation with other departments.

Staff activities are supportive roles designed to improve and maintain the efficiency and effectiveness of the prime purchasing tasks. These include:

- Maintaining product and supplier source files
- Maintaining experience files about vendors

- Developing new sources of supply and enhancing competition
- Materials and component research and analysis
- Standardization programs
- Commodity market trend analysis and projections
- Product design input
- Product improvement input
- Provide information for the make-or-buy decision

A major problem exists in many prchasing departments with regard to the line and staff functions and pertains to the priorities placed upon the devlopment and efficiency of the purchasing function itself. A short-sighted view of purchasing is that it is to perform the line activities at minimum purchase and administrative costs to the firm. Many purchasing personnel are overly burdened with day-to-day line activities, with little time left to devote to or investigate some of the staff function opportunities. The farther-sighted management view of purchasing is that it is to seek such ends while maintaining long-term efficiency and competiveness in materials management and support of corporate strategy. These longer term goals are generally attained through use of the staff functions outlined above. These staff functions are sometimes difficult to justify to top management when seeking resources for implementing and using them. The payback to the firm is often long term and difficult to quantifiably measure.

Purchasing is the management of the process of acquiring goods and services for the firm within its stated goals and objectives. For the most part it is fulfilling the item/product requirements of other departments. That is, purchasing has little responsibility over actually setting the specification for the goods being acquired. But, within this setting, purchasing has four prime prerogatives. First, it selects the source. If the product specification is equal from several sources, it has the task of selecting the source with the best quality and lowest cost. Second, its job is to maintain buying-firm contact with the vendor. Purchasing is the buying arm of the entire firm. Communications and buying processes should go through it rather than between each user department and vendors. Third, purchasing may determine prices and appropriate terms of buying. This is its specialty, while the specification of the product itself may be the specialty of the user department. Fourth, purchasing may question the specifications requisitioned by the user department. This is not to say that purchasing may veto such specifications. What is appropriate is for purchasing to inquire as to the necessity of very tight specifications when slightly relaxed ones may permit purchase of lower cost goods of comparable quality. This point comes into play when vendors seek to influence engineering to specifying their particular item for the firm's product so that no other vendor will be considered by purchasing. This "back door" practice can cause the firm to use innappropriate items when others might provide the needed quality at a lower cost.

The administrative cost of purchasing is basically an overhead cost to the firm. It is difficult to trace each and every cost of the purchasing department to a particular good. It appears that there are economies of scale when relating the cost of the purchasing function to the cost of acquiring goods for the firm. The administrative cost does increase as the firm becomes larger or buys greater amounts of product, but the cost of the purchasing department generally grows at a less proportionate rate. That is, small firms might experience administrative purchasing costs of two to four percent of the cost of the product being acquired, but larger firms generally experience administrative costs of less than one percent of purchases.

The administrative cost of purchasing is largely made up of salaries and wages. Various surveys point to this component as being about three-fourths of the total departmental administrative cost. Other costs are phones and communications, travel, overhead, printing, and employee benefits. The overhead nature of purchasing can be seen in the cost of ordering two separate lots. One might be for $100 of packaging tape for use in a mail room. Another might be for four company trucks totalling $100,000. Others might include cost of soliciting phone bids, examining a sample of each unit with a person in each user department, evaluating the bids, preparing a purchase order, performing follow-up calls, and inspecting the delivered items. Approximately the same amount of time and effort might have been expended with each, yet the dollar amounts of each may be vastly different.

Future emphasis in purchasing is upon systematic processes for routine functions. This reduces the cost and steps necessary for routine activities, enables the overall function to become more objective in approach, and releases purchasing talent to be used in productive staff and research functions. The future indications are that purchasing is becoming more integrative with the rest of the firm in both routine and planning activities. And, the tasks are evolving more toward managerial issues and less toward technical and procedural issues.

Conclusion

The role and activities of purchasing are changing. A new integrated emphasis with materials management is now evolving. Further, purchasing is being integrated with overall corporate activities. The processes and management information systems used in purchasing must reflect these trends.

FOOTNOTES

1. George A. Steiner, *Top Management Planning* (New York: Macmillan Co., 1969), p. 473.
2. Lamar Lee, Jr. and Donald W. Dobler, *Purchasing and Materials Management* 13 ed. (New York: McGraw-Hill, 1977) p. 415.
3. Paul V. Farrell, ed., *Aljian's Purchasing Handbook*, (New York: McGraw-Hill, 1982), p. 5–20.

SOURCES FOR FURTHER READING

Bonfield, E. H., and Speh, Thomas, "Dimensions of Purchasing's Role in Industry." *Journal of Purchasing and Materials Management* 13: 10.

Cooley, James R.; Jackson, Donald W. Jr.; and Ostrom, Lonnie L. "Relative Power in Industrial Buying Decisions." *Journal of Purchasing and Materials Management* 14: 18.

Doyle, Peter; Woodside, Arch G.; and Michell, Paul. "Organizational Buying in New Task and Rebuy Situations." *Industrial Marketing Management* 8 (1979): 7–11.

Erickson, Robert A., and Gross, Andrew C. "Generalizing Industrial Buying: A Longitudinal Study." *Industrial Marketing Management* 9 (1980): 253–265.

Lopez, Frank P. *Model Purchasing Policy Manual.* Woodbury, NY: National Association of Educational Buyers, 1982.

Wind, Yoram. "The Boundaries of Buying Decision Centers." *Journal of Purchasing and Materials Management,* 14: 24.

QUESTIONS FOR REVIEW

1. What is the overall or macro-purchasing process?

2. What factors enter into the make-or-buy decision? What things favor make versus buy?

3. When is the purchase order system used rather than systems contracting?

4. How might bartering be found more in the future?

5. What is a requisition, and how is it different from a traveling requisition?

6. What terms are often found on a purchase order?

7. When are acknowledgements used in the entire purchasing process?

8. Distinguish between followup and expediting.

9. It is often said that purchasing is involved with too many forms and documents. Evaluate this comment.

10. What means of payments are best for buyers versus vendors?

11. What record systems are typically used in a well-functioning purchasing system?

12. What are the responsibilities and prerogatives of purchasing?

INTRODUCTION

QUALITY: WHAT IS IT?

WAYS OF DESCRIBING QUALITY

External Descriptors
Buyer-Firm Descriptors

PRODUCT QUALITY: PROBLEMS AND IMPROVEMENT APPROACHES

Quality Problems
Quality Correction and Assurance
Inspection Economics and Overview
The Mechanics of Measuring the Results
    of Inspection
Managerial Approaches to Quality
    improvement

CONCLUSION

CHAPTER OBJECTIVES

After reading this chapter you should:

- Understand the role of quality in the purchase decision.

- Be able to describe quality through its various means.

- Appreciate the tools used in inspection and quality measurement.

- Understand the managerial approaches useful for reducing quality problems.

Quality Decisions

Introduction

Quality is a word that refers to the attributes of a product or service. These attributes may be physical or aesthetic. Consumers often think that the word quality always applies to the highest standards or the best possible product on the market. Quality is a relative concept. It is not necessarily the highest possible quality. "Optimum" quality applies to the suitability of a particular set of attributes for whatever requirements the product is to serve.

Purchasing has the objective of acquiring optimum quality in the products it buys. This means that the products must meet whatever performance standards or other minimum attributes that are established. This is accomplished by seeking "maximum value," which is defined as the required physical or aesthetic quality at the lowest possible cost. Quality can exist in a very wide range of choices between products. A purchaser will have a minimum set of attributes to obtain in the products he or she is buying. Optimum quality, or maximum value, is found in the lowest cost product that meets the established quality requirements of the firm.

Quality is only one of the objectives purchasing is to attain in its vendor and product selection activities. Others are price, delivery, timing, and assurance of supply. All five relate to each other. This chapter presents many of the concepts and analytical tools used in quality specification and measurement. These include ways of describing quality, using standardization as a simplification process for manufacturing and purchasing, and approaches to quality improvement and measurement.

Quality: What Is It?

"Quality" refers to the attributes or characteristics of something. It can be applied to physical products, services, or processes. In a more specific sense, quality relates to physical form, performance, taste, color, durability, smell, or how something is perceived by people. It is a variable concept that can mean different things to different people.

A firm generally has a wide choice of products available from the supply market. Likewise, it can produce a wide range of quality products to sell to its customers. The major task for purchasing and design engineers is to establish the minimum quality characteristics necessary to satisfy the firm's market, and do so at the lowest possible cost. Each possible supply choice available to purchasers has a configuration of 1) suitability, 2) reliability, and 3) cost. The key is to determine which one of the choices meets the minimum requirements of the firm and its product at the lowest possible final cost to the firm.

Ranges of product quality are usually available to buyers when analyzing various choices of products from different vendors. Exhibit 3–1 presents general relationships that are often found between various sets of quality products and their cost to the buyer.

Quality/cost relationships for various products will often exist in one of three possible types of ranges. Higher quality is often only attainable at higher costs. Value analysis and altered product design can provide exceptions to this rule. But, in this analysis, existing alternative brands or vendor products are being compared in various quality and price configurations. In one context, higher quality is attained at proportionately greater cost. That is, higher quality is possible at costs that are proportionately higher than measurable increases in quality. In another context, there can be a rough linear relationship between quality and cost. This is shown in the middle chart. And, quality/cost relationships also can be found in a relationship that provides higher quality at small increases in cost in the lower ranges, but proportionately higher costs are necessary for small increases in quality at the higher ranges.

The relationships shown in Exhibit 3–1 are general in nature. They are illustrated to show how three possible relationships can exist in various ranges of quality and price. Others are possible, but the key point here is that buyers need to quantify the quality and cost of the products they are acquiring for the firm. They need to know what is "optimum" or provides "maximum value." Firms sometimes prescribe too much quality into the goods they are acquiring; in other instances firm's cost reduction efforts are attained by great losses in product quality. By knowing the relationship of the acquired products to others available on the market, the buyer can make sound judgements in product selection, and he or she can provide valuable input to the product design it-

■ **EXHIBIT 3-1.** *Quality/Cost Ranges Generally Available in Products*

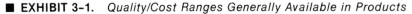

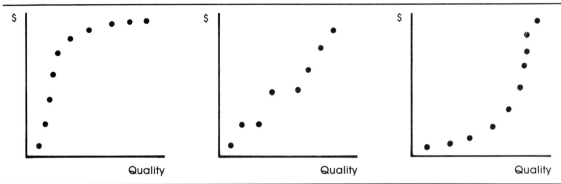

self. This becomes important during product conception stages and later when the product reaches maturity and value analysis becomes appropriate.

Ways of Describing Quality

Quality attributes can be described in many ways. Purchasing often must translate quality requirements of the firm into the communications used with vendors who will supply the products.[1]

External Descriptors

Brand Names
This method of describing goods is done simply by stating the product name and company that produces them. For example, there are many liquid cleaning compounds on the market, but one might be called Ready-Clean. The specification of Ready-Clean in a requisition or purchase order is sufficient description in this situation. There are many pros and cons of using brand names as a quality selection criteria. On the plus side, brand name specification is simple to administer and communicate. It is also useful when the vendor has a patent on the item or the process is secret and competitors have no close alternative items on the market. It is also a useful specification and ordering method when the purchase lots are small and testing and other detailed product evaluation processes are not practical.

However, specification of orders by brand name can have some drawbacks. One is the fact that brand names generally are higher in price due to the expense of marketing associated with them. In another way, user specification by brand name in requisitions might not be based upon sound analysis and evaluation. Direct vendor-to-user marketing efforts might have resulted in the user specifying the brand to the buyer. In this instance, the buyer should have the prerogative to question such specification.

Market Grades
This manner of describing goods is generally based upon government standards applying to the goods. The U.S. Department of Agriculture has created extensive standards and grading systems for grains, vegetables, fruits, meats, cotton, tobacco, and many other agricultural goods. The consumer can readily see these grades in the supermarket whenever a can or box of fruits, vegetables, butter, or eggs contains a label similar to Exhibit 3–2.

In the fruit and vegetable area, the USDA uses many criteria to determine the grade of product. Some of these are flavor, general appearance, color, type, symmetry, absence of defects, texture, tenderness, and other factors. Points are assigned when evaluating each of these factors, and a grader determines the USDA grade that the canner or packer may then apply to the consumer package. This process is voluntary on the part of the food processor and marketing firm; grading is a service for which they must pay the USDA.

■ **EXHIBIT 3-2.**   *Example of USDA Grade Mark*

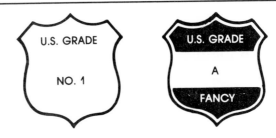

The grain industry heavily relies upon the USDA grading and inspection processes for assuring known quality in purchasing decisions. Grain is graded using such factors as minimum test weight per bushel, minimum percent mixtures with other grains, and maximum limits of such elements as heat damaged kernels, damaged kernels, foreign material, shrunken and broken kernels, and other defects.

Electrical, safety, and many construction codes have been developed by federal and local government bodies, and these are forms of market grades. Electrical component and construction requirements are often stated as minimum design specifications in machinery and construction.

Commercial Grades

Quality can also be described according to norms and standards established by various industries. These descriptions evolve over time as the need for consistent terms and measures arise. Examples are the 48″ x 40″ wood pallet used in the grocery industry, the 16″ center stud measure for internal walls in the housing industry and the different sizes of coal used in various industry. Two examples that can be easily seen by the student in the supermarket are can sizes and eggs. Can sizes for fruits, vegetables, and juices are fairly standardized according to industry-established norms. Examples are the no. 3 can, which holds 46 ounces, and the no. 303 can, which is the standard supermarket one pound can. Efficiency and uniformity in the food processing, tin plate and can manufacturing, and food distribution industries would be difficult without some common measures such as these.

Buyer-Firm Descriptors

The previously discussed ways in which item quality may be specified are developed from outside sources. They are either created by the vendor, as in the case of brand names, or by the government or the industry as a whole. There are many instances when these forms of quality description are not sufficient, and buyer-created descriptions are necessary. The following methods are ways in which the buyer and purchasing firm may specify quality attributes.

Blueprints

This is a very detailed method of describing goods to be acquired. Blueprints are technical drawings with all measures and construction details indicated on them. They are useful when the buying firm knows exactly what is needed and the best method of describing it is through such drawings. Two key drawbacks exist with blueprints, however, and these stem from their very detailed nature. One is that any error made by the person drawing the blueprint might cause an improper design to be made in the physical form of the product. The vendor's responsibility is to follow the exact design and measures of the prints. Any error will be built into the product, and the buying firm will have no recourse but to accept the final product. The other drawback is that this method assumes that the buying firm is very knowledgeable as to what it needs in the final product. That is, there is little room for the vendor to suggest slight alterations in design, measures, or materials that might result in improvements. If blueprints are used, a valuable approach is for the selected vendor to review them with an eye toward providing suggested improvements before actual construction or machine work commences.

Method of Manufacturing

This quality specification applies to the way in which the product is to be produced. Plastic and steel sheeting, for example, can be extruded, pressed, stamped or rolled. The temper, edges, and strength of the sheet will be slightly different depending on the method used. A sophisticated buyer should know the attributes available from each one, since each form of manufacturing will cost different amounts.

Physical Descriptions

This specification includes a listing or bill of materials that the item is to consist of in completed form. It often contains a maximum or minimum specification for certain items. A box frame, for example, may carry the required description of wood dimensions, grade, and bracket and screw sizes to be used.

Performance Specifications

This specification stipulates the maximum or minimum limits of performance of which the final product is to be capable. These might include weight limit minimums, hot and cold operating ranges necessary, speed of output on a piece of machinery, etc. Performance specifications are minimum requirements; they leave the task of creating the specific product up to the vendor. Military weapon systems are often specified with this method. These specifications relieve the purchasing firm from much of the designing tasks, since the vendor is free to develop the product within the limits of performance requirements.

Sample Testing

This method of quality description starts with a sample of an item from a vendor. The measures, qualities, general attributes, etc. are then either acceptable or not acceptable to the buyer. Future purchases are then made with the quality of the tested sample(s) as the expected norm of future lots.

In most instances a blend of many quality descriptions is used. That is, material requirements might be supplied with blueprints for part of a new machine, with the requirement that the vendor develop a component to be included within it that meets certain minimum performance ratings. Some construction requirements include brand-name electrical components.

Specifications are the means for describing quality that is sought in a purchased product. They are the communication means by which a firm seeks a particular performance or other quality attribute from a purchased item. They are developed by many functions within the firm. In many other instances, manufacturing, engineering, and sales are the parties determining specifications.

Specifications are useful when the buying firm is knowledgeable about the item being acquired and is assured that the specification will satisfy a need. They provide tangible means by which to measure compliance with the purchase order or contract requirements. Inspection uses these specifications as the measures for compliance detection. Specifications are valuable for communicating the firm's needs to a wide range of potential suppliers. By having the quality description in detailed form, suppliers may review them and possibly become interested in bidding on the firm's orders.

There are some drawbacks to the use of specifications. One, errors in blueprint drawing was mentioned above, and this danger carries over into all other tightly specified buyer requirements. Further, too tight a set of specifications might cause the firm to miss the lower cost opportunity of using an alternative item that is produced in stock by one or more vendors. Very restrictive specifications might also discourage some vendors from being interested in bidding or negotiating for the work.

Product Quality: Problems and Improvement Approaches

Quality Problems

Product quality is often discussed in the form of defective items, the wrong components included in a product, inconsistency in products or service, or poor workmanship. These factors incur unnecessary costs on the production line through breakage, waste, and stockouts. If a product line was to produce 1,000 units in an eight-hour period for a total operating cost of $12,000, then each unit should cost the firm $12.00. But, if quality problems occur on five percent of them, then the firm only produces 950 units for a total cost of $12,000 and the unit cost is now $12.63. Defective purchased products cause higher than necessary transportation costs, inventory holding costs, and the danger of producing fewer output units at a higher than necessary unit cost.

Poor quality also affects the firm on the outbound product distribution side. Poor quality incurs service costs, lost customer goodwill and perhaps real costs of downtime, and the opportunity for domestic and foreign firm competition. Some of the tangible costs incurred here are product return transportation, lost cash flow if the customer does not pay for the product until it is fixed, and extra marketing costs in attempts to reduce customer dissatisfaction.

Some observers have noted that deteriorated quality will occur at certain identifiable times. One time is when a vendor attempts to apply cost-reduction programs. Outbound inspection is one of the immediate areas in which a firm can cut costs while still maintaining production and sales. Note that this is not always a problem. In fact, a cost reduction program by a vendor can result in improved quality if better substitute items are used. A second time is when an economic downturn causes firms to seek cost savings. The firm might reduce costs at the risk of deteriorating quality. A third time is when the supplier's management changes. This often occurs when the firm is purchased by or merged into another. New management personnel might change methods and processes within the firm, and inspection or adherence to production standards can often deteriorate during these times.

The ways in which poorer inbound product quality appears are many. Failure to adhere to buyer specifications is a major problem in this area. Lax or nonexistent vendor production-line inspection and rough transportation handling are other ways in which quality problems can result. And, vendors might also make unauthorized substitutions in materials or parts.[2]

Quality Correction and Assurance

Quality problems on purchased items can generally be approached through one of several means. Instituting tighter specifications on purchase orders and contracts is one method. Though this might not correct the problem, the tighter specifications that the vendor is attempting to meet might lead to smaller variances that the buying firm can tolerate. That is, the purchased good tolerance range is specified tighter than what is absolutely necessary so that the vendor-supplied range is within the usable range of the buying firm.

Returning goods for rework by the vendor is another approach to reduction in quality problems. This also includes charging the vendor for the returned goods freight, requesting replacements, and even charging the problem units back on the vendor's account.

Inspection is another way in which defective or undesirable units can be prevented from reaching the production line. This requires inspection processes within the firm. Inspection is discussed in more detail in the following section.[3]

Plant visits to vendors who are presenting quality problems can often help reduce them. A visit serves to reinforce the seriousness that the buying firm attaches to acceptable quality products. The visit acts to present the need for higher quality or reduced poor quality. It might also bring to light ways in which the buying firm could help the vendor reduce problems through engineering assistance, altered specifications, etc. The visit can also be used to indicate that alternative vendors might be considered if the problem is not cured.

Quality assurance is an overall process that includes establishing specifications that can be met by suppliers, using vendors that have the capabilities of providing adequate quality within those specifications, utilization of processes, creating incentives and penalties that assure high quality products, and finding the means for measuring the product, service, and cost performance of vendors.[4]

This concept pervades the entire macro-purchasing process from the determination of the make-or-buy decision through to vendor evaluation and selection and the experience stage. It is one of the criterion used in establishing material and other specifications in the first place. Quality enters into the negotiation processes when ranges of quality and price are part of the nature of production. Vendor selection is often based upon the ability to provide the quality of product called for in the specifications. And, finally, the experience a firm has with each vendor causes them to either continue using that vendor or find a replacement.

Inspection Economics and Overview

Inspection is the process of detecting the true quality of purchased goods. It is one of the core elements of quality assurance and very often occurs at the inbound receiving stage, as described in Chapter 2. In other instances, inspection is conducted just prior to use of the goods in production so that defective units will not be used. Inspection is a costly process. Ideally, it should not have to exist, but the penalties for using defective units in production or allowing them to move through to sale are often too high in relation to the cost of in-house inspection.

Inspection serves to divert defective or undesirable units from use in production or sale. The resulting store of poor quality units can be disposed of in several ways. One is to use the good units and return the problem ones to the vendor for rework, replacement, or credit. Another method of disposition is to accept those goods that meet the specifications and to reject those that do not. Still another method is to reject the entire lot if too many units in it do not meet the firm's requirements. This is the most drastic alternative, but it is one that if often practiced where high quality requirements are in use. Food industry processors often do not accept possession of raw ingredients until they have been inspected for quality. In this instance, the cost of rework is either too high or is not possible to perform at all.

The firm has three alternatives with regard to the process of inspection. One is no inspection at all. This alternative relies upon the vendor to supply product units that meet the quality requirements of the company, or assumes that any defective units will not represent significant penalty cost to the buyer firm. This alternative presents no inspection cost to the firm, but does create penalty costs in the form of defective units that are used and/or later sold. Complete inspection is a second alternative. This choice incurs a cost of inspection for each unit, but no penalty cost will result for using defective units. The third alternative is sample lot inspection. This is based upon a sample of units being drawn and inspected. The decision as to whether to reject or accept the lot is based upon the number or percentage of units in the sample found to be defective.

The decision as to inspecting no units or one hundred percent of the units can be based upon a simple analysis. Several items of data are required and these are shown as follows:

- Number of units in each lot, 2,500
- Percent of units expected to be defective (based upon past experience, or vendor admission, etc.), 4%
- Cost to inspect each unit, $1
- Cost of using/selling defective unit, $100

The cost of no inspection is found as follows:

Cost of No Inspection
Alternative = (Lot Size) × (Percent Defective in Lot)
 × (Cost of Using Defective Units)
 = 2,500 × .04 × $100
 = $10,000.

The complete inspection alternative has the following cost components:

Complete Inspection Cost = (Lot Size) × (Cost of Inspecting Each Unit)
 = 2,500 × $1
 = $2,500.

Note that the first alternative contains no term for inspection cost, and the second alternative has no cost for using/selling defective units. In this instance, the firm would find the lower cost alternative of the two to be the complete inspection of units.

Both of the above alternatives represent costs to the firm that ideally should be minimized or eliminated. Complete inspection is not always desirable to perform; it is tedious work that involves much human error. There is no guarantee that complete inspection will find defective units. Even in situations where both the vendor and buyer firm conduct complete inspection on all units, there is still the possibility of defective units being used in the final stage.

The costs of this alternative and the human problems often associated with complete inspection stem from the quality control of the manufacturing process itself. Inspection is the process of determining good or bad units after they have been produced. Process control, on the other hand, is the activity of maintaining close monitoring and control of the actual production. To the vendor, trade-offs exist of whether to 1) tightly monitor the production machinery in order to prevent production of any defective units, 2) inspect all inbound units before they enter into production, 3) inspect all outbound units, or 4) let the buyer inspect or incur the penalty cost of using/selling defective units. Alternatives one through three will tend to reduce the chance of defective units reaching the buyer. Very close attention to the first one will reduce the need to use any of the inspection alternatives.

In the buyer's setting, however, the decision pertains to whether to inspect or not inspect. The formulas presented earlier show how one or the other can be determined as the lowest cost choice. A question often arises as to at what point does one alternative trade off against the other. That is, if the percentage of defective units was to be reduced, at what point could the buyer cease inspecting all units? This can be found by the following formula:

$$\text{Break-even Defective Percentage} = \frac{\text{Unit Cost of Inspection}}{\text{Cost of Using Defective Unit}}$$

$$= \$1/\$100, \text{ or } 1\%.$$

That is, if the vendor was to reduce the actual defective rate from four percent to one percent, then the buyer could eliminate the use of inspection. The cost of no inspection would be $2,500 \times .01 \times \$100$, or $2,500, and the cost of complete inspection would be $2,500 \times \$1$, or $2,500.[5]

This analysis points to several trade-off situations. First, as the penalty cost of using defective units increases, the need for complete buyer inspection increases. Second, as the percentage of defective units increases, again the need for buyer inspection increases. Third, if the cost of inspection or the penalty costs from no inspection are high, the buyer might direct cost-savings attention to either 1) vendor process control that would tend to reduce the defective percentage or 2) negotiate a higher price in exchange for a reduced defective unit rate. In some instances, buying firms will lend their engineering talent to a small-or medium-size vendor in order to reduce or solve a quality control problem in production.

The third major alternative with regard to the process of inspection is sample inspection or acceptance sampling. This is the process of taking a sample of a lot and determining whether to accept or reject the entire lot based upon the results of the sample. Acceptance sampling is an attempt to predict the number of defects in the entire lot. It consists of taking several individual samples of the entire lot and inspecting them in order to determine the defective percentage.

The sampling process starts with the definition of an acceptable quality level, or AQL. The AQL is the number of defects that would be acceptable in the lot a majority of the time. The buyer either accepts or rejects the lot based upon the samples. In basic form, sample inspection starts with a sample or samples being taken and measured for acceptability. The sample or collective samples are then compared to the tolerance allowed in the quality specifications. If the sample has a *smaller* defect limit than required, the lot will generally be accepted. If the defective rate of the sample is *equal* to the tolerance specified, than a second sample is often taken, and the first and second sample results are combined. If the sum of defects is *greater* than the acceptable defect rate, then the lot is either rejected or again is completely inspected to obtain the good units.

For the vendor and buyer, sampling has associated with it two possible errors. They are quantified in what is called an operating characteristic curve, or OC curve. An OC curve is a statistical presentation of the accuracy of decisions made from a specific sampling method. The OC curve is determined using the binomial distribution of statistics. The buyer and vendor can use the curve, however, in order to make decisions with regard to sampling and in-process control. Exhibit 3–3 shows a general OC curve.

The prime feature of this curve is the risk that the buyer incurs with the associated sampling plan in accepting a lot that in reality has more defects that the acceptable quality level, or AQL. On the other hand, the OC curve also shows the risk the vendor incurs with the plan in rejecting a lot for shipment and sale that in reality has less defects that might be led to believe through sampling. In other words, sampling is not perfect. A sample may contain a greater percentage of defects than is in the entire lot.

Exhibit 3–4 illustrates the phenomenon that as the size of the sample increases, the chance of a buyer accepting a bad lot decreases. But, as the chart shows, larger sample sizes do not have a very great effect upon reducing the vendor's risk. This gives insight into why some vendors do not place much significance upon sampling plans conducted in the plant. Buyer rejection and return might often be the less costly alternative from the standpoint of the seller.

■ **EXHIBIT 3–3.** *Illustration of an Operating Characteristic Curve*

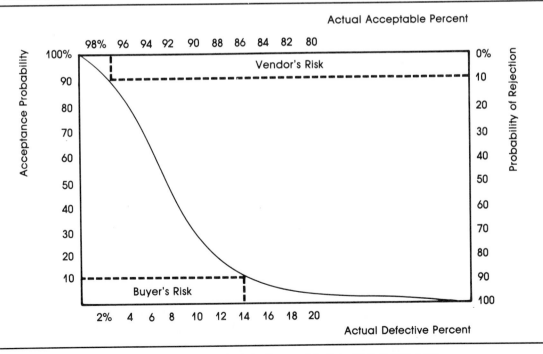

■ Source: Acheson J. Duncan, *Quality Control and Industrial Statistics* (Homewood, IL, Richard D. Irwin, 1974), p. 162.

■ **EXHIBIT 3-4.** *OC Curves for Samples of Increasing Si?*

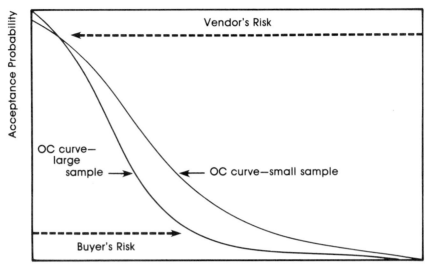

The Mechanics of Measuring the Results of Inspection

An important part of the inspection process is measuring and reporting the results of it. Two key distinctions must be made relating to inspection; these are attributes and variables. Attributes are the characteristics being measured, such as length, strength, weight, color, heat tolerance, etc. Variables are the measures of specific characteristics; examples are inches, pounds, degree of tinting, etc. Attributes tend to be either-or type inspections, such as a go or no-go gauge on the length of casings. On the other hand, variables are measured that might take on any value, like millimeters.

The control chart is a common means of reporting the results of inspection and forming the basis of decisions from sampling. This device is usually used for showing the means of samples or their ranges. The sample data shown in Table 3–1 will be used to illustrate the use of control charts. Ten samples of five each were taken from a large lot of inbound units. The inspection process measured lengths of tubes. Since these are very small medical items, the sample measures are shown in terms of thousandths of millimeter's difference from the specified length.

A *Control Chart of Sample Means*, as shown in Exhibit 3–5, is constructed by first noting the average of all units. This is 443/50 or 8.86 mm. The standard deviation is then determined using the ten means of the samples (9.6, 8.4, 10.6, etc.). This standard deviation is 1.63 mm. The Upper Control Limit (UCL) is then computed using +3 standard deviations from the mean of samples or 8.86 + 3(1.63), which is 13.75. The Lower Control Limit (LCL) is computed by subtracting 3 standard

☐ **TABLE 3-1.** *Samples of Tubing Length in Thousandths of Millimeters from Specification*

Subsample	Observed Values 1	2	3	4	5	Total	Mean	Range
1	10	14	9	6	11	48	9.6	8
2	2	10	8	15	7	42	8.4	13
3	9	12	11	10	11	53	10.6	3
4	3	14	7	4	12	40	8.0	10
5	18	11	9	13	10	61	12.2	9
6	12	7	6	4	7	36	7.2	8
7	7	9	8	3	6	33	6.6	6
8	14	5	3	9	10	41	8.2	11
9	12	8	14	7	9	50	10.0	7
10	6	8	5	11	9	39	7.8	6
						443		81

deviations (or 3 x 1.63) from the sample means. This limit is 8.86 − 3(1.63) or 3.97.

A control chart of range is also useful to indicate the amount of total variability measure between units. Referring to Table 3-1, the ranges for each of the ten samples are 8, 13, 3, etc. A control chart is also made using the mean of all ten ranges and ±3 standard deviations from this mean of 8.1 mm. This is shown as 8.1 ± 3(2.7) or an UCL of 16.2 and a LCL which happens to be in this case 0.0. A lower control limit can not extend below zero because range cannot extend into a negative scale.

Control charts show patterns of variability and visually indicate the degree of this dispersion. They are useful in detecting whether a certain production line is shifting toward better tolerance groupings or worse ones. The upper and lower control limits indicate the range of three standard deviations above and below a mean, or a total of 99.73 percent probability of statistically expected occurrences. If several actual samples begin to be found out of this range, then it can be interpreted that a machine, for example, is, in all likelihood, producing units that are not within the specified norm.

Managerial Approaches to Quality Improvement

The statistical measures and tools presented previously relate to the actual measurement of goods received and how they are used to determine vendor quality performance. Inspection is an after-the-fact phenomenon. That is, it is a measure of goods after they have been produced, shipped, and received by the buyer. It is a process of finding those units that are defective and would disrupt production or harm sales. This section deals with some of the approaches used by buyers and others in the firm to improve quality prior to production of the goods by the vendor.

A trade-off exists here in the form of efforts and costs expended prior to placing the order versus the cost of inspection or the penalty cost of using goods already produced and received in the firm from the vendor.

■ **EXHIBIT 3-5.** *Control Chart of Means, Tubing Length Variation in MM (thousandths)*

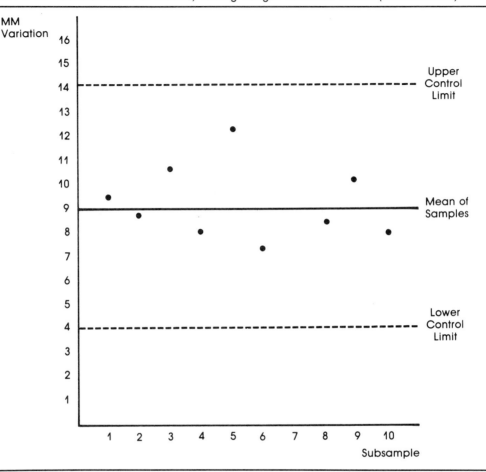

By improving quality on the vendor's production line, there is less chance for defective goods being received and used in production or sale. Received goods that are defective are costly from the standpoint of transportation, special handling, inspection, and harmful costs of possible use. A lesser expenditure might be incurred by the buying firm through quality efforts with the vendor prior to order placement.

Quality Goals and Performance by Vendor

Buyers have several possible indicators to measure when attempting to determine the quality performance of vendors. A recent survey by *Purchasing* magazine presented the quality-related goals buyers strive for when choosing vendors, and are noted as follows in descending order:

1. Consistently meets all specifications on materials and components
2. Improves performance of an end product
3. Improves buyer's in-plant productivity through lower labor or inventory costs

4. Reduces an end product's maintenance cost
5. Reduces buyer firm's maintenance costs.[6]

These are positive factors. They relate to the product and its impact upon the entire firm. They indicate a more encompassing selection decision than product price alone.

The survey also showed how many of the quality-related factors were measured by buyers. These included rejects (90 percent), rework in dollars or hours (66 percent), production stoppages due to poor quality (54 percent), end-customer complaints (52 percent), and amount of material accepted on waivers (50 percent).[7] These measures require information feedback from production and sales to purchasing about the performance of the products being bought and used by the firm. It should not be exceptions data alone. That is, this communication should not relate only to problem goods. A continuous flow of feedback relating to all products purchased and used in production will provide information about fairly good quality materials that might be improved.

Zero Defects Programs

This type of quality improvement approach is a communication from buyer to all vendors emphasizing the need and requirement for quality improvement. It does not necessarily single out any one vendor, rather it is a program of communicating to vendors that the firm seeks lower defects in the future.

Zero defects programs generally stress the acceptance quality level, or AQL, that the firm will tolerate in the future. Where recent performance might have been three percent, a zero defects program might call for one percent or less. Some firms first identify major problem goods and concentrate efforts with the vendors, then move on to those lower on the list. In many instances the firm provides engineering assistance to vendors with quality problems who do not have the engineering talent to reduce or correct such problems. Some quality problems are inherent in the design, while others stem from production processes. In many instances quality problems require one-time correction efforts, with monitoring and minimal attention to fine-tuning thereafter.

Zero defects programs should also extend backward into the purchasing operation as well. Some of the problems that production faces when attempting to use purchased goods might arise from errors in communicating specifications to vendors. Order corrections and changes often require several clerical steps, many of which might not always be changed for an outstanding order. This creates differences in what production expects and what purchasing records indicate the firm is buying. Even the records in purchasing may contain inconsistencies. Attention to this area might include purchase process simplification and a monitoring of clerical performance.

Quality Circles

The concept of quality control circles, or quality circles, has become widely known in recent years as a tool of management successfully used by Japanese firms. These circles are approaches to improving the quality of goods, production, or processes either directly or indirectly involved with the problem areas. The early literature cites use of these groups in areas involving quality control, but their use has been expanded into other problem areas, even interdisciplinary ones in the firm.

The organization of a quality circle usually consists of volunteers from the firm. A team leader is selected who directs the efforts of the group. The group either seeks solutions to a problem defined by upper management, or is free to define and investigate a problem on its own and propose solutions to management. The group members are often given training in quality control and financial measurement tools so that their work is based upon sound measurement and decision tools. The key to the use of quality circles is that the work and proposals are made from lower personnel ranks upward in the firm, rather than from top management down. In this way, persons close to the problems area are better able to attack them and propose correction or improvement approaches. Members of these teams are often compensated monetarily, but in many instances the training, attention, and recognition of the task is sufficient reward.

Quality circles are often useful in attacking problems that exist between two or more departmental disciplines in a firm. These problems are often long-standing, with neither department having the incentive or ability to correct them. The problem might pertain to a practice by one department that minimizes its costs but incurs higher than desirable costs in the other. Or, the problem might be one of item quality that production, engineering, design, and purchasing all have felt is minor to each one of them but cumulatively is large to the firm as a whole.

Purchasing is often involved in quality circles. In this way it provides insights into the attributes and costs of goods being acquired by the firm. Information and paperwork processes are often subjects of quality circles, and purchasing is part of this line activity.

These circles usually are created for specific problems and then are dissolved. They are not always successful. Problems of management commitment, training of the persons in them, cooperation from various departments, and other factors are often cited as reasons for ineffectiveness. But, business literature in the early 1980s mentions quality circles as an effective means for approaching problems that include the input of line personnel. It is on this level that problems can exist for long periods without the attention or knowledge by persons in top management. Efficiency and quality are often created on the line level, and quality circles are a potential means of correcting or improving these while developing the talent of the persons involved.

Vendor Communications
There are several approaches used by firms to improve or assure high quality performance from vendors. These center around communications systems between the firm and vendors. One such approach is part of an overall process at Xerox Corporation. Early Supplier Involvement, or ESI, is one part of the Xerox program. This involves the use of vendor

talent when Xerox is designing new products. Prior to the use of this approach, Xerox would primarily design an entire product, then seek goods of a very specific design from vendors. The ESI system seeks vendor input as to how the product can be designed in as efficient a means possible and serve its intended function. This is a way of utilizing vendor knowledge.

The Xerox approach also includes Pre-Order Supplier Involvement, which it calls POSI. This entails meeting with suppliers about the design soon to be ordered. Vendors review the design and any possible misunderstandings that might arise later during the term of an order are cleared up at this point. These meetings include Xerox purchasing, production, engineering and quality personnel as well as counterpart personnel from vendor firms.[8]

This approach involves vendors in ways that reduce quality problems afterward, as well as the total cost of buying and using a product. Firms might often design a product with specifications that, if followed, would require special production processes by vendors and would incur high costs and prices. By involving the vendor, his/her knowledge and capabilities will enter into the process. The vendor might state that a certain specification might cost $1.00, but a small percentage alteration could be produced for a fraction of that amount. The POSI approach also clears up potential problems before the order cycle period where they might cause high production and marketing penalties for the buying firm.

Plant Visits Regarding Quality Control

Plant visits should also include a review of vendor quality control processes. Important information factors to obtain relate to whether the firm has a quality control staff and what its duties and powers are. A firm might have a person overseeing quality control, but this person might not have the power to reject defective goods or change production processes. Another key factor here is to whom does the quality control group report. If it is to production, the ability to affect production processes might be limited.

Quality control investigation processes should seek to determine where control checks are made. Ideally, these should occur on incoming goods, prior to production, inprocess control, and prior to packaging or shipment. If the vendor buys goods without checking them and assembles them into a unit that the buyer firm sells, the vendor's vendor goods might not be inspected until final preparation for use by the ultimate consumers.

The plant visit also can be used to determine the overall commitment of the vendor to quality. Indicators of this factor include whether there is a quality manual used in the firm and whether all production employees receive training in this area. General maintenance and inventory control practices are visual clues to plant management that affect quality in a pervasive sense.

Conclusion

Quality is one of the prime objectives of purchasing. It relates not only to the product the firm is producing and selling, but it stems from the vendor and the vendor's vendors. Inspection is one aspect of quality that receives much attention, but this is checking after the fact. Attention to the design of the product and the production processes of vendors is often a cost-effective effort that can reduce quality problems or enhance quality altogether in the first place. Quality is one of the basic considerations in the purchase decision of the ultimate consumer. The final selling firm, and all previous firms in the chain-of-product flow, depend upon the competitiveness of the final product.

FOOTNOTES

1. Lamar Lee, Jr. and Donald W. Dobler, *Purchasing and Materials Management* (New York: McGraw-Hill, 1977), chapter 3.
2. "Buyers Resist Attempts to Cut Corners on Quality," *Purchasing*, May 29, 1980, p. 29.
3. Ibid.
4. Lee and Dobler, *Purchasing and Materials Management*, p. 167.
5. Ibid., p. 176.
6. "Quality Extends Way Beyond Reject Rates," *Purchasing*, January 28, 1982, p. 84.
7. Ibid.
8. "Xerox Launches Four-Point Program to Eliminate Defects," *Purchasing*, December 10, 1981.

SOURCE FOR FURTHER READING

Patchin, Robert I., *The Management and Maintenance of Quality Circles*, Homewood, IL: Dow Jones-Irwin Books, 1981.

QUESTIONS FOR REVIEW

1. How would you define the word quality?

2. What is quality assurance?

3. What are the pros and cons of using externally created specifications versus those designed by the buying firm?

4. Discuss the ways in which poor quality increases the cost of production.

5. What are some of the critical points in time or events to watch for in possible quality deterioration from vendors?

6. What are the primary elements of a quality assurance program?

7. What are the trade-off elements and decision factors related to the total-inspection, no-inspection, or part-inspection decision?

8. What are the features of an operating characteristic curve?

9. What are control charts, and how are they useful in purchasing? Should a buyer request them from a vendor for the lot of goods being purchased?

10. Distinguish between attributes and variables and give examples of each.

11. Why have zero defects programs failed or not attained the benefits for which they were designed?

12. What are the elements of a quality circle program?

Lillian Parry is considering whether or not to inspect certain products when received. Information gathered that is needed in this analysis is as follows:

Problem 3-1

Lot size	7,500 units
% Expected defective	2%
Cost to inspect	$.25 per unit
Cost of using defective units	$40 each

Questions:
1. What is the cost of inspecting?
2. What is the total cost of the no-inspection option?
3. Where is the break-even point of the above two alternatives?
4. What is the effect of
   a. decreases in defective rates?
   b. decreases in the cost penalties of using defective units?
   c. increases in the cost of inspection?
5. Draw a chart of the full costs of total-inspection and no-inspection for the following defective rates: 1%, 5%, and 10%.

A shipment of inbound parts was received by a firm. The buyer requested a sample inspection of the goods received. The inspection group took five samples each with five units. The results of this process are as follows.

Problem 3-2

Samples of Unit Weight in Grams
of Deviation from Specification

Subsample	1	2	3	4	5
1	3	7	0	5	1
2	9	4	3	5	0
3	1	4	2	2	1
4	2	6	3	1	1
5	0	1	3	1	1

Questions:
1. Construct a control chart of means and a control chart of ranges for this data.
2. The firm's policy is to reject any shipments in which any two of the subsamples exceed three standard deviations from the mean. Is this the situation with the above data?

INTRODUCTION

METHODS OF PRICE DETERMINATION

    Published Price Lists and Market Data
    Competitive Bidding
    Two-Step Bidding
    Negotiations

COST ANALYSIS — A MAJOR WORKING TOOL OF PURCHASING

    Basic Costs
    Cost Construction and Analysis
    Summary of Cost Analysis

PRICING ARRANGEMENTS

MANAGING INFLATION AND COST INCREASES IN PURCHASING

    Evaluating the Need for a Vendor Price
      Increase
    Long-Term Contracts
    Escalators
    Surcharges
    Evaluating the Profitability of a Volume
      Discount
    Methods of Blunting Price Increases
    Price Freezes and Their Impacts

CONCLUSION

CHAPTER OBJECTIVES

After reading this chapter you should

- Understand the basic cost concepts in purchasing,

- Be able to apply the various price-determination techniques,

- Appreciate the various pricing systems in use,

- Understand how to meet the various price increase tactics in use.

Managing Purchasing Costs

Introduction

Purchasing decisions impact the department's own operation as well as production, marketing, customer service, and the cash resources of the firm. "Lowest final cost" means lowest total cost to the buying firm. This does not always mean lowest cost to the purchasing department. This objective, as well as others, relies upon the systems view and total-cost concept of the firm.

This chapter investigates the major cost-based decision elements of purchasing. These include the ways in which prices are determined, how costs behave, pricing arrangements that are used in the field, and how to act in the face of price increases.

Methods of Price Determination

There are four primary methods of determining the price a firm will pay for goods and services. These are price lists, competitive bidding, two-step bidding, and negotiation.

Published Price Lists and Market Data

This system of price determination is largely imposed by suppliers through the publishing of prices, rates, charges, etc. Price lists generally are found with standardized products. Transportation services, eggs, and oil are examples. Freight rates are published in tariffs for all shippers and receivers to see and use. The egg industry largely sells its products based upon prices that are published by an industry association source. Though the prices published represent summaries of the most recent sales, this publication greatly affects the price charged over the next few days. Oil is often posted at a certain price by OPEC, and this price serves as a single price for most firms in times of tight oil supply or high market demand.

Price lists are posted prices. Many of them can be found in the Wall Street Journal, the Journal of Commerce, or other publications. These are the prices at which sellers seek to make sales. However, there are many instances when these prices are not the ones actually used. One example is trade discounts offered to middlemen for distributing the product to the market. Wholesalers receive a discount as compensation for the services performed by them. Other discounts might be in the form of seasonal or cash discounts. These are discussed in greater detail in Chapter 18.

Another posted price exception occurs when the market becomes soft for the seller. In this instance, a posted price of $100 might still remain in effect, but the seller now offers to pay for freight and allow sixty-day payment terms. The seller did not reduce his/her price, but the true cost to the buyer might now be $85 with these other considerations. This tactic is often used in periods of price freezes and is discussed later in the chapter.

The buyer facing a price-list market conducts price investigation. This is the act of determining the price and total cost of acquiring goods from the range of vendors possible or desirable. Price analysis might require the adjustment of prices that include or exclude certain services in order to determine common total costs of acquisition from each source. In the end a buyer might create a price list for their own firm to use.

Competitive Bidding

While the price-list method of price determination is common with standardized goods and services, competitive bidding is useful in providing competition among sellers for both standard and specialized items. This process of price determination is initiated by sending vendors "Requests for Quotes." The RFQ should contain all the key information needed by the vendors to prepare replies and offers (quotes) for the goods at prices they are willing to charge. Detailed specifications are necessary in the RFQ so that vendors reply with quotes on the actual goods the firm is seeking to acquire.

The bidding process requires that quotes be received in final form by a certain deadline. At that point in time, the buyer opens the bids and makes comparisons among them to determine which one promises the best quality and best value. The bidding process should be objective. In order for it to be effective, many criteria must exist. These are: 1) the RFQ be clear and contain all details needed for the potential vendors to make a valid bid; 2) there should be a sufficient volume being transacted in order to make the cost of the process worthwhile; 3) many sources should exist with the market being responsive to the RFQ's; 4) sufficient lead time for the entire process should exist; and 5) the suppliers should not be collusive.[1] Bidding is a process that requires time and some buyer costs, but it is a very good one for determining which source to use. The quotes from potential vendors are legal offers.

Some problems can arise in the competitive bidding process, however. One of these is that the specifications might be so tight and restrictive that few or no vendors present quotes. Another is that errors in the specifications that are discovered later cause the initial RFQ and bid process to be wasted. Some bidders might wish extensions of time in order to prepare a bid, or they might seek the ability to submit a second bid based upon information received from the buyer about other bids. This situation can be tempting for buyers. One bidder might wish to obtain the business and might do so by underbidding others once he or she has knowledge of what the others have bid. This tends to cause future problems in that the bidders who did not receive the work will eventually lose interest in bidding. The firm seeking the business might bid below its true costs only to cause problems in delivery or quality during the term of the purchase.

The competitive bidding process is designed for objectivity, and it should be managed as such. It provides a consistent method for comparing the quality, price, and total costs of acquiring a good from each of many potential vendors. Bids also provide information about vendors that is useful for future reference, even about those vendors who not selected for the present order.

Two-Step Bidding

Two-step bidding is useful when the vendor will develop some or much of the product being sought. As such, it is often used in high-technology purchases and in some construction settings. Two-step bidding seeks initial bids from potential vendors along with preliminary designs and plans proposed by each one. The vendor presenting the best technical design and acceptable price is then approached in order to establish a final detailed design and a negotiated price for the specific details of the work.

This process of price determination is used for goods or services for which the buying firm is not fully knowledgeable about as to the constructs of the final product. Vendor research and engineering knowledge and talent is used to develop it. The process utilizes a blend of competitive bidding and negotiation. It is useful when there is sufficient lead time for initiation of the actual work.

Negotiations

Negotiation is the fourth method of price determination. It is useful in situations where the other methods might not have been appropriate or have failed and is covered in greater detail in Chapter 6. The advantages of negotiation are that it is flexible in creating the design of the work, determining the split of duties between the vendor and buyer firms, and determining the final price. The drawbacks to this method are that it requires much time and expense in preparing and conducting. A negotiated price is only valid in relation to the negotiated work. It does not assure the buyer that the best possible price was attained since no competitive comparison was conducted.

Price investigation is the comparative analysis of prices charged by the market either through price lists or somewhat through competitive bidding. A related concept is cost analysis. This is the process of the buyer constructing what appears to be the best estimates of a vendor's costs. This information is then useful in the two-step bidding and negotiation processes.

Cost Analysis—a Major Working Tool of Purchasing

Cost analysis requires the use of financial and costing techniques in order to plan and make decisions. It is important for evaluating competing bids and for preparing and managing a departmental budget. This section discusses 1) basic cost definitions that are necessary in the construction and understanding of costs and their behavior, 2) how costs can be constructed in order to make valid decisions pertaining to vendor production activities, 3) break-even analysis, 4) target break-even analysis, and 5) the learning curve.

Basic Costs

A cost in one situation is not the same as in another. A cost can behave differently throughout various ranges of activity or volume. This section presents some insights into the basic behavior of costs and how this behavior might be illustrated. Table 4-1 presents and discusses each of the key costs faced by buyers and planners. Exhibit 4-1 presents these costs in terms of how they behave.

Cost Construction and Analysis

This section presents ways in which specific cost components are collected and analyzed. Ways of determining the direct costs of producing a product, the decisions relating to allocations of overhead and other fixed expenses, break-even analysis, target break-even analysis and the learning curve are discussed.

Direct Product Costs

The direct costs of producing a product are those of labor, material, energy, movement, and any other costs important to the seller. Some of these costs are discussed as follows.

1. Direct Labor Rates. This factor is the cost of labor directly involved in the production of the product. It is the hourly or other dollar measurement of the cost of labor to the vendor. This is not merely the wage rate. It is the total hourly cost of the labor and includes the cost of fringes, benefits, and direct supervision. Thus, an employee earning $7.50 per hour in actual wages might have true or effective wages of $9.75 per hour. Sources for this information are industry associations, unions, departments of labor, chambers of commerce, and local newspapers.

2. Labor Estimates. This is the total number of hours necessary to produce the items by the necessary employees. This measure requires an estimate or calculated standard as to the amount of labor input required for each unit or for the job in total. Productivity and the learning curve become important in this cost component. The arithmetic product of the labor estimate times the labor rate equals the total cost of labor for the work.

3. Materials Evaluation. This is the material and product inputs required for the work. Key decisions to be made here pertain to product

□ **TABLE 4-1.** *Basic Costs and Their Behavior*

Cost	Form	Key Points
Total variable cost	Sum of all variable costs Exhibit 4–1a	A cost that changes in direct proportion to activity or volume. Most material costs are variable.
Per-unit variable cost	Cost per unit of variable items Exhibit 4–1b	The total variable cost at a given volume divided by that volume. The number of units of material or energy need to produce each item of output.
Total fixed cost	A constant cost that is incurred regardless of volume or activity (e.g, rent, depreciation) Exhibit 4–1c	A constant cost throughout an entire range of output or activity.
Per-unit fixed cost	The share of the total fixed cost that is prorated over each unit of output Exhibit 4–1d	Decreases as more units are handled. Determined by dividing total fixed cost by the total number of units handled.
Total fixed and variable cost	The sum of total variable and total fixed costs Exhibit 4–1e	Also called full cost. Full cost = Total fixed cost + (Variable cost per unit) × (number of unit). Most cost functions are of this form.
Fully allocated cost	The total fixed and variable cost on a per unit basis Exhibit 4–1f	Fully allocated cost = Variable cost per unit + (total fixed costs)/(number of units). Tends to decrease as more units are added.
Step cost	Fixed for short spans; variable over long spans Exhibit 4–1g	Basic illustration of how production shift-run costs are incurred. Truck runs also appear in this manner.
Per-unit step cost	Step cost divided by number of units handled. Exhibit 4–1h	Decreases within range of each step; rarely economy over range of many steps.
Marginal or incremental cost	The increase in total costs associated with additional output only	Can be merely an increase in variable costs for producing a few more units at end of existing production line. Can be additional variable costs and some new fixed cost if another shift is required to produce the goods.
Common costs	Cost necesssary for the production of two or more products that cannot rationally be allocated to either	Cost of factory overhead to two or more products. Same problem with corporate overhead. Allocations can be done in number of ways based upon percent division of revenue, direct cost, labor, space, investment, etc. Problem is that each form of allocation produces different final cost for each product.
Joint costs	Cost of an activity that unavoidably produces two or more different products (e.g, refining oil makes gas, diesel, naptha, and other chemicals)	Problem is that cost of one activity automatically produces another, and costs cannot be divided rationally between the two. Specific cost determination of the products is subject to allocation method used. Allocations can be as with common costs.

■ EXHIBIT 4–1. *Cost Illustrations*

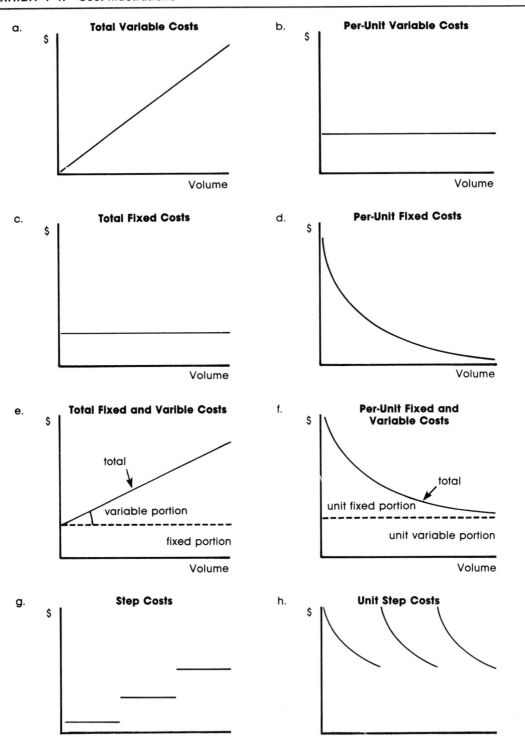

■ **EXHIBIT 4-2.**   *Shift Work Step Function Costs*

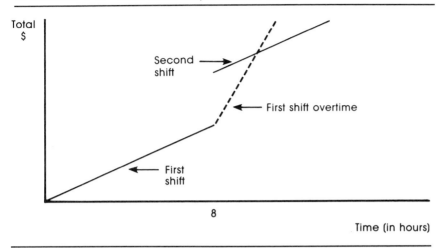

quality and fair prices to be paid for the goods. This process is made simpler when the buying firm actually provides the materials for the vendor. A part of this cost, in either case, is that of allowable scrap, defects, or waste from problems with the product quality or production efficiency.

4. Materials Mix. This step requires a determination of the specific blend of materials or components parts. This is often necessary when chemicals or construction work can be performed using different formulations or methods of using materials.

The above costs must also be used to determine the specific manner in which production will take place. For example, Exhibit 4-2 shows how a shift operation will incur labor costs for a particular job. Since the job will require more than an eight-hour period, a choice must be made as to whether to use the original shift in overtime or use a second shift that might also be used on other work.

Allocations of Overhead and Other Costs

The next step in cost construction involves treatment of the fixed and overhead costs. If there is a set up step required in production that cost is fixed regardless of the number of units to be produced. This creates a semi-fixed cost function with the variable costs of each unit produced being incurred only after the initial fixed cost is encountered.

Overhead cost allocations are added to job costs in any number of ways, many of which were presented above in the common and joint costs sections. Some firms add overhead according to a fixed percentage over and above variable expenses. That is, each $1 of variable expense might have $.20 added to cover overhead. The buyer should seek to determine the method of overhead or joint cost allocation used. In one setting a very large allocation might be applied in order to show high costs and the need for a higher price. Another cost allocation might be of lesser amount and result in a lower negotiable price from the vendor. The basis of overhead allocation is often accepted by buyers as a cost that is not flexible, but in actual practice it is a difficult cost to determine and is subject to close examination and negotiation flexibility.

One example of how fixed costs are not always a cost that the buyer must necessarily bear is as follows. A large equipment manufacturer incurs an expense of $50,000 in setting up production to produce one line of items. The line is now producing Product A for Customer J. Customer K is seeking to buy some units of Product B and A. If the order was first placed for B, then the vendor would incur a $50,000 set up cost to switch over from A to B. Another $50,000 would be necessary to later switch back to A. The buyer who knows his requirements far enough in advance might be able to negotiate a special price without $50,000 built into the job cost for an order of A first that represents a "tack-on" job to the end of an existing production run. Savings such as this are possible when the buyer knows his purchasing requirements far in advance, is knowledgeable as to the production activities of the vendor, and is capable of adjusting purchase timing decisions throughout the year.

Another way in which overhead costs come into play for the buyer is by purchase timing within the fiscal cycle of the vendor. If the total overhead costs of the vendor were covered by normal production in the early part of the year, this cost element can sometimes be negotiated out of the price when goods are bought toward the end of the year. Again, this calls for the buyer to be knowledgeable about the vendor's production operations, cost structure, and financial practices.

Still another useful way in which overhead cost knowledge can be of benefit to the buyer is in determining whether or not his firm represents a submarket to the vendor, in which case these costs can possibly be avoided completely. Many firms determine variable and fixed costs as well as profit targets based upon a normal expectation of sales. If a firm has excess capacity at the end of a period and all overhead and profit targets have already been met, then that firm might be willing to sell additional goods without charging for overhead costs or the normal profit rate. This is a common practice in export sales. A firm might use its excess production capacity for sales at lower prices to overseas markets that do not compete against existing vendors in the domestic market. The separation of these submarkets is a necessary component for this form of economic price discrimination.

Break-Even Analysis

Break-even analysis is useful in determining appropriate lot sizes to purchase. Many vendors use it in order to determine appropriate order size requirements and unit overhead costs on runs of different sizes. The break-even tool can be used in a revenue-cost sense or in the analysis of two cost functions.

The mathematical tool that determines this break-even point is based upon the fact that at the break-even point total costs and total revenue are equal. At no other point are these two equations equal. For example, a vendor's price is $5.50 per unit. Total revenue is equal to $5.50X, which is $5.50 times the number of units. The total costs for a production run are equal to $1,000 in fixed costs, plus $4.00 times the number of units. This cost equation is $1,000 + $4.00X. The volume of units at the break-even will be equal for both the total revenue and total cost lines, so the X quantity term can be used for both equations. To solve the problem, place both equations equal to each other and solve for X, the unknown number of units.

$$\text{Revenue} \times (\text{units}) = \text{Total Fixed costs} + (\text{Variable Cost per Unit}) \times (\text{units})$$
$$\$5.50X = \$1,000 + \$4.00X$$
$$\$1.50X = \$1,000$$
$$X = 666.67 \text{ units.}$$

At 666.67 units the firm breaks-even on total costs with total revenue. To check, determine the amount of the deficit if 500 units were produced and sold, and the amount of profit if 800 units produced and sold; see how there is neither a loss nor a profit when 666.67 units are sold.

This tool is also useful in the analysis of which production process to use when two or more are possible. For example, a buyer is assisting a production analyst in selecting a machine for use in the shop. Data from two vendors indicates that Unit A costs $500 to set up each time it is to be used, and the unit costs of operation are $3.00 per unit. Unit B costs $1,000 to set up, but its variable costs of operation are $2.30 per unit. The break-even point is that volume level at which the total costs of both machines are equal.

$$\$500 + \$3.00X = \$1,000 + \$2.30X$$
$$\$.70X = \$500$$
$$X = 714.28 \text{ units.}$$

At volume levels below 714 units, Unit A is least costly to operate. At levels above 714, Unit B is more economical. Now the choice is based upon what the normal volume usage level will be in production. Exhibit 4-3 shows how the total costs of both these units compare to each other.

■ **EXHIBIT 4-3.** *Total Cost Break-Even Analysis*

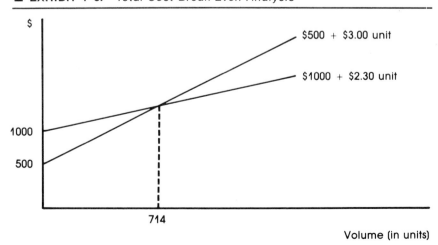

Target Break-Even Analysis

This tool is also useful for the buyer when some of the production costs of the vendor are known. Target break-even can be used to determine the lot size that will be necessary in order for the vendor's costs to be reduced to a point that allows a favorable price to the buyer. This is a key factor when the vendor must incur large costs to set up a production line for the job the buyer is seeking.

To illustrate this tool, assume that a buyer is seeking goods that require the vendor to incur a $5,000 tool and die set up cost. Known variable expenses are $45.00 per unit. The vendor has normally sold the units at $75.00 each. The buyer is willing to buy a much larger quantity, but the price must be lower than $75.00. Target break-even can be used in this situation to determine what volume is necessary in order for the vendor to break even at a lower price. The buyer is seeking a price of $60.00. The volume necessary for the vendor to break even at that price is computed as follows:

$$\$60.00X = \$5,000 + \$45.00X$$
$$\$15.00X = \$5,000$$
$$X = 333.33 \text{ units.}$$

Of course, the vendor is not receiving any profit at that price and volume. A profit factor would then be built into the price of the goods in order to compensate the vendor for the profit element. If the vendor wishes at least a $10.00 per-unit profit on volume jobs, and the buyer seeks a $60.00 price, then the profit is added to the variable cost term for a total dollar amount that must be recouped in each unit. The calculation then is as follows:

$$\$60.00X = \$5,000 + \$55.00X$$
$$\$5.00X = \$5,000$$
$$X = 1,000 \text{ units.}$$

The buyer seeking a $60.00 price would then have to order at least 1,000 units in one run.

Learning Curve

Another key factor in cost analysis is the learning curve. It is the relationship between the number of units produced and the time required to produce each unit. It is a labor concept that states that as more units are produced each successive unit will require less labor time. Exhibit 4–4 shows the basic idea of the learning curve. The learning curve is stated in terms of the following: the full effect of the learning curve is attained with the doubling of volume. For example, in the above 90% learning curve, as unit volume doubles, the time required is only 90% of what it was at the previous volume point. Table 4–2 shows how the 90% learning curve appears along with an 80% and a 70% when the first unit requires 20 man-minutes to produce.

The learning curve shows that each successive unit requires less time to produce than the one before it. The absolute amount of the reduction for each unit decreases, however, as more of them are produced. That is, the most dramatic improvement in efficiency occurs in the first several

■ **EXHIBIT 4-4.** *Learning Curve—90%*

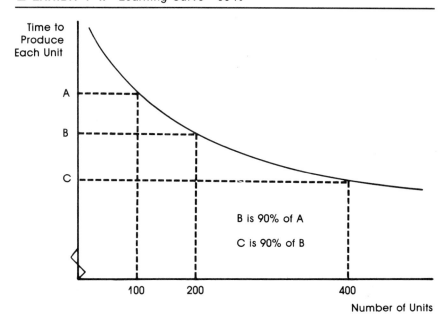

units. The effect of the learning curve approaches a flat line as a large amount of units is produced.

Buyers use the learning curve concept in order to determine appropriate labor estimates on work that has never before been performed. The question that arises is, by the time the 1,000th unit is produced, how much labor time is required for it. Further, how much total time will the vendor consume to produce all 1,000 units. Estimates of the learning curve can be roughly made based upon an evaluation of similar type work that the vendor has performed in the past.

Summary of Cost Analysis

Knowledgeable buyers must be aware of the primary cost structures of the vendor industries they have available to them. This information can be obtained in several ways including research sources such as

☐ **TABLE 4-2.** *Examples of 90%, 80%, and 70% Learning Curves—20 Minute Task*

		Minutes Required	
# Units		**90% LC**	
80% LC		**70% LC**	
1	20.00	20.00	20.00
2	18.00	16.00	14.00
4	16.20	12.80	9.80
8	14.58	10.24	6.86

Moody's and Standard & Poore's financial publications, annual reports, subscriptions to the trade journals in the vendor's field, visits to firms in the industry, attendance at industry association meetings and shows, and by monitoring labor matters in the field. This information can be supported by data in past bids that have been submitted by various vendors. Another source is by interviewing persons in their own firm who may have been employed in the vendor's industry. These sources collectively provide the buyer with insights into the trends, events, and costing structure of the industry from which he or she is acquiring goods.

Pricing Arrangements

There are many ways in which price is established or fixed in a buying-selling arrangement. This section presents the major ways used, with insights into how they provide protection or incentives for both buyers and sellers. Such arrangements are typically contract terms related to prices and charges.

Table 4-3 presents many of the pricing arrangements that are in use between buyers and sellers. Each has certain features designed for the protection of either the buyer or seller. The relative market strength of each party determines the use of each. Some are in favor of the vendor and not the seller. In many of these instances, however, these arrangements are accepted as ways in which the vendor may obtain protection from loss and the buyer still obtain the needed goods.

Managing Inflation and Cost Increases in Purchasing

Evaluating the Need for a Vendor Price Increase

A new buyer at a major manufacturing firm was informed by a prime vendor that its price was being increased because of a wage hike. While the reason was plausible, the buyer wondered if the price increase was totally justified. The buyer applied some industry analysis to determine exactly how much of the price increase was truly due to the reasons stated in the price increase announcement.

The following analysis can provide insights into the need for a price increase. The information used to evaluate this increase is found from sources about the vendor and its industry. Some of this information can be found in summary form in Table 1-1. For example, a vendor paper firm has costs equal to the industry average stated in the table. That is, direct labor is 12.1 percent of that industry's total revenue. A price increase of 10 percent is announced due to an increase in labor rates of 14 percent. Using the following formula, the buyer can determine how much of the price increase is justified by the wage increase:

Justifiable Price Increase = (Labor as % of Industry Cost Structure) × (Amount of Wage Increase)

$$? = (12.1\%) \times (.14)$$

Justifiable Price Increase = 1.694%.

☐ **TABLE 4–3.** *Analysis of Pricing Arrangements*

Form of Arrangement	Key Points
Firm fixed price	One price in contract. Any cost overruns or inflation during the work are at risk of vendor. Best protection for buyer.
Price subject to escalation	Fixed price, subject to upward revision if any of the stipulated cost factors increase greatly during work—labor and materials most commonly. Escalations protect vendor from eroded profits.
Fixed price with redetermination	Used when some cost components cannot be projected when work being planned; only determined during and at end of work. Allows final price to be determined later.
Cost plus fixed fee	Vendor total costs to be paid plus a fixed fee for overhead and profit.
Cost plus percent of cost	Similar to cost plus fixed fee, except that this arrangement provides a fee for overhead and profit that is a percentage of whatever the primary costs finally total. Used when costs of project are unknown or involve new and unknown technology. Perhaps the worst possible pricing form for buyers—all risk of costs passed on to buyer. Incentive is for maximum cost for the vendor.
Cost plus incentive fee	Used in construction work and machinery design. Higher fee for profit provided for early completion or savings in design.
Fixed price incentive	Same elements as above, except that the cost element is fixed.
Cost plus overhead	Used in consulting services hired by not-for-profit institutions like universities. No profit is charged, but surplus is charged through an overhead fee.
Cost-share	Found in contract research settings. Low or nonexistent fee is charged in exchange for sharing in benefits of research results. Found in construction work in underdeveloped nations in which no fee or a small fee is charged; firm shares in output from the work, such as oil output.
Firm price/level of effort	In consulting or research, fee is fixed for a specified amount of work, regardless of findings.
Time and materials	Similar to cost plus percent, price is sum of labor and materials used to complete work. Features similar to those of cost plus percent.
Cost at delivery or price in effect at time of shipment	Found in product shortage or critical mineral settings. Price is set at the prevailing market price on the day of sale and not what was paid by vendor when items were purchased.

That is, labor is only a small part of the industry cost structure. When only 12.1 percent of the costs of the business increase by 14 percent, the total firm impact is only 1.694 percent in additional costs. This is the amount of price increase that is justified by the labor cost raise; the remaining 8.306 percent is pure profit increase.

In another setting, a plastics manufacturer experienced a 20 percent increase in material costs in the 1979 energy crunch period. The 20 percent increase on top of the material cost component of 48.1 percent means that total costs to the firm have increased 9.62 percent. Any price increase above that was not justified on the grounds of the material increase reason. The unjustified portion of this material cost and the above labor cost is subject to negotiation if the market is not totally in favor of the seller.

Long-Term Contracts

Contracts for goods over long periods are useful in creating price certainty in the future. The price arranged can become fixed through the contract in a way that protects the buyer from price increases that might occur in the interim. But, while this approach is a useful tool, there are three prime cautions with it. One, the price might drop and the buyer may be forced to buy at what is now a higher than market price. Two, the price of materials might climb so high as to make it impossible for the vendor to provide the goods. In this instance the buyer has a contract entitling him to the goods, but the seller cannot provide them. And, three, the quality of the goods provided by the vendor might be a problem during the entire period.

Escalators

Escalators are clauses placed in contracts to protect the supplier in the event of price increases during the term of the work. While they serve a necessary role in many instances, the buyer should also seek to protect his/her position by assuring that the escalator is sound and not over-compensating the seller.

Features that buyers should strive for in situations where escalators are demanded by vendors are as follows. *Objectivity*—The amount of the increases should be measurable and based upon objective factors. *Verifiable*—The cost increase charged by the vendor should be verifiable by the buyer. *Beyond Control of Vendor*—The factor subject to escalation should not be one controllable by the vendor. Examples are national labor contracts and raw material sources that are not owned or controlled by the vendor. *Escalator Based Upon Actual Costs*—A common basis of requesting an escalator is an index such as the wholesale price index. A vendor might request this whenever a contract is long in duration. This measure is very general and does not necessarily represent the true costs incurred by the vendor. The escalator factors should be based upon only those costs actually incurred by the vendor.

Another factor in the use of escalators is the cut-off date or date of determination of the amount of escalator to be used. In a period of rising prices, an escalator that provides for costs of labor and materials at the date of shipment to the buyer overcompensates the vendor. In a six-month contract, the materials were purchased in the early months of the contract, not at the end of it. Similarly, labor should not be charged at the latest rate; the proper rate should be weighted to specific actual rates incurred in each month of the job.

Surcharges

Surcharges are extra charges added onto a base price. In recent years they have been found in goods containing precious minerals and in transportation rate settings. Not only do they cause higher costs to buyers, but they represent unknown cost increases that the buyer must incur on very short notice, if any at all.

In the precious metals context,. surcharges are typically based upon the amount of the metal that is contained within a product and the price of the metal in the week of final product shipment to the buyer. Some approaches that may be used in attempting to diminish the impact of these unknown cost factors include negotiating a higher base price for the product in the first place. This new base price would be firm. Another is by not paying for the portion of the surcharge that has been added due to a long order backlog. In this setting, the buyer minimizes his/her harmful impact from the vendor delay. Another is through auditing the amount of the surcharge. One firm that buys products from vendors requiring such metals actually supplies the metal to the vendor just prior to the vendor's scheduled production of the good.[2]

Surcharges exist in transportation with regard to fuel cost recovery. In these settings, the rate for transportation is a base. The cost for fuel is charged on top of the rate to compensate the carrier for whatever the fuel cost was during the week or month of shipment. Though it is not possible to obtain fuel-cost concessions like the above from steamship companies, it is relatively easy to do so with motor carriers. One major grocery chain in the Midwest negotiates a basic transportation price for goods movement that is fixed for a year. The firm reimburses the carrier within three days of delivery for its fuel, based upon the prevailing diesel fuel market and the efficiency of the trucks. During the first year of the arrangement, 1979, the grocery chain paid fuel bills to the carrier based upon a 5 miles-per-gallon consumption rate. In 1980 the rate was 5 1/4 miles per gallon. The rate gradually is being increased in order to induce the carrier to reinvest in more fuel-efficient equipment.

Evaluating the Profitability of a Volume Discount

Large lot buys are one way purchase costs can be reduced. The lower purchase price advantage must be considered in light of the added inventory investment cost.

An example illustrates this decision. A buyer of packaging normally purchases one-month lots from a particular vendor. The vendor offers a five percent discount for a lot purchase quantity equal to two months. The buyer firm's annual cost of holding inventory is twenty percent.

The following formula can be used to determine whether or not the two-month supply purchase is worthwhile for the buyer.

$$ROA = \frac{24 \times \% \text{ Discount without Decimal}}{[(1 - \% \text{discount})(\# \text{ regular months stock} + \# \text{ extra months stock})]}$$

$$- \# \text{regular months stock}$$
$$- \text{ annual } \% \text{ cost of inventory}$$

The return on assets (ROA) obtained from the discount savings when considering the firm's annual cost of holding inventories is:

$$ROA = [24 \times 5\%]/[[(1.00 - .05)(1 + 1)] - 1.00] - .20$$
$$= 113\%.$$

The discount applies to the entire larger lot, both this month's goods and those for next month. But, the added carrying costs only apply to the added inventory.

If the example was extended to two month's additional inventory, the problem computes to a return on assets of 44.9 percent. Buyers often assume that a mere 5 percent discount is small in relation to prime interest rates or the firm's required investment return for new asset acquisition. But, the 5 percent shown above applies to the purchase price of the goods, which are one month or two months in duration, while the annual carrying cost of inventory is 20 percent, but only 1 2/3 percent for one month or 3 1/3 percent for two months.[3]

Methods of Blunting Price Increases

There are many approaches that buyers can use in order to reduce the effects of actual price increases imposed by vendors. The following are some that are used in practice and consist of a blend of tactics that include negotiation, attention to financial details, and use of logistic's principles.

Price increases are usually communicated by vendors in advance of the effective date. This being the case, the buyer can forward buy in order to avoid the future increase. Vendors often announce such price increases in order to obtain orders now in order to fill up production capacity. The effect is often to shift what would otherwise have been future months' work to near-term months. That is, the period just after the price increase date will often be a slack one for the vendor. In this instance, a vendor might also be willing to negotiate a long-term contract at the present price that covers deliveries at the same price into the period in which spot sales are to be made at the higher price.

Buyers can also hold off the effects of price increases by negotiating for the price not to go into effect, for example, on the next order or an outstanding one that is yet subject to redetermination. This tactic has some limited success depending upon the relative strengths of the buyer and seller with each other.

Buying on the spot market when possible can provide some cost savings in comparison to posted price increases. This will often occur when one vendor seeks a price increase to make up for a recent period of low profit, or if it thinks its specific product will bear a higher price market. Prices are rarely established upon complete knowledge of the market; they are often determined through trial and error. By shifting to another vendor or by buying on the spot market at a lower price, a signal is sent to the vendor increasing its price that the buying firm has alternative choices.

Consignment buying is a method used by some to stall off price increases. This is an extension of the long-term contract concept. In this method the vendor delivers goods to the buyer who only pays for them once they are used. The availability of the goods and the fact that they are not on the buyer's financial statements as inventory until used provides very high inventory turnover, low investment, and the ability to hold down a price increase.

Smaller lot size purchases can also have the effect of reducing the effect of price increases. If, for example, a firm purchased $10,000 worth of goods per month at a price of $50 each. The average inventory held is $5,000 during the month. If the price is increased to $60, then the average inventory would normally become $6,000. Instead, if the firm was able to buy in smaller lot sizes, of say, two weeks' supply, then the average inventory becomes $3,000. The firm experiences an increase of inventory turnover and reduces its investment in the goods. If the firm's cost of carrying inventory is twenty percent, then the total cost of inventory holding over a year would be $600 instead of $1,200. The smaller lot size also often permits the firm to sell the final product before the vendor must be paid. Thus, an increase in working capital may more than offset the price increase. But, the impact of this tactic is only felt when reductions in current inventory levels can be attained. It will no longer work when the inventory is reduced to an absolute minimum.

Cash flow might also be a reason for price increase. The buying firm might have in the past delayed paying the vendor due to maximization of cash investment opportunities. The buyer might be able to eliminate a price increase by arranging a shorter payment period. On the other hand, the vendor might have increased its price because the buyer firm delayed payment for many weeks. Negotiation with the vendor and the buyer's own financial managers might result in faster payment and cancellation of the price increase.

Substituted product input is a long-term price increase alternative. Through value analysis or substitute materials, the firm might be able to continue production of the final product without the price increase of the product in question. This is a common occurrence when railroads raise their rates and motor carrier rates become less costly in comparison. Many products have substitute products. Examples are plastic-/wood, plastic/metal, rubber/plastic, and many exist in chemical and food situations.

Price Freezes and Their Impacts

Many national governments impose price and/or wage freezes upon firms and individuals in their societies. The reasons usually involve curbing inflation or reducing the effects of monopolistic practices by some industries. Price freezes have been applied recently in the U. S., most notably in 1971 by the Nixon Administration. That freeze was centered around prices and wages, and the primary requirement was that neither could rise by more than seven percent yearly. Firms had to post prices and prove that price and wage increases did not exceed that amount.

Price freezes affect buyers through the behavior they tend to cause in vendor firms. The general effect of a freeze is that most firms are restricted from increasing their prices, but their costs continue to rise thus diminishing profits. This is particularly a problem when many of the material sources are not subject to the freeze. International sources are one example, since world market prices still continue to rise. The domestic firm, faced with increasing costs but not able to pass them along in increased prices, will either withdraw from the domestic sales market, sell only in international markets where the freeze is not in effect, or will shift the use of those materials to other products.

Price freezes tend to encourage demand while discouraging supply. The effect, then, is often a diminishing of suppliers willing to produce the product for domestic consumption. Another impact is a drop in quality or purity of the material. That is, firms might effectively raise the price through lowered standards or quality. In the end, price freezes tend to delay the price movement to the world market level. In many instances, the price shifts to the real level anyway once the freeze is lifted.

Sellers will often position themselves in various ways if they feel such a price freeze might be forthcoming. One tactic is to raise posted prices and charge these amounts so that they are protected in the event that the real price level moves up to that point. In the meantime, the vendor might offer a series of discounts or services that effectively lower the true cost to the buyer down to the current price. Such items include freight concessions and extended payment terms.

Buyers can use a variety of approaches in an attempt to protect their firms during these periods. Forward purchasing is one basic tool, if the vendor is one that might be able to provide the product. Another approach is for the buying firm to obtain the short-supply material for the vendors. This is possible when the buying firm has more strength in the market than the vendor. Foreign sourcing is another way to obtain supply when the price mechanism does not encourage the product to be produced domestically. Some purchasing managers contract with vendors to supply a percentage of the allocation amounts that the vendor's vendors impose. A major long-term solution used by a few firms in the 1973 period was to acquire the firm that is the vendor of the short material. In this way, the new parent can guarantee itself a full supply of the goods from the previous vendor who imposed allocations upon its customers.

Conclusion

This chapter presented many of the basic approaches useful in cost reduction or minimum cost assurance. The approaches discussed are generally confined to the purchasing and materials management areas. Most actions by buyers, however, impact upon other areas of the firm.

Lowest final cost is one prime objective that is sought by buyers, along with optimum quality and assurance of supply. The range of activities in this area include selection of pricing methods, cost analysis, contracting arrangements, and several topics pertaining to inflation minimization. While these are micro-type practices, they have long-term implications for the firm's corporate strategy.

FOOTNOTES

1. Edward J. Bierman, ed., *The New Study Guide* (Oradell, NJ: National Association of Purchasing Management, 1982), p. 17.
2. "Angry Buyers Protest Precious Metal Adders," *Purchasing*, 8 May 1980, p. 21.
3. Alan Silver, "Calculate Your Own Return on Quality Discounts" (Highland Park, NJ: Alan Silver & Associates, monograph).

SOURCES FOR FURTHER READING

Browning, John M., and Andrews, M. A. "Target Purchasing: the Price-Volume Distinction," *Journal of Purchasing and Materials Management* 14:2.

Dolan, Robert J. "Pricing Strategies That Adjust to Inflation," *Industrial Marketing Management* 10 (1981): 151.

Ibbs, C. William Jr. "'Or Equal' Clause Procurement in Engineered Construction" *Journal of Purchasing and Materials Management* 18 (1982): 29.

Long, Brian G. and Varble, Dale L. "Purchasing's Use of Flexible Contracts" *Journal of Purchasing and Materials Management* 14 (1978).

Tersine, Richard J., and Gengler, Michele, "Simplified Forward Buying with Price Changes," *Journal of Purchasing and Materials Management* 18 (1982): 27.

Tonkin, Lea, "Use Strategy Planning to Keep Purchasing on Track," *Purchasing World*, September 1982, p. 52.

VanDyke, James E.; Roering, Kenneth J.; and Paul, Robert J. "Guidelines for Competitive Bidding," *Journal of Purchasing and Materials Management* 11 (1975): 27.

van Eck, Arend; van Weele, Arjan J.; and de Weerd, Henk, "Price-Performance Evaluation: A Conceptual Approach," *Journal of Purchasing and Materials Management* 18 (1982).

QUESTIONS FOR REVIEW

1. Why do nearly all decisions pertaining to purchase costs have some impact upon other departments of the firm?

2. What are the pros and cons of each of the four forms of price determination?

3. What conditions are desirable or necessary for competitive bidding?

4. When are negotiations appropriate?

5. What is the difference between cost analysis and price determination?

6. What is the difference between variable cost and marginal cost?

7. What is the behavior of a fully allocated cost? List at least three functions or activities that have this type of cost behavior.

8. How is break-even analysis useful in buying situations involving large set-up costs?

9. What is the learning curve, and where is its use appropriate?

10. What three forms of buying arrangements are most favorable for buyers? What ones are least favorable from the buyer's standpoint?

11. How can you evaluate whether or not a vendor's price increase is totally justified?

12. Why are price freezes detrimental to both buyers and sellers?

Problem 4-1

A buyer is investigating three machines with a production engineer. They have developed key information about each of three machines that are available from three different vendors. This information was obtained from the vendors, through engineering studies, and by talking with current users of the equipment. The following data represents summaries of the key cost information they feel they need to determine which machine is best for their firm.

	A	B	C
Set-up cost for each shift	$1,000	$1,500	$2,000
Variable cost per hour	$40	$50	$50

Questions:
1. Which one is the cheapest at 1,000 units per shift?
2. Draw a chart indicating the break-even points in total costs for these machines.

Problem 4-2

A specialty parts manufacturer has been selling goods to your firm at a price of $11.00. Your purchasing team has learned that the vendor's variable cost per unit is about $7.00 and the fixed costs of each purchased lot production run are $1,000. The company currently buys in lots of 300. You seek to reduce the price you pay by offering to purchase in larger lots thereby spreading the vendor's fixed cost per order out over more units.
Questions:
1. What is the vendor's current profit per unit?
2. You approach the vendor with the offer that you are willing to allow a contribution margin of ten percent over and above the variable costs per unit of production. With this in mind, what size lot would you have to buy in order for the vendor to reduce its price to $9.50 per unit.

Problem 4-3

You just received notice that a firm you do much buying from is increasing the price on Product LJM-2 from $10.50 to $11.05, or 5.2 percent. The announcement states that a new labor contract signed in the vendor's industry has just raised wage costs by 10 percent and that the price increase is needed to maintain healthy profits for reinvestment purposes. You know that the vendor's wage costs are 22.4 percent of its total sales revenue on the LJM-2 product line.
Question:
Is this price increase justified? Why or why not?

A firm normally buys lots of 500 units of an item which are used for two pro-   **Problem 4-4**
duction runs per month. The price per unit is $15.00. The vendor also has a
volume price of $13.80 for a minimum of 1,500 units. The firm's annual cost
of carrying inventory is thirty percent.
Question:
Should the firm buy the volume size lot? Why or why not?

The detailed cost information for two vendors is determined as follows: **Problem 4-5**

Category	Vendor A	Vendor B
Cost of production run set-up	$500 per run	$600 per run
Labor cost per hour	$9.42	$9.27
Units produced per hour	71	65
Material cost per unit	$3.11	$3.14
Overhead and profit	30% of labor	70% of materials
Packaging	$4.02 per 10 units	$9.50 per 25 units
Freight	$.625 per unit	$700 for lot of 1,500 units

Question:
*What is the least costly firm to buy from for 100 units, 500 units, 1,000 units, 1,400
units?*

5

INTRODUCTION

VENDOR MARKET CHARACTERISTICS

General Approach
Specific Vendor Qualities
Sources of Product and Vendor Information

EVALUATING VENDORS

Untried Vendors
Vendor Rating Approaches

SPECIAL TOPICS IN ASSURANCE OF SUPPLY

Communication with Nonselected
  Vendors
Vendor Stocking Systems
Consignment
International Sourcing
Purchase from A Manufacturer or
  Distributor?
Sole Source or Many?
Vendor Cost-Reduction Programs
Vendor Lists

PROACTIVE APPROACHES TO SUPPLY ASSURANCE

Altered Emphasis Upon "Selling"
Developing Emergency Contingency
  Approaches
Developing Goodwill for the Firm as a
  Purchaser

CONCLUSION

CHAPTER OBJECTIVES

After reading this chapter you should:

- Understand the basic rationale for developing supply sources for the firm.

- Understand the primary approaches for evaluating untried and existing vendors.

- Apply proactive approaches to assuring supply for the firm.

- Understand how the firm should approach various situations in the supply market.

Assurance of Supply

Introduction

Assurance of supply is the third primary purchasing objective in the balanced-value approach. Purchasing managers must not only seek optimum quality and lowest final cost, but they must also seek an assurance of supply for the firm's product input needs. Assurance of supply means having a good availability of products from competitive vendor markets.

This factor is perhaps more important today than in the past, due to the changes that have taken place in the world economies. Shortages of goods and wide variations in raw material prices have made some firms turn away from a heavy marketing emphasis to one of coordinating the firm's assets with opportunities in both supply and customer markets.

Vendor Market Characteristics

General Approach

A general approach to viewing the overall supply market includes an analysis of the vendor firms. The basic considerations here include reliability of supply, size of the work being sought, number of suppliers, development potential of the vendors, and alternatives available to buyers.[1]

Reliability of supply pertains to the ability of one or more vendors to provide a quality supply at a good price over a long-term period.

Size relates to the size of the orders or work being considered. If future purchase lots are small, then only certain suppliers will no doubt be interested in the work. This will narrow the scope of suppliers, since very large ones will probably not be interested. On the other hand, large orders will be within the operating scope of large volume producers, and smaller vendors are often not able to compete in price. This factor segments the buying market into supplier groups that are possible to use for upcoming orders.

The number of suppliers is another key component of the general approach to an assured supply of goods. Many buyers seek at least two possible vendors for immediate use. Orders are often divided up in such a way that a large order is placed with a large vendor while a smaller is placed with a smaller vendor. This general rule provides orders to firms in terms of lot sizes that interest them as well as fit in with their capabilities. Additionally, the smaller vendor is kept interested with the possibility of larger orders in the future. The large vendor, on the other hand, is aware that another is competing for the work.

Development potential is another general factor considered by buyers and refers to the ability of the vendor to create present and future goods to meet the present and future needs of the purchasing firm. Research and development potential is important here, as is the willingness of the vendor firm to adapt to special needs of the buyer.

Alternatives are those choices that a buyer has available in addition to the primary methods of buying. Some alternatives include the decisions to buy locally versus afar, domestically or internationally, or from a manufacturer or a distributor.

Specific Vendor Qualities

An ideal vendor is one that is responsible, responsive, and meets certain expectations. Responsible means financial fitness. It also pertains to the firm's willingness to fill the right quality, price, and delivery requirements. Responsive refers to how well the vendor reacts to inquiries by the buyer and how well the firm meets the specifications of purchase orders and other buying arrangements. Expectations are long-term factors that deal with the vendor's helpfulness in developing alternatives and solving problems.

In particular, vendors are often evaluated in terms of the following basic items: meeting specified quality, charging an acceptable price, and meeting an agreed-to order cycle time. These are basic components or evaluative criteria with regard to the handling of orders. Other items of importance to buyers deal with the vendor's assertive actions; that is, positive reactions to unforseen events, e.g. providing advance notice of problems, and taking the initiative to improve products for the buying firm. Such actions are not always present in a buyer-seller relationship, but they are features sought by buyers.[2]

Sources of Product and Vendor Information

Obtaining knowledge about products and possible vendors is an on-going activity in purchasing. This information serves as the basis for the eventual selection of a vendor for an order. In some instances, this process entails the building of a library of product and vendor information. In other settings, it is merely a collection of information for a file to be used only once. The information sought is continuously analyzed in light of the vendor evaluative factors.

Buyers gather data about sources and products through many means.

Industrial Registers
These are publications that contain listings of firms and products. One major source is the *Thomas Register.* This series of books is published periodically in three basic forms. One is the *Products and Services* vol-

ume, which indexes by product the names and addresses of firms selling that product. Another is the *Thomas Catalog* volume, which shows drawings and specifications of products from over 1,000 companies. These are cross-referenced with the *Products and Services* volume. A third series in the Thomas set is the *Company Profiles.* This listing presents information on over 100,000 firms in terms of addresses, plants, asset ratings, company executives, and other detailed management information.

Industrial registers are also published for different industries. These are sometimes published by an industry association to which firms in a certain product line belong. An example is the National Highway and Airline Directory. This shows the addresses, routes, and some points-served information for major air and truck firms.

One factor to keep in mind with respect to registers and other industry directories is that they are not all-encompassing. These publications are sold to subscribers, but inclusion of firms in them is on a purchased-space basis. Only firms that elect to buy space are included in these publications. As such they are not always complete lists of the entire supplier industry of a particular product line.

City Directories

Many organizations e.g., the Chamber of Commerce, in cities publish city directories of firms located in these locales. These publications are similar in form to the above industrial directories. They list firm names, addresses, and products sold.

Supplier Catalogues

These include publications, promotional literature, drawings, and price lists that are made available by suppliers.

Trade Journals

Nearly every industry is covered by a magazine in the field. Examples are *Iron Age, Distributor, Railway Age, American Nurseryman*, etc. While these publications contain articles of interest to those in the field, they are valuable sources of new and existing product information through the advertisements. It is not uncommon for a buyer in one firm to subscribe to the trade journals covering the industry of the vendors from which he/she buys from. This keeps the buyer up to date on technology, equipment, and practices in the supplier industry.

Yellow Pages

The telephone directory is another prime source of product information. In some cities this part of the phone directory is so large that a separate industrial edition is published apart from the consumer listings for restaurants, dentists, etc. The industrial edition lists firms of all types that have paid for advertising space within the publication.

Mail Advertising

Direct mail information is a constant part of the inbound mail to a purchasing department. This literature is often unsolicited in that it is sent via the use of mailing lists purchased or maintained by the vendor firm sending the items.

Trade Shows

Many industries conduct trade shows and exhibits in various locations throughout the U.S. For example, the textile equipment manufacturers conduct a periodic trade show in the Greenville–Spartanburg, South Carolina area. The food machinery manufacturers often conduct shows in New York and Chicago. Similarly, container manufacturers and materials-handling-equipment firms hold yearly shows. The latest equipment is often on display at these shows. The advantage of attending these events is that a wide range of manufacturers' equipment is on display in one location. Physical comparisons can often be made here in ways that would otherwise be more costly. This is an important and valuable use for some purchasing department travel funds.

Company Personnel

Many persons inside the buyer's own firm have personal knowledge of products and companies. Engineering and manufacturing personnel are often aware of the current state-of-the-art and firms supplying this technology. In many instances, vendors approach these internal personnel directly. Periodic checking with these people is often a useful way of obtaining up-to-date information about product areas not always possible in the purchasing department.

RFQ's and Bids

The use of requests for proposals and the bids that potential vendors return are also useful avenues for the information gathering process. Bids contain technical, cost, and managerial information about the vendor. This information should be crossreferenced in some way so that it may be accessed for future analysis involving other goods and orders.

Purchasing Associations

Many local purchasing associations publish magazines, provide vendor fairs, and act as contact points for obtaining knowledge about possible sources. In many instances, personal contacts at association functions can provide leads to possible vendors.

Foreign Freight Forwarders

These organizations act to move products for importers and exporters. They are a valuable source of information about possible vendors in overseas nations. They are generally located in major seaport cities such as New York, San Francisco, New Orleans, etc.

Department of Commerce

A part of the U.S. Department of Commerce acts as an information source for U.S. firms seeking to obtain products from overseas countries. Foreign vendors list their names, addresses, and products with the agency, and this information is readily available for any U.S. buyer.

These information sources are starting points for obtaining data about vendors and their products. An important part of this process is the maintenance of a purchasing library of literature and information about vendors.

Evaluating Vendors

Untried Vendors

The untried vendor represents an opportunity as well as a risk. The use of vendors with which there is no previous experience requires some initial work by the buyer. This is especially critical if the dollar value of the purchase is large and/or the quality of the goods is tightly specified. That is, the greater the dependency of the buying firm upon the vendor, the greater the need for initial analysis into the background of the vendor. Buyers use four basic sources of input for this process.

Vendor Financial Background

The financial strength of a vendor is of concern to a buyer. Vendors can discontinue operations due to poor financial condition thereby leaving buyers without needed goods. Poor financial strength can also mean that the vendor might cut corners in production and quality, even though specifications are tightly worded on the purchase order. The lack of a good credit rating will mean that the vendor might not be able to procure raw materials for the buyer's job until the vendor pays for past purchases.

There are two primary approaches useful in evaluating a vendor's financial strength. These are financial rating services and a financial evaluation performed by the buying firm. Dun & Bradsteet is a long-standing financial rating service. For a fee the buyer may obtain information that D&B might have compiled about the vendor. The information supplied generally includes the corporate officer's names, some basic product information, and the credit rating. The D&B service is of primary use by firms considering extending credit to a firm in question. The rating provides an indication of past credit worthiness and the overall financial background of the firm. Buyers can rely upon the D&B rating as an indication of a firm's financial strength as well as its reputation with its creditors.

The buyer can also perform a financial evaluation of a vendor, if such information is available. Sources include vendor annual reports and financial sources such as the Standard & Poors financial directories. The three primary documents needed for a sound financial evaluation are the income statement, balance sheet, and the statement of sources and uses of funds.

The income statement shows the profit or loss the vendor incurred during a recent span of time. Usually these are stated in annual terms, but quarterly reports and semiannual reports are also published for firms in which the stock is publicly held. Annual reports cover an entire year and tend to include both high and low seasonality periods. Quarterly statements can be misleading, if they are viewed for only the good or bad portion of the vendor's product season.

The balance sheet shows the financial posture of the vendor at a given moment in time. It shows the firm's cash, receivables, securities, inventories, plant, and equipment. On the other hand, it also shows all forms of debt and owner's equity. The balance sheet provides many insights into the firm's inventory holdings in relation to its total assets; it also shows to what extent the vendor may need to obtain credit in order to accept more work. Both this form and the income statement can be used to evaluate the strength of the vendor in terms of profitability, return on assets, and asset turnover. The approach for this was presented in Chapter 1.

The sources and uses of funds statement shows the inflow and outflow of cash for the previous year. This statement provides insights into whether the firm's liquid position is stronger or weaker than the last statement. The income statement shows what has occurred in terms of operating sales, expenses, and extraordinary items. The balance sheet shows the firm's financial position at one given moment. The sources and uses of funds statement presents all changes in cash or other liquid assets. That is, it shows whether the firm earned cash from operating profits, sales of assets, selling off land and equipment, or through the use of tax benefits. It also shows how cash was used, for example to pay off a long-term debt, to increase inventories, or to buy back some of the firm's stock.

Each of the three statements provide information to the person evaluating them that the others do not contain. Each has a special purpose. Buyers are interested in such factors as inherent profitability and the ability to produce his or her order without straining the vendor financially. That is, can the vendor pay for materials and labor for a two-month period without resorting to borrowing or extreme means of cash conservation, or can the inventory stand the storage without deteriorating or obsolescence. The level of inventories also give insight into whether or not there is some negotiating potential. A firm that has a large holding is often more likely to negotiate than one that must produce the goods from start.

Plant Visits
Buyers can gleen much information from visits to vendor plants. This is a key element in a purchasing department's budget. Without the ability to visit vendors, the buyer is often making decisions in a blind manner about untried and existing vendors. Many elements of vital information are gained on such visits.

Equipment capabilities is one key facet of information gained on a plant visit. The type of equipment, its age, and how well it is maintained are all important items that relate to the ability to produce certain goods within the tolerances and specifications that the buyer seeks. The current level of operations in relation to the vendor's total capacity is another item of data that is gathered from such visits. This provides insights into backlogs and the ability to grow with the buyer's firm, if large volumes are planned in the future.

The condition of the plant and its equipment is another key indicator of the management quality of the vendor. A plant that is kept clean and maintained well indicates that the firm considers maintenance important, and employees will tend to treat equipment and goods with greater respect than otherwise. Plant visits can be used to note whether or not there are large piles of scrap and waste at various work stations, or whether process control and quality control measures are being applied in the plant.

The technical competence of employees and management can also be determined by such visits. An interview with a salesman in the buyer's own office can give little true insight into this facet of the vendor. At the plant, the buyer can meet with engineers and production personnel, quality people, and persons who operate the warehouse, docks, and transportation system. The attitude of the employees is important to detect. A good morale and attitude toward the vendor's customers indicates that a good level of attention is paid to the firm's products and its service to customers.

A plant visit is usually arranged in advance, and there is sufficient time for the vendor to clean up the plant. A tactic that one specialty metal buyer on the East Coast uses is to visit the vendor again unannounced a few weeks later with another person from his own shop. This is done to familiarize the other person with the vendor as well as to note whether or not the original visit was a special clean-up effort for that particular visit.

Other Factors to Consider

The untried vendor is being sought for all the same reasons that any other purchase is made. The key points in evaluating the total realm of any vendor include things such as 1) geographic location, which has a bearing upon buyer/vendor ease of communications, transportation, and the ability to provide rush orders, and 2) capacity in relation to the present level of business handled, which indicates whether the vendor can grow with larger volumes of orders being considered by the buyer. The vendor who is currently operating at much less than full capacity can handle the business with relative ease. One that is now at or near capacity would have to drop other business or spend extra time and effort to invest in new, expanded facilities in order to grow further.

Management and employees are other key factors to consider with the untried vendor. Management expertise, experience, and technical capabilities are important factors in the vendor selection decision. One element to consider is the age balance in management. If all key persons are at the same age near retirement, then a troublesome turnover might take place in the near future. If, on the other hand, there is a balance of ages in the top structure, then there is less likelihood of major management problems from this factor. Another element of management structure to note is whether the firm is managed by one dominant person. This might work well for many years until the firm grows too large for it to be managed in this manner or until that person retires or is replaced. Successors to such managers often find it difficult to provide smooth transitions.

The Initial Small Order

One common industrial tactic in the use of an untried vendor is to place a small order with the firm. Some points to consider here include communications with the vendor and the degree to which the buyer will or could become dependent upon this source. Key communications include an understanding of specifications and quality requirements. In this area, standardized goods are often safe for initial orders. Other key points to state to the vendor include transportation terms, packaging, payment terms, delivery dates, and what services might be expected along with the goods.[3]

Untried vendors are opportunities for expanded supply options. They can remove a buyer from a single source situation. Costs might be lowered by using the new vendor. Quality might be improved, and faster delivery might be available over current vendors. The new vendor might also provide technical services not currently available from existing ones. But, any planned shift in supply sources should be made with caution. Firms eager to gain new business might apply special efforts to provide superior service. They might also bid low in order to have the buyer gain a dependency upon them. This was the case with a profesisonal association in logistics. It shifted mailing and member record-keeping services from one vendor to another on the basis of a low bid. The new vendor returned the following year with a higher contract price based upon "new and increased costs," and the organization had no place to turn because the original long-standing firm had discontinued operations. This "low balling tactic" can be a very tempting trap to fall into, but it can be avoided by not allowing too strong a dependency to develop with a new vendor or any other vendor.

Vendor Rating Approaches

Existing vendors should be evaluated by some means, and the systems used should be as objective as possible. The reason for such an evaluation is to provide the buyer with a sound base to judge the relative merits of each vendor. Vendors who know of such evaluations also know that their products and services are subject to measure, and future business might depend upon high performance.

Rating systems can be developed along any number of lines; the most popular ones are presented here. These are generally constructed in order to select or highlight vendors on the basis of a single dominant characteristic, categorical perferences, a weighted-point scheme, or a cost-based evaluation method.

Dominant Characteristic

This approach first requires a major item or characteristic to be identified for evaluation. In many settings this might be lowest bid price. Or it might be highest quality or shortest order cycle time. In government purchasing settings, lowest bid price is often the overriding selection criteria, unless some other compelling factor prevents this from being the best choice.

An example of how this method would be applied can be illustrated in the bids received from three vendors. Vendor 1's bid is for $10.10 per unit in a 1,000 lot purchase. Vendor 2's bid is $10.05, and Vendor 3's bid is $9.50 for the same lot size. In this situation the selection probably would be made for Vendor 3 with Vendors 2 and 1 following in preference.

Simplicity of application is the major advantage of this method. Only one factor is used, and it is easy to determine and apply. A prime drawback is that other factors are ignored in this system, unless they are major, obvious items. Examples would be an extremely long order cycle time, or very poor quality. Vendors who are aware of this type of evaluation method might strive to perform well within the one selection factor and let slide the other features of their total performance with the buying firm.

Categorical Rating System

This evaluation method seeks broad input about many elements from many sources within the firm. For example, production might be requested to evaluate vendors on the ease of using items in production; quality control might be asked for information about and preferences for each vendor. The buyer might consider the total order cycle times that each vendor has provided in the past. These might be stated in terms of the total cycle lengths or the reliability of original estimates in comparison to actual performance. The buyer might also construct a measure of the original bid against the final total billing price and the total costs of using the product. There are many other evaluative factors that can be used in this method, and some of these will be illustrated in the following example.

Each department that is involved with the use of products from various vendors is polled with regard to positive, neutral, or negative preferences for each vendor. Following are four factors and the results of these preferences as they were obtained from various sources within one firm.

Factor	Vendor A	Vendor B	Vendor C
Quality (defect %)	+	+	+
Price/Total Cost	+	−	−
Production Ease of Use (% problems)	+	−	0
Order Cycle Time Reliability	0	−	+

On this basis a ranking probably would be constructed showing Vendor 1, 2, and 3 in descending order. Advantages of this method are that many factors are evaluated, there can be broad input from many parties in the firm, and the method is objective in nature. A drawback is that it treats each factor equally, when in reality the firm might wish to place more emphasis on some factors and less on others.

Weighted-Point Approach

This method reduces the drawback of the categorical approach by assigning weights to each of the various factors. It also treats specific elements of performance within each factor. For example, the buyer might treat the quality percent of defects with a weight of 40, the bid cost to final cost factor with a weight of 30, percent of production problems with a weight of 20, and average variability of planned order cycle time with a weight of 10. All of these weights total to 100.

Factor	V #1	V #2	V#3
Quality (1.00 – defect %)	40 (.99)	40 (.98)	40 (.93)
Bid (Bid/Total Final Cost)	40 (.99)		
#1: $10.10/$10.11	30 (.93)		
#2: $10.00/$10.80		30 (.93)	
#3:$ 9.50/$10.60			30 (.90)
Production (1.00 – % defective			
units)	20 (.99)		20 (.96)
Order Cycle Time Reliability		20 (.92)	
(1.00 – .10 each late day)	10 (.90)		10 (.90)
Weighted Sum	98.1	10 (.70)	92.4
		92.5	

On this basis, vendors fall into a descending order of 1, 2, and 3. This system is very objective, but it is dependent upon the relative weights assigned to each factor.

Cost-Based Approach

This system is often called the cost-based or cost-ratio approach to vendor evaluation. It is a subset of the weighted approach in that it uses much of the data supplied by the weighted point method and applies it to a presently considered vendor selection decision. For example, each of the vendors bid the following: Vendor 1, $10.10; Vendor 2, $10.05; and Vendor 3, $9.55. The cost based method then divides each of these bids by the weighted score found above. The following shows the results of this treatment:

Vendor #1:	$10.10/.981	= $10.30
Vendor #2:	$10.05/.925	= $10.86
Vendor #3:	$ 9.55/.924	= $10.33

This shows the total paid plus compensating costs that the buyer firm will have to incur with purchases from each vendor. That is, Vendor #1 has a higher bid price than all the others, but it is reliable in order cycle time, its product quality problems are low, and it traditionally costs the firm about what was originally bid in the first place. The cost-based evaluation approach indicates that the total final cost of using Vendor #1 will be about $10.30 per unit. The other vendors might be less costly from a pure bid standpoint, but the total projected costs of using these other firms make their total costs higher than that of Vendor #1. This ranking in preference is now #1, #3, #2.

The cost-based approach is very inclusive in terms of factors and costs. It attempts to identify the total cost of selecting each vendor. Though it is a rough estimate, it is a useful approach. The problem with this method is that it requires a large amount of information input and calculations about each vendor. For this reason it is generally found only in large firms at the present time.

These tools attempt to reduce many evaluative factors down to a single indicator of the relative benefits and drawbacks of each vendor. Some firms include such things as financial stature, technical assistance provided by each vendor, willingness to negotiate, quality of transportation service between the vendor and the receiving site, ease of purchase order change, special order handling, and many others as evaluative factors. Each method provides buyers with a perceived objective basis upon which to evaluate vendors. However, each method can involve some error because of the attempt to use subjective factors in objective mathematical ways. Further, the issue of relative weight assignments is crucial to the proper use of them.

Firms can extend the use of vendor rating systems into communication devices with vendors. For example, Exxon has created such a system that first ensures each vendor is fully knowledgeable about the specific features of products and services that Exxon is seeking from them. That is, Exxon first meets with vendors to provide them with specific aspects of price, service, and product expectations. Vendors are then informed that Exxon collects performance data to use in an evaluation method. The system is similar to personnel performance evaluations in that vendors are provided feedback as to the perceived results of their work. A series of annual awards is made to vendors that provide outstanding work and service. This includes a dinner, awards, pictures, and press releases. Though this system involves extra expenditures, Exxon has found it to be a positive cost in relation to the short- and long-run benefits derived from it.[4]

Special Topics in Assurance of Supply

There are several special topics relating to the activity of finding, developing, and maintaining adequate supply sources for a firm. Though not necessarily line purchasing activities, they can be considered part of the strategic and tactical approaches useful in developing an effective purchasing function in the firm.

Communication with Nonselected Vendors

One often overlooked aspect of the purchasing process is follow-up with vendors who sought business with the firm through bids, negotiations, etc. but were not selected for the present order. This topic borders on courtesy. But even more important, it creates perceptions with vendors that affects their future interest in doing business with the buyer's firm.

There are good routine reasons for communicating with vendors after the award to one of them. One is to request return of blueprints, specifications, etc. If the buyer has released documents that are proprietary in nature, then this request also should include a reminder as to the confidential nature of the data.

Several long-run positive benefits are gained when buyers follow-up with losing vendors. A sound approach here is to provide the vendors with realistic reasons why they did not obtain the order. These reasons can be stated in positive terms such as quality, order cycle time, price, etc. It is often a good practice to inform not only the vendor's salesman, but also company's upper management. Salesmen do not always enjoy high credibility inside their own firms. Sometimes good information supplied by them fails to go far inside their own offices. If a technical reason was the cause for not selecting a vendor, the buyer can possibly further develop that source by informing its higher management, whereby changes might be integrated into future product or service decisions.

Vendor Stocking Systems

This approach is useful in reducing the order cycle time as well as assuring high availability of the goods. A vendor stocking system consists of contracting with the vendor to buy a range of goods over a period. The agreement stipulates that the vendor will store the goods near the needed receiving point. In some situations, this storage location is leased or provided on site of the buyer.

Vendor stocking systems often are part of systems contracting. The terms of the arrangement include some agreed-to amount of goods, which can be adjusted when the final total amount of goods needed is determined. That is, there are often allowances for under- or over-buying from the original contracted amount.

Consignment

This is an arrangement of contracting for special or standard goods with a vendor who stores them inside the buyer's facility. Payment for the goods does not take place until they are used, or until the end of the contract period if all are not used.

This system provides instantaneous order replenishment for the buyer. The advantage of volume buying is attained, and the goods are on-hand for use when needed. Volume transportation movement economies are also experienced when the goods are moved into the site. The buyer firm must provide space, but, the capital cost of holding the goods is directly borne by the vendor until the goods are actually sold. This system can be beneficial when the cost of capital for the buyer firm is higher than that of the selling firm. Another benefit is that this system freezes the price of the goods over a long period. It further makes the buyer firm stronger on the market than it is normally when smaller separate purchases are being made.[5]

Consignment has some drawbacks. One is that it commits the buying firm to the amount of goods stipulated in the contract. This is a problem when exact requirements are not known for the products. The goods might not be in the quantity eventually needed; overages might have to be bought, and underages still represent extra purchases throughout the year. Further, if the quality of the goods is not as the firm desires, there is the issue of how to resolve this once they are in-house. Finally, there is the risk of obsolescence or shifting needs of the buying firm. All of these factors must be evaluated before entering into a consignment arrangement.[6]

International Sourcing

The question as to whether to seek sources overseas or remain domestic in orientation carries several pros and cons. On the side of international sourcing, it represents an opportunity to find wider source markets. Other markets might be lower in price or more plentiful in quantity. Some overseas sources might also provide higher quality than is available domestically. In the same vein, overseas sources represent competition to domestic ones, which can have an overall effect of reducing price increases from the domestic sources. Or a foreign source might be required when the firm also sells finished goods to that country. That is, countertrade or bartering might be part of the arrangement, and a sale is contingent upon a purchase being made as well.

On the domestic side, the close proximity of the vendor to the buying firm poses several advantages. For one, closer links mean that transportation costs might be lower and more reliable. In another context, the closer link means that issues between the buyer and vendor might be more easily resolved than in the international setting. The closer link also often allows a lower overall total inventory investment due to the more reliable and shorter order cycle time. All of these pros and cons are presented in further detail in Chapter 11, International Purchasing.

Purchase from a Manufacturer or Distributor?

This issue of supply assurance has many ramifications that go beyond price alone. If a firm can buy in large lots, then purchases direct from a manufacturer might be possible at lower prices. The manufacturer might also provide a level of quality or a specific item not always available from standardized lines through distributors.

On the other hand, distributors are a local source of a wide range of goods. They represent a rough equivalent of a vendor stocking system with no risk of having to buy or contract for any specified amount. Arrangements can be made with local distributors to handle direct requisitions from user departments in the firm. Distributors also provide a wide range of brands and quality goods for evaluation and selection.

Sole Source or Many?

This issue relates to the decision of whether to use one source or many. The sole source might be the only one possible when a patented item or some specialty is required that is only provided by one firm. On the other hand, the use of one vendor is often a conscious action by buyers. It can have the cost advantages when special tools and dies are required for set up or when one vendor possesses a special technology that presents benefits not available elsewhere.

The single source can present problems that are often avoided when the firm seeks product from many sources. The multiple source decision removes the firm from monopolistic tendencies that one vendor might begin to display. Further, multiple vendor sourcing reduces the problems that can arise from fires, strikes, supply disruptions experienced by one firm, etc. That is, the multiple vendor choice spreads the risk of supply problems.

Vendor Cost-Reduction Programs

Cost-reduction programs can be a positive force in reducing prices for buyers. They can lead to improved products, lower prices, and new material ideas. Some buyers make a practice of encouraging vendors to continually perform this activity upon the products they are buying. The use of cost-reduction programs is one of the facets of evaluating existing and potential vendors.

Cost reduction programs can have negative aspects, however. They are frequently used in firms when revenues slacken or costs are increasing at a rate that is deemed undesirable by top management. One of the immediate buyer impacts experienced is a decrease in product quality, less attention to purchase order details, or changes in specifications. In many instances, cost-reduction programs are applied across the board with little regard to the relative impact caused by such efforts. In other settings, the costs that are reduced are short-term in nature, with little attention being paid to the long-run effects of these decisions.

Vendor Lists

Buyers and purchasing managers often use vendor lists as a systematic means of selecting vendors for particular orders. These are lists or files that contain suggestions or decision rules for selecting vendors. The file might: 1) contain an approved list for the buyer to select from; 2) present a priority ordering of firms to check first, second, etc.; or 3) show an approximate allocation of volume that should be sought from each throughout a time period.

Vendors are placed onto such lists through various means. Some firms have formal evaluation systems for vendor listings. These might require the vendor to provide financial information, product samples, presentations of organizational structure, and possibly references. The list then is distributed to the firm's many buyers. This has the advantage of one initial investigation about the vendor firm that relieves buyers at many sites from having to do the same. It also simplifies the purchasing process for the individual buyers.

The use of vendor lists can, however, present some drawbacks. One is that it can require much time and effort by the person maintaining it. It must also be kept up to date to assure that vendors continue to provide adequate levels of service and product performance. Feedback from various buyers is very important for this listing system to remain effective. Another drawback is that it can place too much authority over vendor selection into one person, who might be subject to unethical behavior.

Proactive Approaches to Supply Assurance

There are three major areas in which a purchasing manager can actively maintain a posture for his or her firm that is favorable for supply assurance. These include a shifted view of the buying and selling relationship between them and vendors, the development of contingency approaches for use in the event of emergencies, and the creation of goodwill with vendors.

Altered Emphasis Upon "Selling"

The former situation of numerous suppliers, low inflation in prices, and the marketing emphasis of vendor firms is gradually subject to change. The commodity disruptions and energy and capital-related impacts of the 1970s have changed the nature of the buying power of purchasing managers.

Supply assurance in many instances requires purchasing managers to develop a selling stance with regard to their firms. That is, no longer can it be assumed that vendors will seek the buying firm. There are many situations in which some buying firms are too expensive or not otherwise profitable to sell to. Vendors might require some "selling to" in order for the buying firm to access their goods and services. This is particularly important during a commodity shortage period.

Proactive supply assurance actions in this area often require buyers and managers to travel to vendors, trade shows, exhibits, etc. It further means that the purchasing person must begin thinking in terms of how to make his or her firm more competitive in ability to attract goods at reasonable prices. Later chapters will show some actions that are possible in this area, including close buyer-seller links in which costs are shared or minimized between them.

Developing Emergency Contingency Approaches

Production downtime penalties are extremely expensive and represent lost marketing opportunities from stockouts as well. These are two major constraints placed upon the timing, quality, and price selection decisions made by buyers. Quite often problems in supply or price are not the fault of the buyer, but corporate attention is directed there when a vendor fails.

A program of contingency development should be a part of the overall managerial role of purchasing. These include decision rules that can be used in the event that a vendor fails to meet a critical delivery date, a fire or strike prevents the vendor from producing and delivering, or transportation systems break down between the vendor and buyer firm. Contingency systems should be designed so that purchasing is made aware of pending problems as early as possible. That is, communications from the vendor and transportation firms should be open and free with purchasing. Similarly, effective buyers and managers in this area often make primary decisions, with backups or alternatives available in the event that basic operations do not go as planned or expected.

Developing Goodwill for the Firm as a Purchaser

Selling firms often can make a choice of whether or not to seek sales with certain customers, or they can actively create priorities of firms they wish to serve versus those of lower desirability. Buyers and managers are often the focal point of such decisions. In this realm, much of the firm's entire goodwill is centered upon the purchasing department.

There are many forms of buyer behavior that are seen as being supportive of goodwill between purchasing firms and vendors. Many of these are stated in the NAPM Code of Ethics statement, which is covered in detail in Chapter 20.

Conclusion

Assurance of supply includes any and all activities that are designed to determine, develop, and maintain competitive sources of products and services needed by firms. Inherent to this entire process is the make-or-buy decision that was presented in an earlier chapter. Adequate supply can no longer be assumed by buyers. The nature of relationships between buyers and sellers is no longer as one-sided as it might have been at one time. A current plentiful supply of goods at very low prices, in fact, is a danger that the total amount of that supply might diminish as some vendors drop product lines in the future.

A major part of this entire supply decision area includes the timing of product acquisition or commitment. This includes forecasting of future prices in the near term as well as supply over longer periods. Purchasing is expected to be able to obtain products today, but it must also have an eye toward the long-term markets its firm will need to utilize.

FOOTNOTES

1. J. H. Westing, I. V. Fine, and Gary Joseph Zenz, *Purchasing Management* (New York: John Wiley, 1976), chapter 5.
2. Ibid, p. 12.
3. Somerby Dowst, "Get Off On The Right Foot With New Sources," *Purchasing*, 8 October 1981, p. 93.
4. Vern H. Goodwin, "Improving Vendor Performance in the Business Logistics Network," *Logistics Issues for the 1980s*, proceeding of the Logistics Resource Forum (Cleveland, OH: Leaseway Transportation Co., 1982), p. 171.
5. "Beef Up Buying Clout With Consignments," *Purchasing*, October 9, 1980, p. 52.
6. Ibid.

SOURCES FOR FURTHER READING

Brokaw, Alan J., and Davisson, Charles N. " 'Positioning' a Company as a Preferred Customer." *Journal of Purchasing and Materials Management* 14 (1978):9.

Dempsey, William A. "Vendor Selection and the Buying Process." *Industrial Marketing Management* 7 (1978): 257.

Dowst, Somerby. "General-line Firms Feel a Lot of Heat." *Purchasing*, 9 September 1982, p. 53.

Drozdowski, Ted E. "Make Vendor Rating a Two-Way Street." *Purchasing*, 11 March 1982, p. 19.

Fowler, M. J. "Buying What's Never Been Bought Before." *Purchasing World*, April 1983, p. 60.

Lamberson, L. R., Diederich, D., and Wuori, J. "Quantitative Vendor Evaluation." *Journal of Purchasing and Materials Management.* 12 (1976): 19.

Klebba, Joanne M., and Dwyer, Robert. "Environmental Impact on Purchase Decision Structure." *Journal of Purchasing and Materials Management.* 17 (1981): 30

Monczka, Robert M., Giunipero, Larry C., and Reck, Robert F. "Perceived Importance of Supplier Information." *Journal of Purchasing and Materials Management* 17 (1981): 21.

Sibley, Stanley D. "How Interfacing Departments Rate Vendors." *Journal of Purchasing and Materials Management* 14 (1978).

QUESTIONS FOR REVIEW

1. What are the various ways in which buyers can determine vendors on the market?

2. How is the untried vendor more of a risk than one that has never before been used by the firm?

3. What financial information is generally sought about vendors?

4. What information can be determined from vendor financial information?

5. What does a plant visit tell the buyer?

6. What are the pros and cons of the various vendor rating systems?

7. Why is it so important to communicate with vendors that have *not* been selected for a specific job.

8. Why would firms seek vendors internationally or afar in the U.S. versus domestically or locally?

9. What are the advantages and disadvantages to the use of vendor lists by buyers?

10. Why is it important for buyers to adapt contingency approaches?

11. How might ethical or unethical behavior affect the buying effectiveness of the firm?

12. "The purchasing department is a part of the firm's public relations image in the market." Evaluate this comment.

Problem 5-1

In preparing a year-end audit report of purchasing department activities you request a listing of all vendors used by the firm for its primary raw materials. This information is combined with the number of vendors in the field who are known to provide the same products but were not used by the firm during the past year. This table is as follows.

PRODUCT/COMMODITY FILE SUMMARY

Vendor	$ (thou's) Purchased By Firm in 1983	# Sources Used	Others Possible
1	$ 500	1	0
2	540	2	not known
3	180	3	4
4	55	6	10 +
5	5,000	7	4
6	1,000	1	2
7	2,000	1	2
8	2,400	2	5
9	1,100	5	8
10	1,200	3	6

Questions:
1. Which of these products would you direct attention toward first? Why?
2. What long run plans would you suggest for the department based on the information presented?

Problem 5-2

A buyer traditionally has paid $8.00 per unit to a carrier. It has been offered a discount plan which is as follows:

Cumulative Quantity
Per year   **Unit Rate**
The first 100 units $8.00 each
The next 100 units
    (#'s 101 to 200) $7.50 each
the next 300 units
    (#'s 201 to 500) $7.00 each
Units 501 and up   6.50 each

The buyer knows that the carrier's variable cost per unit is $4.25, and that fixed costs amount to an additional $3.25 per unit. The firm can use the carrier for about 750 unit movements per year.

Questions:
1. What will be the total cost of 750 units?
2. What is the unit cost to the buyer of all 750 units?
3. Explain why the carrier can move product below its full cost and still remain in business.
4. Can the carrier do this in the long run? Why or why not?

6

INTRODUCTION

WHEN NEGOTIATIONS ARE APPROPRIATE

NEGOTIATING OBJECTIVES

SCOPE OF NEGOTIATIONS

APPROACH TO NEGOTIATIONS

Background Steps to Negotiations
Planning Stage
The Negotiation
Aftermath of the Negotiation

SPECIAL NEGOTIATION TOPICS

Buyer Pricing Strength and the Maximum
  Price Objective
Timing of Negotiations
The Sole Source Situation
Negotiating Transportation Rates and
  Services

CONCLUSION

CHAPTER OBJECTIVES

After reading this chapter you should:

- Appreciate when and for what reasons negotiations are used.

- Understand the basic component items that can be negotiated.

- Appreciate the general process of negotiation.

- Be able to approach negotiations for transportation rates and services.

Negotiations

Introduction

Negotiating is the art and science of communication in order to obtain a desired performance or commitment from another person. In purchasing it is meeting with suppliers in order to obtain a certain price and/or quality commitment from one or more of them. It is perhaps the least scientific or precise of all functions performed in purchasing. Most of purchasing's other activities involve objective data, analyses, and decision rules. Negotiating includes some of these, as well as information of differing degrees of reliability, psychological tactics, and pressure. The realm of negotiations is approached by knowing when it is appropriate, what the key objectives can be, and the primary approaches useful in them, as well as knowing how far to go.

The topic of negotiations is presented at this point in the book because negotiations must be approached with quality, price, and source availability in mind. It is a key factor in the timing of purchases. Transportation represents a new area for negotiating price and service advantages for the firm, and this subject is also presented in this chapter.

When Negotiations Are Appropriate

Negotiations are time-consuming and costly; they require that the firm have a relatively long lead time to conduct negotiations prior to order placement and goods receipt. Further, they are expensive from the standpoint of analyst and management time and costs. Negotiations require preparation, data collection, position development efforts, and sometimes travel. This method of price determination or goods availability is not to be used in all settings. It is not an ideal method to use in all possible buying settings.

The economics of negotiations can be likened to a break-even chart situation. Some purchases are small in volume, dollar expenditure, and quality concern. The cost of the transaction might not be large, and for this reason it might be uneconomical for the buying firm to enter into negotiations. Though the buyer might be able to obtain a better price through negotiation, it is less costly to pay the current higher unit price than spend resources on negotiations. On the other hand, some purchases entail large quantities or other special needs. An expenditure for negotiations might result in major savings over current prices; this is even more advantageous when the cost is spread over many units. The higher transaction cost might bring about lower unit price.

In a relatively competitive setting, negotiations are useful when the features of competitive bidding are not present. Such features are a large number of willing sellers in the market, and clear and definite specifications with which to communicate to vendors. If these are lacking, then an approach to one or more willing vendors for a negotiation would be necessary. Further, negotiations are often useful when the buyer is not fixed in terms of the specifications that will be needed. In this instance, the vendor's knowledge will be used to develop some or all of the specifications as well as to produce the product.

Negotiations are useful in situations in which the quantity sought is large enough to encourage a seller to provide a price advantage, either through volume revenue or cost-economy considerations. Negotiations are also useful in settings in which the job being sought requires a large amount of set-up costs and effort. Further, they are used in long-run work requiring many time periods or many separate jobs over a year or so.

Negotiating Objectives

Buyers use negotiations to attain desired price, quality, or service ends that are not always possible or not possible at all from other means. Some of these prime objectives are:

- A price better than one available from other methods.
- Quality that is either better or of a different level or type from what is currently on the market.
- Quantity different from normal practices.
- Vendor distribution service inbound to the buyer's firm that is of special features.
- Concession for delivery, payment, or other selling/buying arrangement.
- Cooperation or communication reinforcement about the relationship between the two firms that is desired by the buyer.

Negotiations are often considered as price-oriented processes. However, many other features, in fact any other one, can be sought through this process.

Scope of Negotiations

Nearly any facet of a purchase may be negotiated. The individual components of the goods or service being acquired all sum up to the total cost and quality of the final item. The rudiments of negotiations do not bear totally upon the full price of the goods; rather, specific costs, features, and services are more fruitfully discussed individually to build up to the final price to be paid by the buyer. Table 6–1 presents most of the components involved in the production and delivery of goods to a buyer.

Various negotiating features are part of the total package of product and price paid by a buyer for goods supplied by a vendor. Profit is sought by vendors, and this factor is often included through mark-ups to some costs or as a fee added to the total. Many of these individual components can be provided by the buyer firm. That is, there are more alternatives than merely making or buying the total product. Differences in the cost components will exist due to the relative efficiencies of each firm, their locations, their respective tax rates and costs of capital, as well as their skills and experience. Some of these components are hard, tangible costs, and others are "soft." That is, a buyer might negotiate a specific price on one component and in return allow the vendor to use a buyer-supplied die on other work. Another concession element that does not cost as much for the buyer is to allow the vendor to use designs on other work. The benefit to the vendor greatly outweighs the cost to the buyer. These are some very subtle elements in the negotiating process.

The overall requirement is that the buyer know what each component would cost to produce or provide by his or her firm. This gives insights into whether or not a vendor statement about a cost is appropriate. It also gives the buyer the ability to offer his or her own firm's services or goods as part of the work. One major consumer goods firm uses a certain raw material in one of its product lines. It buys the product on the open market in a very competitive manner. The consumer goods division of the same firm acquires some parts from a small vendor who must buy this same raw material on the open market at very high prices. In this instance, the buyers for the consumer goods plant arrange shipments of the raw material to the vendor from the plant of the firm's other division.

One last point about negotiations is the cost of the relationship. Firms undergo a learning curve in dealing with each other. Switching from one firm to the next often incurs the penalty costs of buyers and sellers getting to know each other and their respective firm's policies and procedures. One overriding feature of negotiations is that they can lead to long-term relationships that can reduce costs and problems for each firm. A feature in one negotiation can relate to a feature in a later one. That is, the vendor might agree to a short-term concession today for the benefit of the buyer firm only to expect like treatment in return in the next round of work. Such considerations are very important in the long-run costs and profitability of both firms.

Approach to Negotiations

There are four basic steps to negotiations. First is the background or spadework step. This is the process that leads the buyer up to the need for negotiations. Second is the planning step, in which the buyer prepares specific information for the negotiation with a particular vendor. Third is the negotiation itself. And, fourth is the aftermath. Most of all the activities involved with negotiations fall into one of these four steps.

☐ **TABLE 6-1.** *Analysis of Negotiable Component Costs and Services*

Item	What Included	Key Points
Designs	Plans and blueprints required for the work	Buyer firm might more economically produce these. A cost item not to be included in price, if buyer firm provides for work. An item to "sell" to vendor, if firm does not need after work is completed.
Dies	Forms, molds, etc. for use on production machinery	Vendor might already possess one, something that might not have to be charged for on current work. Buyers sometimes supply dies. Investigate whether less costly for vendor to produce die or for buyer firm to make or obtain for the work.
Tools and machinery	Production equipment needed for the work	Same points as with dies. Buyers firm might supply these items when it previously made the goods, but seeks to have other firms produce them in future; way to test vendor.
Training	Cost of training vendor workers	Can be performed by either buyer firm or vendor when new work needed on new technology machinery.
Raw material freight	Inbound goods movement cost	Freight sometimes moved at less cost in buyer firm's truck or arranged movement. Useful when buyer firm supplying raw goods for the work.
Raw materials	Goods needed for work	Buyer firm might be able to obtain these at less cost or in better ways than vendor.
Labor	Labor in production Rate of pay and time required	Some finishing, etc. might be performed at less cost or higher quality than vendor. Buyer to ascertain hourly rate of pay for actual workers needed by vendor to do work.
Labor benefits	Fringes for production workers	These costs sometimes paid once by firms at start of each new period. The work needed by buyer might not cause some of these fringes to be paid workers during the work in question.
Overhead basis	Factory and overall vendor overhead costs	Method of allocation should be examined. See costing section in Chapter 4, since each method of allocation causes a different "cost."
Supplies	Materials needed for work, but not part of output	Can be a separate negotiable element in runs.
Packaging/loading	Method of packing, loading, and shipping goods	Sometimes can be performed better and at less cost by buyer firm personnel doing this at vendor's plant.
Freight	Movement costs	Seek to determine whether vendor or buyer firm freight arrangements are least costly.
Inventory holding and storage cost	Capital cost, storage cost	Alternatives to explore are vendor stocking, consignment, or any other system.

☐ **TABLE 6-1.**   *Continued*

Item	What Included	Key Points
Insurance	Risk coverage over the goods	Important in transportation of fragile items.
Freight terms	Determines which firm pays the carrier	See Chapter 18 on freight terms.
Escalators	Cost elements that might increase during the work	See Chapter 4.
Returns	Goods returned from buyer to vendor, usually due to poor quality	Alternatives are rework and charge-back, return for rework, return for immediate replacement.
Payment terms	Payment for the goods	Length of time to pay. Shorter time should affect lower price.
Lot size	Size of shipment	Seek what is optimal to ship in carrier; some units can be carried free if shipment is a very large less-than-truckload move.
Vendor lead time	Time between order or requisition and delivery	The longer time required by the vendor, the less the price should be.
Quality	Quality of goods	Some buyers use "bracketing," which consists of a price for a acceptable level of quality as well as prices for higher and lower quality goods.

Background Steps to Negotiations

The background step entails price investigations, consideration of competitive bidding, or attempts at competitive bidding that led to poor results. Similarly, buyers might be led to negotiations through the use of two-step bidding in which the first step is bidding by potential vendors and the second step is final, detailed negotiations. Negotiations are useful for situations, other than pure price attainment. They are often necessary when special tooling or quality features are necessary. This is especially true when the tools or dies are not transferrable to other work that the vendor might perform for other customers.

The background stage leads up to the decision to negotiate. Negotiations are often expensive and time-consuming. They require long managerial lead times and much preparation on the part of the buyer. This stage involves the decision of whether to negotiate or rely upon one of the other methods of price determination.

The information necessary for this decision falls into three basic groups. One is the price that might possibly be paid by using one of the other forms of price determination. A second is the time and cost of conducting negotiations with one or more vendors. And a third is the best estimate of the price that might be obtained through negotiations. The difference between the first price and the final negotiated price is the price advantage gained through negotiations, but the investment required to obtain this advantage must be considered. The purchasing manager or buyer must then determine whether there is sufficient payoff in either the short or long run for using negotiations.

Other factors that come into the decision at this point are the overall price, quality, and availability trend of goods on the market. The general trend in the economy, whether tightening or shifting into a slump, is important from a timing standpoint. If the economy is loosening, then negotiation might not be needed. If, on the other hand, production capacity is becoming tighter and prices are rising, then it might be appropriate to do so.

Planning Stage

This is the preparatory stage to the actual negotiation. In this area the buyer is establishing that a particular vendor is the best potential for the negotiation and the work. This requires prior analysis into the vendor's financial position, the condition of its plant, the quality and balance of its management, and finally the nature of the vendor's initial proposal for the work. The buyer must be assured that the particular vendor is one that would normally be selected in any other type of purchase decision.

Information the buyer should collect prior to the actual negotiation includes the needs of the buying firm, cost analysis of the vendor as well as the buying firm, an estimate of the vendor's needs, the alternatives available to the buyer, and how the buyer firm is a responsible customer. Each one of these items of information establishes a position of relative strength for the buyer.

1. Needs of the Buying Firm. This data consists of all the volumes, timings, seasonalities, etc. of the product being sought. It consists of the quality needed, as well as bracketed quality levels higher and lower than the base level. This provides some flexibility in the entire negotiation processes within the quality production capabilities of the vendor. The needs of the buying firm present the exact work the firm is seeking from the vendor. Further factors about the work being sought, which can be brought out in the form of buyer concessions or additional negotiating features, are larger volumes, longer production run lot sizes, less seasonality, buyer provision of key materials or problem components in the entire work, or any other feature that is beneficial for the vendor.

2. Cost Analysis. This is the prime information needed by the buyer entering into negotiations. Cost analysis consists of information relating to the buying firm's own cost to make the product in question, an estimate as to what the specific cost components are for the vendor, and a determination of negotiating objectives. The maximum objective is the lowest possible price being sought from the vendor. The minimum objective is the highest possible price that the buyer firm will settle for, and the prime objective is one between the two that provides optimal services, quality, etc. in addition to the price. It is known that the maximum objective for the buyer might cause the vendor to cut corners on quality, delivery or other factors. In the end,

■ **EXHIBIT 6–1.**   *Negotiating Objectives*

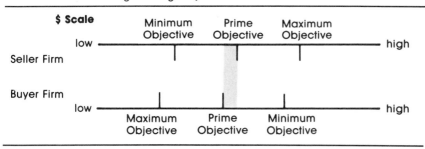

the total cost to the buyer would be higher because of the sum of the price paid and compensating efforts to make up for vendor deficiencies. Figure 6–1 shows how these objectives relate to both the buyer and seller in a negotiation.

Cost information includes any data the buyer firm might have compiled in the past in a make or buy study for this product. This information provides the buyer with indications of reasonableness of price being stated by the seller. Other information in the cost analysis area needed by the negotiating buyer are cost estimates of the vendor's costs for labor, materials, overhead, transportation, capital cost overhead, and any other key cost components as discussed in Chapter 4. The buyer attempts to learn much about the cost structure of the seller so that each cost factor can be evaluated in terms of reasonableness.

3. Estimate of Vendor Needs. This information relates to the power the vendor has in relation to the buyer. That is, the buyer seeks to determine the degree to which the vendor needs the work in question. During times of price increases and business booms, this power will be largely in the hands of the vendor. On the other hand, if the buyer knows that the vendor's business is soft or that the vendor is seeking additional work of the type being sought by the buyer, then some relative bargaining strength is in the hands of the buyer.

4. Buyer Alternatives. This is a determination of alternatives that the buyer firm may resort to as negotiating factors or as other avenues of approach in the event the negotiations are not favorable. Items to note here are other vendors, the possibility of doing all or some of the work in-house, the possibility of delaying the purchase, using other technology or parts, etc. This gives the buyer the option of obtaining a price from more than one negotiating vendor. It also lets that vendor know that if all fails for the buyer, he or she has other alternatives to fall back upon instead of merely relying upon the one vendor.

5. Noting How the Buyer Firm is a Responsible Customer. These are points about the desirable nature of the firm in terms of it being a sound and good customer for the vendor to deal with. Some common points here that are good to remind the vendor of during the entire process are as follows: the fairness and ethical nature of the buying firm, how it pays its bills promptly, the fact that it only resorts to claims in sound situations, and sharp practices are not used, as well

as any other facet of the buying and selling arrangements that can make the buying firm a desirable customer.

Information is the key strength of the buyer in a negotiation. It must be sound, easily accessible, and credible. The greater the detail of such information, the more easily the buyer can use it in the give and take of the negotiation. Other points of value are those factors that the buyer is willing to use in concessions. They are individual points about quality, timing, payments, etc. that the buyer may concede in the negotiation in exchange for concessions from the vendor that might be of greater dollar value.

The Negotiation

Many points that are useful to keep in mind here are frequently mentioned in literature about negotiations. While many of these points might not actually provide an advantage to the buyer, they can represent disadvantages if used against him or her.

- Prepare an agenda for the negotiation. This is a listing and timing flow of the points sought in the negotiation. Of importance here is the timing of when certain factors are introduced into the negotiation.
- Be sure that the person negotiating for the vendor has the authority to negotiate for the vendor. That is, the person negotiating should be able to commit his or her firm to whatever is settled during the negotiation.
- Prepare a negotiating team with a leader. This team can consist of many persons from law, engineering, production, finance, marketing, or any other area of the firm from which some expertise might be needed during the negotiation.
- Attempt to conduct the negotiation on home ground. This means that the buyer should try to have the negotiations conducted in his or her own offices. The person who must travel to another location to negotiate will undergo a disadvantage in being uncomfortable with their surroundings, not having complete access to information needed in their own offices, and not being able to control many of the daily schedule events. Coffee breaks may be set by the host party when things are not going well for them, or they can be delayed if the momentum of the negotiation is in their favor, etc.
- Be sure to sit together with other persons of the same side. In other words, do not allow the group to be broken up with persons of the other firm in between. This cuts off communications that might then only take place at coffee breaks, lunches, after hours, etc.
- Set sights high in the initial round of negotiation. Rarely, if at all, will one party finally obtain more than what was originally set as a stated goal. The final settled point will be somewhere between the buyer's and seller's original goals, but it will not be outside either of these.

- Establish momentum by first stating what is needed by your side. Seek the supplier's reaction and then ask the supplier to justify his/her position. This creates a slight advantage in favor of the buyer in that the seller must justify his/her goals. Part of this justification should be price or cost analysis by the vendor.
- Use various means to indicate the buyer's position of strength. This might include the ability to produce the product in-house, the existence of recent communications with other vendors, or any other way to let the vendor know that there are other options available to the buyer. It might even consist of alluding to future work after the current job.
- When it is time for the buyer to offer a concession, do so only after the seller has done so. Further, the buyer's concession might be of lesser dollar value or some nondollar item that appears to be equal. For example, if the vendor offers a drop of 5¢ from his/her original position, the buyer should increase something less than 5¢ with his/her concession. In some instances, the buyer might offer a quality or payment term item in concession that is of lesser than 5¢ value to him or her. The reason for this approach is that the buyer who can exercise this tactic will generally cause the final price to be on their side of the 50 percent dividing line of the original goal statements.
- Use sound and convincing data in arguments and discussions. The greater the detail and perceived validity, the greater the ability to obtain a convincing result from the other side.
- Discuss costs and not always price. Center the discussion about dollar figures as much as possible around the vendor's costs. If price is discussed, there is always the clouded element of profit or other margins present that can complicate full understanding of the amounts discussed. By discussing costs, the arguments can be directed toward data the buyer might also possess about the vendor's industry. Besides, a profit figure should often be a separately discussed factor in the total negotiation.
- Use silence and delay tactics for good use. Silence is often perceived as deep thinking or dissatisfaction with what was just presented by a vendor. This might prompt further concession or discussion from them.
- Sometimes mask the true importance of some points. If a certain point is critical to the buyer, it is often wise to not let that fact be known to the seller. Rather, by treating it as a minor point, the vendor might concentrate on other things and let the "minor point" be part of an offering along with what he or she thinks is important elsewhere.
- Keep good notes and records as to what has been agreed upon. These points will form the basis of a future contract or letter of agreement at the terminaiton of the negotiations. It is critical that each of these points be clear.
- Be firm and fair. Deal from a position of strength or at least from the outward impression of strength. This often means being firm

and deliberate in action. On the other hand, being fair and honest is important for the entire process to be successful now and in future negotiations.

A successful negotiation should be one in which both sides feel they have won. In reality, one side will have won more than the other. But, both must feel that something positive was gained, and that they can show their own employers that they were successful for them. This is an important point to keep in mind when a buyer has nearly total strength in a negotiation. That is, it is not always good policy to seek maximum results from a vendor to their detriment. The vendor's negotiator must be able to satisfy his or her own employer that the negotiations had some positive features for them.

Aftermath of the Negotiation

The negotiation will finally end with all or most points being agreed to, or at least being disposed of in some manner. It is important at this point to establish the key points of the negotiation for complete understanding by both parties. This is often accomplished through a "memo of agreement." This is a statement that describes the final points and terms of the negotiation. It is often signed by both parties, and it becomes the basis of a final contract that is later drawn up.

Several points should be considered in these memos. One, it is often wise for the buyer's side to draft them. This assures that the full understanding of the buyer is put into the wording. It should also be reviewed by all the other persons on the negotiating team of the buyer. This reduces the possibility of incorrect terms, etc. Finally, the memo should be in simple terms that indicate the intent of the agreement rather than attempting to be a legal contract. The full working of a legal contract should be left to lawyers.[1]

Special Negotiation Topics

There are several key topics in the area of negotiations pertaining to buyer pricing strength, the timing of negotiations with a vendor, the single source situation, and the new scene in transportation negotiations. Each one of these represents an opportunity for buyers.

Buyer Pricing Strength and the Maximum Price Objective

The long run viability of a vendor is important for a buyer to consider, since each supplier represents a source of supply as well as a competitive force in the entire marketplace. This viability primarily depends upon adequate revenues. These revenues are determined by the firm's pricing practices and its negotiating strength with buyers. Figure 6–2 presents the relationship of price to the profit and the cash position of the supplier in a hypothetical cost situation.

In this situation, the firm produces goods at a variable cost of $5.00 per unit. The total company overhead for the period is $10,000, and the company volume is 4,000 units for the period. The fully allocated cost is $7.50 per unit at this price and cost configuration.

■ **EXHIBIT 6-2.** *Price/Cost Relationships*

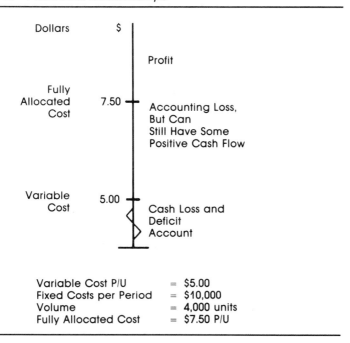

Variable Cost P/U	= $5.00
Fixed Costs per Period	= $10,000
Volume	= 4,000 units
Fully Allocated Cost	= $7.50 P/U

The price might be negotiated anywhere on the dollar continuum shown in Exhibit 6–2. Four primary zones exist in this entire dollar range and each represents different situations for the vendor. First, the price might be above the fully allocated cost. This represents actual profit to the extent of the amount above the cost. Second, a settled price that is below the fully allocated cost, but above the variable cost will result in a loss or deficit, but the firm might still recoup a positive cash flow for the work if some of the fixed expenses do not represent a cash outlay. Third, is a price at variable cost. While this covers the direct costs of producing the goods, it does not contribute to the overhead or profit of the vendor. It is too risky a price, because a cost overrun of just 1¢ will result in a true cash loss to the vendor. Fourth, a price below variable cost will produce a cash loss and a profit loss for the vendor.

The operating and investment factors relating to pricing are presented in Table 6–2. This shows the four zones and the operating and investment decisions relevant for the vendor in each. A price above fully allocated cost is the best possible situation. One below fully allocated cost but above variable cost is often desirable in the short run if there are no other better uses for the assets involved and if the work will result in a positive cash flow. But, this pricing area will not recoup sufficient cash funds in the long run for the vendor to reinvest in new or replaced equipment. That is, there are some times when it might be a good practice for both the buyer and vendor to settle upon a price between $5.00 and $7.50. With this price range in the long run, however, the vendor will not have sufficient resources to replace the assets, and it will drop from that line of business when its assets cease operating.

☐ **TABLE 6-2.** *Price/Cost Relationships*

Price/Cost Situation	Vendor Operating Decision	Vendor Investment Decision
Price at or above fully allocated cost	OK to produce and sell goods	Generally OK to invest in new assets or replace existing ones.
Price below fully allocated cost but above variable cost	Operate only in short run (no longer than one year and certainly no longer than life of assets) Try to raise revenue or fing better use for assets	Do not invest further into this segment of business; generally do not replace assets at end of lives.
Price at variable cost level	Too risky! Try to raise revenue or find better use for assets	Do not invest further into this segment of business; do not replace assets.
Price below variable cost	Do not operate. Try to raise revenue or find better use for assets	Certainly do not invest more into this business segment.

Timing of Negotiations

The timing of the purchase is another key facet of negotiations. Using the above costing situation, assume that the vendor's variable cost per unit of $5.00 is stable throughout a long time span. The $10,000 overhead or fixed cost is determined to be a cost incurred by the vendor for six-month periods. The 4,000 unit volume used to compute the fully allocated cost represents a volume level the vendor felt it could sell during that period. It is only a part of the vendor's total capacity. The 4,000 unit volume is reached by the end of the fourth month. This means that any other units produced during the six-month time span will not have to bear any additional overhead cost allocations of $2.50 each. The fixed costs for the period were already recouped on the originally planned 4,000 units.

Exhibit 6–3 illustrates this cost situation. It shows how the first 4,000 units cost the firm $5.00 each in variable cost plus a $2.50 allocation of the overhead cost for a total of $10,000. Once the 4,000th unit was produced, any additional ones only cost the firm $5.00 each. That is, no additional overhead allocation is needed on each unit until another six-month time span begins with a new overhead cost.

Herein is an opportunity for a buyer to negotiate a low price on an extra run of goods. If the buyer knows that the seller's fiscal period allocation was already reached and there is still some remaining capacity to produce more units, then there is a true opportunity for the seller to cut its price to somewhere between $5.00 and $7.50 and for the buyer to obtain a special price cut on some units. The seller gains from extra production and profit. The buyer gains as well.

■ **EXHIBIT 6-3.** *Overhead Cost Allocation During Fiscal Period*

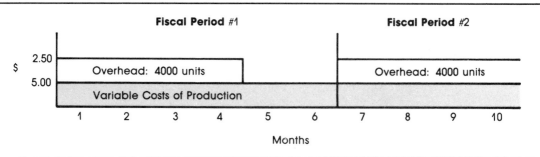

This situation requires the buyer to be aware of the seller's fiscal periods, amount of regular producton, and its accounting practices. This illustrates that the more information gathered from and about suppliers, the stronger the buyer will be in the long run.

The Sole Source Situation

This setting is perhaps the most disadvantageous for the buyer. The power of the relationship is mostly in the hands of the seller firm. Price is often administered and terms of sale are defined by the seller. This does not mean that the buyer is at total disadvantage from price and service standpoints. There are several approaches and areas of investigation that are available to the buyer.

The "make" decision is one that can be investigated when attempting to obtain price reductions or quality improvements in a sole source setting. This is most common with utility sources. Firms will often investigate their own gas, electricity, and water sources. Even communications is now possible without the sole source of the original AT&T Company. The make decision will often involve an investment that represents a "threshold" cost entering into the line of activity. That is, a high initial cost will have to be incurred to begin the operation. This investment cost will have to be evaluated against the savings from the operation versus continuation with the sole source. The basic concept involved here is investment payback, which is presented in Chapter 9.

The firm can also develop power against a sole source by openly pursuing the "make" decision. This has long been a tactic traffic managers have used with private trucks in order to hold down for-hire carrier rates. It might not be required to enter into the activity, but the actual movement toward doing so can provide negotiating leverage with the sole source to reduce its price or improve its product. Thus, the perceived threat of dropping the sole source is sometimes sufficient to gain concessions.

Alternate materials is another avenue of investigation in breaking the price and product power of a sole source. By shifting to other materials, the buyer can seek other sources that might be more competitive. This step can only be taken after initial research into the feasibility of using other materials. Further, this step includes investigation into reducing, if not replacing, the product of the sole source.

Another possible area of price and product improvement investigation is to seek an advantage by working through the sole source's weakest conditions. The source might have a slow period through the year or may experience slumps from time to time. It might face periods of cash outflows or other conditions that might be advantageous for the buyer. By working with the sole source during these periods, it might be possible to adopt to other purchasing timings that the source might be willing to provide concessions for.

Negotiating Transportation Rates and Services

Rail, motor, water, and air transportation rates and services can now be negotiated. Prior to the late 1970s most transportation firms were created and managed within a utility concept. They were protected from competition and collectively set prices; new firms were limited from entering the field. Cost increases were passed on through the use of general price increases on all traffic for all firms in the industry. There was little or no bargaining strength for the purchaser or distribution manager. Embarking upon the use of the firm's own private truck, water, or air operations or using another transport mode were the only negotiating strengths available to the manufacturing firm.

Deregulatory moves by various agencies and Congress have changed transportation from having utility concept to that of a competitive environment. Carriers are limited from collective pricing, new firms can enter into the marketplace with relative ease, and pricing and services are now very flexible. All of this opens the way for purchasing managers to negotiate transportation services and prices with carriers. Carriers are very competitive today. Buyers can often obtain most or all of the terms they seek in a negotiation. This is not necessarily sound in the long run, because the carriers must survive in order to provide consistent low-cost service to the firm.

A sound approach to negotiating for lower transportation rates, more carrier equipment, or better service utilizes the same concepts applied in negotiating for goods from a producer vendor. It begins with an analysis and statement of the buyer's traffic patterns inbound, between the plants, and outbound to customers. Much of this information is available from the firm's distribution department, but a large part of it is dependent upon the purchasing department's vendor selection, timing, and other product-flow decisions. The purchasing department can use production plans, lead times, vendor locations, forward buy decisions, etc., to create a statement of inbound transportation needs over a coming year or so. This will show traffic volumes, origin-destination lanes, and type of commodity needed to be hauled.

The total cost of transportation must also be treated in terms of vehicle utilization and flow. For example, dense loading of a vehicle will spread the total costs of the move over more units and reduce the cost per unit of inbound goods. Here is where the buyer will look to such things as larger lot size, different packaging from the vendor, better loading techniques by the vendor, etc.

Vehicle utilization also affects the transportation cost through the backhaul. A shipment in one direction produces a backhaul for the carrier. It is a joint cost situation for a carrier. A loaded one-way move with no backhaul will have to bear the total roundtrip cost of the vehicle movement. This move will be expensive for the shipper or buyer. On the other hand, a move that is balanced with another move (inbound purchase balanced with outbound shipment from the same plant), will serve to reduce the prorata share of the total cost for each leg of the move. It is critical that buyers match up their decision options with carriers and vendors with those of the outbound distribution movements of their own firm.

Conclusion

Negotiations are becoming more and more important in the job of purchasing. Not only is it useful with vendors, but it is now a commonplace practice in transportation service procurement as well. Negotiations involve time and can be costly in terms of data collection, analysis, and preparation. Further, they can entail travel costs. It is a pricing mechanism that can be beneficial to the firm, but it is not always a sound one. Buyers still do not know if the price and product/service features obtained are the best possible ones that could have been obtained. There is also the risk of conducting negotiations that do not result in desired ends, and in the meantime time is lost that reduces the supply options of the buyer in light of the product deadline need.

Negotiations are both an art and science. They rely greatly upon the availability of information and the determination of the negotiator's position of strength. Many psychological approaches and tactics are used. Though a buyer might not be forceful or aggressive in negotiations or might never be involved in them at all, this chapter presented many of the tactics that are valuable to know in the event they are ever used against them.

FOOTNOTE

1. Chester L. Karrass, "Memos of Agreement," *Purchasing*, 5 November 1981, p. 41.

SOURCES FOR FURTHER READING

Bartos, Otomar J. *Process and Outcome of Negotiations*. New York: Columbia University Press, 1974.
Hanan, Mack *Sales Negotiation Strategies*. New York: AMACOM, 1977.
Morley, Dan E. *The Social Psychology of Bargaining*. London: G. Allen & Unwin, 1977.
Nierenberg, Gerard I. *Fundamentals of Negotiating*. New York: Hawthorn Books, 1973.
Young, Oran B. *Bargaining: Formal Theories of Negotiations*. Urbana, IL: University of Illinois Press, 1975.
Zartman, I. William. *The Negotiating Process: Theories and Applications*. Beverly Hills, CA: Sage Publication, 1978.

QUESTIONS FOR REVIEW

1. When are negotiations an appropriate price determination technique?

2. What are the common objectives of negotiations?

3. What specific items can be negotiated within the scope of work being sought?

4. Is the buying firm constrained by the only alternatives of either making or buying?

5. What is so important about the overhead basis and overhead rate in a negotiation?

6. Why should costs be negotiated as separate from price?

7. What are the different stages of the negotiating process?

8. What are the differences between minimum, prime, and maximum objectives?

9. How does a memo of agreement come into play in a negotiation?

10. Must a vendor always obtain a price that is at or above its fully allocated cost?

11. What features about transportation can be negotiated?

12. How is a transportation rate or service negotiation approached?

Problem 6-1

A buyer traditionally has paid $8.00 per unit to a certain truckline for inbound movements. Deregulation of the trucking industry has led to sharp price cutting by all motor carriers. A discount program is being offered by the carrier. It is as follows:

Cumulative Quantity per year	Unit Rate
The first 100 units	$8.00 each
The next 100 units (#'s 101 to 200)	7.50 each
The next 300 units (#'s 201 to 500)	7.00 each
Units 501 and up	6.50 each

The buyer knows that the carrier's variable cost per unit is $4.25 and that fixed costs amount to an additional $3.25 per unit. The firm can use the carrier for about 750 unit movements per year.

Questions:

1. *What will be the total cost of 750 units?*
2. *What is the unit cost to the buyer of all 750 units?*
3. *Explain why the carrier can move the product below its full cost and still remain in business.*
4. *Can the carrier do this in the long run? Why or why not?*

7

CHAPTER OBJECTIVES

After reading this chapter you should:

- Understand the basic points of
  contract law.

- Appreciate the primary concepts
  relating to antitrust and pricing laws
  in the United States.

- Understand product liability and the
  legal facets of transportation.

- Appreciate the legal requirements of
  many public policies and
  noneconomic laws applying to
  purchasing.

The Legal Realm of Purchasing

Introduction

The legal realm of purchasing is both wide and varied. Laws and liabilities in the field stem from many different sources and involve many types of actions. There is no one single source of law. Influences upon the purchasing task come from federal, state, and even local levels; from laws, administrative regulations, and past case decisions of both courts and regulatory agencies. Legal constraints exist regarding buyer-vendor relationships, pricing and other business practices, product liability, policies toward the use of small companies and minority-owned firms, product control laws, transportation, hazardous waste movement and storage, and even the personal liability of the purchasing agent or manager.

Legal Influences in Purchasing

The laws, regulations, and policies that shape the buying practices and functions of purchasing personnel come from many areas. The Federal Constitution set the stage for laws and regulations over business practices through its Commerce Clause. State constitutions generally established the powers to create laws for the health and welfare of citizens. Such laws included means for adjudicating issues between two or more parties. Other laws and regulations stem from these two constitutional areas.

The laws of agencies and general buying-selling relationships in the marketplace were first defined by common law. This was a body of court decisions stemming from English practices that evolved into a generally consistent pattern over the years. These practices and rules were eventually codified into what is known today as the Uniform Commercial Code. It has been accepted by all states except Louisiana, which still applies Napoleanic law for contracts between merchants. Court issues involving contracts and other business transactions are evaluated in light of the Uniform Commercial Code.

Federal laws often were written to encourage, outlaw, or otherwise shape certain business practices. Such laws, known as administrative laws, are general in nature, with government agency created or empowered to administer the law and fill in the details of how the law should be carried out. Congressional acts often empower the agency to create specific detailed laws. The Congressional acts are found in the *United States Code.* Various agency regulations are found in what is called the *Code of Federal Regulations.* These government agencies are empowered to enforce the laws, thereby acting as prosecutors; they also act as courts before which two or more parties subject to the laws may have issues decided. For this reason, regulatory agencies are often referred to as being quasi-legislative and quasi-judicial in nature.

Court cases also shape business practices. When laws are enacted; they are often tested in issues brought before courts. The specific interpretation of the laws by the courts eventually becomes a body of knowledge that shapes future practices by firms and persons. Case decisions indicate the direction in which courts will decide issues relating to the laws.

The Purchase and Contract Law

Purchasing law mainly stems from contract law. The purchasing agent and manager act as legal agents of the firms that employ them. Their daily processes revolve around contract law. Offers and acceptances are fairly well-defined by this law, as is contract satisfaction and nonperformance, which includes defective goods, rejection, and measures of damages.

Common Law and the Uniform Commercial Code

Commercial transactions and relationships originally were subject to common law. Common law was the body of case precedents dealing with disputes between two or more parties over matters of business transactions and relations. Each state, except Louisiana, created legislation basically following the concepts behind English common law. Through the years, however, specific differences between various state laws complicated business transactions, and this led to the establishment of the Uniform Commercial Code.

The Uniform Commercial Code consists of ten Articles, which are as follows:

1. General Provisions
2. Sales
3. Commercial Paper
4. Bank Deposits and Collections
5. Letters of Credit
6. Bulk Transfers
7. Warehouse Receipts, Bills of Lading, and other Documents of Title
8. Investment Securities
9. Secured Transactions; Sales of Accounts, Contract Rights, and Chattel Paper
10. Effective Date and Repealer

Article 2 contains many of the contract provisions that will be discussed in further detail in this part of the chapter.

The Law of Agency

Purchasing buyers commit their firms to accepting goods in exchange for monetary obligations. Sales persons, on the other hand, commit their firms to provide customers with output in exchange for monetary resources. In both instances, the buying and selling persons are acting as agents for their employing firms.

The term *agency* indicates that a person is acting for another person or firm called a *principal*. In this capacity, the person is acting as an *agent*. The agent is a person who 1) acts on behalf of another person or firm, 2) is under close supervision of the principal, or 3) has an obligation to act in the principal's best interest. In one sense, agents can be employees such as purchasing persons. In another sense, agents can be independent parties or contractors, such as real estate agents, sales agents, or insurance agents. The discussion here is limited to the relationship between the purchasing person and his or her firm.

An agent obtains the ability to act for a principal through the *authority* granted him or her by the principal. This authority can exist, or may come into existence, in three ways— 1) by having acted as an agent in the past, 2) by establishing the relationship in writing (e.g., an employment contract or a contract stating the authority is granted), or 3) through the act of employment in which the person hiring the buyer states that he/she is to purchase goods for the firm up to certain dollar amounts.

Authority can be either actual or apparent. Actual authority may be express or implied. Express authority is that which the principal has expressly granted to the agent. Implied authority is that which might not have been expressly stated, but is normally required in the regular conduct of the responsibilities imposed upon the agent. Apparent authority is that which might be beyond express authority. It is the authority that third persons assume the agent possesses, even though he or she might not actually possess it. Apparent authority arises: 1) from an appearance of its existing, 2) when the decision is within the agent's area of responsibility or 3) when the third party is justified in assuming that the agent does, in fact, have the authority. In these three situations of apparent authority, the agent has the power to bind the principal. The third party can assume apparent authority if other agents in similar settings possess authority to act in the same manner.[2]

The law extends certain responsibilities for an agent in his/her relationship with their principal. One aspect of the agent's responsibilities is a duty of obedience. The agent is required to follow the instructions of the principal. Duty of loyalty is another requirement and stems from the fact that the agent is in a position to bring harm to the principal through misdeeds or neglect. The prime areas of prohibition here are: 1) an agent may not have personal interest in a contract negotiated for his/her principal, 2) an agent may not obtain gains from the business transacted for his principal, 3) an agent may not act on both sides in a negotiation, and 4) an agent may not misuse confidential information relating to the principal.[3]

Contracts

Contracts are agreements involving a promise or a set of promises that the law will enforce. The Uniform Commercial Code has defined rules by which agreements shall be created, and it establishes in the ways they shall be enforced.[4]

Contracts may exist in many forms. An *express contract* can be either oral or in written form. The terms can be explicitly stated in their entirety, or they may be *implied;* that is, not all terms must be reduced to writing or oral statement. Implied terms are those that both parties of the contract understand are necessary in order to carry out the provisions of the contract. *Bilateral contracts* are those in which one party is to fulfill one provision, while a second party is to fulfill another. It is necessary for both parties to fulfill their obligation in order for the contract to be satisfied. Breach or nonperformance can arise when one of the parties fails to fulfill his/her requirements. An *executed contract* is one in which all the terms have been carried out by all parties. This contrasts an *executory contract*, which is one that still has not been carried out in its entirety.[5]

The prime elements of a contract are:

1. Manifestation of intent,
2. Consideration,
3. Capacity,
4. Reality of intent,
5. Legality of purpose,
6. Compliance with the statute of frauds.[6]

Each element is discussed individually in the following paragraphs.

Manifestation of intent requires that both parties have some form of agreement. That is, both parties must agree that each is to perform in some specific way. Both parties must have a mutual understanding of the activity required of each other. The factors relating to offer and acceptance are important here, and these are presented below.

Consideration is the price paid for promises. In a buying and selling contract, it is the promise that one firm will ship products to another firm that will, in turn, pay for the material in some way.

The *legal capacity to act* is another element required for a contract to be enforceable. This element deals with the legality of minors entering contracts, and the question of persons having or not having the authority to act on behalf of a principal. Actual and apparent authority become the issue in purchases entailing very large amounts. A production manager entering into a contract to buy large capital assets might be questioned. Does he or she have the authority to commit the firm, or does that authority rest only with the purchasing manager and president of the firm. Can the purchasing manager make such purchases without the consent of a minimum number of vice-presidents?

Reality of consent is involved when questions of mistakes enter into the understanding of the offer and acceptance or if inducement of fraud or use of duress were present making the contract.

Legality of purpose means that the contract cannot require actions that involve crimes, torts, usurious interest, gambling, or the violation of licensing statutes.

Compliance with the statute of frauds states that oral contracts may be used for agreements of under $500 in value. Above this amount, the contract should be in writing. This area of contract law deals with the need to protect persons from false testimony. Evidence in writing reduces the possibility of such an occurrence.[7]

Offer and Acceptance

The offer is the action by one person of providing another the ability to create an obligation for him or her or their principal. Purchase orders, and some proposals, are a form of offer. The person making the offer is called the offeror, and the person to whom it is sent for acceptance is called the offeree. An offer is an expression of intent as to the kind of contract and terms by which the offeror is willing to be legally bound. An offer must be explicit; it can remain outstanding until 1) a stipulated time period lapses, 2) it is withdrawn, or 3) after a reasonable time.

Acceptance is the action by the offeree of creating a contract, which becomes effective when transmitted back to the offeror. Acceptance must be a specific action designed to signal the intent of the offeree to abide by the offer. This is usually accomplished through transmittal of a signed copy of the offer back to the offeror. In purchasing settings acceptance is often signaled by a confirmation order or a signed copy of the buyer's purchase order returned to him or her. The acceptance must be made by the person to whom the offer was made, or by his or her principal.

Acceptance is often made with minor changes added to the original offer. Sometimes this can create a cross-play of offers and counteroffers. The Uniform Commercial Code permits minor changes to be made in an offer by the person accepting it. Such minor changes do not negate the offer terms unless three criteria exist. Section 2–207 of the Code states these three criteria as 1) the offer expressly limits acceptance to the terms of the offer, 2) the changes materially alter the offer; or 3) notification of objection to the changes has already been given or is given within a reasonable time after notice of alteration is received. Section 2–207 further states that conduct by both parties that recognizes a contract is sufficient to establish one even though written evidence may not so indicate it.

The Code also recognizes that contracts can be formed through *one way communications*. An example of this type of contract is one party sending written notice to another that goods will be shipped on a certain date. Physical acceptance of such notice is not mandatory between merchants; however, with individuals and consumers there must be some form of acceptance. Section 2–201 states that such a statement shall become a contract unless the addressee notifies the addressor within ten days that he or she is objecting to the original notice.

Letters of intent often raise questions in the offer/acceptance area. A letter of intent is a communication from a buyer to a seller regarding terms he or she would like to obtain agreement upon prior to a formal contract. In other words, a letter of intent is used prior to a commitment to purchase. It can be used to establish a price or to seek a position in production scheduling. The letter of intent from a customer provides the seller with a tentative planning basis upon which to seek purchased goods for a possible future job.

A letter of intent can obligate the buyer to consummate a purchase, if it is designed in such a way as to cause the seller to initiate production or purchase of goods. This action is often taken in order to facilitate faster production or to obtain a place in the seller's order books. In foreign purchase settings a letter of intent seeks a commitment prior to full financial and legal terms being solidified, which might take several weeks. Letters of intent are also used when a buyer learns that a seller has a current production run of a certain product, and the buyer can obtain a low price by tacking on to the end of that current production run. By such action the buyer can avoid the production set-up costs of a new run later. The letter of intent can be transmitted in one day whereas other more formal purchase documents might take several days to be sent. As stated, the letter of intent can, in fact, become binding. The issues of actual and apparent authority again come into play here. If the seller has accepted this type of letter in the past from that particular buyer, then it is assumed that apparent authority exists.

Unpriced orders are another area requiring careful examination. Many times orders are placed without a specific price or without total costs being known by the buyer. This often occurs when cost calculations would consume too much time, or if the price of materials for the item being purchased is unknown by the seller. Such purchases are often called "price advise" orders. They are legal orders and do constitute the basis for valid contracts. The final price is determined later and the invoice amount becomes the "consideration" or payment sum. The Uniform Commercial Code contains a section relating to disputes arising from this type of purchase. If the buyer and seller dispute the final price, the Code states that the courts will determine a price based upon a reasonable value of the goods and services rendered. In addition, Section 2–305 of the Code states that upon failure to determine a price through fault of one of the parties, the other party may cancel the contract or determine a reasonable price. If the price cannot be agreed upon, the buyer has the option of returning the goods.[8] If the buyer cannot or will not return the goods, the seller may set a price that is equal to the market value of the goods at the time of contract came into dispute.[9]

Price protection for goods and services being produced often creates a legal problem. Both the buyer and seller might agree to certain price terms in an offer, acceptance may have been received, and a contract drawn; however the seller may face a situation of rising costs that were not known at the time of the contract agreement. Normally, both buyer and seller are bound to the prices, quantities, and qualities stipulated in an agreement. But, the Uniform Commercial Code provides protection for the seller in situations that are impossible for him or her to perform. Such is the case when raw material prices are suddenly increased due to war, commodity disruptions, or other uncontrollable events.

"Price protection," or holding price at one point, is a concern for buyers as well. When contracts are written with time, labor, and material rate terms, with costs-plus contracts, or other terms that leave the door open for uncertainty in the final price, the buyer is in a precarious position. One way in which the buyer may seek protection in such a situation is to stipulate terms that certify the seller will charge the lowest price provided to other customers. This includes the price being lowered during the term of the contract, if the price is lowered for other customers during that time span. Further, price protection may be gained and the degree of price uncertainty limited through a clause requiring notification in the event of price increases and demanding the right to inspect the records of the seller.[10]

Performance and Nonperformance

The problem of one party not complying with the terms of a contract is a common concern. This noncompliance is often referred to as *breach of contract*. The concept of breach exists in two forms. *Actual breach* occurs when one party does not abide to the contract terms. In buying and selling contexts, this usually occurs when the seller does not meet the quality or delivery timing terms. Technically, the seller breaches the contract if he or she does not meet the delivery date in the contract. In this instance, the buyer may refuse to take delivery of the goods. However, the buyer generally has a difficult time seeking damages in late shipment situations. At best, the damages would amount to the difference in the value of the goods at the time of actual delivery and their value at the agreed-to date of delivery. The damages awarded can include such items as production cost penalties, added overtime, or premium transportation costs required to move the goods to the destination, etc.

Anticipatory breach is the second type of nonperformance. Anticipatory breach means there might be a breach in the future or near-future. Examples of this type of breach are: 1) the seller informs the buyer in advance of the delivery date that he or she will not uphold those terms of the contract or 2) it becomes known to the buyer that the seller will not be able to fulfill the contracts. An example would be insolvency; either the seller or the buyer may not be able to financially fulfill the contract. In such instances, it is possible under the Uniform Commercial Code to seek written assurance that the contract will be fulfilled. During this period the party seeking the information may withhold performance of his or her part of the contract. The party from whom the assurance is sought must reply within thirty days. If no word of assurance is received within that time, the first party may assume a breach by *repudiation*.[11] This means the buyer assumes the seller will not fulfill the obligation.

Rejection of goods falls into the area of performance and nonperformance. Again, goods may be rejected at delivery if the seller took too long to deliver them. The Uniform Commercial Code lists key ponts for rejection. One, the buyer is permitted to inspect the goods prior to actual acceptance. For example, goods are delivered and the buyer signs a carrier delivery receipt, but the goods are still subject to inspection. If rejected, they must be set aside for the seller to inspect as well. Acceptance of the goods is final when the buyer begins to exercise normal ownership rights over them; that is, they are unpacked, moved to storage, to the store shelf, or into production. Once goods are accepted in any of these manners, the buyer has, in essence, waived the right of rejection. Rejection, however, may be total or in part.

The second point about rejection is that a positive action must take place. Merely leaving the goods on a dock and not paying the invoice a month later is not sufficient rejection. Also, rejection must be made in a "reasonable period of time." If the goods do not conform to those specified in the purchase order or contract, the buyer may reject them. However, the act of rejection must be timely, and the cause of rejection must be specifically stated. The goods should be segregated to prevent their becoming part of the normal inventory of the buying firm. They should be available for identification and inspection by the seller.

Damages from nonperformance fall into four basic groups. *General damages* amount to the difference between the value of goods at the time of delivery versus their value at the time of specified delivery, or when the buyer learned of breach. *Incidental damages* involve the actual costs of rejection, and include the cost of inspection and holding the goods while they are being rejected. However, the cost of inspection for accepted goods is not recoverable. *Consequential damages* are those resulting within the firm from not having the goods at the time expected or in the form specified. Damages here result from production downtime in order to reshift machine and manpower schedules, or any premium transportation required to honor the buyer's own contract with his/her customers. The key here is to specify on the purchase order just what the goods are intended for. This serves as notification to the seller that the goods are earmarked for a specific purpose and that damages could result if the contract terms are not met. *Liquidation damages* are those that arise if the terms of the contract are not met. These damages are usually stipulated in advance in the contract. For example, the contract might state that for every day of late delivery there will be a damage amount assessed that reduces the price by 10¢. However, the cost of seeking damages through a court is high, and good faith negotiation is a sound practice here.[12]

Warranties

Warranties are linked to the concept of performance and nonperformance. Warranties define the quality of the goods and establish the extent to which the producer is responsible for defects. Warranties are one liability area that manufacturers are subject to in their relationships with customers. Other areas are negligence, misrepresentation, and product liability. Warranties can be stated by the manufacturer or seller determined from the Uniform Commercial Code or from laws in the state in which the goods are sold.

Four basic types of warranties exist; these are: express warranty, implied warranty of merchantability, implied warranty of fitness for particular purpose, and implied warranty of title. Warranties carry from the manufacturer through to resellers to the eventual buyer-user. An express warranty is one that makes a specific statement about the product. Examples are that a paint will not peel, a battery will last five years, a light bulb will burn for 2,000 hours, or a carrier will provide overnight delivery. An express warranty is one that the manufacturer makes specifically about a product. It is a contractual promise or stipulation about the quality of the good or service. If the user finds that the product or service is not what is expressed in the warranty, then the manufacturer is in a breach liability situation.

Implied warranty of merchantability states that the item being purchased is of standard specification and is fit for the ordinary purpose for which it is normally traded. For example a copying machine has an intended purpose of providing copies from originals. Implied warranty of merchantability assumes the unit is free of defects and is capable of producing copies. The Uniform Commercial Code states that goods must be salable, or merchantable, and this concept is implied when the unit is sold.

Implied warranty of fitness for particular purpose states that the manufacturer sells the product for a particular purpose or to be used in a specific manner. This type of warranty comes into play when the buyer is not totally knowledgeable about the features of the product or its components. Two key points are important here: 1) the seller must have known the use to which the buyer planned to apply the product, and 2) the buyer must have relied upon the seller to provide him/her with the proper item. It is implied that when a purchase is requested in this manner, and the seller provides the product, that product must be suitable for the purpose intended.

Implied warranty of title deals with questions of the right of the seller to sell the product. It is assumed that when someone sells a product, he or she has the right to sell it, and the product comes without infringement upon patents, copyrights, etc. The seller must have the legal right to sell the product. This type of warranty also states that the goods must be free of any question of title. A question of title arises when an unknown supplier arrives at a plant with a truck filled with goods and offers to sell them at a low price.

The Role of Boiler-Plate Terms in Contracts

Contracts and purchase orders often contain what are called "boiler-plate" terms. Such clauses are designed to protect the buyer from certain actions as well as to assure that the seller will conform to certain practices that the buyer wishes. A good review of boiler plate terms is presented by Ammer, and some of these are as follows:[13]

Price—This term states that if the purchase order is unpriced, the goods will be sold at the last quoted amount or at the prevailing market price, whichever is lower. It is a protection in the event that time does not enable the buyer to determine the price when placing the order.

Payment Terms—The credit period and early payment discount, if any, are stated and shown to begin at either the date of delivery or the invoice date, whichever is later.

Packaging and Shipment Preparation—This term usually states that the seller is to prepare the shipment for safe movement and delivery. This expense is to be borne by the seller and can include shipment bracing, dunnage, packing materials, and pallets.

Identification—This term states that a packing slip is to be shipped with the goods in order to identify them upon delivery. The packing document is to show the purchase order number. This number is required to determine whether or not the shipment should be accepted on the inbound delivery dock. Good receiving practice requires dock personnel to determine whether or not shipments should be accepted prior to signing delivery receipts and accepting the goods. Carriers often make deliveries to the wrong address of a firm, or to the wrong firm altogether. By identifying the shipment through the packing list and a copy of the original purchase order, dock personnel can avoid accepting incorrect incoming goods.

Warranties—Purchase orders may contain warranty statements that the buyer desires. A general boiler-plate warranty statement might be one that states the buyer wishes the strongest warranty the seller provides.

Assignment—This statement obligates the seller to not assign any rights or claims to any other parties without prior permission of the buyer.

Partial Shipments—Many times a buyer will not wish to receive partial shipments. A boiler-plate statement might be used to state that all shipments must be in their entirety.

Arbitration—This clause states that in case of legal dispute, arbitration is to be used in place of court litigation. This point is discussed further in this chapter.

Boiler-plates and other preprinted purchase order terms and vendor acceptance statements often give rise to conflicts or questions of priority. General rules for resolving basic conflicts are as follows:

1. Typewritten insertions in a contract or purchase order take precedence over printed items.
2. Handwritten insertions supercede typed of preprinted items.
3. A conflict between a spelled out number and one that is a different numeral is resolved in favor of the number that is spelled out.
4. Conflicts between terms and clauses are resolved in favor of the one appearing first in the document.
5. Ambiguities are interpreted against the party inserting the term in question.[14]

Arbitration

Arbitration is a relatively useful system of settling disputes involving contract issues between buyers and sellers. The American Arbitration

Association provides expertise in many areas of possible dispute. Commercial transactions between buyers and sellers is one area in which this service may be used. Issues are brought before an arbitrator, and arguments are heard in much the same way as a court case. The decision of the arbitrator is not binding under common law, but it is often a sufficient hearing with enough valid consideration to put the issue to rest. The prime benefit of arbitration is the avoidance of more costly and time-consuming court litigation.

Pricing and Business Practice Laws

Four basic regulatory laws in the U. S. address the conduct of sellers and buyers in pricing and selling practices. These laws are known as antitrust laws, they are designed to prevent market abuses that create monopolies or allow price discrimination between buyers in the marketplace.

The original antitrust law is the Sherman Act of 1890. This law prohibits practices that create or tend to create monopolies. Key components of this law are as follows:

1. Trusts, etc., in restraint of trade illegal; penalty. Every contract, combination in the form of trust or otherwise, or conspiracy, in restraint of trade or commerce among the several States, or with foreign nations, is declared to be illegal. Every person who shall make any contract or engage in any combination or conspiracy declared by Sections 1 to 7 of this title to be illegal shall be deemed guilty of a felony, and, on conviction thereof, shall be punished by fine not exceeding one million dollars if a corporation, or if any other person, one hundred thousand dollars, or by imprisonment not exceeding three years, or both said punishments, in the discretion of the court. 2. Monopolizating trade a felony; penalty. Every person who shall monopolize, or attempt to monopolize, or combine or conspire with any other person or persons, to monopolize any part of the trade or commerce among the several States, or with foreign nations, shall be deemed guilty of a felony. . .[15]

The Sherman Act was designed to prohibit price fixing among competing firms, eliminate monopolization of a market or business sector, prevent refusal to sell to or deal with certain firms, avoid geographic allocations of markets, and disallow territorial customer restrictions.[16]

The Clayton Act of 1914 strengthened the laws in this area by prohibiting additional practices. Exclusive dealing arrangements were prohibited, including arrangements whereby a buyer purchases all his/her business needs in one product area from a single seller during a period of time. Tying contracts were also prohibited. A tying arrangement is one that requires a buyer of one product to also buy others sold by the seller. An example can be shown in a typewriter situation. If a customer buys a typewriter, a tying arrangement would obligate the buyer to purchase ribbons from the same firm.

The Federal Trade Commission Act of 1914 created the FTC as an overseer and enforcement agency in the business trade area. It is the primary agency serving as a watchdog in unfair business practices and works with the Justice Department in investigating and prosecuting violations.

The Robinson-Patman Act of 1936 prohibited price discrimination in interstate selling situations. Section 2 of the Clayton Act originally stated that it was unlawful for a seller to practice price discrimination where the effect might be to substantially lessen competition or create a monopoly. Price discrimination arising from differences in grade, quality, or quantity sold, or from allowances for difference in the cost of selling or transportation were not illegal. Prior to the Robinson-Patman Act quantity discounts were a common practice that benefited large buyers. This was a problem between local, small grocery stores and the large supermarket chains that were coming into existence. The Robinson-Patman Act sought to eliminate the buying advantage of a large buyer over a smaller one, except where the price difference could be justified by true differences in the seller's costs from volume manufacturing, packaging, delivery or sale, or by the seller's good faith effort to meet competition. The Act further made it illegal for purchasers to knowlingly seek price discriminatory practices from sellers.[17]

To show price discrimination, complicated proof is necessary. There must be 1) two sales, 2) of products, 3) of like grade and quality, 4) to two different buyers, 5) in the same competitive market, 6) at the same or nearly the same time.[18] The price difference takes into account all allowances granted. To prove price discrimination, the sale must have been completed; mere offers to sell are not sufficient. Competitive injury must also be shown. This can be proven by showing how the discrimination 1) substantially lessened competition, 2) tended to create a monopoly in a line of business, and/or 3) injured, destroyed or prevented competition with any person who received the benefit.[19]

Defenses for price discrimination, or situations in which price differences may be justified are: 1) differences in cost, 2) the need to meet competition, and 3) changing market conditions. Differences in cost of manufacturing, sale or delivery as well as different methods or quantities fall under the defense of cost justification. These include costs of differing lot sizes, the cost of producing and storing a product for one customer compared to another who buys well in advance and takes immediate delivery off the production line. The key factor here is that the seller must back up the cost difference with a cost study, and the different prices must be available to anyone who seeks to buy under each condition.

Meeting competition as a discrimination defense was the subject of a recent Supreme Court decision in the Great Atlantic and Pacific Tea Company case. A&P received a bid for a product from Seller B after it received one from Seller A. Seller B's price was higher than A's. A&P did not divulge the price bid to B, but it did tell B that it was not in the ballpark of A's. B then returned with a second bid that was below A's. This appeared to be an inducement of price discrimination. The Supreme Court in 1979 stated that B's actions were legal in that it was meeting competition in good faith efforts. It did not rule that the tactic used by A&P was illegal which the FTC originally stated was unfair inducement of price discrimination. The Supreme Court interpreted otherwise.

Changing conditions is a third defense of price discrimination. Practices here can include lowering the price in order to prevent further deterioration of value in perishable goods, the need to clear seasonal stock, and the selling of inventory for a product being discontinued. In effect, these fall under the different time period defense mentioned above.

The Clayton Act also prohibits interlocking directorates; persons may not sit on the board of directors of two or more firms where they might eliminate competition by agreement between the two firms. For example, Person A sits on the board of companies M and N. Company M produces a raw material that is needed in N's production. This interlocking directorate situation could lead to influence inside N to buy only from M. N would tend to limit purchases on the market in order to favor only M. This is illegal under the Clayton Act and calls for competitive bidding procedures with good records. It is not illegal to buy from M; it is just that Firm N must maintain records that it buys from M because it is the best source. Firm M, too, must protect itself by maintaining adequate records to show that it is not practicing price discrimination.

Reciprocal purchasing is another topic in this area that affects purchasing decisions. Company X is a large trucking firm. Company X has a large shipper customer, Company Y, who is a major truck manufacturer. Reciprocal purchasing takes place here; that is, Truck Firm X buys a large part of its yearly fleet needs from Y, and Y ships a lot of its freight via X. This is technically a form of reciprocal purchasing, it is illegal if the agreement is coercive or if it prevents competition from outsiders.

The personal and corporate penalties from antitrust and price discrimination practices are quite severe. Penalties can be avoided by being open to dealing with the general buying and selling market. Maintenance of good records will defend actions that might appear to be discriminatory but are, in fact, justified cost defenses.

Product Liability

The product liability issue has grown in the past two decades. The old standard of *caveat emptor*, or buyer beware, has given way to an expansion of liability on the part of manufacturers, distributors, and retailers. The threat of liability can and does reach back to the original producer of a product. Firms are more careful today in product development and manufacturing control to see that sound design and safe component materials are applied. Firms are being held more liable for their product(s), and they recognize that bad publicity about one product in a line can affect the sales and reputation of all others produced by the firm. *Caveat emptor* has shifted to *caveat venditor*, or "let the producer beware." This shift has implications not only for product design, marketing, and production personnel, but it also affects purchasing.

There appear to be three general areas of product liability that arise from the American judicial system. One is negligence. This pertains to careless manufacturing that leads to a defect in the goods that cause harm to a user. The point here is that the claimant must prove that the manufacturer was careless and that this led to the injury. This liability extends into the field even though several intermediate buyers handled the product and it may have changed hands between final users.

Breach of warranty is another product liability area. Warranties may be express; that is, they state a fact about the product in advertising, promotion, labeling, etc. They can also be implicit. This is the case with safety. It is implicitly assumed that a product is safe if it is marketed to the general public.

Liability also arises from a principle of strict liability. This type of liability deals with the fact that a product sold on the market may contain a defect and that the ultimate buyer may use it without inspecting it for defects. If the product does, in fact, have a defect but the buyer did not inspect it for such, the producer can still be held liable. All that is necessary here is to prove that the product is defective. Proof of manufacturer negligence or carelessness is not necessary.[20]

Another area of product safety and liability stems from the Consumer Product Safety Act of 1972. This law created the Consumer Product Safety Commission, CPSC, which studies products that pose safety problems. Toys for small children are common products examined by this commission. The presence of lead in paint was a major issue handled by this Commission. The Commission has set safety standards on a variety of products. Violating any of these standards exposes the firm to a series of fines and other legal actions. The specific standards set by this Commission for products are found in Title 16, *Code of Federal Regulations* published yearly and updated by the weekday publication called the *Federal Register.*

Product liability enters into the purchasing area in several ways. Raw material specifications must conform to the CPSC as well as to regulations of the Food and Drug Administration, the Department of Agriculture and other agencies that set standards for products. It is not enough to accept specifications from a company product development group and purchase materials on the market for use in production. Purchasing should make one last check within the firm to determine the final use and handling of commodities, especially when chemicals and edibles are involved.

Purchasing is being called upon more and more to build part's traceability systems. Such records are often necessary when the final product is subject to recall. Recordkeeping as to the sources, lots, and disposition of parts and components in the company's products is becoming a necessity.

The use of substitute components and materials must be strictly defined in purchasing contracts. A substitute item might not be visible upon inspection, yet it might have a drastic negative impact upon the use of the final product. Quality assurance is naturally tied to this entire area. This includes specifications, inspection, ethical standards of the vendors, and close communication between the firm and the vendors as well as with its customers who use or resell the product. Finally, liability terms in purchase contracts must be carefully defined. Liability obligations can extend far into the future if a product is defective of of faulty design.[21]

Small and Minority-Firm Sourcing

Public Law 95–507, which amended the Small Business Act of 1978, seeks to promote greater government use of small vendors as well as those that are minority-owned and operated. The law is intended to develop economic opportunities for these firms.

The purpose of the law is to have large suppliers to the government develop programs that specifically include subcontract sourcing from small, minority-owned firms, or those owned by economically disadvantaged individuals. Specifically, the law states that bidders for Federal contracts over $500,000, or one million dollars in construction contracts, must submit a plan that shows how the firm will meet percentage goals for using subcontracting firms in these categories. The contracting firm must name a person who is responsible for establishing such a system, and it must include the specific plan for sourcing, developing, and using minority firms. The law states that no contract will be awarded unless the firm's approach "provides the maximum practicable opportunity for (these firms) to participate in the performance of the contract."[22] The process of developing an "acceptable plan" to include minority firms generally consists of the following approaches: 1) develop a company-wide awareness for the program, 2) establish review programs for the system, 3) train and motivate small and minority firm personnel, and 4) provide assistance to such firms in the form of describing opportunities for selling to the prime contractor. Firms use various techniques and incentives to reach out to potential subcontractors in this area. Such techniques include allowing longer lead times, requesting smaller quantities within the capabilities of the small firms, providing progress payments, providing assistance in obtaining raw materials, developing technical expertise for them, broadening product specifications to fit the firm's ability and providing financial assistance.[23]

The plan and approaches to be used by the firm must be provided in advance of the bid award. Usually this part of the bid package is prepared by the firm's marketing department, but much of the input will come from purchasing which often oversees the program.

Product Control Laws and Influences

Many forms of governmental influence exist over the buying, selling, handling, and consumption of products. These regulations are in addition to the laws governing trade as found in the Uniform Commercial Code antitrust and transportation areas. Most of these influences are called noneconomic regulations, since they do not pertain to price, trade, or buying and selling transactions. Instead, these regulations are found on both the federal and state level pertaining to the movement, specification, distribution, and recordkeeping of products. The areas, agencies, and basic realm of these influences are summarized in Table 7.1.

Legal Aspects of Transportation

Transportation is playing an increasing part in purchasing. Two major concerns of buyers are rate overcharges and shipment loss and damage.

□ **TABLE 7-1.** *Summary of Product Control Laws*

Area	Location in Code of Federal Regulations	Key Points
Employee safety	Title 29	Occupational Safety and Health Administration; agency responsible for employee safety. Affects specifications of safety items in any employee setting. Problem when importing; many foreign goods do not conform to OSHA rules.
Hazardous materials transportation	Title 49	Administered by the Department of Transportation. Covers how any hazardous goods shall be shipped, labeled, and documented.
Hazardous waste products	Title 40	Coverd by Environmental Protection Agency. Specifies how waste products that are dangerous shall be stored and moved.
Motor carrier safety	Title 49	U.S. Dept. of Transportation. Can affect purchasing manager if responsible for company truck fleet. All aspects of truck safety are covered by these rules.
Animal and plant inspection	Title 9	Any movement of plants and animal over state lines comes under these rules of the Department of Agriculture.
Customs	Title 19	Customs Service, Department of Treasury. Deals with importation, drawback, collection of duties, sampling, etc.
Food and drug safety	Title 21	Food and Drug Administration. All aspects of safety in ingredients, packaging, and labeling of food and cosmetics.
Alcohol possession	Title 27	Bureau of Alcohol, Tobacco, and Firearms. Jurisdication over movement, storage, and use of alcohol.
Drug movement	Title 21	Drug Enforcement Administration. Rules for labeling, accountability, and distribution of drugs.
Product grading	Title 7	Department of Agriculture; food grading.

□ Note: The *Code of Federal Regulations* is updated yearly. Weekday changes made by each agency can be found in the *Federal Register*, which is published by the Government Printing Office, Washington, D.C.

Overcharges and Undercharges

The bill of lading for transportation is a contract of carriage that contains the commodity being moved, origin and destination points, and the desired route. The carrier uses this document to determine the freight charges for the shipment. Five items can cause the wrong charges to be billed that constitute an overcharge or undercharge. Vendors and receivers are naturally interested in collecting for overcharges, while carriers are interested in undercharges. In either instance, rail, motor, and freight forwarder freight bills may be audited for up to three years for over or undercharge claims. The five actions that can cause an over or undercharge claim are as follows.

1. Error in rate. This can occur when the billing clerk applies a rate of say, $4.80 when the proper rate should have been $4.50.

2. Error in weight. By verifying that the weight charged on the bill was not the same weight of the shipment a claim of this type can be filed. Proper weight tickets and product counts are necessary here.

3. Error in commodity description. Tariffs generally state rates according to the commodity being hauled. It is easy for some products to be misdescribed by the shipper or the carrier billing clerk. Tariffs often contain many different categories of commodities, each with different rates. Choice of the wrong category can give rise to a claim of this type. For example, a shipment of canned soup might have a rate of $7.75 per hundredweight (cwt) while another commodity category entitled edibles might have a rate of $8.00 cwt. If the product is canned soup, but the rate charged is $8.00, the paying party is entitled to an overcharge claim settlement. The rate with the more specific description of the goods is the one that applies.

4. Error in tariff interpretation. Tariffs contain many complex rules and regulations. These rules relate to forms of packaging, routing, pickup and delivery processes, and a host of other transportation-related items. If any provision is improperly interpreted when applying rates, a claim may exist.

5. Clerical errors. Such errors occur with incorrect extensions of the carrier or the weight or number of packages in the shipment. They can also occur with improper addition of several specific charges on a shipment.

Overcharge claims may be made up to three years from the date of the bill. Many firms send freight bills to auditing firms that seek to uncover overcharge situations. Payment for such services comes from a percentage split of any overcharge claims settled with the carriers. In many respects this is a no-risk source of file maintenance for overcharge detection and settlement.

Loss and Damage Claims

Another key area of concern to purchasing personnel is the filing of loss and damage claims against carriers. Such actions arise when the goods are damaged in-transit, are lost or stolen, and the vendor does not immediately replace them or file for the claim. The terms for settling such disputes are determined in the sales agreement. Ten various shipping terms are presented in Chapter 18, since they relate directly to the price structure of each product.

The delivery receipt that is signed by the receiving party is the prime document used at the beginning of loss and damage claim processes. Very often obvious damage to the goods is noted upon delivery. Also, any shortages of boxes, drums, etc. should be noted here. Notice of expected inbound shipments should be on file at receiving docks. The reason behind this is that the delivery receipt of the carrier can be matched against the goods as well as the purchase order, or notification of inbound goods movement. Otherwise, a shipment of eight boxes that is so noted on a delivery receipt would be accepted at face value, yet the original order might have been ten boxes. Very often, the inbound carrier makes up the delivery receipt at the final terminal based upon what is present on their dock. This type of system does not catch the fact that ten boxes were originally tendered and two were lost enroute. A good carrier documentation system is based upon the original bill of lading and pickup driver count of the goods. These two inputs then become the enroute carrier manifest and act to create the delivery receipt.

A bill of lading signed by the pickup carrier indicates that the goods were as described and in apparent good order upon pickup. Inbound dock personnel who sign the delivery receipt are also implicitly stating that the goods were received in apparent good order. Therefore, it is imperative that any obvious damage, loss, or shortages be noted on this form prior to acceptance of the shipment. The bill of lading, freight bill, delivery receipt, and inspection report become the basis for claims filing and settlement.

A claim process should be initiated as soon as possible after delivery of goods. This includes noting any problems on the delivery receipt, calling the carrier terminal, and following up with written notice. An inspection report should be made out objectively. A good practice is to note any damage using a camera and dating/timing the pictures. The sooner after delivery the claim is initiated, the easier it is to prove that the carrier is liable.

The law for surface common rail and motor carriage states that a claim may be initiated up to nine months from date of action. Many carrier tariffs will state that claims for concealed loss and damage must be filed within fifteen days of delivery. This is not legally significant, since the nine-month rule still applies. However, concealed loss and damage is difficult to resolve, since it is subject to question as to whether it occurred within the vendor's plant or the buyer's own warehouse and production facility. It is a good practice to set up inspection systems for transportation damage for inbound goods in much the same way as quality control inspection is used to monitor vendor performance.

Recourse against a carrier for not settling or completely settling a claim can only be taken before a court. The Interstate Commerce Commission has no jurisdiction in this realm. Generally speaking, this is a matter of contract compliance, and most states have statutes of limitation of six years in this area. Another course of action might be to take a claim dispute to the Transportation Arbitration Board. This is a body of shippers, carriers, and attorneys specializing in the claims area. A brief report of the issues seen by both the carrier and claimant is presented, analyzed, and decided. This is often a less expensive board to finally resolve an issue before than a court of law.

Contract carriage and air loss and damage claims are subject to whatever is stated in the contract or tariffs of the air carriers. Contract carriage is specifically defined by the contract agreed to and signed by both the carrier and shipper/receiver. Claims are a major part of the creation of the contract. Air freight is completely deregulated, and liability and claims are defined by each carrier's tariff and the air bill of lading.

Claims filing processes can entail a substantial investment in manpower and time. Many firms shift this responsibility onto vendors by requiring that any claims be filed by the shipper, and that the goods be immediately replaced in the meantime. Firms also will set a policy of not filing any claim under certain amount, such as fifty or twenty-five dollars. The rationale here is that the claim process can often cost more than the amount involved. Still other firms will insure the goods in-transit with the same insurance firm that covers inventories within the firm's plants and warehouses. In this setting, a claim can be easily filed and the insurance firm who will in turn deal with the carrier.

Personal Liability of Purchasing Managers, Buyers, and Agents

The purchasing agent and manager act as "agents" for the firms employing them. This is a legal relationship that consists of the purchasing person having the power to represent his/her employer in actions with a third party, usually the vendor. While the purchasing agent is not a distinct legal party, the law of agency recognizes his/her actions as binding in transactions between the firm and vendors. A prime point arising from this employee-employer relationship is that the law of agency requires loyalty by the agent.

There are many ways in which buyers, purchasing agents, and managers can be held personally liable for their actions. This liability is distinct from the protection afforded them by law for actions by their employing firm. In such a setting, the company might do something in its relationship with a vendor that would cause a lawsuit. Breach of a volume contract or other similar action can expose the firm to liability from a lawsuit. In situations as this, the firm and not the purchasing manager is the liable party. There are, however, many situations in which the purchasing agent can be personally liable to civil or criminal action.

The basic principles of personal liability are initially defined by the authority granted the purchasing agent. Actual and apparent authority are again part of the question here. *Actual authority,* that authority stated in agreement or employment contract, defines the limits of actions the firm is allowing the person to operate within. *Apparent authority* is the authority vendors and other outsiders perceive the purchasing person to possess. Apparent authority is that scope of authority possessed by others of similar stature in other firms in the industry. This might consist of, say, the maximum limit any one purchasing manager might order on the power of his/her single signature alone. The question of actual or apparent authority gives rise to personal liability. If the purchasing person exceeds actual authority but not apparent authority, his/her employer generally is bound by those actions but may seek action against the person. On the other hand, if the buyer acts beyond both actual and apparent authority, the vendor or other outsider may hold the purchasing person directly liable. In this area, it is important for the purchasing person to always be sure the vendors knows that his/her actions are for, and on behalf of, his/her employing firm. A legal distinction device can be used whenever signing letters, contracts, and orders; that is, a signature "by" the purchasing person "for" the principle firm/employer generally removes any personal liability.

Deception for personal gain is another area that exposes the purchasing agent to liability. Any action that involves personal gain while behaving as an agent for the principle firm can cause the agent to be liable. False statements concerning his/her authority that have the result of creating deception opens the door to personal liability. Further, any action that assists a competing company can bring liability to the person from his/her own employer.

Damaging and illegal acts comprise other areas of personal liability. If an agent performs a damaging act without authority of his/her own firm, even though he/she believes they possess such authority, the agent can be personally liable. Liability can also exist if the agent performs damaging acts outside the scope of his/her authority, even though the acts were performed with the intention of aiding and benefiting their employer. Further, any act that is illegal can result in the agent being personally liable, even if he/she are acting upon authority granted by his/her employer. In fact, any act that causes damage to another person can bring personal liability to the purchasing person.[24]

Violating the lawful protection of items owned by others can also expose the purchasing agent to liability. An example is patent infringements. If an agent willingly buys from a firm that is known to be infringing upon the patent of another firm the agent is liable. However, case law is not entirely clear about situations in which the purchasing person was not aware of the actual or possible infringement.

Another liability area involves the use of proprietary information. If such information gained from one vendor is provided to another vendor, the purchasing agent can be held liable. The use of copyrighted items and trademarks can involve personal liability as well.

The antitrust laws involving the Sherman, Clayton, and Robinson-Patman Acts make the purchasing agent as well as the firm liable for violations. This liability carries over into the transportation area with rebates and other forms of discrimination which are unlawful by the Elkins Act of 1903.

Noneconomic regulations in the transportation area involving hazardous materials and toxic wastes can also involve the purchasing agent and the firm in a liability suit. The original laws in this area held either the agent or the firm liable, but not both together. This resulted in firms forcing employees to violate such laws, or employees acting unlawfully because their employing firm and not them would be held liable. When both the agent and the firm are liable, however, there is no room for shifting responsibility in order to avoid liability.

Conclusion

The legal realm of purchasing is composed of law, regulations, and liabilities from many different sectors. They have a major influence upon the daily operation and planning of purchasing activities. There is no one source of these legal influences. The buyer must be aware of federal and state laws, regulations of both federal and state regulatory agencies, contract law within the jurisdiction of courts, and many requirements imposed through policies of the government.

FOOTNOTES

1. Paul V. Farrell, ed. *Aljian's Purchasing Handbook* (New York: McGraw-Hill Book Co., 1982), p. 4–5.
2. Benjamin N. Henszey, Barry Lee Myers, and Reed T. Phalan, *Introduction to Basic Legal Principles*, 3rd ed. (Dubuque, IA: Kendall/Hunt Publishing, 1982), p. 373.
3. Ibid., p. 368.
4. Ibid., p. 118.
5. Ibid., chapter 4.
6. Ibid., p. 122.
7. Ibid., chapter 7.
8. See Farrell, *Aljian's Purchasing Handbook* p. 4–26.
9. Dean S. Ammer, *Materials Management and Purchasing* (Homewood, IL: Richard D. Irwin Co., 1980), p. 127.
10. Michiel R. Leenders, Harold E. Fearon, and Wilbur B. England, *Purchasing and Materials Management* (Homewood, IL: Richard D. Irwin Co., 1980), p. 437.
11. Dr. Russell Decker, "Get Assurances When You Suspect a Breach," *Purchasing*, 18 September 1980, p. 75.
12. Donald A. Wiesner, "Don't Let Inaction Rob You of Your Rights, *Purchasing*, 30 April 1981, p. 63.
13. *See* Ammer, *Materials Management and Purchasing* pp. 155–158.
14. "Contract Priorities: Boilerplate to Bafflegab," *Purchasing*, 30 April 1981, p. 59.
15. John D. Jackson, "Negotiate With Knowledge of the Law on Your Side," *Purchasing*, 30 April 1981, p. 47.
16. Ibid.
17. Robinson-Patman Act, Sections 2 (a) through (e), amending the Clayton Act, United States Code.
18. John D. Blackburn, Elliot I. Klayman, and Martin H. Malin, *Legal Environment of Business*, (Homewood, IL: Richard D. Irwin, 1981), chapter 8.
19. Ibid.
20. Lawrence A. Bennigson and Arnold I. Bennigson, "Product Liability: Manufacturers Beware," *Harvard Business Review* 52 (May–June 1974): 122–32.
21. Dr. Russell Decker, "You Can Be Picky With Nonconforming Goods," *Purchasing*, 12 June 1980, p. 59.
22. Rand L. Allen, "Public Law 95-507 Affects Government Contractors Small and Minority Subcontractors," *National Purchasing Review*, November-December 1979, p. 13.
23. Ibid., p. 15.
24. *See* Leenders, Fearon and England, *Purchasing and Materials Management* p. 429.

QUESTIONS FOR REVIEW

1. What is an agency? How is the buyer an agent of the firm he/she is employed by?

2. How can there be apparent authority without actual authority? What is the legal distinction between the two?

3. What are the prime elements of a purchase contract?

4. How do the purchase order and confirmation play roles in creation of a contract?

5. How may a buyer break a purchase contract?

6. Distinguish between the four types of warranties presented in the chapter.

7. What constitutes price discrimination under the Robinson-Patman Act? Was there illegal inducement under the A&P case?

8. How may a firm be held to product liability?

9. What are the requirements of Public Law 95-507?

10. What constitutes an overcharge in a transportation setting?

11. What processes are available for loss and damage claims against a common carrier of transportation?

12. In what ways are purchasing personnel personally liable?

PART II

STRATEGIC PURCHASING:
MANAGEMENT ESSENTIALS

Section I presented most of the basic concepts needed for a sound buying operation. But, the demands of today require much more from a purchasing department. Production and service organizations lose much when purchasing is passive in its activities.

This section presents many of the skills and activities required for purchasing in addition to the basic buying functions. Many of these activities have always been present in purchasing, but perhaps to minor degrees. These practices are now management essentials that have become more important in the past decade.

The timing of purchases and forecasting future needs are critical topics today in that the times at which goods are needed by a firm do not always correspond with the best times of product availability on the market. Capital asset acquisitions is another area in which purchasing can and does provide valuable input. Deregulation of the transportation field has brought many new opportunities and problems that were not previously of major concern to buyers. This is an area that requires active attention today. International purchasing is important, because the world is the sourcing realm today and not just one nation. Value analysis is an area where purchasing can save the firm money as well as reduce quality or supply problems. And, supply strategies are critical in that firms can no longer assume that a constant, adequate supply of goods will be available in the world.

INTRODUCTION

PURCHASE TIMING FACTORS

FORECASTING AND TIME-SERIES ANALYSIS

EXTERNAL DATA IN THE FORECASTING AND BUDGETING PROCESSES

LONG-RUN ANALYSIS AND PLANNING

CONCLUSION

CHAPTER OBJECTIVES

After reading this chapter you should:

- Appreciate the need to consider timing in the purchase decision.

- Be able to supply the basics of forecasting to purchase decisions.

- Understand the basic role of index numbers in the field.

- Appreciate the basics of external forecast and economic data sources.

Purchasing Timing and Forecasting

Introduction

The timing of purchases is a basic consideration in the purchasing decision process. Timing is involved in the decision of whether to seek a long-term arrangement or make a single purchase on the spot market. It is involved in determining and obtaining the right price and proper quantity in a shifting market. Buyers need considerable information in order to make judgements in this area.

Forecasts are useful in the purchasing department budget process. Managers must make projections about future prices so that relatively accurate budgets can be prepared. Forecasting in the budgeting process is important because it provides a benchmark against which departmental performance can be compared. Additionally the firm needs to have some insights into future cash flow needs for routine and extraordinarily large buys.

This chapter presents many of the approaches that are used by firms in determining the right moment for placing orders. Forecasting and time-series analysis, which includes the mathematical approaches used to focus upon the nature of trends and point decision makers into the right directions, are discussed. Externally available forecasting data sources are also presented. Price freezes, which are sometimes implemented in times of very high inflation, are explored in terms of their impacts upon selling and buying markets. And, the chapter ends with some insights into the need for studying long-run markets that the firm currently or most probably will be buying from in the distant future.

Purchase Timing Factors

The nature of a supply market includes available supply, prices, number of firms, and the relative power of both buyers and sellers. In most settings, the market is continually shifting. Trends might appear at some times only to have sudden turns occur in the other direction. Many of these events can be explained by examining some of the cycles and other factors that affect the market. The topics that follow relate to what is occurring in the market within the context of optimal purchase timing decisions.

Business Cycles

The overall long-run business activity of a nation's economy tends to shift up and down in what are called business cycles. These cycles can be of varying lengths, and the turning point from one stage in a cycle to the next is not always identifiable until long after it has occurred. Study of the overall cycle, however, gives some insight into buying market opportunities and constraints. Exhibit 8-1 presents a general illustration of overall economic activity in a business cycle.

A business cycle contains four basic periods of interest to economists, businessmen and buyers. These periods are 1) recession, 2) pick up 3) boom, and 4) contraction. There are many other names attached to these periods, but those listed are common terms that easily explain the nature of each.

A recession, or trough, is a period of low activity. Many plants are closed and layoffs are common. Prices are usually at a low point, unless foreign material supplier or other uncontrollable factors push costs upward. Many concessions usually can be obtained from suppliers, and in many industries it becomes a buyers' market. During a recession some plants are permanently closed, and some firms withdraw from product lines or business altogether. It is a period of many bankruptcies.

The pick-up stage is typified by increasing activity. Sales and production rise. Inventories tend to decrease, since sales are rising faster than production. Prices tend to become firmer, fewer concessions are available from vendors, and order cycle times lengthen. This is the time when buyers will often seek long-term contracts from vendors. The long-term contract can fix the current price for a long period, while the spot market continues to increase. Such contracts commit the vendor to supply a certain productive capacity in each of several months into the future.

The boom is the time when overall activity is highest. Businesses are operating at high levels of production, and sales are brisk. The least effi-

■ **EXHIBIT 8-1.** *A General Business Cycle*

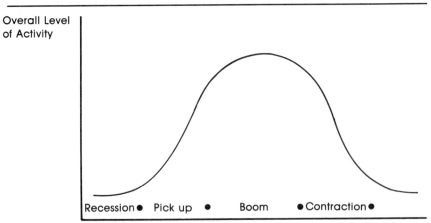

cient factories are again brought on-line during this period. Profits are often high; and it is a seller's market in many industries. Buyers find this period perhaps the most difficult for them. Prices tend to be controlled by the sellers, competition is high among buyers for the production capacity of sellers and their output. Bottlenecks occur in some industries. During this period a firm can be in the situation of having orders, but either cannot obtain the raw materials or does not have sufficient production capacity to produce the goods.

The contraction stage is signaled by economic activity dropping. Sales and production decrease. Inventories might temporarily become large because production has continued while sales have dropped. Prices begin to soften, and order cycle times decrease. Buyers often purchase small quantities at this time, since each subsequent buy is often made at a lower price than the previous one and with a shorter lead time.

The overall business cycle provides insights into what buyer tactics are appropriate in each buyer-seller market situation. The price cycle is related to the business cycle, and it is presented in the following section.

Price Cycles

The upward and downward swing of prices in raw material and component markets is an important trend for buyers to note and adapt to. Price increases and decreases often correspond with the overall business cycle, but that is not always the case. Some price cycles occur separately from economic cycles. The price cycle has important implications for buyers in the timing of purchases. Exhibit 8-2 shows a general price cycle. This example shows the January price of an item to be $1.00 per unit. The buyer requires 1,000 units per month over the next year. The price is shown to rise by $.10 per month to a high in June and July of $1.50. Prices then drop $.10 per month back to $1.00 in December.

■ **EXHIBIT 8-2.** *General Price Cycle*

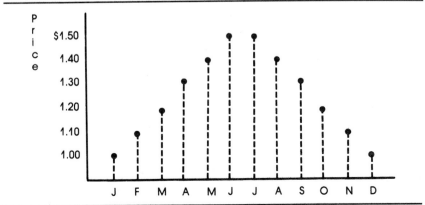

There are many purchase timing options available for obtaining the 12,000 units over the entire year. These options are first presented below in the context of the price increase picture that faces the buyer in January.

OPTION #1: Buy monthly lots from January to June

January	$1,000 \times \$1.00 = \$1,000$
February	$1,000 \times \$1.10 = \$1,100$
March	$1,000 \times \$1.20 = \$1,200$
April	$1,000 \times \$1.30 = \$1,300$
May	$1,000 \times \$1.40 = \$1,400$
June	$1,000 \times \$1.50 = \$1,500$
	Total = $7,500

OPTION #2: Buy in two-month lots from January to June.

January	$2,000 \times \$1.00 = \$2,000$
March	$2,000 \times \$1.20 = \$2,400$
May	$2,000 \times \$1.40 = \$2,800$
	Total = $7,200

OPTION #3: Buy in three-month lots from January to June.

January	$3,000 \times \$1.00 = \$3,000$
April	$3,000 \times \$1.30 = \$3,900$
	Total = $6,900

OPTION #4: Buy entire six-month supply in January.

January	$6,000 \times \$1.00 = \$6,000$

These options show that in a price upswing situation, the buyer can save the firm money through forward buying for known future monthly needs. The total economic worth of such a decision must be weighed against the certainty that the goods will be needed in those months, along with the cost of warehousing, the opportunity cost of the funds tied up in the forward-brought goods, and the expectation that prices will continue to rise through the period. A problem occurs when a large supply of goods is on hand when the current spot price begins to drop. It is crucial to have some knowledge of the market in order to be able to detect when downturns in prices might begin to occur.

In the downward price swing situation, the firm should not have large supplies of goods from forward buys at relatively high prices. When prices start to drop, the purchaser should institute hand-to-mouth buying practices. Following our example in Exhibit 8-2, in July only one month's supply should be bought. Otherwise, a two-month purchase in July would cause an expenditure of $1.50 for July's goods and $1.50 for August's goods, when in August the market price will be down to $1.40. The firm would overpay $.10 per unit plus holding costs for August's goods. Taken to the extreme, a six-month purchase in July would cost the firm $9,000, whereas monthly purchases for the rest of the year on the spot market would cost the firm only $7,500.

Production Capacity

Price fluctuations are a major concern throughout the entire business cycle and during price cycle shifts. Another key facet of buying is the availability of products during these periods. Buyers must be concerned not only with optimal timing to capture price advantages for their firms, but they must also look to an assurance of supply during these times as well.

During upswings, production capacity begins to become utilized fairly quickly. Higher sales rates tend to deplete the present store of finished goods inventories fairly quickly. Vendors will begin production in order to satisfy present demands. This situation will lengthen the order cycle times rather quickly. Where buyers were used to ten-day to two-week deliveries from on-hand inventories, vendors now begin to backlog orders for many weeks because they will have to make them in production.

Buyers can often obtain protection for their firms during these periods by placing orders for standardized goods for future month's production and delivery. That is, a buyer might place an order for goods that will require one production shift of the vendor for the first week of each month for the next ten months. When the actual production time nears, the buyer might transmit a purchase order changing the amount of the product the buyer will need in each month. This is similar to making a reservation for production capacity, and is often a better practice than placing orders each month only to find that subsequent orders have longer backlogs. In this situation, however, the buyer must be sure that the specific vendor is a favorable choice from quality and price standpoints.

Lead Times, Order Cycle Times, and Backlogs

These three terms are key features in the buying decision. Hopefully, inventory control or user departments will requisition goods from purchasing with sufficient time allowances for the buyer to obtain them from a vendor. Lead time and order cycle time involve the same concept, and refer to the total length of time required from original order transmission until the goods are received. Lead time begins with the discovery of a need within the firm and transmission of this need to purchasing, often referred to as administrative lead time. It includes the time needed to transmit the order to the vendor, as well as to complete vendor order processing activities, production, shipping, transportation and receiving. Inside the buyer firm on the inbound side, lead time can also include the time required to inspect the goods and actually deliver them to the user.

Backlog, on the other hand, refers to the time it will take for the vendor to actually schedule and produce the goods. It is the lag between vendor order processing and production scheduling and the time in which the goods will actually be produced. A backlog can be as short as a few hours or as long as several months. The vendor's other orders, production capacity, availability of goods, and quality of machinery and worker efficiency play roles in backlog.

Buyers will generally notice that order cycle times will lengthen as a vendor's sales increase and inventories become depleted. On the other hand, during a downturn, order cycle times will decrease as orders can be satisfied from inventories. The trade magazines in purchasing routinely provide information about lead times for many industries. This information is highlighted in terms of whether times are the same, lengthening or decreasing, it can be a valuable warning indicator for buyers. Order cycle times should be monitored with specific vendors even when orders are not being made at a specific time. The buyer should then inform materials management and inventory control of any increase in order cycle times.

Hedging

Firms incur price risks whenever lead times are long. A firm might budget for the cost of goods for a certain amount, only to find that the price has risen drastically by the date of final purchase transaction. Firms can take one of four actions to reduce this form of price risk. One is to buy the goods and physically hold them until needed. A second way is to contract for a fixed price to remain in force through delivery of the goods. In this instance, the vendor will experience the risk, and he/she will normally build price "padding" into the original price. A third action, used frequently with foreign purchases, is to contract for the purchase to be payable in U.S. dollars. And, finally a fourth risk-reducing action use the futures market in what is called hedging.

Hedging is the practice of using an organized commodity exchange to transfer the risks of forward or long lead time buying onto other parties. It is different from plain forward buying, which is the ordering and obtaining of goods in advance of known production or resale requirements; and, it is also distinct from speculation, which is the buying of goods or contracting for them with the intent of reselling for a profit, but with no plan for use in production or in normal reselling contexts. Several situations are presented here to show how firms experience risk from long lead time purchases, and how they can use hedging to minimize it.

A U.S. firm seeks to purchase an item from a British firm. The price of the item is 10,000 British pounds, and that amount must be paid via letter of credit the day the vendor delivers the item to the dock for loading onto a ship bound for the U.S. The lead time will be about four months. The buyer knows that the current dollar to pound relationship is $1.80

for each pound. That is, the U.S. firm must pay $18,000 to be equivalent to 10,000 pounds. During the lead time, the pound drops in relation to the dollar. Now the pound is at $1.57, and the buyer experiences a windfall the day on which the goods must be paid. Instead of the goods costing $18,000, they will only cost $15,700.

But, the risk can shift against the buyer. Suppose, for example, that the buyer places an order with a German firm for goods that are priced at 100,000 German marks. The current dollar to mark relationship is $.42 for each mark. The goods, if transferred today, would cost the buyer $42,000. The lead time is long, and the mark could rise against the dollar. By the time the goods are transferred and payment becomes due, a mark might cost $.52. In this situation, the buyer would have to pay an additional $10,000 in order to obtain sufficient marks to pay for the goods.

The risk of prices or currencies falling during the lead time is not always of major concern to buyers. The problem exists when the buyer places an order and budgets a certain amount of funds to pay for the item. The buyer, then, is exposed to currency or price shift risk. Hedging can be used to reduce or avoid that risk.

The German mark situation will serve as an example of how buyer firms can use hedging to their advantage. On the day that the 100,000 mark order is placed with the German firm, the dollar to mark relationship is such that the goods would cost the buyer $42,000. On the same day, the buyer firm will purchase a futures contract in dollars for 100,000 marks to be delivered for about $42,000 several months from now. In the meantime, the mark climbs. The purchase price increases now to $52,000 for 100,000 marks, but the buyer is not worried, because the counterpart futures contract that he/she bought for $42,000 will collect 100,000 marks at the end of the same time span. Near the date of transferring the goods, the firm settles the futures contract for $42,000, collects 100,000 marks, and pays the German firm the 100,000 marks. The risk has been transferred to whomever sold the futures contract for marks to the firm.

A firm is also exposed to price risk when it accepts an order for work it will not perform for several months. For example, a firm might bid on a job for which the calculated cost of a certain metal is $ .75 per pound. The metal will be ordered four months from now for delivery in the fifth month, for use in production and delivery on the first of the sixth month. The metal price could rise between now and Month Five. The firm wishes to obtain price protection so that it does not have to pay more than that amount by the delivery date of the metal. The current price of the metal is $.75, so the firm buys a futures contract for that amount, for delivery in Month Five at that price.

During the five month-period the actual daily delivered price of the metal increases to $.90 per pound. Without the hedge, the firm would have lost $.15 per pound for the metal that was used in production. The futures contract, however, protected it from this problem. In Month Five the firm settles the futures contract and collects a sum equivalent to $.90 per pound for the metal. This money is then applied to the actual purchase of metal on the open market at $.90. If the firm was purely speculating, it would have made of profit of $.15 per pound. Instead, it applied the entire proceeds to the purchase of metal at $.90. Thus, the entire set of transactions cost the firm $.75 plus commissions and fees. In this instance hedging is not speculation or risk taking; it is risk reduction.[1]

Hedging is conducted through organized commodity exchanges. These trade commodities include such things as wheat, corn, soybeans, rye, feeder cattle, hogs, cocoa, coffee, cotton, orange juice, sugar, copper, gold, heating oil, platinum, silver, lumber, plywood, foreign currencies, and government securities. Exhibit 8-3 shows what a futures market standing might be on any one day.

The price for corn in the next delivery period is about $2.45. May futures are $2.54, July is $2.60, etc. These prices are different from the *spot price*, which is the price of that commodity that is being delivered at to final users today. The spot price for corn on the date of the futures listing shown was $2.26.

There are special terms that are found in the realm of commodity exchanges. A *futures contract* is a contract created by the organized exchange that requires a stipulated quantity and grade of goods be delivered at a specified future date. *Margin* is the money a futures contract buyer must pay to guarantee that he or she will settle the account when due. It is a form of deposit that must be paid. Margins are often five percent to fifteen percent of the total contract amount. A *normal futures market* is one in which the differences in prices for each period are about equal to the cost of holding the goods for that amount of time. A market in which the subsequent futures prices are higher than the actual cost of holding them is said to have been bid up by increased demand or fear of product shortages in future periods.

Hedging serves many useful purposes for the public. One is reduction in corporate risk in obtaining goods in future periods. Another is that these markets tend to smooth out price fluctuations as compared to the prices that would otherwise exist. The exchanges are a relatively efficient market mechanism through which such transactions and supply and demand relationships can be settled. The exchanges also have rules that provide assurances as to product grades, qualities, and quantities.

■ **EXHIBIT 8-3.** *Futures Prices—Corn*

FUTURES PRICES—CORN

	Open	High	Low	Settle	Change	Lifetime High	Lifetime Low	Open Interest
—GRAINS AND OILSEEDS—								
CORN (CBT)—5,000 bu.; cents per bu.								
Mar83		245½	243½	245½	+ 1¼	320¾	227½	68,625
May	252½	254¾	252½	254¼	+ 1¼	322½	236¼	27,230
July	260	262¼	259¾	261½	+ 1¼	316½	243	19,256
Sept	265½	268	265½	267	+ 1	291	247	2,838
Dec	274½	277½	274½	276¼	+ ¾	277½	253	13,568
Mar84	285	288¼	285	286¾	+ ½	288¼	278½	339

Est vol 21,007; vol Wed 24,199; open int 131,856, +2,045.

Finally, the futures market provides a free forecast of market prices to both the active hedging buyer as well as one who does not engage in it.

Labor Negotiation Cycles

Pending labor negotiations at vendor firms is another key factor buyers must consider in timing purchases. New labor contracts generally mean that the cost level and prices of the vendor's product will rise. Pending labor negotiations might result in a strike, which would disrupt the buyers own inbound supply. Of course, the labor cycle is also being watched by buyers at other firms, and industrywide concern over a labor situation will often cause a rise in orders, which might extend order cycle times up to the labor contract date.

The impact of labor negotiations can be great, and they often extend across a majority of a vendor industry. For example, 60,000 aluminum workers are employed by four major suppliers in the U.S.; this contract is on a cycle for May renewal. Longshoremen affect entire seacoasts when a strike occurs in this area. Ships with inbound goods can sit offshore for several weeks when these negotiations dissolve into strikes. About 300,000 steel workers are covered by contracts that are up for renegotiation every three years in August. Similarly, teamster truck drivers are covered by contracts that are renewed every third year in April.

Corporate Constraints

Conditions within the buyer's own firm affect the timing of purchases as well. Not only are production plans part of this timing decision, but other corporate constraints exist as well. A firm's capacity for storage will hinder the ability to buy in large volumes. Similarly, the firm's cash flow might be seasonal in nature, thereby preventing buyers from seeking favorable buys in forward settings at certain times of the year. The accounting fiscal cycle also can constrain purchasing timing. Firms often want low inventories on the date the annual balance sheet is computed. The rationale for this is explained further in Chapter 14, but for now this practice can prevent buyers from placing forward buys and even some regular orders at or near these cycle dates.

Public Policy Constraints

Actions by the federal government can also affect purchase timing. Quotas for imports the buyer seeks will impact greatly upon the time of the year in which the goods are purchased. Further, changes in import duty tariffs can either prevent, speed up, or delay importation decisions. In another realm, actions by the Federal Reserve Board with regard to the interest rate will cause the firm to react accordingly. A high interest rate will cause corporate officers to seek lowered inventories. This will force smaller and more frequent orders. On the other hand, the firm will delay payment to vendors in order to conserve cash and earn money market funds from the high rates. Such action places buyers in a difficult position with vendors with whom they are seeking to maintain a good relationship.

Forecasting and Time-Series Analysis

Forecasting and time-series analysis are tools that attempt to project into the future as well as quantify what has occurred in the past. Forecasting is the science and art of determining, with some degree of accuracy, what events will likely take place in the future. Time-series analysis consists of many various tools that describe what events took place in the past. For this reason, they are often used in forecasting settings.

Forecasting is conducted to provide management with information upon which to make sound decisions about the future. The role of forecasting is to provide an accurate picture about the future so that maximum profit or minimum cost decisions can be made. Forecasts are not always totally accurate, but they aid in narrowing the uncertainties about the future. Forecasting assists management with projections about sales expectations, timing of demands by the market, costs of future expenditures, and the availability of goods on raw materials markets.

Time-series analysis, in addition to being used in forecasting, is often utilized in the budgeting process. Purchasing managers face the task of budgeting a minimum of once per year. Quantity demands are often presented to them in the form of manufacturing plans and requirements. The key problem at hand is to determine what prices will be in effect for these goods at the times in which the orders for them will be placed.

The Firm's Forecasts

Purchasing forecasts generally follow an overall forecast of the firm for sales activity over a coming period. This forecast is then used to create production activity plans and general schedules. Distribution is linked with this same production plan for planning uses and costs of warehouses, outbound transportation facilities, and inventory levels. Purchasing often uses this same production plan in order to obtain information for the timing of raw material requirements. Purchasing is also interested in developing future price information in order to determine optimal timing of buys in light of production needs. This information is critical in the form of prices, availability, and lead times. This short-run purchasing forecast also relates to inbound transportation costs, inventory levels, and the ability to seek opportunities such as forward buys, systems contracting, consignment, and other cost-effective tactics.

Purchasing is also interested in long-run forecasts and should be a part of the firm's overall long-run planning activity. Purchasing will be responsible to obtain the goods the firm wishes to use in production five and ten years from now. Buyers should know what the prospects of supply markets will be at that time so that their own managements can make decisions about current or prospective products. For example, some critical minerals are projected to be in very short supply towards the turn of the century. And, similarly, energy supplies of all forms will present differing advantages and disadvantages ten years from now. Purchasing is in a position to analyze future supply and price conditions, and this information is critical to the long-run planning efforts of the firm.

Forecasting has undergone varying degrees of respect and reception by management. Throughout the 1950s and 1960s forecasting was favored because it provided fairly accurate data about coming years. New tools to aid in forecasting were being developed with the aid of the computer and management science techniques. In the 1970s problems with energy, product shortage, capital, etc. caused many well prepared forecasts to be grossly out of range from actual activities. Major disruptive and unpredictable events in that decade could neither be predicted nor were similar impacts ever experienced in recent history prior to this time. However, use of forecasts continues to rise.

Characteristics of Forecasts

Forecasting is seen as a valuable tool in spite of the major problems with it in the 1970s. Many managers feel that any forecast is better than no idea at all about the future. They state that it is better to plan within the context of a wrong forecast than to have absolutely no future direction for a firm's activities. In line with these thoughts, several characteristics of forecasts are important to keep in mind when approaching and using them.

One, forecasts will rarely be completely accurate. There is no way in which the future can be projected with certainty. As such, forecasts should be used knowing that the makers are not infallible nor are the forecasts. However, forecasts should not be criticized or cast aside for this reason. They do narrow the uncertainty about the future and provide some basis to direct management activity and evaluate performance within the original plans.

Two, forecasts should be presented in the form of ranges. Exact pinpointed prices, sales volumes, etc., cannot be determined. It is less inaccurate for a range of estimates to be made. That is, a forecast might be stated in terms of an estimated sales figure with likely highs and lows presented as well. This is similar to the concept presented in the control chart discussion in Chapter 3.

Three, the greater the aggregation of forecasts the more accurate they will be. That is, a forecast about Product 1DK-7 is very difficult to project with close accuracy. On the other hand, it is often easier and more accurate to project the future about the entire product line of which Product 1DK-7 is a part. Differences in daily demands for specific products, exact actions by company customers, etc. are all nearly impossible to predict with accuracy. This is akin to attempting to predict the exact weather for a day in December versus making a prediction about the average weather for the entire month. Overall estimates about product lines, customer groupings, territories, etc. tend to be more accurate than specific ones.

Approaches to Forecasting and Time-Series Analysis

There are five basic approaches to forecasting. Overview summaries of these are explained in an excellent manner by Dakridakis and Wheelwright.[2] These five approaches are described as 1) informal, 2) causal or regressive, 3) time series, 4) subjective assessment and 5) technological. They are summarized in Table 8-1.

☐ **TABLE 8-1.** *Overview of Forecasting Methods*

Method	Construction	Key Points
Informal forecasting	Made from a few opinions	Based upon judgement. Can be very good, depending upon quality of persons' input. Opinions not in quantifiable measures.
Causal or regressive approaches	Links of data in independent and dependent form Regression (simple and multiple) See Exhibit 8–4	Explains degree of change in one variable in relation to change in another. Quantifiable, provides an equation for extension. Purely statistical association, not cause and effect.
Exponential smoothing	Time-series tool that smooths out variations in past data in order to help project next period	Places greater weight on recent events more than past ones (a weakness with regression). Purely statistical, no cause and effect.
Decomposition	Breaking a time series into basic parts: base, trend, season, and "noice" See Exhibit 8–5	Gives insights into underlying components of past events.
Subjective approaches	Compilation of executive or other broad-based opinions Use correct and past data to make decisions about future.	Can be very good for predicting near term events. Examples are NAPM *Commodity Reports* and monthly *Report on Business* with changes in production, new orders, prices, and inventories. Examples are *Purchasing* and *Purchasing World* features on prices and lead times.
	Decision trees	Finds likelihood event as well as quantifying all probable events. Problem is subjective use of probabilities.
Technological approaches	Delphi Method to forcast future technology	Form of expert opinion of future events and technologies. First seeks to determine possible future events. Then seeks to determine likelihood of these events. Process handled in objective manner.

Trend extrapolation, decomposition, decision-tree analysis, and the Delphi method are also approaches discussed in some detail here.

Trend extrapolation is one of the major time-series methods of forecasting. The monthly prices of a raw material for the past ten years can be shown in a table or along a Y-axis on a chart. The months are the independent variable , and the prices are the dependent variable. A general trend or line might be obvious from the data or chart. Trend extrapolation is the mere extension of the line or trend. This is a simple process, but it is not based upon anything more than numbers on paper. That is, no real world factors are taken into account in making this estimate other than the use of past data.

Trend extrapolation is used in a manner similar to regression. For example, assume a buyer has the following data pertaining to prices for a particular raw material.

Year	Price per Pound
1977	50¢
1978	53¢
1979	55¢
1980	62¢
1981	70¢
1982	72¢
1983	70¢

A general upward trend is noted here, with prices becoming soft in the last year. The regression approach can be used on this time series data with what is called least-squares equation.

The least-squares equation can be determined by using the data shown here in the following manner. First, array the information by year and price. The years can be represented by 0, 1, 2, 3, etc., instead of 1977, etc. This makes it simpler to handle the data. The representative years, 0, 1, 2, etc. are the X variables, and the prices are the Y variables. The X's and Y's are multiplied together and summed for a third term. And, the X's are squared and summed for a fourth term. These figures are then treated in two simultaneous equations as illustrated here.

Year	Year times Simplified X	Price Y	Price XY	Year Squared X^2
1977		50¢	0	0
1978	1	53	53	1
1979	2	55	110	4
1980	3	62	186	9
1981	4	70	280	16
1982	5	72	360	25
1983	6	70	420	36
	21	432	1409	91

The simultaneous equations that use the above data to solve for the least-squares equation are as follows.

I. Sum of Y = (Number of years) × A + (Sum of X) × B
II. Sum of XY = (Sum of X) x A + (Sum of X Squared) × B

In numbers these are:

I.   432 = 7A + 21B
II. 1409 = 21A + 91B

To solve, multiply Equation I by − 3 and solve for the "B" term. Once this is determined, then use the "B" term in either of the equations to solve for the "A" term. The final equation is

$$Y = 48.15 + 4.04B.$$

This is interpreted to mean that the base point price is 48.15¢, and in each year the price rose by an average of 4.04¢. An extrapolation for 1984 would be made by taking the 1983 price and adding 4.04¢. Exhibit 8-4 shows this data and equation.

Again, this tool provides a mathematical equation to describe past experience, but it does not necessarily relate to future occurrences.

Decomposition methods of time-series analysis and forecasting break down trend data into four basic parts which are base, trend, season and "noise." Exhibit 8-5 illustrates how series data for a material price might statistically be decomposed into the four basic parts.

Forecast Perspectives

Forecasting is not an accurate undertaking because too many factors are uncertain or cannot be controlled. And, some elements of forecast preparation exist that must be kept in mind by both the preparer and the user.

■ **EXHIBIT 8-4.** *Least Squares Analysis of 1977–1983 Prices for a Material*

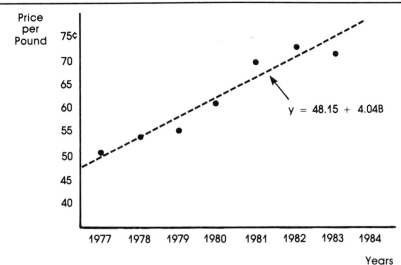

■ **EXHIBIT 8-5.** *Illustration of Data Decomposition*

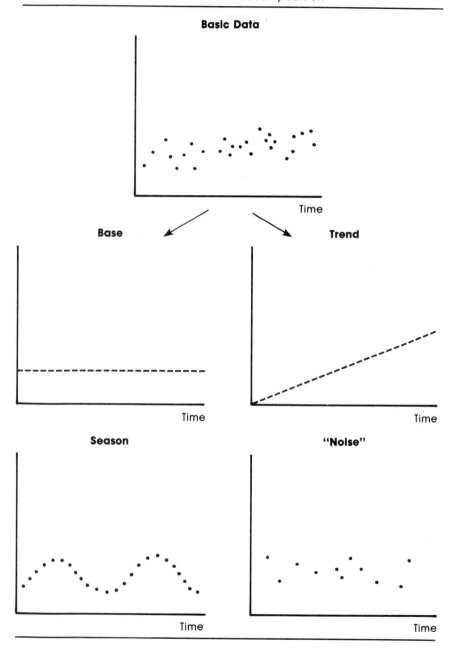

The making of forecasts for corporate use should be based upon sound managerial approaches. For not only is the data collection and computation important, but the way in which the process is carried out must be sound as well. Several points affect this process. Forecasting is an art as well as a science. For this reason it is important that forecast preparation be undertaken by a team or group. Wide input and expertise should be utilized instead of relying on one person. The objective of the forecast should also be recognized and accounted for in the entire process, including the use and users of the forecast. A forecast that is prepared for sales projections will often have a different scope and content than one prepared for distribution inventory control. Whatever assumptions were made in the preparation of the forecast should be made known to its users. A sound forecast should also be backed up with sound causal factors as well as solid qualitative factors from expert sources.

On the other side, users of forecasts would do well to approach the forecast with several perspectives in mind. One is the objective of the forecast. A forecast prepared for regional sales managers can often serve as a quota communications medium. This forecast would not necessarily work well in the materials management area because some of the data might be desired goals rather than expected results. Understanding the assumptions and methodology used in preparing the forecast is another key perspective. This includes the qualitative factors as well as those linked to reliable quantitative elements. Further, forecasts rarely predict accurately the actual turning points in business activity. It is relatively easy to project current trends or even shifts in trends, but the prediction and forecasting of turning points is very difficult.

External Data in the Forecasting and Budgeting Processes

Three prime external sources of information on the state of the economy are the U.S. Government, the National Association of Purchasing Management, and purchasing magazines in each respective field.

Government Information

The Census Bureau in the U. S. Department of Commerce compiles statistics and publishes reports through various media to the public. One prime information source is the Leading Indicators Composite Index. This index is composed of many specific items of data that collectively point to the current and immediate future direction of the economy. The individual items that are used in this composite index require some understanding by the buyer and manager, for some are key indicators for particular industries.

Manufacturing experience is captured in the average workweek length in hours as well as the layoff rate of workers in manufacturing. Changes in these two manufacturing-related factors give insights into steady, increasing, or decreasing activity in this area.

Business activity is noted by statistics on new goods orders. This index shows whether or not a new orders for goods from all forms of manufacturing entities are changing or remaining steady. Similarly, new building permits for construction give an indication as to near-term future demands for products used in constructing homes, buildings, and factories. Contracts for capital equipment is another key item used in this overall composite index. Capital equipment purchases not only indicate how much business will be transacted in these areas, but it presents a relative direction of the expectations of all businesses that purchase and use this type of machinery.

Inventories are another key part of this composite as well. The inventory-to-sales ratio is a major element of interest to industry watchers. This figure is a measure of the total inventory reported in the economy divided by the current months' sales. The resulting ratio is stated in terms of months' of inventory on shelves in relation to the sales. Thus, a 1.80 inventory ratio states that 1.8 months of inventory is on hand.

The inventory-to-sales ratio will drop when businessmen expect the economy to drop and sales are expected to drop as well. It will also drop if sales increase faster than the ability to increase production. The ratio will rise when businessmen produce in expectation that sales will increase, it will also rise as sales drop and production continues.

Financial measures are also captured in this analysis. One of the major elements here is the money supply in the economy. Money supply refers to the amount of money in circulation available for transactions of all kinds. The Stock Price Index is included because it reflects an overall economic concensus as to the health of the economy and expectations for the immediate future. Another indicator used is changes in liquid assets of firms. Liquid assets are cash, investments, accounts receivable, and other very short-term assets. The relative strength of these assets point to the ability of firms to invest in current operations or embark upon new investments.

Vendor market factors include prices for key commodities and vendor delivery performance. Key prices are concentrated upon major raw materials used throughout the economy, as well as energy. Delivery performance that is shortening indicates a greater capacity to supply the market, larger inventories, or a decrease in sales. A lengthening of order cycle times indicates sales outgrowing inventories and production capacity.

Business changes also point to the overall direction of the economy. The two key data items here are the number of new business formations and the number of business failures.

National Association of Purchasing Management Information

The National Association of Purchasing Management (NAPM) publishes a monthly *Report on Business* that is widely received in the business and economic community. The reason for this reception is that it polls purchasing managers throughout the U.S., and these persons are in a position to make valid statements about the immediate future of the economy. A purchasing manager who knows that his or her firm will produce an item three months from now must plan for placing an order to obtain the raw materials in advance of the three months. Thus, purchasing managers' current opinions and comments are considered leading indicators about sales, employment, and the overall activity in the economy.

The NAPM report shows four prime charts each month. These are: production, new orders, inventories, and prices. Each chart includes a trend line and the latest reporting of the percentage of buyers who report each of these in their firms as "same," "better," or "worse" than last month.

Vendor deliveries and the buyers' future expectations are also captured in the report through reporting of purchase timing policies. A trend and latest reporting is made as to how far in advance the collective buyers place orders for production materials, MRO supplies, and capital expenditures. The periods reported are hand-to-mouth, 30 days, 60 days, 90 days, and 6 months and longer. A lengthening of these times indicate increased business activity and a tightening of vendor capacity or decreased vendor performance.

The *Report on Business* also highlights any commodities that are reported by the respondents as being in short supply, down in price or up in price. Specific industry features are included in each month's report ranging from the paper industry, to metals, energy, and other fields.

Trade Press Sources

Purchasing and *Purchasing World* magazines are current sources of information about prices, availability of goods, and trends in the field. Monthly features in these magazines include information about inventory changes, lead times and vendor performance, directions of the gross national product, prices, forecasts for basic industries, and projections about prices. These publications also have articles of interest about new products, processes, and the trends in the field.

Long-Run Analysis and Planning

Purchasing is a key component in the overall operations of a firm. The strategic advantage the firm enjoys on the market is directly tied to its purchasing effectiveness. This is true in the short run with daily, weekly, and yearly operations, but it is also becoming more important in long-run contexts as well. A part of the purchasing function should be actively devoted to addressing matters of a long-run nature.

One important activity in purchasing is to periodically measure, analyze, and report overall trends in supply markets. Buyers and managers see many of these trends on a daily basis, but it is important for managers above purchasing, as well as many in interfacing departments, to become periodically aware of these trends. This is a necessary communication to others about the changes in the markets from which the firm buys, and the information serves to warn about pending problems, rather than have them appear as a fault of purchasing when they become critical, and point to areas that other departments might see as opportunities in the future.

Another context in which long-run attention by purchasing is effective for the firm is suggesting value analysis areas. Major price increases, trends in tightened supply, and permanent quality problems with goods currently bought are key areas to suggest interdepartmental efforts in value analysis.

Long-run analysis in purchasing must also include investigation, study, and reporting of the nature of the basic industries and firms that are current and future sources for the firm. This includes forecasts of long-run prices and availability. Some of this analysis seeks input about the future of politics in foreign lands from which goods are now bought or may be bought in the future. One major firm in the U.S. viewed the long-run picture of energy and decided that it might be wise to purchase a firm that is in the energy business. Although the basic energy product was in adequate supply at the time of the purchase, the firm's analysis pointed to a major tightening in supply and increases in price of that source in the 1990s. In this context, purchasing forewarned the firm about a future supply assurance problem, and the firm reacted with an investment decision.

Conclusion

Purchase timing is a key supply and cost-effective factor. It is highly dependent upon the needs of the firm and opportunities and constraints in the field. This chapter presented most of the factors relating to timing that are within the purchasing managers sphere of decision making. These include both short and long run elements, trends in the field, the use of external data, and the need for long run analysis.

The specific timing of goods availability is also tied to production and marketing. These elements are presented in further detail in Part III where manufacturing needs, marketing plans and logistics factors come into play as well.

FOOTNOTES

1. "Hedging—Industry's Risk-Reducing Factor," *Purchasing*, 29 January 1981, p. 164A17.
2. Spyros Dakridakis and Steven C. Wheelwright, "Forecasting: Issues & Challenges for Marketing Management," *Journal of Marketing* (October 1977), p. 24.

SOURCE FOR FURTHER READING

Armstrong, Jon Scott. *Long Range Forecasting: From Crystal Ball to Computer.* New York: Wiley, 1978.

Cantor, Jeremiah. *Pragmatic Forecasting.* New York: American Management Association, 1971.

Chrisholm, Roger K., and Whitaker, Gilbert R., Jr. *Forecasting Methods.* Homewood, IL: Irwin, 1976.

Nelson, Charles R. *Applied Time Series Analysis for Managerial Forecasting.* San Francisco: Holden Day, 1973.

Paradiso, Louis. "How to Forecast," reprinted monograph from *Purchasing World*, (1983).

"How to Build Your Own Materials Cost Index." *Purchasing*, 10 June 1982, p. 51.

"NAPM Adds New Composite Index to its Report on Business." *National Purchasing Review*, March-April, 1982, p. 6.

"Price Forecasting," reprinted monograph from *Purchasing World*, (1983).

    Routine features from these sources also provide valuable information

    NAPM's *Report on Business:*

        Monthly Report

        Trends in Production, New Orders, Inventories, Prices, and Vendor Deliveries

        Specific Commodity Changes

        Commodity Reports

Purchasing Magazine:

        Hotline: Economy

                Markets

                Leadtimes

                Forecasts

Purchasing World Magazine:
PW Predicts
Business Databank

QUESTIONS FOR REVIEW

1. Why do firms forecast?

2. What do firms forecast? What is important to forecast in purchasing?

3. What are the best and worst periods for buyers in the business cycle?

4. What strategies are appropriate in a cyclical price movement of a particular commodity?

5. What do increases and decreases in backlogs and order cycle times indicate to purchasing managers?

6. A firm signs a contract to sell goods to a customer in December. It is now June and the price of the raw material needed in this job is $1.00 per pound. How can hedging be used to protect the firm from price increases and decreases?

7. What are the advantages and disadvantages of using regression or least squares in forecasting?

8. How does decomposition analysis help purchasing managers understand price activity for a particular product?

9. How is a regression equation interpreted?

10. You are a purchasing manager for an electrical supply manufacturer. What government and NAPM data would be of interest to you?

11. What valuable information is provided by the NAPM in its *Report on Business?*

12. Why should a purchasing manager attempt to analyze markets for goods that are ten years into the future?

Problem 8-1

A firm buys a product on the world market for production throughout the year. A seasonality exists in the supply of the product with July and August being the low point of the year. It is now early July and planning is taking place for the August purchase as well as preliminary estimates of buys from September through December. The price is now $1.15 per cubic foot. The August price is expected to be $1.17 with normal seasonal increases of five percent for each of the next six months.

Question:
What is the total cost of acquisition if buys are made monthly through December? Every two months? For the entire lot?

The prices paid for a commodity by a firm over the past several quarters are as follows.

Problem 8-2

1st Q	1982	$1.23
2nd Q	1982	1.16
3rd Q	1982	1.10
4th Q	1982	1.10
1st Q	1983	1.15
2nd Q	1983	1.21
3rd Q	1983	1.26
4th Q	1983	1.32
1st Q	1984	1.37

Questions:
1. What is the least-squares equation for this data?
2. Chart the time-series price data presented.
3. What modification might be appropriate in order to use this data for more reliable results in recent times?

A certain vendor industry that your firm buys from has the following inventory-to-sales ratios over the past several months

Problem 8-3

Month	Ratio
1	1.90
2	1.92
3	1.95
4	1.88
5	1.80
6	1.72
7	1.64

You depend upon several firms in this industry for timely deliveries of a product you use in production. All indications are that the trend shown in the above table will continue or at least remain the same.

Questions:
1. What does the inventory-to-sales ratio measure?
2. What does the trend indicate? What other things occur when the ratio behaves in this manner?
3. What actions are appropriate by buyers in this situation?

9

CAPITAL INVESTMENTS: A SPECIAL PRODUCT/ASSET MANAGEMENT ANALYSIS

What Is Investment Analysis?
Why Is It a Special Topic?
The Investment Analysis Process

PRIVATE FIRM PROJECT ANALYSIS

Basic Financial Information
Financial Worth of a Project

LEASING VERSUS PURCHASING

PROJECT INVESTMENT ANALYSIS IN PUBLIC AGENCIES

CONCLUSION

CHAPTER OBJECTIVES

After reading this chapter you should:

- Understand the basic approach used in capital budgeting

- Be able to compute the financial projections of a project

- Understand the impacts of purchasing upon the capital project

- Appreciate the differences found in public sector capital project analyses.

Purchasing and Capital Acquisitions

Capital Investments: A Special Product/Asset Management Analysis

A firm is concerned with long-run profitability of products and any other project idea that requires a commitment of funds with long-term financial benefits. The new product development approach requires a large investment in research, testing, introduction efforts, and often new machinery and even factories and distribution systems. A firm does not wish to invest scarce funds into any idea or project that will provide a long-term rate of return less than what it could have earned by investing the funds elsewhere. The same basic logic follows through into the purchase or acquisition of a fixed asset that will be on the books for several years. The asset investment must provide a good competitive rate of return.

What Is Investment Analysis?

Investment capital, financial analysis, or capital budgeting are terms used interchangeably for the same basic concept. For simplicity sake, we will refer to it as investment analysis. It is the process of evaluating the expenditure in a project or long-term asset to determine its financial worth over its life or the period of commitment by the firm. It consists of relating the initial investment expenditure, or investment, to the longer term benefits derived from the project. It is used in the decision process for new products, factory buildings, equipment, machinery, and distribution facilities. Investment analysis also includes the decision process related to the lease versus purchase decision.

Why Is It a Special Topic?

Investment analysis is presented here for several reasons. One, it is an area that requires much long-term planning, the benefits of which are often years in coming. Purchasing is often called upon to provide cost and availability estimates for capital assets as well as materials that will be needed during project life. Two, capital assets are bought infrequently, and they often involve very large expenditures. Capital assets are not like the repetitive goods purchases made in normal raw material processes. Capital items often involve costs that are not specifically known at the time of purchase thus complicating this problem further. And, three, capital goods must be carefully analyzed with a total life cycle cost approach. That is, the least costly asset might be the most expensive to operate over its life. This entire area is heavily involved in engineering, market planning, and financial analysis. The different nature of investment analysis often causes some firms to make it a separate function in purchasing.

The Investment Analysis Process

The entire cycle of capital projects falls into roughly nine distinct stages.

1) Idea Generation. This is the initial conception and planning stage by a person or group. This stage does not generally last long. The cost of actually analyzing the worth of a project idea is high, so little hard development work will take place beyond cursory idea generation.

2) Initial Screening. If an idea appears promising, it usually will undergo some form of top management screening before progressing much further. The purpose of the screen is to turn down ideas top management does not wish to pursue before too much time or money is spent on them. Additionally, approval from a screening often will provide funding and work assignments necessary for full detailed analysis. Purchasing is often involved in these first two stages by being asked for purchase prices, freight costs, and lead times for items necessary in the project. This information is known to be subject to change; only close ballpark estimates are necessary at this point.

3) Technical/Financial Analysis. After top management approval, very technical engineering and financial data gathering and analysis begins. The person or group within marketing, distribution or production wishing the new asset or project usually conducts the analysis. Information is gathered from all areas such as marketing, production, accounting, finance, engineering, and purchasing. Here, purchasing is again requested for information about available machinery on the market, only this time more detailed cost and lead-time data is sought. The specific features of each item are analyzed in detail. This stage typically ends with a tentative idea as to which model or approach to obtain, the total initial capital cost necessary to acquire it, and the estimated annual net benefits of the project into future years. Computations as to project payback and rate of return are also made.

4) Proposal. This is the formal request document onto which the above cost, benefit, and rate of return information etc. is placed. It is usually a summarized form that is supported by back-up information. The proposal is what is used to formally request capital funds from top management for the project.

5) Accept/Reject Decision. This is the step at which top management decides whether to go ahead with or turn down the project. Purchasing is generally represented at these meetings. The approval is often in the form of signatures from all or a majority of all on these boards or committees. This is the purchasing department's authorization to begin acquiring the needed items.

6) Financing Decision. After project approval is obtained, then the decision of financing the project is often made. Financing might entail outright cash purchase, borrowing, selling stock or bonds, or any one of many types of leases. Purchasing usually provides specific information on prices and leases here.

7) Implementation. The construction or acquisition phase is one in which purchasing is heavily involved. The physical task of acquiring the capital goods and optimally timing their arrival is a purchasing responsibility. Close coordination must exist in this phase with the person or group who is launching the project.

8) Post Audit. Many firms conduct audits of project performance once they are on stream. These audits are designed to ascertain whether the project is living up to initial projections and whether refinements are necessary in its operation. Purchasing will be called upon to provide an historical summary of all costs expended to acquire and set up the asset.

9) Replacement. Eventually the asset will require replacment or phasing-out. The cycle begins all over again with purchasing being asked what an estimated replacement unit will cost as well as how much the old asset will generate in net realizable value.

Purchasing is involved in most stages throughout asset or project life. The tasks are nonrepetitive. They often involve estimates, since hard information is often not available, and often concern vendors who only are used a few times in a decade. The skills, approaches, and disciplines here are different from those of raw material or repetitive component purchasing.

Private Firm Project Analysis

Private firm project analysis is divided into three areas. First, is the basic information needed for financial analysis. This is the initial acquisition cost and the annual net cash benefits. Second, the financial worth of the project is determined using basic product/project information in a series of financial tools. Such approaches are employed by private firms that are seeking financial return analyses. Third, the evaluative approaches used in not-for-profit and government settings is presented. These are often different than those used in private settings.

Basic Financial Information

Two key bits of information are required before the financial feasibility of a project can be determined. These are: 1) initial capital cost, and 2) annual net cash benefits.

The initial capital cost consists of all costs required up to the actual start of the machine, operation, or product sale. The following listing shows the items that are typically included in computing the initial capital cost.

Purchase price	$ 95,000
Freight	5,000
Site preparation	10,000
Installation	25,000

Training	15,000
Construction Interest Cost	5,000
Development Costs	5,000
Sub.	$160,000
Less: Investment tax credit	(10,000)
Total	$150,000

First, and always, is machinery purchase price and inbound freight. In addition, the firm will spend money for preparing the site, installation, training of workers and managers, interest on the construction loan, and the engineering and analytical work that goes into designing the project. If an old machine is to be replaced, then its dismantling costs are to be added, less whatever scrap value will be obtained from its disposition. A final and often overlooked element in this analysis is the investment tax credit. This is a reduction in income taxes normally payable by the firm due to fixed asset acquisitions made. The tax credit is ten percent of the purchase and freight costs on all six-year and longer assets, and six and two-thirds percent on assets of shorter depreciable lives. This tax credit, $10,000 in the above example, is an amount of taxes that the firm will not have to pay because it acquired this asset. The asset's initial capital cost, then, is $150,000.

Annual net benefits is the second bit information needed in this analysis. These are the net cash flow results in each year of asset life. It is determined as follows.

This is a two-step process that first requires project net profit to be determined. This is done using the standard income statement information used in accounting. The second step requires adding the "net after taxes" to the amount originally deducted for "depreciation." The sum is the net amount of cash that will result from the project during the year. This is the annual net benefit.

If a project has no actual cash flow, then it can be still justified by determining what net savings in expenses the firm will gain by switching to the new machine. This is a common approach used when new replacement machinery is being considered in a factory. Savings-type projects are perhaps easier to justify than new product ones because the former do not require estimates for revenues. Cost savings are perceived as easier to measure than a revenue and cost bearing project.

Financial Worth of a Project

The initial capital cost and annual net benefits are the two key items needed in financial investment analysis. A third is the present value rate, but this will be presented later. The common analytical tools used by industry are 1) simple payback, 2) discounted payback, 3) net present value, and 4) internal rate of return.

Simple payback states how long it will take the initial investment cost to be recouped by the net benefits of the project. This can be computed as follows.

YEAR	ACTUAL CASH FLOW	CUMULATIVE CASH FLOW
0	($150,000)	($150,000)
1	60,000	(90,000)
2	60,000	(30,000)
3	60,000	30,000
4	60,000	90,000
5	60,000	150,000
	$150,000	

The cumulative column shows that at the end of Year 2 the project will still have a deficit of total cash flows, but it will be in a surplus by end of Year 3. The exact payback point is two years plus a fraction of a year. The fraction is determined by using the deficit in Year 2 without the brackets as a numerator over the total inflow in Year 3. This is 30,000/60,000 or .5. Thus, the simple payback is two and one half years or two years and six months.

Simple payback has the benefit of being easy to understand. It is a basic measure of risk. The answer is in terms of time, the lesser the time is the better; the longer it is, the worse. If a project still has a cumulative deficit at the end of its life, then it will not return its entire initial cost to the company.

Simple payback has a disadvantage, however. It does not account for inflation, decreases in purchasing power of money over time, or the opportunities a firm might have in investing its funds elsewhere. In the above example, each dollar of $60,000 returned in Year 5 is assumed to have the same dollar-for-dollar purchasing power or value as those returned in Year 1. This, of course, is false in any inflationary period.

The present value factor, PVF, is a convenient tool to account for the above time value of funds. Table 9-1 is a present value table for rates up to 40 percent and up to ten years. Many firms do not use the benefits accruing in a project beyond Year 5 even though a project might still be in existence. The rationale here is that the project must break-even in five years or less for the project to be approved. This is consistent with the long-term planning horizon in many firms.

Discounted payback uses the above payback concept while accounting for the time-value of funds. It is computed using the firm's investment cut-off rate as supplied by the finance department. This rate is used to ascertain specific present value factors for each year from the table. In the example project, twenty percent is the rate used.

YEAR	CASH FLOW	20% PVF	VALUE STREAM	PRESENT VALUE STREAM
0	$(150,000)	1.000	($150,000)	($150,000)
1	60,000	0.833	49,980	(100,020)
2	60,000	0.694	41,640	(58,380)
3	60,000	0.579	34,740	(23,640)
4	60,000	0.482	28,920	5,280
5	60,000	0.402	24,120	29,400
			29,400	

The present value factor for the initial capital investment is 1.000 since present dollars each having one dollar value, are being spent.

The discounted payback is 3 + 23,640/28,920 or 3.82 years. In simple terms the project broke-even in two and one half years. But, when the firm's time-value of funds is considered, the return takes place in three years and ten months. Again, discounted payback is expressed in time, the shorter the better. It is a measure of project risk.

Net present value is the next financial evaluation toll. It seeks the total surplus of cash return from the project over and above the firm's opportunity rate. In the sample project, the net present value is $29,400, which is the sum of the fourth column or the last figure in fifth column. It is interpreted as the total surplus dollars earned from the project considering the firm's time value of funds or opportunity rate that could have been earned elsewhere. If the net present value is zero, then the project just breaks even on this measure. If it is negative, then the firm would do better to invest in another project that would at least earn the cut-off percent rate of earnings, in this case twenty percent. But, the sample project is promising with a large surplus.

Internal rate of return is the last investment tool. It is a percent figure of return. This can be compared to interest costs other investment alternatives or the inflation rate. It is found by multiplying various percent present value factors by the actual yearly cash flows until one of the percent PVFs results in the cumulative column summing to zero. The present value percent that accomplishes this is the internal rate of return. At twenty percent a positive $29,400 results. The following table shows the results of other present value factors, PVFs.

P.V.F.	Cumulative Present Value Stream
20%	$29,400
22%	21,840
24%	14,700
26%	8,100
28%	1,860
29%	− 1,026

The internal rate of return for this project is about twenty-nine percent.

These tools are often considered together because each one has a strength that the others do not possess. Risks in a project are evaluated by discounted payback. Project scale, magnitude, and feeling of surplus purchasing power earned is provided by net present value. Project "return" is illustrated with internal rate of return.

Purchasing is involved with investment analysis in several ways. One, purchasing must use these various approaches when it seeks investments for itself such as computers, private fleets, or communications systems. Two, purchasing's effectiveness in acquiring the sought items in a project is important. This means obtaining the capital item at

☐ **TABLE 9-1.** *Present Value Factors*

Yr	\	\	\	\	Interest Rate	\	\	\	\	\
	1	2	3	4	5	6	7	8	9	10
1	0.9901	0.9804	0.9709	0.9615	0.9524	0.9434	0.9346	0.9259	0.9114	0.9091
2	0.9803	0.9612	0.9426	0.9246	0.9070	0.8900	0.8734	0.8573	0.8417	0.8264
3	0.9706	0.9423	0.9151	0.8890	0.8638	0.8396	0.8163	0.7938	0.7722	0.7513
4	0.9610	0.9238	0.8885	0.8548	0.8227	0.7921	0.7629	0.7350	0.7084	0.6830
5	0.9515	0.9057	0.8626	0.8219	0.7835	0.7473	0.7130	0.6806	0.6499	0.6209
6	0.9420	0.8880	0.8375	0.7903	0.7462	0.7050	0.6663	0.6302	0.5963	0.5645
7	0.9327	0.8706	0.8131	0.7599	0.7107	0.6651	0.6227	0.5835	0.5470	0.5132
8	0.9235	0.8535	0.7894	0.7307	0.6768	0.6274	0.5820	0.5403	0.5019	0.4665
9	0.9143	0.8368	0.7664	0.7026	0.6446	0.5919	0.5439	0.5002	0.4604	0.4241
10	0.9053	0.8203	0.7441	0.6756	0.6139	0.5584	0.5083	0.4632	0.4224	0.3855

Yr	\	\	\	\	Interest Rate	\	\	\	\	\
	11	12	13	14	15	16	17	18	19	20
1	0.9009	0.8929	0.8850	0.8772	0.8696	0.8621	0.8547	0.8475	0.8403	0.8333
2	0.8116	0.7972	0.7831	0.7695	0.7561	0.7432	0.7305	0.7182	0.7062	0.6944
3	0.7312	0.7118	0.6931	0.6750	0.6575	0.6407	0.6244	0.6086	0.5934	0.5787
4	0.6587	0.6355	0.6133	0.5921	0.5718	0.5523	0.5337	0.5158	0.4987	0.4823
5	0.5935	0.5674	0.5428	0.5194	0.4972	0.4761	0.4561	0.4371	0.4190	0.4019
6	0.5346	0.5066	0.4803	0.4556	0.4323	0.4104	0.3898	0.3704	0.3521	0.3349
7	0.4817	0.4523	0.4251	0.3996	0.3759	0.3538	0.3332	0.3139	0.2959	0.2791
8	0.4339	0.4039	0.3762	0.3506	0.3269	0.3050	0.2848	0.2660	0.2487	0.2326
9	0.3909	0.3606	0.3329	0.3075	0.2843	0.2630	0.2434	0.2255	0.2090	0.1938
10	0.3522	0.3220	0.2946	0.2697	0.2472	0.2267	0.2080	0.1911	0.1756	0.1615

Yr	\	\	\	Interest Rate	\	\
	21	22	23	24	25	26	27
1	0.8264	0.8197	0.8130	0.8065	0.8000	0.7937	0.7874
2	0.6830	0.6719	0.6610	0.6504	0.6400	0.6299	0.6200
3	0.5645	0.5507	0.5374	0.5245	0.5120	0.4999	0.4882
4	0.4665	0.4514	0.4369	0.4230	0.4096	0.3968	0.3844
5	0.3855	0.3700	0.3552	0.3411	0.3277	0.3149	0.3027
6	0.3186	0.3033	0.2888	0.2751	0.2621	0.2499	0.2383
7	0.2633	0.2486	0.2348	0.2218	0.2097	0.1983	0.1877
8	0.2176	0.2038	0.1909	0.1789	0.1678	0.1574	0.1478
9	0.1799	0.1670	0.1552	0.1443	0.1342	0.1249	0.1164
10	0.1486	0.1369	0.1262	0.1164	0.1074	0.0992	0.0916

Yr	28	30	32	34	36	38	40
1	0.7813	0.7692	0.7576	0.7463	0.7353	0.7246	0.7143
2	0.6104	0.5917	0.5739	0.5569	0.5407	0.5251	0.5102
3	0.4768	0.4552	0.4348	0.4156	0.3975	0.3805	0.3644
4	0.3725	0.3501	0.3294	0.3102	0.2923	0.2757	0.2603
5	0.2910	0.2693	0.2495	0.2315	0.2149	0.1998	0.1859
6	0.2274	0.2072	0.1890	0.1727	0.1580	0.1448	0.1328
7	0.1776	0.1594	0.1432	0.1289	0.1162	0.1049	0.0949
8	0.1388	0.1226	0.1085	0.0962	0.0854	0.0760	0.0678
9	0.1084	0.0943	0.0822	0.0718	0.0628	0.0551	0.0484
10	0.0847	0.0725	0.0623	0.0536	0.0462	0.0399	0.0346

or below the cost used in the original justification. Cost overruns will cause decreases in the net present value and rate of return as well as a lengthening of the payback periods. For example, if the above project was $10,000 more than planned, the rate of return drops to twenty-five percent. Three, a delay in acquiring the assets impacts the firm detrimentally as well. A six-month delay in project operation causes all the benefits to slide six months farther into the future. This makes the rate of return for this project twenty-four percent. Cost overruns and delays by purchasing have a great impact upon the total life returns of projects.

Leasing versus Purchasing

A financing decision follow the project acceptance step. Financing can be gained through outright purchase or through one of many buying arrangements. Leasing has become a popular form of acquisition financing. It has been made even more attractive with the advent of "safe harbor" basing provisions in U.S. tax laws that permit firms incurring losses to still take effective advantage of depreciation and investment tax credits.

Purchasing is often called upon to make the buy-or-lease decision. It is like an apple-orange comparison because there are benefits and drawbacks to each choice.

Purchasing has the advantage of total control over the asset throughout its entire life. The purchase decision is often the least expensive, since a leasing firm's profits are not being paid. The asset belongs to the owner after its effective life is past. This is an advantage with land, buildings, and airplanes, which can appreciate over time. Finally, purchasing often involves a single cash outlay with none thereafter and only annual depreciation benefits coming to the firm.

Leasing, on the other hand, provides the advantage of low initial cash commitment. A lease payment is paid rather than an entire purchase amount. The lease payment also can correspond to the earnings of the asset. That is, after the first lease payment, earnings from the asset can pay for the subsequent ones. A lease arrangement might provide for machine installation earlier than a purchase. The buying power of the leasing firm might be so great as to pass on this economy to the lessee. An accounting benefit can also be obtained through a lease in the form of not having either the asset nor the lease obligation on the company books. This serves to increase the return on assets ratio. Leasing is a low-risk way of entering into new areas. If the firm decides that the experience does not warrant continuation, a lease often can be easily terminated. Finally, many lease arrangements include training, administrative services, as well as maintenance and repair services.

The problem at hand in many settings is to weigh the benefits of a lease against the additional costs typically associated with them. For example, truck or copier leasing is often more expensive than outright purchase, but the lease often avoids training, recordkeeping, personnel hiring, and maintenance necessities. The following approach can be used to evaluate how much the lease costs over and above the purchase on a time value of funds basis so that a comparative benefit and cost decision can be made by the firm.

An approach to evaluate the lease versus purchase includes 1) determining the after-tax cash flow costs of the lease, 2) calculating the after-tax cash flow costs associated with the purchase, 3) subtracting the purchase cash flow from the lease cash flow to determine the annual and total cost difference of the lease over and above the purchase, 4) determining the above, after-tax cost difference in percent terms, and 5) evaluating this percent in relation to the after-tax cost of borrowing the funds for a purchase option. The following example illustrates the analysis using the project from the capital tools.

An asset can be purchased for $100,000, or it can be leased for $30,000 per year for five years. The costs of installation, etc. would be the same with each choice, but maintenance and training would be provided by the lease. The company tax rate is 30%.

Step 1: Determine after-tax lease cost.

Year	Before Tax Cash Flow	+	Lease Tax Shield	=	After-Tax Cash Flow
0	$ 30,000				$ 30,000
1	30,000		($ 9,000)		21,000
2	30,000		($ 9,000)		21,000
3	30,000		($ 9,000)		21,000
4	30,000		($ 9,000)		21,000
5			($ 9,000)		(9,000)
	$150,000		($45,000)		$105,000

Note that the lease payment is at the beginning of each year. Since the company is in the thirty percent tax bracket, each lease payment shields $9,000 of funds from being paid in taxes. Year 5 is beyond the life of the lease, but the tax effect of the lease payment in Year 4 is included in it.

Step. 2: Determine the after-tax purchase cash flows. The asset costs $100,000 and will be depreciated over five years for $20,000 per year. At thirty percent taxes, the tax shield affect will be $6,000 per year for years 2 through 5.

Year	Before Tax Flow	+	Purchase Tax Shield	=	After Tax Cash Flow
0	$100,000				$100,000
1			($ 6,000)		(6,000)
2			($ 6,000)		(6,000)
3			($ 6,000)		(6,000)
4			($ 6,000)		(6,000)
5			($ 6,000)		(6,000)
	$100,000		$30,000		$ 70,000

Step 3: Subtract the after-tax purchase cash flow from the after-tax lease cash flow.

Year	After-Tax Lease Cash Flow	After-Tax Purchase – Cash Flow	L. Minus P. Difference
0	$30,000	$100,000	($70,000)
1	21,000	(6,000)	27,000
2	21,000	(6,000)	27,000
3	21,000	(6,000)	27,000
4	21,000	(6,000)	27,000
5	(9,000)	(6,000)	(3,000)
	$105,000	$ 70,000	$35,000

Step 4: Determine the time-value percent difference between the lease minus purchase cash flows.

This is done in much the same way as the internal rate of return is computed. That is, by trial and error, various percent value factors are applied in order to find which one creates a present value stream that sums to or close to zero.

TRIAL 12%	L–P	12%	Present
0	(70,000)	1.000	(70,000)
1	27,000	3.038*	82,020
5	(3,000)	.567	(1701)
			$10,325

*PVFs can be added and multiplied as one when the cash flows for several years are equal.
The sum is too high on the positive side:
Attempt second trial using 16%.

TRIAL 16% Year	L–P Flow	16% PVF	Present Value Stream
0	(70,000)	1.000	(70,000)
1–4	27,000	2.798	75,546
5	(3,000)	.476	(1,428)
			4118 too high

Trial 19% Year	L–P Flow	19% PVF	Present Value Stream
0	(70,000)	1.000	(70,000)
1–4	27,000	2.638	71,226
5	(3,000)	.419	(1,257)
			(31)

Nineteen percent is the cost of the base over and above the purchase in percent time-value terms.

Step 5. Compare the extra cost of lease to cost of borrowing. This last step requires subtracting the after-tax cost of borrowing funds for a purchase from the after-tax cost of the lease.

Company cost to borrow 14% before taxes
At 30% tax rate, after tax
cost to borrow is 9.8%

Cost of lease over purchase (from Step 4)	19%
Cost to borrow for purchase	9.8%
= True cost of financing by lease over and above purchase	9.2%

Purchasing, finance and the managers seeking to obtain the asset can now evaluate the convenience of having maintenance and training included on the lease. The cost of this service feature is $35,000 or 9.2% over five years. In some instances, a lease actually can be less than the cost of a purchase. This can occur when leasing company buying power is great and/or its cost of capital and tax rates are different than the leasee. Of course, if the leasee cannot take advantage of the investment tax credit or depreciation for tax shield purposes, leasing can still bring these total cost reduction elements to bear positively for the lessee.

Project Investment Analysis in Public Agencies

The previous analyses are used in private, for-profit firms. The intent of these tools is to evaluate the financial return, or cash profit, to the firm. In government settings, these tools generally are not appropriate because profit is not the sought after reason for a project. Instead, minimum total life cost is a more appropriate approach.

Life cycle costing is applicable when the original purchase price is high, the asset has a long life, operating costs are large, and/or energy use is high. The basic concept allows two or more capital good alternatives to be evaluated on the basis of total purchase and operating costs over their entire lives.

The key information needed for this analysis includes 1) initial cost, 2) length of life, 3) salvage value, 4) maintenance and repair costs, 5) operating costs, 6) taxes and related benefits from depreciation, if any, 7) a discount rate for selected present value factors, and 8) escalation rates for operating and maintenance costs. Taxes and depreciation are not used in this analysis in public agencies, but should be included if used in for-profit firms. An example of two alternative machines will show how this can be applied. Table 9-2 shows the initial price of Machine A as $80,000 and Machine B as $100,000. On the surface, Machine A often would be the one sought by purchasing managers because it has the least total initial cost of $107,500 versus $125,000 for B. However, Machine A has a higher energy cost that has an expected inflation rate of

☐ **TABLE 9-2.** *Life Cycle Cost Analysis*

Machine A

Cost	0	1	2	Year 3	4	5	
Purchase Cost	$ 80,000						
Life	5 years						
Engineering Cost	$ 10,000						
Instal. Cost	$ 10,000						
Training	$ 4,500						
Labor		40,000	42,000	44,100	46,305	48,620	
Energy		50,000	55,000	60,500	66,550	73,205	
Downtime %	4%						
Downtime Cost		12,000	12,960	13,997	15,117	16,326	
Total Costs	$104,500	102,000	109,960	118,597	127,972	138,151	= $701,180
@ 12% PVF	1.000	.893	.797	.712	.636	.567	
Total Present Value Cost	$104,500	91,086	87,638	84,441	81,390	78,332	= $527,387

Machine B

Cost	0	1	2	Year 3	4	5	
Purchase Cost	$100,000						
Life	5 years						
Engineering Cost	$ 10,000						
Instal. Cost	10,000						
Training	5,000						
Labor		50,000	52,500	55,125	57,881	60,775	
Energy		40,000	44,000	48,400	53,240	58,564	
Downtime %	2%						
Downtime Cost		5,000	5,400	5,832	6,299	6,802	
Total Costs	$125,000	95,000	101,900	109,357	117,420	126,141	= $674,818
@ 12% PVF	1.000	.893	.797	.712	.636	.567	
Total Present Value Cost	$125,000	84,835	81,214	76,862	74,679	71,522	= $514,112

ten percent per year and a higher maintenance cost, which is expected to climb by eight percent per year.

Life cycle costing analysis requires adding all costs per year after they have been adjusted for inflation. The total yearly costs are then discounted using a present value rate appropriate for the organization. Even government agencies should use a discount rate, since they must often borrow funds on commercial markets. The sample problem uses a twelve percent rate, which is not an unlikely local, state, or federal government cost of borrowing. On a total cost and present value basis, the operating cost of A is higher than B, thereby over shadowing the benefit of a lower purchase cost. Thus, in this case, the asset with the higher purchase price has lower operating and downtime costs. Over the lives of both assets, Machine B costs less than Machine A.

Life cycle cost analysis is built into the initial capital cost and annual net benefit analyses of the financial tools used in private firm settings. It is appropriate to use in public agency, and not-for-profit organization settings. It recognizes that the least purchase or lowest initial capital cost alternative is not always the best to acquire. Instead, the entire total life performance is pertinent for economic capital asset decisions.

Conclusion

Product creation, management, and termination decisions are a major strategic area of the firm. Purchasing is involved with marketing at every stage of produce life. Too often managers in each area view the other at arms legth. The ties must be close for the firm to benefit. Capital asset acquisition is also a part of the strategic planning processes of the firm. Capital assets are used to carry out strategic planning goals in the form of producing products for the firm. Capital analysis throughout asset life is a form of product management. Capital assets either assist the firm in reaching strategic goals, or they can restrict it by only being able to produce something the market no longer demands. Therefore, product management must be closely coordinated with capital asset use. Capital asset decisions are similar in public organization settings, though the use of capital assets there are somewhat different. Life cycle costing in public agency decision making considers more than purchase price alone.

SOURCE FOR FURTHER READING

Anderson, Paul F., and Bird, Monroe M. "Marketing to the Industrial Lease Buyer." *Industrial Marketing Management* 9 (1980):111.

Brown, Robert J. "A New Marketing Tool: Life-Cycle Costing." *Industrial Marketing Management* B (1979):109.

Cavinato, Joseph L. *Finance for Transportation and Distribution Managers.* Washington: Traffic Service Corp., 1977.

Department of Defense. *Life Cycle Costing Procurement Guide.* Washington, D.C.: U. S. Government Printing Office, 1970.

Johnston, Wesley J., and Bonoma, Thomas V. "Purchase Process for Capital Equipment and Serivces." *Industrial Marketing Management* 10 (1981):253.

Semich, J. William. "Look to Leases When Profits Turn to Losses." *Purchasing,* 7 October 1982.

QUESTIONS FOR REVIEW

1. What is capital project analysis?

2. How is purchasing involved prior to the vendor and item selection decision in a capital project?

3. Why is there an initial screening and another accept/reject step used in most firms?

4. What technical and financial information is used in project analysis?

5. What is the "Initial Capital Cost" of a project? How is it different from the price of the asset?

6. What is the "Annual Net Cash Benefit" of a project, and how is it different from the profit term typically reported on income statements?

7. What are the pros and cons of simple payback?

8. Explain the concept of "present value" in layman's terms.

9. What are the distinguishing features of a) discounted payback, b) net present value, and c) internal rate of return?

10. How is investment analysis different in a public agency from that in a private firm?

11. How are leases and purchases different?

12. What is the basic objective of the lease versus purchase tool presented in this chapter? That is, what is the measure it seeks to ascertain?

Problem 9-1

A company is considering a capital investment project in the form of new production machinery. The initial capital cost is $140,000, and annual net benefits are $40,000 for each of the seven years of project life. The company cost of capital is fifteen percent.

Questions:
1. What are the:
   a) discounted payback?
   b) net present value?
   c) internal rate of return?
3. What would be the effect of a purchase price overrun of $10,000 on the initial capital cost in terms of impact upon the internal rate of return?
4. The equipment is slated to begin service on January 1 of this coming year. What would be the impact in terms of internal rate of return if the project was delayed through lengthened delivery and the equipment would not start service until next July 1?
5. What impact upon the internal rate of return would occur if the annual net benefits were actually $30,000 due to an error in estimating maintenance costs by someone in purchasing?

Problem 9-2

An analyst gathers information pertaining to a possible capital acquisition. The information gathered is as follows:

Acquisition-related costs

inbound freight	12,000
engineering and set up	43,500
training	15,000
inbound freight	12,000
interest cost in construction	5,500
investment tax credit	6-2/3%
depreciable life (straight line)	5 years

Performance-related costs (annual):

energy savings	$ 50,000
labor savings	110,000
maintenance savings	15,000
scrap and waste savings	10,000
pollution and disposal cost savings	20,000
overhead costs	20,000
company tax rate	30%

Questions:
1. *What is the initial capital cost?*
2. *What is the annual net benefit of this project?*
3. *Using a twenty percent value factor, what is the project's discounted payback, net present value, and internal rate of return?*
   Note: Round the initial capital cost and annual net benefits to the nearest thousand.

A firm has a choice of buying or leasing an asset. The purchase price is $32,000, and the lease cost is $10,000 for a four-year term. The company is in a twenty percent tax bracket, and its cost of borrowing on a before tax basis is ten percent.

Problem 9-3

Question:
Is it least costly to purchase or lease?

Refer to the information in Problem 9-2. Assume this project is being considered by a government agency. What is the life cycle cost of this asset to an agency that pays no income taxes nor gains any benefit from investment tax credits?

Problem 9-4

10

CHAPTER OBJECTIVES

After reading this chapter you should:

- Understand the basic forms of transportation available to a firm.

- Be able to take advantage of some of the new opportunities brought about by deregulation.

- Understand the activities of traffic management for purchasing benefits.

- Be able to determine the total cost of transportation in the entire purchasing decision.

Purchasing Opportunities in Transportation

Introduction

The transportation industry in the United States was relatively stable from the late 1940s to the middle 1970s. Traffic managers, those charged with the task of shipping a firm's product, enjoyed a consistent and gradually expanding supply of carriage forms during this period. Rates, or prices charged by carriers, were uniform and changed in relatively small and often predictable amounts each year. Carriers experienced many productivity gains in the form of larger and better engines and equipment, expanded highways, and other benefits that all served to blunt rate increases from wages and other inflation items.

Fuel and capital cost spirals, supply shortages, and a push to deregulate U.S. transportation started to affect the stable carrier situation in the middle 1970s. By 1980, four major legislative acts were passed that greatly altered rail, motor, and air carriers. The impact within the industry has been great; major changes in services and pricing resulted. The long-run impacts have yet to unfold, and the full extent of these changes might not be known for another decade. Changes will continue throughout the 1980s that will greatly affect the services available for moving goods as well as the cost of moving goods.

This chapter explains why transportation is now more than ever a key element to purchasing and the firm as a whole. An overview of the basic legal and carrier forms of transportation is presented initially. The major changes that have taken place in transportation are next explored from a purchasing standpoint. The role of traffic management which is becoming more important with respect to inbound shipments, is discussed. Finally, several specific topics of transportation of concern to purchasing managers are analyzed.

Why Transportation Is Important to Purchasing

Purchasing managers can no longer rely upon delivered pricing terms, where the vendor's traffic manager arranges the inbound move. Too many cost and service opportunities that purchasing could otherwise obtain might be overlooked.

Inbound transportation managed from the purchasing manager's standpoint has several strategic implications for the firm. First, the firm's product price advantage might stem from a favorable inbound rate and movement configuration. Second, the transportation link might represent a sourcing advantage. Examples of this are company-owned ships or motor trucks, which provide superior, flexible service over that provided by regular carriers. Third, an inbound transportation function can go far in making optimal timing decisions for the flow of goods into the firm. Fourth, an actively managed inbound flow network can seek out the last channel of procurement.

A general logistics concept applies here that relates transportation costs to the cost of goods. In basic form it states that as goods shift from raw to finished form, transportation is of relatively less value to the product at each stage. Conversely, the raw material stages experience higher relative transportation cost impacts than do finished goods. This can be seen with coal where carrier rates can be over fifty percent of the landed cost of the product. But, with a camera shipped half way around the world, the rate might be high per pound but only five percent of the final price. Transportation, then, is a major factor in absolute and relative terms in goods sourcing.

Transportation is more important to purchasing now simply from the expanded service opportunities that are evolving. More carriers are entering the market in the wake of deregulation. Many offer varied service and price packages that did not previously exist. Whereas a small number of equipment choices were available in the 1950s, today the shipper is offered a myriad of choices. In the past, when choices were few and simple, little effort might have been needed to move goods. Today, the wide choice of method, price, and quality of carriers requires that transportation be actively managed and integrated into the operation of the firm for both inbound and outbound goods.

Supply of Domestic Transportation—Legal Forms

Four legal categories of transportation firms are in service in the U.S. These four categories are subject to federal economic regulation of carrier routes, rates, financial features, and services. The categories are common, contract, exempt, and private.

Common Carriage
Common carriage is the backbone of American transportation. Common carriers serve the general public. Services by these carriers cannot be discriminatory between shippers or receivers. Most railroads and about 20,000 motor carriers are common carriers. Examples are the Sante Fe Railway, Yellow Freight Systems, Roadway Trucking, and Emery Air Freight

Contract Carriage
Contract carriage is defined by contractual agreement between the carrier and shipper, or the carrier and receiver. It is usually for a specialized

service with specific equipment, scheduled service, or a regular service in which the carrier offers a special rate in exchange for a contracted volume commitment.

About 5,000 contract trucking operations are in existence today, and about 5,000 contracts are in effect between railroads and manufacturers and receivers. Whereas common carriage service is provided according to rates that are published in tariffs for all to examine, contract carriage is only between the contracting firm and the carrier.

Exempt

Exempt carriage is free from the regulations of the Interstate Commerce Commission pertaining to rates, routes, services, and financial regulations. However, exempt carriers are still subject to the safety regulations of the highways. Exempt carriage exists today in the movement of fresh fruits and vegetables by both rail and truck, piggyback trailers on flatbed cars on railroads, and any product that moves in a rail boxcar. A purchasing manager must negotiate a rate for each and every movement, and it is difficult to determine what the prevailing rate level is at any moment. As more deregulation of this industry takes place, more transportation modes will become exempt.

Private

Private carriage is transportation provided by the firm that owns the goods. A buyer might notice that some shipments arrive from the vendor in the vendor's own truck. This form of service is usually initiated for cost, service, or control reasons.

Transportation Services Available to Buyers

At the end of World War II, firms had only about twenty forms of carrier services available to them. The choices were few and the rates were all the same. Buyers simplified their jobs by specifying vendor delivery to their sites. Now, however, the choices are expanding, and buyers must be as concerned about the movement inbound as they are about the vendor chosen. A brief review of some of the various forms of carriage are presented in Table 10–1 along with key points of concern for buyers.

Insights Into Motor Contract Carriage

Contract carriage is a major growth form of transportation in the 1980s. Shippers are increasing their use of contract carriers for a variety of reasons ranging from assuring service certainty and equipment supply to eliminating or reducing the effects of industrywide rate escalations.

This form of transportation is obtained by negotiating services and rates with a carrier. There is generally a minimum tonnage obligation upon the shipper that is linked with a carrier requirement to haul it upon sufficient notice at a specified rate per pound, ton, mile, or shipment. The federal laws relating to contract carriage are found in the Revised Interstate Commerce Act (Chapters 101, 105 and 107). Specific ICC regulations are found within Title 49, *Code of Federal Regulations*, Parts 1000 to end. These regulations deal with obtaining permanent

☐ **TABLE 10-1.** *Overview of Domestic Transportation Services Available to Buyers*

Form	Feature(s)	Key Points for Buyers
Rail: plain equipment	Plain box, flat hopper-type cars Distributed by carriers on nondiscriminatory basis	Vendor must often use blocking and bracing and other car preparation efforts and expenses. Plain box car declining; rail firms no longer buying. Future shortages in plain box cars; higher rates as supply gets tighter. Some shipper/receivers provide own cars.
Rail: specialized equipment	Internal features in cars Distributed according to revenue to be earned by carrier	Saves shipper blocking/bracing expenses. Easier loading/unloading. Car very expensive; only tendered for high revenue shippers/receivers.
Rail: leased/owned equipment	Shipper or receiver obtains own cars	Assures car supply. Can have car designed for firm's own goods. Carriers provide allowance for providing car. Necessary in bulk liquid moves; rails won't provide.
Rail contract service	Agreement for service/rate between firm and railroad	Can assure car supply. Used to obtain low rate for long-term volume commitment.
Piggyback	Truck trailer on rail flat car	Combines flexibility of truck with rate of railroad. Opens up the number of railroads a firm can use, since trucks of another carrier can reach the firm but another rail carrier actually has tracks to the plant.
Motor: plain truck	Van or flatbed trailer	Basic equipment of common carriers. New 1982 law allows longer, heavier loads for move economy, but higher taxes on trucks might keep savings to minimum.
Motor: specialized equipment	Tank and other special moves	Primary contract carriage operations. Some firms provide own equipment, hire carrier to move it. 1982 law impacts the same.
Package/courier services	Small package movers Air and bus firms provide also	UPS is basic example. High rate, but OK on high value goods. Fast, frequent service; movers of document and repair parts.
Air freight	Same as package/courier	Service either door-to-door or (cheaper) terminal-to-terminal. Can be less costly when considering cost of inventory in-transit, or penalty of not having item.
Domestic water	Barge movements	Slow, low cost; good for large/bulk moves. Barge can be "warehouse" while in-transit.

☐ **TABLE 10-1.** *Continued*

Form	Feature(s)	Key Points for Buyers
Forwarders	Small package movers	Can be less costly than regular truck and air.
Shippers' association	Small package movers	A nonprofit, forwarder-like operation made up of firms that join in collective membership and operation.
Shippers' agent	Piggyback service	A firm that combines two or more separate trailer moves for a single piggyback move; savings passed on to firm that would otherwise have to pay penalty for shipping only one piggyback tailer to destination.
Brokers	Find shipments for carriers; find carriers for shippers	Common in exempt transportation; will become more popular with more deregulation.
		Act as clearinghouse-type agents for both carriers and shippers/receivers.
		Performs some traffic functions for shipper/receivers.

route permits, contract filing, and other service features. Since 1978 many regulations relating to contract carriage have been repealed or relaxed thereby making it much more flexible to obtain than in the past.

The basic relationship between the shipper and carrier is defined by the contract. An analysis of most of the key features found in basic motor contracts follows.

Agreement—statement naming shipper/consignee and trucker along with addresses of each.

Tender—Shipper/consignee agrees to tender named commodities along certain origin-destination routes or in general regions. Minimum amount of tonnage is also stated. Trucker agrees to haul same.

Receipt—Trucker to issue receipt for each shipment as well as provide evidence of delivery.

Compensation—A rate per package, pound, ton, mile, truckload, or other basis.

Billing—Trucker to submit invoices promptly; shipper/consignee to pay same promptly within specified timeframe.

Transportation—Trucker to supply transportation at cost and expenses; shall comply with all applicable laws and regulations. Terms applying to trucker use of owner-operators usually stated. Trucker has control and responsibility over owner-operators, relationship is not between shipper/consignee and owner-operator. Sometimes special trailers are provided by shipper/consignee.

Liability—A minimum insurance to be provided by trucker; shipper/consignee is held harmless from trucker actions.

Loss and Damage—Terms contained here as to liability of trucker for goods of shipper/consignee. Can range from no liability to absolute. Claim process is specified.

Force Mature—Statement to the effect that major circumstances such as plant fires, etc. that constitute major, unforeseen, harmful events upon either party may temporarily suspend the contract.

Nontransferability—Contract is usually not transferable by either party.

Time and Termination—Length of contract, termination notice, and minimum time for some.

Signatures—By both parties.

Contracts have become very flexible in the past several years. For example, it is very common for a contract to specify "general commodities," for points of service to be shown as "within the 48 contiguous United States," and/or the rate to be stated on a per mile basis, such as $1.00 per loaded mile. Many contract carriers have little or no actual equipment. They rely upon owner-operators who haul freight for any carrier. In these instances there is little need to schedule shipments to assure a return load. Upon delivery the owner-operator is released to find shipments for himself from brokers or other carriers in the surrounding area. Finally, the flexibility of contract carriage is particularly appealing with some carriers who require a minimum tender of one pound or one shipment. Many carriers offer this term as a matter of competitive convenience.

Insights into Private Carriage

Private carriage is estimated by many sources to carry approximately twenty-five percent of all intercity freight tonnage in the U.S. Many firms cite positive reasons for having initiated private carriage. These range from lower transportation costs than that available from for-hire carriers, special equipment needs not readily available elsewhere, or route flexibility not possible from for-hire carriers. Some shippers/consignees are entering into private carriage today in order to be assured service availability through the deregulation shake-out period in which many carriers will probably regroup or withdraw from many markets.

A major caution should be kept in mind with regard to private carriages. While private carriage might present some desirable benefits to the employing firm, it is perhaps the highest risk form of service available. Risks are associated with equipment investment or leasehold obligations, employee hiring and management, and adopting the flow of inbound and outbound goods to it rather than the other way around. This latter phenomenon can often increase inventory and/or decrease service quality in materials management or customer service. For example, a problem arises when the fleet manager holds up shipment in order to accumulate a full truckload.

Private carriage should be regarded as a venture of last resort. The competitiveness of for-hire carriers and the decreased regulatory constraints that are now present provide many opportunities for finding needed service without having to resort to private carriage. In addition, negotiated special services are now possible with common carriers. A wealth of contract carriers enables a wide range of cost/service configurations. And, a myriad of hybrid carriage forms, from piggybacks to shipper associations, might be able to provide the needed service. Private carriage should only be embarked upon if the cost or service objective desired is not available from other, less risky sources.

One recent innovation in the area of private carriage is the use of arms-length contract carriers. An arms-length contract carrier is one who serves only one firm. A variation of this is the owner-operator who obtains a contract carrier permit from the ICC and acts in a close-link fashion with one shipper-consignee. These options provide many of the benefits of private carriage without the long-run commitment or risk.

Dynamic Changes in Regulation

Political winds and pressures for changes in transportation laws and regulations started in the late 1960s. Deregulation, or reregulation, became a serious issue in each congressional session in the 1970s, and it accelerated under the Carter Administration from 1976 to 1980. The pressure for change was reinforced by fuel shortages and capital problems of motor, rail, and air modes as well as bankruptcies in the rail industry. Air freight was deregulated late in 1977; passenger carriers and large freight carriers were greatly deregulated in 1978. The Motor Carrier Act of 1980 and the Staggers Rail Act of 1980 are of major importance to purchasing managers.[1] Both of these acts greatly amended the Revised Interstate Commerce Act.[2] These laws have caused extensive changes in service availability and rate practices to industry in general. And, these impacts are still unfolding as the ICC amends and writes specific administrative regulations that correspond to the 1980 acts.

Table 10–2 presents the major motor, rail, and air transportation regulatory changes since the late 1970s that have or will affect purchasing and materials.

Released Rates

A normal common carrier rate places liability upon the carrier for the full value of the goods being shipped, unless they are lost or damaged by an act of God, public enemy, or public authority; by the inherent nature of the goods or through shipper negligence. A released rate is a lower than normal rate in exchange for a reduced level of liability. Released rates now may be offered without ICC approval. Careful analysis is required here, however. Released rates have been known to result in some carriers becoming lax in the handling and security of goods. In some instances, though, the goods owner can realize a savings. The following information presents a real example from the glassware industry.

```
Shipments = 1,000,000 lbs. yearly
Product weight: 1 pound
Product value: $2.00/unit
```

☐ **TABLE 10-2.** *Regulatory Changes of Importance to Purchasing*

Feature	Former Setting	Importance of Change
Motor transportation policy	All services/rates of common carriers had to be the same.	Price/service offerings to reflect needs of shippers and receivers. Negotiated prices and services now possible with common carriers.
New or expanded motor carrier service	Very difficult to enter into trucking or expand routes. Required ICC hearings.	Only financial fitness and shipper or receiver support is now needed. New services or expanded ones are now easily and quickly obtained if current carriage is not adequate.
Private carriage operations	Many restrictions on how service provided; even service from one subsidiary to another was prohibited.	Private truck operation can haul for other firms on what would otherwise be empty backhaul. Can serve other subsidiaries, if one hundred percent owned by parent firm. Can more easily obtain owner-operator as contractor and utilize as private carrier without having to own equipment and employ driver.
Contract carriage	Limited to only eight shippers/receivers. Must apply for rights from ICC for every new route. Same carrier could not also provide common carriage.	Common/contract services possible by same firm. Unlimited shippers/receivers. Rights are general in nature; no new application needed for new routes, plants, shippers, receivers. Negotiated, stable rate makes budgeting easier.
Released rates	Only a few commodities	Any commodity; see discussion.
Rate bureau changes	Carriers could collectively set rates. Most rates the same. Negotiation very difficult. Tariffs covered all carriers.	Carriers immunity from antitrust is now limited. Carriers cannot collectively set rates that apply only on their own line. Easier to negotiate with carriers. Requires separatae tariff for each carrier. More difficult to determine rates of all carriers.
Rate changes	Very few rates change with less than thirty-day notice. Shippers/receivers and competing carriers could protest rates.	Rates can change more quickly. Ability to protest now severely limited. More difficult to budget for freight costs.
Rail rates	Subject to ICC review. Relatively easy for user firms to protest if too high.	Carrier flexibility is enlarged; shipper-receiver ability to protest now limited. Little recourse if rates too high.
Contracts (Rail)	Not allowed until 1978.	Opportunity for car supply, service, or rate break by buyers.

☐ **TABLE 10-2.** *Continued*

Feature	Former Setting	Importance of Change
		Confidentiality of contracts means buyer cannot determine what competitor is paying for inbound moves.
Released rates	Limited until 1980.	Now easily put into place by rail carrier. See discussion.
Route or branch line surcharges	Nonexistent until 1980.	Can mean sudden rate hike on certain lines; buyer or vendor has no recourse. Means higher rates on certain routes or on branch lines; might suddenly make a vendor uneconomical to procure from.
Abandonments	Difficult to drop lines until 1980.	Low traffic lines now easily dropped by carriers. Shippers/receivers have to seek alternative services.

    Carrier loss and damage experience: 1/2 of 1%
    Full Rate: $6.00 per 100 units
    Released rate: $3.50 per 100 units, maximum liability $.50/lb.
Full rate analysis:
    Transportation cost: $60,000
    Loss/damage: 5,000 units
                       $10,000 value
    Carrier reimbursement: $10,000
    Total cost: $60,000 plus value of outstanding funds during loss and damage claim settlement
Released rate analysis:
    Transportation cost: $35,000
    Loss/damage: 5,000 units
                       $10,000 value
    Carrier reimbursement: $2,500
    Total cost = $35,000 + $10,000 − $2,500 plus value of funds outstanding in claims process or about *$42,500*

The portion of liability not covered by the carrier, however, might be covered through company-secured insurance.

Line Traffic Functions in the Firm

Traffic is the function of purchasing transportation services for the firm. The specific activities conducted in traffic correspond to the purchasing process outlined in Chapter 2. The following areas are of prime importance:

1. the specific tasks of traffic,
2. the total cost of a transportation service choice,
3. carrier selection criteria,
4. carrier evaluation methods.

Traffic Tasks

Traffic departments generally perform eight basic functions, and occasionally a ninth. These are as follows.

1)*Shipment Planning*—This activity involves forward planning to ensure that the proper type and quantities of carriage will be available at the time needed. This often entails negotiating with carriers for service and price packages, arranging adequate car or truck capacity, and stipulating the timing of service. For short-term commitments, planning involves scheduling equipment and service in order to maintain a smooth, noncongested flow of goods inbound and outbound. Materials Requirements Planning can be used to forward-plan carriage supply needs. One firm uses MRP on exceptions report to indicate any future inbound flows that will exceed the weekly capacity of the regular carrier firms serving that plant.

2)*Carrier Selection*—This is the process of selecting the actual railroad, rail route, or motor carrier for each specific move. The process is conceptually similar to that presented in Chapter 5, Assurance of Supply. On the whole, traffic managers seek to maintain a competitive price and service posture among several carriers serving each facility. Carrier selection is presented in greater detail later in this section.

3)*Ordering Service*—This is the act of contacting the selected carrier in order to arrange each shipment. Usually this is accomplished through a phone call to a railroad car distributor, motor carrier city dispatcher, or broker. The information sought by these carrier personnel includes shipment point, destination, commodity, form of packaging, weight, and sometimes on approximation of cubic size. The required piece of equipment is often stipulated. Scheduling of vehicle arrival is often necessary to facilitate the shipping dock flow efficiencies.

4)*Tracing/Expediting/De-expediting*—As in purchasing, tracing is a constant traffic activity in order to determine inbound shipment arrival at a plant, distribution center, or customer. Tracing involves phone communication with carrier terminals; some shippers-consignees are directly computer-linked with rail carriers. One facet of carrier marketing and customer service is on-line shipment tracing systems that can instantaneously report shipment location and estimated time of arrival.

Expediting is the process of speeding up shipment arrival. In some motor carrier instances, expediting is not possible due to speed and driver road-time limitations. Some motor shipments can be speeded up by tagging them and having them specially handled through intermediate terminals. Rail movers, likewise, can sometimes be expedited by contacting carrier sales or customer service personnel who are knowledgeable about terminal processes and capabilities. Such actions can cut transit time by as much as one day per major enroute terminal.

De-expediting means slowing up shipment arrival. This is often requested in order to avoid unloading dock congestion, smooth out unloading labor activities, even out dock work loads (e.g. avoid overtime on one day just to have slack time the next), reduce warehouse congestion, and to improve cash flow if the credit period begins on day of delivery. Carriers will often abide by de-expediting requests. They do so by slowing down the shipment travel or by holding it at the last enroute terminal. Care must be taken here, however, since carrier detention and demurrage charges often begin to accrue on goods held up enroute. Even if such charges are not applied by the carrier, the free holding of goods can be construed as an illegal discriminatory service that can cause both receiver and carrier to be liable to federal laws governing such practices.

5)*Preauditing/Rating*—Freight bills for carrier freight charges are often preaudited, and in some instances shippers insert what they believe to be the correct rate on the bill of lading. This latter act is called rating. Many shippers, and receivers conduct pre-auditing in order to verify the accuracy of the charges. The advantage of preauditing is to avoid incorrect charges and a later claim. Even if shippers pay the freight bills and pass on the charges to the buyer in an invoice with the goods, it is wise practice for the buyer to verify the charges.

6)*Paying the Freight Bill*—Another traffic function is to initially process the freight bill prior to payment by accounting. This usually entails matching up the carrier delivery receipt with the freight bill and a prepared voucher that contains budget codes for commodities, plants, etc.

One advantage of vendor freight bill payment and inclusion of these charges on the invoice for the goods is the cash flow benefit for the buyer. Carrier credit regulations currently require common carrier rail bills to be paid within 120 hours, and common motor carrier bills within seven days from their receipt. If these bills are paid to the carrier by the vendor and charged back on the invoice to the buyer, then buyer payment for freight charges can be affectively lengthened to thirty, forty-five or however many days the invoice for the goods is outstanding. In essence, the buyer has taken, say, forty-five days to pay the freight bill without violating transportation credit regulations. A disadvantage of this practice is that the vendor might not place great care or attention to rate costs or freight bill accuracy. Several pointers here are: freight rate negotiations might not be sought by the vendor, economical transportation alternatives might not be explored, bills might not be audited, and the gross freight charge might be passed on to the buyer with the vendor receiving an end-of-month discount rebate from the carrier. Good buyer practice here is to request a copy of the freight bill from the vendor and to verify its accuracy. Some firms audit all such bills; some audit only random or systematic samples. Other firms go so far as to seek favorable rates from the inbound carriers but continue to have vendors pay the bills and charge them back. This is often the case when vendor traffic departments are small or weak.

One final point, freight bills can be audited for overcharges for up to three years from their date. Many traffic firms will audit bills and be compensated a percentage of whatever overcharges are collected. This is a low cost, low risk beneficial practice for purchasing managers.

7)*Detention/Demurrage Processes*—These two terms refer to motor carrier and railroad charges to shippers and receivers for detaining equipment beyond a stipulated free period for loading or unloading. These costs are often charged to whomever receives the freight bill in the firm. Fast dock loading and unloading will avoid such charges. But, dock congestion, warehouse manpower assignments elsewhere, plant space shortages, or the use of a rail car or truck for temporary storage due to a production schedule shippage are just a few reasons why equipment unloading will be delayed. A problem often arises here in that the equipment delay is at the request or convenience of production or warehousing personnel, but detention/demurrage charges often accrue to traffic or purchasing. This is poor responsibility accounting, since the latter two might not have caused the delay. Such charges should be passed on to the department(s) causing the delay. Even though many motor carriers do not charge detention, equipment delay will often force rates up due to slow capital utilization of the equipment.

8)*Claims*—Loss and damage occurs with all shipments to varying degrees. Transportation hazards range from theft, mishandling, misrouting, poor stowage to impact, to compression and water damage. All these hazards are tracked down for both claim payment on immediate shipments in question as well as to diagnose causes for preventive measures in the future.

9)*Private Truck or Car Fleets*—Many firms have their own private motor fleets or privately owned or leased rail cars. This entails a substantial administrative activity. Privately owned fleets provide a carriage supply or service not available from regular carriers as well as favorable landed costs in comparison to other forms, but several cautions are relevant here. First, the fleet might not be cost competitive with for-hire carriers or the private fleet of the vendor. A second caution concerns the service attained from the fleet. For-hire carriers can be called for daily service. The private fleet might not be able to handle a shipment on a desired day. Or, the fleet manager might accumulate shipment requests over several days in order to run a full vehicle. A third problem arises for the firm as a whole if the fleet was justified on the basis of two-way hauls; that is, outbound to customers and inbound from vendors in the same area. This can dictate buying from vendors who are no longer cost or quality competitive. These are just three concerns for purchasing managers to be aware of when the firm is considering or using private fleets.

Many traffic departments conduct routine staff activities as well. These include rate negotiations, service negotiations, special equipment planning, budgeting, capital investment analyses, and distribution studies. It is the goal of many traffic managers to, in effect, pay for the total yearly administrative costs of the department through cost savings, payback from studies, and activities conducted by the staff area.

Total Cost of Transportation

Given the changes taking place in transportation, purchasing managers stand to gain many benefits from closer links to this area. One of the major decision tools is the determination of the total cost of transportation. This figure can be used to evaluate whether the purchasing manager or vendor should arrange the move. It is a useful tool in determining which form of transportation to select.

1)*Rate*—The basic carrier charge is the primary starting point. It is the most visable of all cost factors, and it is often the easiest cost factor to determine. All too often this is the only decision criterion used; high-rate carriers often are overlooked, yet they might be the lowest in total cost.

2)*Packaging/Bracing and Dunnage*—These are the costs required in packaging, lumber, strapping, covers, etc. in order to safely move and stow the goods. Rail and steamship movements often require heavy lumber crating in order to comply with tariff provisions designed to reduce damage to goods while in carrier possession. Motor and air freight moves will usually require less shipment packaging and bracing. Rail car or truck preparation costs such as cleaning or sanitizing prior to loading are included here. Even within one carrier mode, different equipment will require different packaging and shipment preparation needs. Grain can be moved in sacks, in bulk in box cars that require expensive shipper-supplied corrugated grain doors, or in large lot size bulk in top-loading, covered hopper cars that require little, if any, preshipment cleaning. The use of specially equipped rail and motor carrier equipment avoids the need for packaging, bracing, or dunnage. The necessary features are built-in for the product being moved.

3)*Access*—The prime mode of transportation and the rate charged by the carrier might include door to door service, or it might require a special movement to be able to load it onto the carrier's equipment. For example, motor carriage can provide door-to-door service, but air and water shipments usually require special pick-up and delivery moves to and from the terminals of those carriers. This is a necessary cost component in the move.

4)*Loading/Unloading*—The act of physically loading and unloading the transportation vehicle is a necessary component, even though the buyer is not paying this cost directly out of his or her budget. A major trade-off exists here between transportation and warehousing that often has an impact upon purchasing and sales. For example, one frozen food shipper in the Pacific Northwest found it best to hand load refrigerator piggyback trailers in order to get as many packages into the trailer as possible. Since the rate was the same regardless of shipment weight, the unit pound rate cost for each box of food was minimized. The buyer was pleased with the dense loading and low unit rate, but was unhappy when his firm started to charge his budget for warehouse unloading that required two persons at eight hours each. The buyer determined that a less densely loaded, palletized shipment could be unloaded in one hour. Further, the faster loading and unloading helped avoid detention charges. So, while the shipment now bears a higher unit rate cost, the total landed cost is lower.

5)*Insurance*—This cost is found in ocean moves and in any shipment involving a very high value product.

6)*Time Value of Goods in Transit*—This is an opportunity cost of the value of goods in transit. The formula for this cost is

$$\text{Cost of Goods in Transit} = (\text{Value of Goods}) \times (\text{Company Cost of Capital}) \times (\text{Days in Transit}/365).$$

This cost will not appear on any one department budget, but accounting and finance personnel are aware of its existence. It is a true economic cost to the firm. Goods in transit represent resources that are owned or committed but are not usable at that time. A $50,000 shipment enroute for ten days with company cost of capital at fifteen percent has a cost of $406, while a three-day move has a cost of $123. This cost has a major bearing upon such company measures as inventory turnover or return on assets. Of course, if goods are being purchased FOB destination and the credit period begins upon shipment arrival, then this cost is minimal.

7)*Loss and Damage*—This is the total cost from goods experiencing damage or being lost in transit. It includes the cost of the claim filing process, but it is tempered by any claim settlement by carriers or insurance firms. The time the claim is outstanding must be included. This is figured as the claim amount times opportunity cost times days outstanding in terms of proportion of the 365-day year.

8)*Documentation*—The process of preparing shipment documents must be included in this total cost equation. Documentation for domestic shipments is relatively simple, but international shipment documents are complex and require considerable expenditure in time and costs. The paperwork process can entail upwards of twenty separate documents, and the access bill of lading alone is often required in the form of five original copies.

9)*Cash Flow in Freight Bill Payment*—Domestic regulations require common rail bill payment in 120 hours and common motor bill payment in seven days. Contract carriage in these modes can be paid in a period defined by the contract. A bill of $500 payable in thirty days versus seven days at a company capital cost of sixteen percent represents a cash opportunity of $5.04. If a rail contract move is involved that costs $10,000, the difference between 120 hour payment and fifteen days is $43.84 in opportunity costs. Granted, these do not appear to be large sums, but they are if such movements are repeated a thousand times in a quarter.

☐ **TABLE 10-3.** *Ship Versus Air*

SAMPLE COST ANALYSIS

$/Lb. Surface		$/Lb. Air	
Tariff	.094	Tariff	.532
Packaging	.064	Packaging	.030
Inventory Costs:		Inventory Costs:	
Shipper	.514	Shipper	.313
Consignee	.719	Consignee	.476
Transit	.086	Transit	.008
Transportation		Transportation	
Insurance	.026	Insurance	.017
Pick-up Cost	.018	Pick-up Cost	.006
TOTAL	$1.521	TOTAL	$1.382

☐ Source: Advertisement-Scandinavian Airlines. "When you ship by water, the only thing that goes fast is your money." *Aircargo Magazine*, March 1982, p. 15.

One major international airline advertises a cost comparison using many of the above factors. Table 10–3 shows the per pound cost of shipping overseas via ship versus airplane in one analysis of a particular commodity and shipment size.

These nine factors comprise the direct total costs of one form of shipping over another. The major point here is that the actual rate charged by one carrier represents only one part of this equation. Although an air rate might be higher than a motor rate, the total costs might favor the air mode, likewise with higher motor rates versus lower rail charges.

Carrier Selection Factors

Selecting one carrier over another in the same mode is another major decision in traffic. Many factors are considered in this decision. The factors considered by purchasing managers are presented from a survey conducted by the American Trucking Association and *Purchasing World Magazine*.[4] Table 10–4 presents the rankings of various factors.

Fifteen various factors are considered by purchasing managers. On time reliability and shipment transit time are shown, along with the shipment car, as being more important than the actual rate charged. Some purchasers will use a superior service carrier who charges a premium rate. On the other hand, rates are the subject of intense negotiation today. A carrier who will not negotiate for lower rates often will not get future business from a buyer. In this instance, the carrier will not be selected on the basis of rates. Once a lower rate is negotiated, this factor becomes of lesser relative importance, and service factors are then considered more important.

The fifteen factors are price and quality attributes of carrier services. Yet, service is an intangible product. Service factors might be ranked one way by one buyer and another way by a second buyer. Similarly, one buyer might feel that one factor is important one day and switch to an-

☐ **TABLE 10-4.** *Carrier Selection Factors*

Motor Carrier Characteristic	Purchasers' Ranking
On-time deliveries	1
Care in handling	2
Time in transit	3
Rates	4
Shipment tracing	5
Insurance Coverage	6
Door-to-door deliveries	7
Claims record	8
Regular schedules	9
Shipment security	10
Through routing	11
Geographic coverage	12
Types of equipment	13
Consolidating/breaking capabilities	14
Intermodal capabilities	15

other the next day. These phenomena point to the difficult nature of carrier management and marketing. For these reasons it is useful, if not imperative, that close communications exist among shipper, carrier, and purchaser with regard to needs and capabilities. It is also necessary for a buyer who prefers a certain carrier to check with his/her vendor regarding the vendor's experience with the same carrier. A carrier might provide superior service in one region but not be so in another where the vendor is located.

Conclusion

The transportation industry has undergone a great degree of change in recent years and will continue to do so throughout the 1980s. Though many of the regulatory changes were made in the interest of transportation consumers, not all will benefit and those who wish new advantages must actively seek them. Transportation and traffic can no longer be regarded passively as a constant "given" by purchasing managers.

Transportation decisions must now be made in tandem with the vendor decision. That is, purchasing is now and in the future faced with "double vendor" concept in each purchasing decision. Not only must each vendor be considered as in the past, but the cost, availability, and quality of inbound movement must also become part of the purchase decision. In the past, three of five vendors in the country might have been the company sources. Uniform carrier rates or equalized vendor pricing might have made the inbound logistics factors comparable for all three. Now these logistics factors are changing and dynamically fluid. One vendor might no longer be economical to purchase from, and perhaps a fourth vendor may now have low cost carrier service available. This analysis cannot be performed just once, it must become a continuous evaluation process.

Transportation is a vital part of the firm's position and advantage in the marketplace. It has long played a vital role in the firm's outbound distribution system, but there are now too many opportunities on the inbound side for this function to be regarded as a responsibility of the vendor's traffic manager. Many of these concepts are discussed further in Chapter 19, Supply Strategies. Purchasing and transportation will, of necessity, evolve closer in the future.

SOURCES FOR FURTHER READING

Blanding, Warren. *Blanding's Practical Physical Distribution*. Washington: Traffic Service Corp., 1978.

Bowersox, Donald J. *Logistical Management*. New York: Macmillan Publishing, 1974.

Cavinato, Joseph L. *Transportation-Logistics Dictionary*. 2d ed. Washington: Traffic Service Corp., 1982.

Coyle, John J., and Bardi, Edward J. *The Management of Business Logistics*. 2d ed. St. Paul, MN: West Publishing, 1980.

Coyle, John J.; Bardi, Edward J.; and Cavinato, Joseph L. *Transportation*. St. Paul, MN: West Publishing, 1982.

Flood, Kenneth U. *Traffic Management*. Dubuque, IA: William C. Brown Co., 1975.

Harper, Donald V. *Transportation in America: Users, Carriers, Government*. 2d ed. Englewood Cliffs, NJ: Prentice-Hall, 1982.

Lieb, Robert C. *Transportation: The Domestic System.*2d ed. Reston, VA: Reston Publishing, 1981.

Morse, Leon Wm. *Practical Handbook of Industrial Traffic Management.* 6th ed. Washington: Traffic Service Corp., 1980.

Sampson, Roy J., and Farris, Martin T. *Domestic Transportation: Practice, Theory, and Policy.* 4th ed. Boston: Houghton Mifflin Co., 1979.

Taff, Charles. *Management of Physical Distribution and Transportation.* Homewood, IL: Richard D. Irwin, 1978.

Wood, Donald F., and Johnsosn, James C. *Contemporary Transportation.* Tulsa, OK: Petroleum Publishing, 1980.

FOOTNOTES

1. Public Law 96-296, *The Motor Carrier Act of 1980*, July 1, 1980; and Public Law 96–448,*The Staggers Rail Act of 1980*, October 14, 1980 (U.S. Government Printing Office).
2. Public Law 95–473, *The Revised Interstate Commerce Act*, as amended; also found in Title 49, *Code of Federal Regulations*.
3. Title 49, *Code of Federal Regulations*, Part 1043, 1982.
4. Richard L. Dunn, ed. "A Basic Guide to Choosing Transportation Services." *Purchasing World*, September 1982, p. 47.

QUESTIONS FOR REVIEW

1. Why is it now important to evaluate and use transportation factors in the purchasing decision?

2. Distinguish between the four legal forms of transportation.

3. What shipper-receiver benefits are found with specialized rail or motor equipment?

4. What are the pros and cons of contract carriage?

5. What changes in services, rates, etc. does a shipper or receiver notice when a form of transportation becomes deregulated?

6. What are some of the benefits and risks of private carriage?

7. How has pricing of transportation changed by rail and motor carriers since 1980?

8. How has rail and motor entry into and exit from the market changed since 1980?

9. How should a consignee evaluate the use of a released rate?

10. What are some reasons why a purchaser should specify the exact method and carrier for inbound movements when the freight is initially paid by the vendor?

11. How are the line functions of traffic similar to those of purchasing?

12. Why is the carrier rate not the only factor to consider in a movement?

11

CHAPTER OBJECTIVES

After reading this chapter you should:

- Understand why firms will source product overseas.

- Be able to analyze and determine the major costs of importing.

- Understand the basic functions involved with letters of credit and other means of goods payment.

- Appreciate the role of many facilitating firms in overseas trade.

International Purchasing

Introduction

International purchasing is widely practiced by many U.S. firms. Many companies are new to the activity, while others have not yet explored nor practiced it. Import sourcing is an activity that presents many new opportunities to a firm. It also presents some risks and necessitates that firms possess some completely different expertise than that needed in domestic purchasing.

International purchasing is becoming a necessary avenue of sourcing for many firms. Trade processes are easing, and foreign markets represent new opportunities for the firm. The strategic position of a firm is very much tied to international activities. The foreign sources may be advantageous in price, quality, supply or even in marketing areas. Unlike the past where most products might have been available domestically, today's contemporary purchasing manager often must have an eye toward international markets.

This chapter explores international sourcing with its contraints, opportunities, and various approaches. It then presents an overview of international logistics activities and systems that are used to move products. The services of various facilitators are useful in foreign trade as well. Finally, several concerns of overall international magnitude are presented that should be part of every long-term foreign sourcing endeavor.

Why Firms Purchase Internationally

Firms seek overseas goods and sources for many reasons. Many of these reasons are opportunity-related, while other companies are forced into it due to the lack of domestic sourcing alternatives available to them.

Broader Markets

As world economies develop and transportation links become less difficult, foreign sourcing becomes more feasible. Many foreign nations are entering into chemical markets in ways that make them viable sources. Brazil, India, Iraq, Nigeria, Saudi Arabia, Korea, and Turkey are just a few countries involved. Their entrance into the market results from many reasons, which range from national employment and export development efforts, favorable export transportation rates, to U.S. domestic firms dropping basic lines due to competitive low margins. These reasons give rise to the need to look overseas for cost savings or quality-enhanced sources.

Small or Reduced Domestic Supply

Many raw materials are not available in the U.S. Others are available domestically, but the composite of labor, refining, and shipping costs allow importers to underprice the domestic sources. Still other materials are not available domestically because some U.S. firms have dropped production due to the high cost of conforming to the provisions of the Occupational Safety Hazards Administration and Environmental Protection Agency regulations.

Import sourcing is continual for many firms, while for others it is only a periodic practice. For example, poor grape and raisin crops in California increase domestic prices above the minimum level at which they may be obtained from Spain and other Mediterranean countries. In bad crop years, overseas sources are often the only ones available.

Price/Quality Advantages

Some foreign sources are price competitive or contain certain desired qualities as compared to domestic sources. Sweden, for example, is a large source of aeronautical equipment, and it is very competitive against domestic suppliers.

Countertrade

Some firms import goods from a certain nation so that the sales group of that same firm may make a sale there. This is particularly important with nations that have a currency that is not easily converted on the world market, or if the country does not possess hard foreign currencies to pay for such purchases. The purchase of raw materials by the firm provides the resource to consumate the sale.

International Sourcing

International sourcing is conceptually similar to that in domestic markets, however, some differences in approach must be employed. Sources should be reliable, creditworthy, provide the product quality needed, be competitive, and have all the other attributes discussed in Section I of this text. The international buying area, on the other hand, has some constraints that must be kept in mind when buying.

Sourcing Approach

Several additional steps or areas of emphasis should be covered by purchasing when buying internationally. The first step is to have a sound idea that foreign sourcing is needed or that the opportunity for doing so exists. The studies that will be required to make this determination will demand extra effort, costs, and even manpower. These studies will have to be justified by reason of high prices, tight supplies domestically, or numerous other factors. Second, a visit to potential foreign sources is often necessary. No amount of sales literature will present many of the tangible and intangible details that a personal visit will uncover. International sourcing involves higher risks, and information obtained on a visit will go far in measuring and possibly overcoming some of this risk.

Third, profiles should be developed and business terms established with potential sources. Exporting experience is a necessity, but it takes many years for a company to become systematic at exporting. Exporting systems, procedures, and legal requirements are often burdensome. A company that does not have to undergo the learning curve with its concurrent and unexpected costs passed on to the buyer is an almost essential asset to the firm entering foreign sourcing for the first time. Potential sources should be asked for references in the U.S. or Canada. Economical information or credit references are also helpful, although these are not always freely available in overseas firms. In this realm, the buyer is seeking insights into the foreign company's ability to withstand the added inventory and distribution costs of overseas selling. A key detail to be determined is the quality of the materials management system in the firm. Many foreign firms are not as sophisticated as U.S. companies in handling multiple, fast deliveries, large volume vendors, or the large production lot sizes that might be required by the purchaser.

A further detail to seek is a U.S. contact representing the foreign source. U.S. contacts simplify communications, time-of-day, language, and even customs differences. This representative should be technically knowledgeable and available for any problems that might arise in the relationship. The purchaser should also ascertain the vendor's long-term commitment to the export market. Because international sales and buying requires some initial and on-going administrative burden, an indication should be sought as to how long or to what degree the vendor intends to sell in this new market. A source that is merely attempting to sell overseas in order to tide the firm over a local recession should be avoided. Finally, the extent and quality of transportation links should be investigated. Some nations require that a certain percentage of their exports be made in national flag ships, but the delay in waiting for such sailings can be weeks or months.

The economy and the political situation in the country is another important sourcing information item. An unstable political setting might lead to plant, transportation, or port closings. Or, the product and country might be prone to joining a cartel in the future. Relying only on this foreign source in the event of one of these events would be a problem, especially if the firm's competitor is strongly allied with a long-standing domestic source that has limited capacity to grow.

A final step into international sourcing is to develop in-house expertise on foreign markets and buying. This expertise should include knowledge of importing processes as well as transportation and financing systems. This step is an expensive, threshold cost, but it is necessary if foreign sourcing is to become a standard practice in the firm. Without it the firm can blindly incur higher costs or lose opportunities in the marketplace.[1]

Importing Constraints

Many additional buying-related elements exist in this realm that are minor or nonexistent in domestic sourcing. These can represent constraints to the foreign sourcing process.

Countertrade Requirement

This situation arises when the firm or one of its customers seeks to sell goods overseas in nations that require countertrade, buy-back, swap, compensation or switch as it is often referred to.[2] A countertrade requirement states that along with the sale, there must be a certain amount of buying from that country. For example, a purchasing department may be required to seek sources in a certain nation because its own sales department or that of a customer is making a sale there. The rationale for this practice is to develop export industries as well as to earn the U.S. currency to make the purchase of goods that the firm is selling. This constraint has led many purchasers to discover good sources that would have otherwise been overlooked, but it can force a search in a foreign country that is not economical to the firm. If this is the case, any penalty or diseconomies incurred in the purchasing realm must be weighed against the value of the sales.

Trigger Prices

Domestic industries that are being harmed by lower-priced foreign sources often can seek trigger price protection from the U.S. government. This protection is designed to prevent undercutting of prices that would harm domestic sources. It is a mechanism used in the steel industry if the prevailing foreign prices drop to a certain point. In that situation, the trigger price will be imposed, which becomes a new price floor for imported steel. The problem often cited here is that the trigger price floor forces the buyer to seek some products that are no longer available domestically and, in this case, it merely raises the price on imported goods.[3]

"Buy American" Terms

Many customers, especially federal, state, and local government agencies place terms into purchase contracts that require the firm to use domestically produced components. This requirement is designed to protect domestic industries and employment. But, it often forces the purchaser to use higher priced vendors who might not provide the quality, service, or lead time available from a foreign source.

Barters

Bartering is an extension of the countertrade arrangement and usually entails buying and selling between two countries where one or both parties has a weak or untradeable currency. Bartering has become useful in the trade of copper from Peru to Hungary in exchange for buses. The arrangement is nonmonetary.

Another example is the Pepsi Cola Co. sale of syrup to Russia. Rather than receive hard currency in payment for the sales it makes, Pepsi Cola obtained a like value of vodka, which it is now selling in the West. In other settings, an industrial firm will build a plant in a foreign country and take back a minimum quantity of this foreign output for hard western currency markets. A more complicated arrangement is the famed Russian gas deal with Europe. Russia has little pipe and pump production capacity. Western Europe has this capacity, and it needs the gas. This arrangement involves two firms or organizations and the central banks of each nation. First, an agreement is made between all six parties. A German pump manufacturer ships pumps and pipes to Russia. It is paid in German currency from the German bank. The Russian pipeline construction agency installs the pump and pays the Russian bank in the local currency. Once gas is shipped by the Russian gas agency, that agency is paid out of the local currency account by the Russian bank. The German gas distributor receives the gas and pays the German bank for it. Once the pumps are paid for, the arrangement reverts to direct German currency payment to the Russian gas company. In the meantime no borrowing of German currency was necessary by the Russian organization or government.[4]

Problems associated with bartering include finding a desirable commodity to take in return, having the acquired goods up to a marketable quality, and being able to actually use them in-house. An additional concern is that the foreign source might learn exporting trade on the arrangement only to begin competing against the firm on the open market with extra output. On the other hand, some firms have gained an edge on sourcing certain products that take competitors many years to copy.

Currency Levels

The relative position of currency exchange between one nation and another affects the price level of traded purchases and sales between them. These exchange rates often pose a benefit and disadvantage to the firm at the same time.

For example, an American purchaser in the 1960s bought components from Germany that cost four German marks each. At the time the German mark was $.25, so the price to the American firm was $1.00 per unit. By the early 1970s the rate of exchange went against the dollar. By 1971 the mark cost $.40. Now the same unit cost $1.60 to the American firm with no actual price increases made by the exporting German manufacturer. In this case an importer could be caught in a cost increase situation when the dollar drops in relation to the exporter's currency. This situation can occur within the order cycle time of one purchase. That is, one expenditure figure might be planned upon for several months only to have to pay a higher figure required on the day of ship's loading from the export nation. On the other hand, a dollar drop will make American exports relatively cheaper to foreign importers.

Currency fluctuations in the reverse can benefit a purchaser. For example, a firm imports an item from Canada in the middle 1970s when both dollars were about equal to each other. The item cost an American importer $2.00 each, and he purchases in lots costing $20,000 or 10,000 units. By 1982, the Canadian dollar dropped to $.80 American. Now the same unit can be purchased by the American for $1.60, or he can obtain 12,500 in each $20,000 lot. Inflation differences in both countries were ignored for simplicity sake in this comparison.

Currency devaluations will produce price decreases for American importers. These devaluations have the effect of lowering the cost of buying from a country, since more of its currency can than be purchased for each American dollar. On the other hand, the company probably will experience a drop or loss of sales to the same country, since the American item costs the foreign importer so much more after the devaluation.

Currency levels are a real cost factor that cannot be ignored by purchasers. The problem is that the changes are often not predictable, and they are totally beyond control of the firm. They constitute a true risk factor in conducting overseas business.

Components of International Logistics

Frequently the cost of inbound logistics from foreign sources can be as much or more than the price of the goods. This is particularly the case with raw ores or other low dollar-per-pound commodities. Also, the movement from a foreign vendor's location to a U.S. plant can involve upwards of twenty separate parties. This situation is distinct from a domestic purchase that involves just the firm, vendor, carrier, post office (for billing and paying), and both firms' banks. This section presents overviews of the total cost components of purchasing from abroad, including the supply of transportation alternatives, insurance and claims, terms of sale, means of payment, documentation, and customs.

The Total Cost of Movement

The cost of moving goods to the U.S. only initially consists of the purchase price. That price must be stated in terms of *where* it is the price. That is, if it is FOB vendor's plant, then the buyer must arrange and directly pay for inland freight to the port, and all costs from there. This is difficult to arrange from the U.S. On the other hand, an FOB port-of-import term provides a price that includes all services up to the port of off-loading. No matter what the terms, the price is just one component with all the other logistics costs borne directly by the buyer or included and paid indirectly in the price.

Inland transportation is the cost of movement of goods from the vendor's plant to the port and from the import port to the buyer's site. These costs include rail, truck, or water moves that involve carriers other than the ocean or air carrier. Port handling and storage are often overlooked but necessary costs. These costs are charges for handling and storing the goods at the port while awaiting the scheduled ship or air carrier. Sometimes this change can be provided conveniently by the inland carrier in a single service or billing. That is, this carrier may hold the goods at its own terminal and only deliver them to dockside within a day or two of sailing. This avoids the often higher cost of dockside warehouse storage. Storage costs can also be levied on the inbound side if the goods are not cleared through customs quickly upon off-loading.

Long haul transportation is an expense incurred for the ship or airplane movement. This cost includes the actual ship or plane loading and unloading and some obligation protection in the event of carrier loss and damage.

Packaging is the cost of crating, blocking, bracing, and loading into the container, etc. In ocean shipping by breakbulk, goods must often be sent to a crating firm that is familiar with the boxing and labeling requirements of the shipping line and country of import. Sea container moves do not require crating, but they do necessitate blocking and bracing. Moves by air require less protection. In each instance, the weight of the packaging is charged by all carriers at the same rate per pound as the goods themselves.

Insurance is a factor that should be almost never omitted. It covers loss and damage and obligations that can arise upon the goods' owner through little or no fault of his own.

Customs duties and taxes are other costs of overseas moves. Some nations assess a tax on exports. Imports are subject to customs by the United States. Linked with this cost is the fee to a customs broker who is often hired to assist the goods through clearance upon landing.

Finally, time in transit and the corresponding costs of financing and the opportunity costs of the involved funds are critical factors to consider. These expenses include the cost of arranging letters of credit and other documentation, as well as any "losses" associated with the funds tied up until the firm actually receives the goods. A formula for figuring this is the value of funds tied up $\times$ the company's opportunity rate of funds $\times$ the number days of funds tied up $\div$ 365. See Chapter 17 for a discussion of this cost concept. This cost component alone often causes a firm to use air transportation rather than ship even though the ship charges a lesser rate. The total costs of air transportation, with less packaging, insurance costs, and time in transit are often less than the costs of using a ship on packaged goods.

The total cost of movement will also include the use of parties such as freight forwarders, consulates, and bankers. These facilitators are necessary for arranging many of the required services in an import move, and their activities are discussed later.

Import movements can be handled in a myriad of buying and payment arrangements as well as transportation forms and routings. There are usually many possible ways of landing goods at a factory. For each, the total cost of all the above factors must be considered and analyzed. For example, the most efficient means of moving goods from the Mideast to Ohio might be not by all-water to Baltimore and then by truck, but rather by water and land across Europe, water to Montreal and then truck to Ohio. Many New York-New Jersey importers from Japan use water to the West Coast then container rail moves across to the East Coast. A coffee firm in California discontinued inbound ship movements from Columbia in favor of a through-container move via New Orleans and then by rail to the processing plant near San Diego. This might appear illogical, but it is possible. Any lower cost/less handling routing opportunity should be explored.

Supply of International Transportation

There are many forms of international carriage available to purchasers. Closer to home, shipments into the U.S. from Canada and Mexico can be transported overland via truck and rail using conventional storing, movement, and receiving procedures. But, overseas shipments must be made either by air or ship.

Air

Air freight generally consists of high value cargo that can withstand the relatively high freight charges. Fine sensitive goods such as stereos, publications, instruments, and even food often are shipped by air. The United States has an advantage of being reached easily within forty-eight hours from nearly all points in the world. Only scheduling and border clearances lengthen the transit time.

Air cargo movements are made in both passenger planes as well as in all-cargo planes. All cargo services are by schedule or complete plane charter. In both forms, the freight either can be palletized or containerized. Usually the container itself will not leave the destination airport, but some high volume air cargo buyers of clothes from the Far East have made arrangements to move the goods in containers all the way to their stores.

Ship

Ship services appear in three basic forms of carriage—liner, tramp, and private. Those categories define the type of service.

Liner ships and firms generally carry freight for the general public with scheduled, fixed route services. One company, for example, schedules service every ten days from Portland, Seattle, and Vancouver to Kobe, Yokohoma, Puson, Inchoa, Keelung, and Hong Kong. Sea-Land, another liner firm, operates weekly service from New York to Europe with large container ships and feeder service on both ends to and from smaller ports.

Liner service exists in five forms. First is breakbulk. Breakbulk means that the ship firm will handle packaging, crating, drumming, or bagging cargo. Freight is loaded onto the ship and stocked manually on the internal docks inside the ship. Nearly all sea freight was moved in this manner until World War II. The second form is container ships. Containers are boxes into which a shipper loads freight. These containers are attached to truck wheels and driven to the port. At shipside the container is lifted off the wheels and stacked onto the ship. The process is reversed at the off-loading port. Container moves reduce many of the packaging requirements of breakbulk service and enables faster transit time. A container ship can be completely unloaded and reloaded in six hours, whereas the same amount of freight in a breakbulk ship might take a week to unload. Container services exist on routes connecting major industrial nations of the world.

A third liner service offered by some firms is a RORO ship. RORO stands for roll-on-roll-off. Containers can be handled with this type of service, but the ship is not restricted to ports that have a container crane at dockside. Rather, freight can be driven on or off a RORO ship. This type of service is commonly used for shipments to underdeveloped nations with ports that lack adequate dock space and handling equipment. Many RORO ships can back up to a dock and load from the rear, rather than occupy wharf space along the entire side of the ship. In crowded ports, this is a major advantage. Lastly, RORO ships can also handle large consignments such as construction equipment.

The fourth mode of liner service is LASH or seabee liner services. LASH or seabee liners are ships that can handle loaded barges. Freight can be loaded on a barge in, say, Basle, Switzerland, floated down the Rhine River, the barge and goods loaded onto a LASH ship at Rotterdam, moved to New Orleans where it is off-loaded and floated up the Mississippi to St. Paul, Minnesota. Savings come from the reduced storage costs at both ports, as well as no handling of the freight.

A fifth liner service is called "open cargo." Open cargo ships are usually "break-bulk" freight liners that will often move goods at negotiable rates. Wheat, scrap metal, and some ores are often moved this way. Usually such shipments are in lots of under 5,000 tons and are handled only when the liner did not fill all its space with packaged cargoes.

Liner services charge according to tariffs that are published and open to public inspection. Liner companies have marketing staffs, and they advertise their sailings well in advance in order to attract bookings. Many liners belong to conferences, which are collective rate-making bodies. Membership in a conference limits the individual liner firm's ability to negotiate lower rates with a shipper. All liner firms in the conference charge the same published rate in the conference tariff.

One recent pricing innovation that has come into use with liner rates is time-volume rates. Time-volume rates are lower than normal rates in exchange for a commitment for a minimum amount of tonnage via one carrier over a time period. In marketing terms, this is a lower price to contracted high-volume buyers and is a brand loyalty tactic. Such rates should be investigated if foreign buying is common and routine over a certain route, and one liner firm is preferred.

A last point on liner prices pertains to the basis of rate assessment. Rates are charged generally on the basis of weight and/or measurement. Weight can be short ton (2,000 pounds), long ton (2,240 pounds), or metric ton (2,204.62 pounds). Measurement weights can be by 40 cubic feet or metric cubic ton (35 cubic feet). The specific ones are stated in each tariff. It is important to note this in preplanning overseas buys. The difference between 2,000 and 2,240 pounds is twelve percent. This can cause a total cost calculation to be off so far so as to mistakenly lead the firm to buy from an uneconomic source. Further, some tariffs charge on "W/M" bases. This means that the charges will be computed on weight or measurement tons, whichever is greater. For example, a shipment weighs 14,000 pounds and measures 5' × 8' × 9'. The tariff uses 2,000 pounds and 40 cubic feet as its weight and measure tons, respectively. The rate is $50 W/M. Since 14,000 pounds is 7 weight tons and the 360 cubic feet shipment in 9 cubic tons, the charge is $50 times 9 tons or $450.00. Containers and LASH barges often charge for each "load," regardless of weight or commodity inside.

Tramp ships comprise the second major group of overseas ship services. Tramp ships move shipload cargoes wherever they might originate or terminate. For example, tramp ships will move whole shiploads of oil, grain, lumber, chemicals, and coal. Like taxis, tramp ships will move freight wherever the market supply and demand is most profitable for them.

Tramp ships are hired through a charter. A voyage charter is a one-way rental of ship and crew. A time charter is a rental for a period of time, e.g. a year. The time charter can be less costly over the long period, and it can assure a steady supply of carriage, which is better than arranging many voyage charters. Another tramp rental form is a bareboat or demise charter. Typically this is a very long charter period during which the goods' owner rents the ship and supplies the crew, fuel, etc. Sometimes this is arranged for the life of a ship. Charters can also be arranged under a contract of affreightment. Affreightment is a split charter in which one shipper uses one half of the vessel and another shipper uses the other half. Split charters can also be arranged with one party shipping one way and another shipping on the return. Such agreements can greatly reduce the total cost of chartering for both shippers.

Charter ship pricing is established by supply and demand. During the early 1970s, grain movements to the Mediterranean Sea were as high as sixty dollars per ton, while in 1981 they were as low as twelve dollars per ton. A glut of shipping capacity in the world is expected to keep ocean charter rates low through the late 1980s. Reduced world oil demand from the Mideast, the reopening of the Suez Canal, along with the large number of ships built in the 1970s are seen as factors keeping shipping rates low for several years.

Private ships are a third form of ocean carriage. Private ships are owned by the firm moving the goods. Examples are found in the banana, automobile, and lumber industries. Private ships are usually designed to efficiently load, unload, and carry specific commodities. Frequently such measures will provide the owner firm with lower shipping costs than can be obtained from liner and tramp services.

Protection Against Perils

Carrier liability in international shipping is drastically limited compared to that in domestic movements. The Carriage of Goods at Sea Act of 1936 limits carrier liability to $500 per package. The law also exempts carriers from obligation if loss occurs from fire (if not the fault of carrier), perils at sea, acts of God, war, intervention of law, acts of omission by shippers, strikes or riots, attempts to save life or property at sea, the inherent nature of goods, insufficient packing or marking, or from acts of negligence of the master navigating or managing the ship. However, law does hold the carrier liable for loss and damage due to neglect or carelessness in storing, handling, or discharging goods. This seemingly low liability enables the carrier to avoid many claims, especially if the firm is foreign-based. Liability in shipping can, in fact, be placed upon the good's owner. If a ship is in danger and must jettison freight to lighten its load, then all the safe goods' owners and the ship owner must make up for that loss. This practice is known as general average loss.

The obligation condition in foreign shipping situations necessitates insurance coverage on goods being moved. Many letter of credit arrangements require insurance. Most shippers merely seek all-inclusive insurance which covers any and all possible perils that can occur anywhere along the route including those associated with inland carriers, wharfs, stevedoring, and aboard ship. Insurance is usually one of the factors stated in the buying and selling terms. Some foreign nations require that all shipments being imported into or exported out of these lands be insured by firms of those countries.

Terms of Sale

The terms of sale are a very important part of any purchase. A $100,000 purchase that is bought FOB-Antwerp rather than FOB-New York means that the buyer must incur several thousand dollars additional expense because freight and insurance are now the buyer's responsibility. Shipping terms define whether the buyer or seller has responsibility for each component in an overseas movement. The terms basically define where one party's responsibilities end and the other's begin. Table 11-1 identifies the key components of common types of terms used in overseas shipping. Please note these terms are discussed from an importing context.

Importing is simpler and more convenient if title passage is arranged as close as possible to the buyer. There are fewer details to arrange in, say, a Cost-Insurance-Freight than a Free Along Side foreign port situation. But, none of the costs are avoided. They are added into the price of the terms by the seller. Many factors are estimated by sellers with "padding" added to allow for uncertainties enroute. In many instances, it might be less costly for the buyer to arrange many of the details and have the selling terms defined at the foreign export port. Insurance might be cheaper from a U.S. firm, or the company might have a lower time-volume rate in effect with one carrier. Further, if the U.S. dollar is dropping daily in relation to the foreign currency of the purchase, it will be cheaper to buy the goods near the origin point rather than two weeks later at the destination. Finally, the buying company's own distribution and traffic department might have foreign trade expertise or relations with a reliable, efficient foreign forwarder who can easily handle the shipment.

Means of Payment

The process of payment for goods and many of the movement services is also different in foreign trade. While open accounts and consignment are possible when buying from overseas, few sellers will allow such terms. The cost of selling overseas is much more complicated than selling domestically. In addition, legal recourse against a nonpaying foreign buyer is much weaker. Consequently, firms selling overseas often will require letters of credit to assure payment.

□ **TABLE 11-1.** *Shipping Term Components*

Term	Basic Responsibilities	Load Inland Vehicle at		Ocean Documents Select Vessel Load Ship		Pay Ocean		Obtain Marine		Risk During	
		S	B	S	B	S	B	S	B	S	B
EX WORKS	Origin specified as to plant		X		X		X		X		X
FOT	Seller arranges inland carrier and loading of vehicle; obtains clean bill of lading from inland carrier	X			X		X		X		X
FAS VESSEL FOREIGN PORT	Same as FOB except seller pays for heavy lift charges	X			X		X		X		X
FOB VESSEL FOREIGN PORT	Seller arranges inland move and pays cost to ship pier	X		X			X		X		X
EX SHIP	Seller to foreign port up to ship unloading	X		X		X		X		X	
EX QUAY	Seller arranges through to import customs	X		X		X		X		X	
C&F	Seller's price quote includes transportation to foreign dock	X		X		X			X		X
CIF	Seller's price quote includes transportation to buyer and insurance	X		X		X		X			X

S = Seller
B = Buyer
In all instances, seller is responsible for export license packing list, certificate of origin and export packing.
Buyer is responsible for import customs in all but EX QUAY.

A letter of credit is a means of payment that utilizes the trust relationships of banks. There are required processes in the logistics system to assure proper goods transferance and payment. In addition to the buyer and seller, letters of credit will involve the buyer's bank, the seller's bank, and the ocean or other enroute carriers or warehouses. Table 11-2 illustrates the general process.

The letter of credit process is outlined rather generally, but Table 11–2 illustrates the basic flow of events. Several facets of this process

☐ **TABLE 11-2.** *General Letter on Credit Process*

	Buyer	Buyer's Bank	Carrier	Seller's Bank	Seller
1.	← Buyer and seller agree to purchase and sign agreement. →				
2.		Buyer deposits funds or obtains line of credit at his bank ("issuing bank")—			
3.		Issuing bank asks foreign banks of seller to advise or confirm credit. Called "advising" or "confirming" book. ←		→	
4.				Foreign bank informs seller that funds are confirmed. This helps seller be assured of funds availability. →	
5.			←	Seller makes shipment knowing funds are assured.	
6.			←	Seller meets terms of shipment as outlined in letter of credit; e.g., obtains ocean bill of lading, etc.	
7.				←Seller sends documents to confirming bank.	
8.				Confirming bank checks documents against credit to see if meets requirements.	
9.		←		Foreign bank sends all documents to buyer's bank.	
10.		Buyer's bank checks for accuracy and validity of documents.			
11.	→Buyer makes payment with his "issuing" bank.				
12.		Issuing bank transmits proceeds to either notifying or confirming bank or direct to seller. →		→	
13.	←Issuing banks presents documents to buyer				
14.	Buyer presents documents to→ carrier as proof of payment				
15.	←Carrier delivers← goods to buyer				

warrant further discussion. One, letters of credit may be revocable or irrevocable. A revocable letter of credit allows the buyer much flexibility. It can be amended or revoked up to the time of payment by the issuing bank. This involves a high risk for the seller, because the letter can be cancelled while the goods are enroute. An irrevocable letter of credit is less flexible for the buyer; it gives the seller the assurance that the buyer's bank will not cancel the order. A confirmed, irrevocable letter of credit provides the seller a double assurance of payment that is also covered by a bank in his own country. This type of letter of credit is slightly more costly for the buyer to obtain.

Letters of credit involve banks as a mechanism for payment. Whereas the buyer and seller might not know each other, additional trust and assurance is given to all when a banking system is used to facilitate funds transfer. Additionally, terms of credit letters require compliance to specific terms that involve the carriers and other enroute logistics parties. For example, dock receipts and bill of lading generally are required before a bank will finally transfer funds to the seller. By producing these receipts, the buyer has proof that the described goods have been shipped, and that they are on their way to him/her. This compliance feature is as important to the buyer as the cash receipt is to the seller.[5]

Funds transfer is becoming simpler as computer and satellite data transmissions are utilized to greater degrees. Funds can be transferred instantaneously, rather than entailing a wait for ocean or even air mail. This fact has great bearing upon cash management for the buyer. If the issuing bank has extended credit to the buyer, then title transfer at the foreign port will speed up payment and keep interest charges to a minimum. On the other hand, if the buyer's credit at the bank has been established through a high-interest-earning certificate or account, then title transfer at the U.S. port is favorable.

Documentation

The buyer should be familiar with the many different forms and documents used in international shipping. Each document has a specific purpose, which is detailed here.[6]

Booking Request
Booking requests are used to reserve shipment space aboard a liner vessel. Typically, this form will include the ship, its sailing date, the port, commodity, weight, cubic size, packaging, and shipper name. The buyer is responsible for making this request on shipments having terms of EX Works, FOT, and FAS.

Shipping Permit
The shipping permit is provided by the liner company to the person arranging the goods' movement to the pier where the ship is loading. This form is proof to pier personnel that the shipment may be received at the dock. Again, the buyer will have responsibility for this in EX WORKS, FOT, and FAS foreign port movements.

Dock Receipt
The dock receipt is a receipt for the goods delivered to the outbound dock. The buyer is involved with this in EX WORKS, FOT and FAS moves. On "FOB foreign port" terms this document is one of the key components in the settlement of a letter of credit.

Packing List
The packing list accompanies the goods. It describes the goods and the method of crating/packaging, names the shipper, consignee, and route of movement. The vendor is always responsible for creating this form.

Bill of Lading
The bill of lading is a receipt of goods and contract of carriage provided by the land carriers on both ends of an ocean move. On FOT terms, this document is used to pass title with a letter of credit upon pick up from the vendor's plant. On EX WORKS moves, the buyer will receive this document from the rail or motor carrier. With shipping terms of all types, the buyer will be involved directly with this document on the move from the port to his receiving plant or warehouse.

Delivery Receipt
The delivery receipt is provided by inland carriers for the consignee to sign upon receiving the goods. When signed by a receiver, this form is proof that the carrier delivered the goods according to the bill of lading.

Ocean Bill of Lading
The ocean bill of lading is a receipt for goods delivered to the ship for movement. Its other legal purposes are that it describes the goods, has the legal significance as that of a contract of carriage, determines the carrier's liability, is used to determine ocean freight charges, and informs the carrier who to notify when ship and goods arrive at port. It is one of the key documents used to actually pass title to goods. In FOB foreign port, CIF, C&F and even in FAS terms, the ocean bill of lading is the key document for letter of credit settlement. The ocean bill of lading is also a prime component for the clearance of goods into a country. The buyer is responsible for it in EX WORKS, FOT, and FAS terms. He/she must pay for its preparation in FOB foreign ports and C&F terms.

Through Ocean Bill of Lading
A through ocean bill of lading is used whenever more than one ship line is involved in the movement of goods. This is frequently the case when moves involve small ports. Goods are often transferred to an overseas inbound carrier at a major port.

Import License
The import license is a document granting permission to import goods into the U.S. This document is discussed in greater detail in the section on customs.

Certificate of Origin

A certificate of origin is required on goods moving to the U.S. It notes the origin of the goods as well as the makeup of the items. It is used to determine the exact import duty, as well as to determine whether the goods conform to U.S. food, drug, and agricultural laws.

Inspection Certificate

An inspection certificate is often required by buyers in order to obtain an independent check as to the specific makeup of the goods being purchased. This certificate is prepared by an independent person or firm.

Charter Party

The charter party form is used in chartering a tramp vessel. It is the "lease" document between the charterer and the ship owner, or his/her legal representative.

U.S. Customs

Goods entering the U.S., and most other nations of the world, are subject to inspection and assessment of taxes or duty fees. Inspections are made to determine the goods' value for duty computation, whether the shipment contains prohibited goods, if it is truly invoiced in the quantities shown, as well as to check proper package labeling. The ocean bill of lading and an invoice must be used to clear goods through customs.

Goods may be cleared through customs only by 1) the goods owner, 2) an employee of the goods owner, or 3) a person licensed by the U.S. Treasury, i.e., a customshouse broker.

Because import clearances are a detailed process and often occur at some distance from the actual buyer's plant, a customshouse broker is a convenient and efficient person to hire for such purposes. A customshouse broker handles the actual customs entry. A legal relationship is created between the buyer and a broker through a document called a power of attorney, which both parties sign.

Import duties are assessed in a number of ways. They vary by commodity as well as by nation of export. Specifically, duties are assessed either on a specific basis, which means per pound or other quantity, or on AD VALOREM basis, which is a percent of value, or a combination of the two methods.

Goods are processed through clearance in one of three ways. The first way is by consumption. This means the goods are cleared, all duties are paid, and the owner is free to remove them. The second way is by bonded warehousing where the goods may be kept for up to five years without payment of duties. They may be reexported in this time without duty payment. But, duty must be paid at the end of three years or upon removal for consumption. A third disposition method is movement to a free trade zone, which will be discussed later in this chapter.

A special topic related to customs is drawback. Drawback is a feature in U.S. customs law that allows an importer to later reexport the same or comparable goods and receive a refund of up to ninety-nine percent of the original duty paid. The items needed to receive drawback are proof of inspection, proof of receipt, proof of use of the goods, specific information as to how the imported goods were used, and proof of exportation. The details relating to drawback and other customs matters are explained in *Title 19, Code of Federal Regulations* and updated in the *Federal Register*.

Facilitators of International Logistics

Facilitators are firms that are a part of the international trade scene and act to help the flow of goods for buyers and sellers. While they are not the actual buyers, sellers or carriers, they very much help facilitate this trade.

Foreign Freight Forwarders

Foreign freight forwarders act to handle booking and other movement services for overseas shipments. They attend to many of the paperwork processes necessary for moving goods across borders. Foreign forwarders do not take possession of the goods nor do they consolidate them like domestic forwarders. The services handled by freight forwarders typically include booking, handling port transfers, arranging packing, marking and paperwork, translating foreign correspondence, and tracing. Freight forwarders are paid a fee based upon a percent of actual charges for pier, ocean, inland handlings and movement, etc. Forwarders are used on a majority of overseas shipments, and they are a good source of information about potential vendors. Only a large firm with much experience in foreign shipping can afford to attend to the activities provided by foreign freight forwarders.

Ship Brokers

Ship brokers represent tramp ship owners and shippers or consignees of loads moved on tramp ships. These brokers act to seek shipments for ship owners or seek ships for potential charterers. Major ship broker centers are located in New York, London, Hong Kong, Oslo, and elsewhere. They are paid a percent of the charter fee.

Ship Agents

Ship agents are used by liner firms and tramp ship operators to arrange port matters such as fees payments, pier reservations and payment, ship mail, crew reassignments, ship provisioning, minor ship repair, and other housekeeping items that are difficult for the ship's owner, charterer, or captain. The agent is familiar with the port and can more easily pay for needed services than can the infrequent operator or ship's captain. A formal arrangement is created between the operator (owner or charterer) and ship agent. It stipulates the services to be provided and fees for them.

Import Agents

Import agents represent foreign sellers of goods. They are salesmen of the firms, except they are paid by commission, have no legal interest in the goods, and maintain no inventory. Buyers can approach import agents as sources for placing orders. The actual purchase process must still take place using letters of credit, etc., and arranging of the move.

Independent agents, on the other hand, actually buy goods from overseas for resale. Price and other purchase details are arranged with an independent agent. Usually such agents have already purchased the goods and have them on hand. Some buyers will use these agents as a way of avoiding the paperwork and arrangement processes of international importing. A purchase from an independent agent is a purchase from a domestic source. Of course, the independent agent's profit and the buyer's possible loss of drawback ability must be evaluated in the decision tradeoff.[7]

Foreign Trade Zones

A foreign trade zone, or FTZ, is a piece of land or a building designated as such by the Customs Service. There are approximately twenty-five foreign trade zones in the U.S. These are locations at which firms may store, assemble, manufacture, or hold goods for sale. The advantage of an FTZ is that goods may be imported, moved to these locations in bonded transportation, and held there indefinitely without paying duty. Goods may also be reexported without paying duty. Goods become subject to duty when they are moved to a domestic location that is not a FTZ. The firm can reexport goods as with drawbacks, except that the FTZ permits avoidance of the duty-related cash flow loss in the first place. Goods intended for manufacturing and domestic sale do not have to have duty paid on them until removed from the facility. That is, imported manufacturing inventories can avoid the duty cost component. It can be held off until ultimate sale of the finished goods.

Future Concerns of Foreign Sourcing

Foreign buying can be necessary or merely desirable for the buyer. Many opportunities in cost, quality, or avoidability arise in this area. Factors affecting this area in the future that can have semipermanent impacts include the strength of foreign sources, shipping supply, and a strategy for alternate sourcing.

The Organization of Petroleum Exporting Countries, OPEC, was one of the first and widely publicized price-fixing and supply-allocating cartels drastically affecting foreign sourcing of a major U.S. consumed product. OPEC is organized by many foreign nations. Many other cartels are in existence or could come into existence on most any standardized raw commodity of importance to industrial nations. The tendency has existed for small mineral rich nations to seek market power with other lesser developed nations through the cartel medium. The need for hard currency income is a motive for such moves. Domestic sources are not directly involved in such cartel systems due to U.S. antitrust laws. But, the market prices set by collective efforts abroad do tend to affect the pricing approaches of domestic sources. Alignment with domestic sources will blunt, to some degree, the price impacts of strong cartels in sellers' markets.

World shipping capacity is greater than demand for reasons that range from speculation ship building, the reopening of the Suez Canal, and a drop in world trade. Rates are soft in such markets. It is estimated by many that this condition will persist through the 1980s.

Tramp rates are subject directly to market supply and demand. The overseas buyer needing such service should approach tramp shipping like an investor. That is, in cyclical price upswings a long-term charter can be used to hold a low rate constant for a long time period. On the other hand, at a downturn in the market, voyage charters are best, since successive ones will be lower in price.

Pricing in the liner trades will be affected by an agreement made by many countries in the United Nations. Known as the United Nations Conference on Trade and Development (UNCTAD), nations abiding by it will apportion liner traffic between them on a 40/40/20 basis. That is, forty percent of liner trade between A and B can be in A's ships, forty percent in B's ships and only twenty percent in other nations' ships. This will severely affect the efficiency of world liner shipping. Third nation shipping might decrease, leaving buyers with long waits or high charges until a ship of A or B can become available.

Finally, foreign sources are far, and many complicating factors can hinder their supply or logistics flow inbound to the buyer. Political, social, and currency factors can lengthen or interrupt this flow. It is, therefore, necessary to develop alternate contingencies to these sources. These might include other nation sources or even development of new domestic sources having shorter logistics links.

Conclusion

International purchasing represents both an opportunity and an additional operational and administrative burden. It opens source markets, presents possible price advantages, and it can increase competitive supply facing the firm. But, it is different than domestic sourcing. International sourcing involves a greater knowledge and involvement in multinational matters, overseas transportation, methods of financing, and different legal arrangements. International trade is becoming easier, faster, and less costly from movement and transaction standpoints. Even buyers who are not now buying from abroad must look to this area as a matter of routine examination and consideration.

FOOTNOTES

1. Peter H. Denning, "Purchasing Internationally," *Aljian's Purchasing Handbook* (New York, NY: McGraw-Hill, 1982), chapter 22.
2. James F. Donohue, "Count on Countertrade to Complicate Your Life," *Purchasing*, 26 June 1980, p. 65.
3. "Buyer's Launch Worldwide Search for Materials," *Purchasing*, 26 February 1881, p. 14.

4. Robert E. Weigand, "Barters and Buy-Backs: Let Western Firms Beware!," *Business Horizons*, June 1980, p. 54.
5. "Financing International Trade," publication of the Marine National Exchange Bank, Milwaukee, WI.
6. Tom Foster, "Anatomy of an Export," *Distribution*, October 1980, p. 75.
7. Alfred Murr, *Export-Import Traffic Management* (Centreville, MD: Cornell Maritime Press, 1977).

QUESTIONS FOR REVIEW

1. Cite the pros and cons of international sourcing?

2. Why might countertrade increase in the future?

3. How might a purchasing manager become involved in a bartering arrangement for his or her firm?

4. What additional costs of purchasing and landing a product must be considered in an international setting versus a domestic one?

5. Your firm imports machines for resale to manufacturing firms in the U.S. What form of transportation would be best for bringing the machines in from overseas?

6. Why is transportation insurance a special feature of international sourcing?

7. Why are the selling terms more important to define and understand in foreign sourcing than in domestic settings?

8. Distinguish between FOB foreign port versus FOB domestic port of entry terms.

9. What terms should be sought by buyers in the following two types of situations:
   a) a buyer of a large multi-national firm,
   b) a buyer of a small firm who is purchasing from a major European manufacturer that sells much of its output in the U.S.

10. What is the role of the letter of credit?

11. Distinguish between foreign freight forwarders, agents, and brokers.

12. What opportunities and problems are on the horizon with respect to international transportation that might affect foreign sourcing?

12

INTRODUCTION

WHEN ARE VALUE ENGINEERING AND VALUE ANALYSIS CONDUCTED?

BASIC APPROACH TO VALUE ANALYSIS

Basic Value Analysis Study Process

CONCLUSION

CHAPTER OBJECTIVES

After reading this chapter you should:

- Understand the concept and role of value analysis.

- Be able to approach a value analysis project with sound techniques.

- Appreciate how value analysis is similar to a capital investment project.

- Understand how value analysis is one of the ways in which purchasing is integrated with the rest of the firm.

Value Analysis

Introduction

Value analysis is the task of studying a product and all of its components in order to determine ways of producing it at a lower cost, with improved quality, or with a material in greater or more stable supply. It is a creative task, sometimes requiring brainstorming and questioning into areas rarely looked at during a product's life.[1] Purchasing is the appropriate place for this activity to take place because it is the juncture for production, engineering, and vendors. Value analysis generally refers to improving existing products or processes. Value engineering, on the other hand, refers to the task of improving product design prior to establishing the final design and specifications.

When Are Value Engineering and Value Analysis Conducted?

Value engineering often includes a purchasing review of the tentative plans and specifications for a product being developed. The intent here, traditionally, is to determine if obvious savings can be realized through standardization, better materials, or use of existing applications. More recently, value engineering in purchasing has involved being part of the original product design team in order to suggest such ideas early in the product's development.

Value analysis, on the other hand, is not always conducted during the life of a product. However, when it is conducted, it generally occurs at one of several specific points in time, or because of certain events. For example, marketing may determine that an improvement in the product is necessary. This might occur while a product is in its introduction stage, or at any other stage in its life cycle. Certain parts might fail during normal use, suggestions for improving the design might come in from users, or the design might require alteration in order to meet a feature provided by competition. Many factors can cause a firm to review a product with an eye toward quality or aesthetic improvement during any stage.

Value analysis is often appropriate when new technology develops in the supply market. This might be a new material, adhesive, control device, coating, chemical, or a change in any other component. The result may be significant quality improvements, a new marketing appeal, reduced costs, or just keeping the product on par with competitive products.

Quality problems during production or with the final product can spur value analysis. Perhaps a certain component represents an increasing waste or scrap problem. Similarly, problems with the product in the field that result in customer dissatisfaction might give rise to complete product value analysis rather than analysis of one particular component.

Another time at which value analysis can be useful is when the product enters the maturity stage of its life cycle. During this period, design improvements in the basic product are often worthwhile, since this stage continues for a long period. Value analysis at this point can be triggered by a cost squeeze experienced due to flattening sales or price competition. This is the time for the firm to look for long-term contracts with vendors to achieve economic gains. Value analysis into any way in which the product can now be made at less cost, with higher quality or aesthetics, or with better materials is an economical or profitable endeavor.

Price increases by vendors are another reason why firms may review a product and its component in a value analysis setting. The component or material experiencing the price increase is looked at with substitution or reduction of use in mind. Similarly, firms will often use value analysis as a means of reducing total product costs when a product is no longer profitable, but the firm still wishes or needs to market it.

Basic Approach to Value Analysis

Value analysis is an approach to improvement. It is a thought process that is not tied to current designs or methods but rather attempts to create improvement in any manner possible. It is neither a pure quality enhancement nor strictly a cost-reduction effort. Value analysis is concerned with the following concept:

$$\text{Value} = \text{Function/Cost.}[2]$$

Optimum value is the lowest possible cost that will accomplish a certain required function.

Value analysis is linked with productivity, where productivity is an index number obtained when the sum of the outputs is divided by the required inputs. There are five basic ways of increasing value (or productivity), and five ways that can decrease it. The following illustration will show how various factors relate to each other and the total value or productivity goal.

```
Value = Function (output)/cost (inputs)
        Function (output) = 50 units
        Cost (inputs)     = 40 cost measures
Current Value = 50/40
              = 1.25 cost units per unit of function
```

Improvements can be attained through the following changes:

increase function/keep costs the same

52/40 = 1.30 The result is larger than the original 1.25 index or value. Emphasis here is upon greater function or output.

keep function the same/reduce costs

50/38 = 1.32 The result again is larger than 1.25. Emphasis here is upon reduced costs at same level of function or output.

increase function greatly/increase costs to lesser degree

53/41 = 1.29 Result is greater than 1.25. This concept is often behind capital investment projects. An increase in costs results in a greater increase in benefits to the firm.

decrease function/decrease costs to greater degree

49/37 = 1.32 Result is greater than 1.25. This is possible when the drop in function or output is acceptable to the firm or marketplace.

increase function/decrease costs

51/39 = 1.31 Result is greater than 1.25. This phenomenon is often possible when new technological advances are used. Computer control that replaces manual control can often produce greater output at lesser unit cost.

Decreases in value or productivity will result with any one of the following five situations.

decrease in function/costs remain same

48/40 = 1.20 Result is less than 1.25. This can occur with machinery or personnel operate slower than before.

function remains same/cost increase

50/42 = 1.19 Result is less than 1.25. Pure wage increases without resulting work rule or flexibility benefits will present this worsened situation. Similarly, sloppiness in production that results in waste and scrap increases can require more materials with the same resulting output.

function increases/costs increase to greater degree

51/43 = 1.19 Result is less than 1.25. Some design changes and capital investments can produce this result.

function decreases/costs decrease to lesser degree

47/39 = 1.21 Result is less than 1.25. Some pure cost reduction programs can produce this type of result upon the firm, unless approached with all trade-offs in mind.

function decreases/costs increase

49/41 = 1.20. Result is less than 1.25. This is the worst of all situations and can occur when price increases are associated with decreases in raw material quality.

Value analysis attempts to increase function or output in relation to costs, or it seeks to maintain function or output with a decrease in total costs. The analyses shown here point out how any one of five possible favorable outcomes can be obtained with relative changes in either function or cost. The initial task for the value analysis team is to identify the need of the study; that is, is function improvement or cost reduction sought, or both? The approach taken during the entire value analysis process will be defined by the established goal. A process that seeks to increase function while maintaining costs will be different from one that seeks to maintain quality while decreasing costs.

Basic Value Analysis Study Process

A basic approach to value analysis is suggested by Dowst and others is composed of five phases: 1) the information phase, 2) the speculative phase, 3) the planning phase, 4) the execution phase, and 5) the reporting phase.[3]

Information Phase

This step in the value analysis process consists of gathering all information pertinent to the product. This includes descriptive data such as assembly drawings, single-part drawings, bills of material, sources, inventories, scrap rates, yield rates, warranty records, annual usage or volume figures, age of present design, problems cited by customers and salesmen, methods of transporting the product, production lot sizes, packaging used, and maintenance records.[4]

Cost information is also needed during the information phase. This includes data available from current record systems as well as some constructed cost data using the descriptive information. Some of this information should be in cost form for the following items: component costs, freight, loss and damage, acquisition costs for ordering, inspection expenses, returns, inventory costs, length-of-life for required manufacturing items, packaging material expenses, energy costs, and manhours required to produce and ship.[5]

The information phase questions the reason for each existing component or step. Examples are as follows:

1. Is paint for decoration or environmental protection?
2. Is a metal shield used for weight stability or protection?
3. Are switches and controls in certain places and of certain sizes for particular reasons?
4. Are there safety requirements needed for the product?
5. Is a shield for sound proofing for the operator or dust protection for the machine?
6. Was part of the original design established for product protection in transit to the site of use or is it entirely functional for its life of operation?

Questions such as these determine why certain factors were built into the original product design. It is frequently worthwhile to gain access to the original design records, which might contain reasons for certain design features. Some may no longer be needed.

Speculative Phase

This phase of the study consists of questioning each and every component, step, method, material, part, etc. Free and open discussions, without criticism, are required. Brainstorming, with persons from many functions and disciplines present, is a technique often used during this phase.

The basic questions asked are:

1. What is the product?
2. What does each part or component do?
3. What does it cost the firm?
4. What alternative item might accomplish the same function?
5. What is the cost of the alternative?[6]

The existence and need for each and every part of a product is questioned. An aid in this questioning process includes labeling each part with a single verb and single noun. Examples are "supports weight," "prevents contamination," "slows movement," "provides grip," "prevents vibration," "holds tube," etc. These basic, almost generic, statements define the purpose, if any, for each part. This practice quickly points out whether or not a need truly exists for each part. It also assists in finding alternatives.

Dowst lists various alternatives for consideration during the questioning process including: 1) substitution, 2) elimination, 3) standardization, 4) combination, or 5) simplification[7]. Further questioning should take place with regard to factors such as maintenance costs, safety features and possible alternatives, and the toxic properties of any of the materials or components.

Other approaches for the speculative phase are suggested by L. D. Miles. One of these is *purchased part function analysis*, which calls for the buyer to assume nothing regarding any part or component. The buyer asks questions about each part until he or she fully understands its purpose and what it contributes to the function of the total product. The key is to determine whether there are any parts, materials, or components that provide little or no value or function to the entire product.

Miles suggested another approach for the questioning phase that he refers to as *purchasing specification function analysis*.[8] Purchasing specification function analysis requires a review of all specifications with the view that each item of specification costs money to obtain. Each specification is then questioned. For example, a buyer required a thin plastic sheet, square on three sides and pointed on the fourth side. (Exhibit 12–1 presents the piece needed.) The original specification established several years earlier called for a particular type of plastic material. The sheeting was extruded and stopped every 28" for a "pointed cut" and a perpendicular cut. Out of 560 square inches of material, 480 square inches were usable, with scrap running about 14.2 percent. Further, the buyer firm provided specialized pointed blades to the vendor for each order. The back of each piece was cut in a second step with a

■ **EXHIBIT 12-1.** *Illustration of Altered Cutting and Materials Specifications*

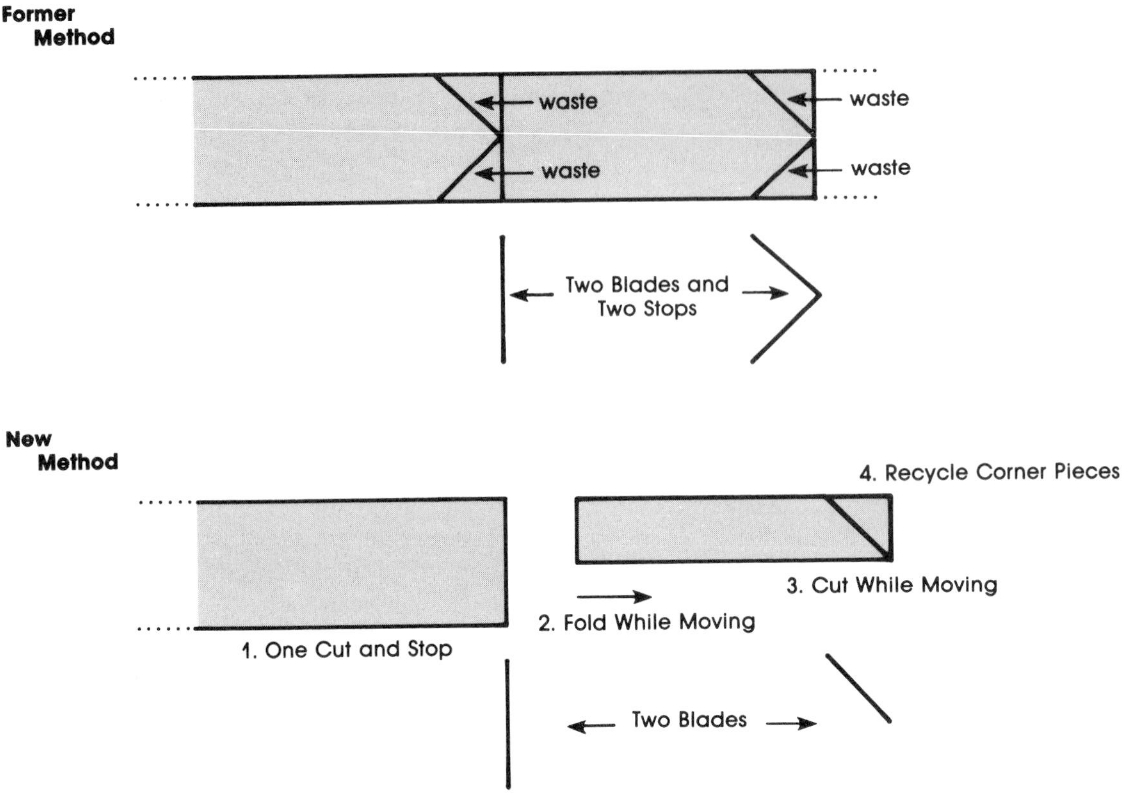

Former Method

New Method

perpendicular blade. The sheeting was stopped for each cut, for a total of two stops and two cuts. A switch to another plastic material enabled the scrap pieces to immediately be recycled into the extrusion machines. The buyer and vendor changed the process to one using a standardized 45 degree blade and a perpendicular blade. By first folding the sheeting over in half, one cut of each is made, and no stop is needed for the diagonal cut. No waste is incurred, since the two small triangle cuts are recycled, and material costs for each run are reduced.

Another area of investigation suggested by Miles is *nonworking cost function analysis*. (Nonworking cost function analysis attempts to determine areas where material cost can be reduced.) For example, an expensive material is needed in one critical area on a particular part; for manufacturing simplicity purposes, the entire part is made of this material. The firm is paying for expensive material where it isn't needed, in a nonworking area of the part. An example is structural "I beams." In many instances, holes can be punched out of the "web" part of the beam, thereby reducing weight and material needs, with little or no loss of strength experienced.

In another example, one value analysis project started because of slow functioning and problem part in the production process. The item in question was a nozzle that was used to apply a small quantity of heated adhesive to every unit of production. The application process involved several physical movements and a squirting action of the nozzle. During a single shift over 10,000 applications were made, and the nozzle head had to be replaced about every 1,000 applications. The nozzle head was relatively inexpensive, but the problem part was halting the production line and adjusting each new head took about ten applications to be accurately set. The problems centered around 1) need for adhesive, and 2) the problem of production halting and replacement.

The solution to the problem consisted of modifying the line so that ten nozzles linked together would apply adhesive to the production units in each of ten rows on a conveyor belt. Each nozzle then functioned about 1,000 times per shift, and it was not necessary to halt production to change any of them. All nozzle changes are now made at the beginning of each new shift and the adjustment process is only performed once during the shift.

Planning Phase

The planning phase is one in which various alternatives are evaluated. In the two examples just presented, several alternatives were evaluated for each project. In the plastic sheeting example, a wider sheet with a zig-zag blade was investigated, but the extra costs of using a very wide die on an extruder were rejected. This option would have resulted in less scrap than the original amount, but the cost of the die would have been high. The final solution included a more efficient blade-cutting system as well as using another plastic material that could be recycled. The adhesive project included analysis of more expensive nozzle systems, slowing down production so that there was less of a disruption when the nozzle head had to be changed, as well as a study of other adhesive systems altogether. In each setting, many alternatives were investigated before the final ones were selected.

Planning requires analysis of the part or component in question with regard to its design costs, material and production costs, and inventory holding costs. All costs are targets for reduction.

Some considerations to be contemplated during planning analysis are presented in Table 12–1.

Planning involves a business analysis investigation of the type used in new product introduction efforts. It requires reviewing each alternative in terms of the product itself, the firm, as well as vendors and customers. A total, or global, analysis is needed. For example, one alternative might diminish the appeal, quality, or perceived usefulness of the product in the market.

Execution Phase

During the execution phase, one or more alternatives are actually tested. This might consist of producing new dies and operating several production test runs. In this testing phase the buyer must work closely with vendors, especially if the alternative being considered will alter the type of goods needed from the vendor.

☐ **TABLE 12-1.** *Key Items of Study in Value Analysis*

Production—
* speed of operation for lower unit cost
* scrap and waste reduction
* tolerance-related costs (degree to which items must be checked, inspected,adjusted, rejected, etc.) and how they might be lowered
* packing materials cost
* the cost of packaging the product
* reduced energy needs
* less pollutants and safety problems
* reduced maintenance requirements
* fewer parts or movements necessary
* improved safety

Purchasing—
* ease of ordering . . . shifting from negotiating specialized part to competitive bidding
* use of standard items rather than specialized ones
* standardization to reduce stockkeeping units and chance for obsolescence

Materials Management and Distribution—
* reduced weight in transit (since weight is charged in freight rates)
* decreased loss and damage incidence
* ease of handling, loading, and unloading
* easier transportation possible
* improved safety
* ability to handle as regular product rather than as hazardous shipment
* fewer stockkeeping units
* smaller size.[1]

Marketing and Product Planning—
* better styling
* easier set up and operation by users
* reduced operating cost for users
* improved safety
* fewer servicing needs

The execution phase might also involve actual market testing similar to that frequently used with new product introductions. This type of testing consists of providing the product for free to certain customers for use and evaluation. Or, the test marketing might take the form of a gradual introduction of an altered product for sale in a defined region or city. Market researchers then conduct a follow-up investigation on consumer reactions to the change. Firms do not want to change an existing product only to experience poor market results.

Reporting Phase

The final phase of value analysis is reporting. Results of full market testing or pilot use are gathered and aggregated with all cost information. The cost information should consist of two basic sets of figures. One set of figures should show the savings or changes in existing costs versus the operating, sales, or other costs associated with the alternative being considered. The second set of figures should detail any costs changes associated with in the production process. This step must include financial analyses similar to the ones presented in Chapter 9 with regard to payback, net present value, and internal rate of return. New ideas must be able to recoup the changeover costs through favorable financial returns to the firm.

Value analysis can be approached in a number of ways. The concepts presented here show the entire range of techniques and methods that can be used. However, some additional sources exist that can be utilized in value analysis, including customers and distributors. They are the users and marketers of a product and are very knowledgeable about how it works, how it might be improved, and what features competitors might have built into their products. Another alternative is to involve vendors. Vendors might be able to provide assistance in developing new materials applications or suggest other ways that the product can be improved. This technical assistance can often be obtained by changing from a design specification on purchase orders to the use of performance specifications. Some vendors attempt to gain knowledge of their customers' needs in order to provide design and improvement service as a part of their marketing effort. In some instances, this might be the only competitive advantage a vendor might have in a market, but it often is a very important one, and one he or she is eager to provide.

Conclusion

Value analysis is a key purchasing management activity. It is a positive, productive process that is afar from the daily order handling routine. Value analysis centers upon cost and quality improvements in ways not addressed elsewhere in the firm. This process can be very useful in advancing the purchasing department as an integrated component needed in the productivity of the firm and a major contributor to corporate profitability.

FOOTNOTES

1. Larry D. Miles, *Value Analysis Principles for Effective Buying*, ed. Edward J. Bierman, Paul V. Farrell, and Joseph R. Megiliola, vol. 3. *Guide to Purchasing* (New York: National Association of Purchasing Management, 1973), p. 1.14.4
2. Somerby R. Dowst, *More Basics for Buyers* (Boston, MA: CBI Publishing Company, Inc., 1979), p. 127.
3. Ibid, p. 130.

4. Tom King, "Vendors Can't Contribute Unless They Know The Facts," *Purchasing*, 29 May 1980, p. 67.
5. Tom King, "Wring Costs Out of Maintenance," *Purchasing*, 25 November 1981, p. 126A17.
6. Dowst, *More Basics for Buyers.*
7. *Ibid.*
8. Miles, *Value Analysis Principles for Effective Buying.*
9. "Quality Rests on an Active Supplier," *Purchasing*, 28 January 1982.

SOURCES FOR FURTHER READING

Fallon, Carlos. *Value Analysis to Improve Productivity.* New York: Wiley, 1971.
Fram, David. *Value Analysis: A Way to Better Products and Profits.* New York: AMACOM,1974.
Miles, Lawrence D. *Techniques of Value Analysis and Engineering.* New York: McGraw-Hill, 1972.
Mudge, Arthur E. *Value Engineering: A Systematic Approach.* New York: McGraw-Hill, 1971.
O'Brien, James J. *Value Analysis in Design and Construction.* New York: McGraw-Hill, 1976.
"Value Analysis: A Plan for All Seasons," *Purchasing*, 31 March 1983, p. 77.

QUESTIONS FOR REVIEW

1. What are the differences between value analysis and value engineering?

2. What are the typical goals of value analysis?

3. At what points in time is value analysis appropriate?

4. Why isn't value analysis totally appropriate during the product decline stage?

5. What are some of the reasons why a firm would look to vendors for ideas in value analysis?

6. What are some of the reasons why buyers cannot look to vendors for new ideas, or count on vendors to come up with savings ideas for them?

7. How and why are requisitioners and buyers sometimes guilty of overlooking savings ideas?

8. How is value analysis similar to productivity?

9. What key information should be gathered in the information stage of value analysis?

10. What are the basic questions that should be asked when conducting value analysis?

11. How are value analysis ideas similar in implementation to any capital project idea in a firm?

12. Why should value analysis techniques be applied to transportation of the firm's goods?

Indicate whether the following actions will result in an increase or decrease in productivity or whether it is merely a lateral shift with no resulting benefits or harmful effects?

Problem 12-1

1. Material price decrease
2. A decrease in material price of $1.00 with an increase in freight costs by $1.00 from buying from overseas. The goods must be paid at port of embarkation, and a two month inventory of raw materials is now necessary where a one-month was previously held.
3. Cost savings by purchasing that results in a 4% total acquisition cost decrease but scrap and waste in production increase by 4½%.
4. Price increase by vendor by 3% with modifications in the item being acquired that enables your firm to reduce its scrap and waste from $6.67 per unit to $6.34.
5. Production changes a process that enables a unit cost reduction from $9.18 to $9.10, but materials management must shift from a $3.13 component to one that costs $3.21.
6. Your firm incurs a material price increase of 10% on an item that makes up 60% of the product total cost. Total costs of the firm are about 95% of total revenue. The firm raises the price of its product from $11.25 to $11.70 as a result of the material cost increase.

13

INTRODUCTION

SCRAP/SURPLUS GOODS MANAGEMENT

Sources of Scrap and Waste
Alternative Channels of Disposal and Use
Recapturing Value from Surplus Capital
  Goods

MANAGEMENT OF CRITICAL COMMODITIES

Long-Run Mineral and Commodity Strategy
Micro-Tactics to Provide Product Supply

INFORMATION—THE KEY TO EFFECTIVE PURCHASING MANAGEMENT

Purchasing Research Needs
Purchasing Information Systems
Research of Areas Often Overlooked

CONCLUSION

CHAPTER OBJECTIVES

After reading this chapter you should:

- Understand the problems and opportunities of scrap/surplus goods management.

- Be able to identify the causes of scrap/surplus goods.

- Understand the nature of supply management with critical minerals and other key commodities.

- Appreciate the need for information in purchasing strategies.

Supply Strategies for the Future

Introduction

Purchasing has long been regarded as a passive managerial function, reactive to whatever occurred within the firm or its supply markets. That outlook is changing, however, and purchasing is being viewed more today as part of the strategic information input in defining the firm's current and future resources, problems and opportunities.

Purchasing can no longer assume an existing stable supply of materials and goods on either the domestic or international market. Communications, transportation, and corporate relationships are making the world smaller. No longer is there just a domestic market for sales or buying. What occurs in one part of the world affects supplies and markets in others. Even if a firm does not acquire goods internationally, foreign supply markets affect competing firms' buying practices, which in turn can affect the domestic market.

The supply markets available to a firm consist of and are shaped by many factors. Exhibit 13–1 shows many of the primary influences in supply markets. A first major influence is technology and new product development. Changes in these factors can cause existing supply markets to shift dramatically. Evidence of this is the fast growth of firms in the micro-processing area that have come into existence only within the past five to ten years. Many of these firms did not exist previously; computers have created vastly different markets than were ever present before. Even with existing firms, new technology can cause some firms to become the strong and new dominant forces in the market. A firm's supply market is shaped largely by the primary sources it currently uses as well as others that are purchased from to a lesser degree or not at all. Even an unused supplier can affect those from whom a firm does buy. Another influence in this area is that of competing firms' buying practices, strategies, and directions. A company can find itself in a weak buying position by actions of competitor's as well as other firms that are not competing with it. This is especially the case when the raw material or component in question is needed by many diverse industries. International markets are another major influence in the supply markets available to a firm. Even when the company acquires goods only from domestic sources, foreign suppliers can cause the domestic source to competitively drop from the market.

■ **EXHIBIT 13-1.** *Elements Affecting Company Supply Markets*

```
                    ┌─────────────────────────┐
                    │  Government Legislation  │
                    │      and Regulations     │
                    └─────────────────────────┘
                                 │
  ┌──────────────────┐           │           ┌──────────────────┐
  │ General Economic │           │           │    Technology    │
  │    Conditions    │           │           │ and New Products │
  └──────────────────┘           ▼           └──────────────────┘

┌──────────────────┐                         ┌──────────────────┐
│  Competitors' and│                         │ Prime, Alternative,│
│   Other Firms'   │       ┌─────────┐       │ and Other Suppliers│
│  Buying Practices│──────▶│   The   │◀──────└──────────────────┘
│    and Other     │       │  Firm's │
│    Strategies    │       │  Supply │       ┌──────────────────┐
└──────────────────┘       │  Market │       │ Fiscal, Monetary,│
                           └─────────┘◀──────│     and Other    │
┌──────────────────┐                         │ Government Policies│
│  Labor Relations │                         └──────────────────┘
└──────────────────┘

  ┌──────────────────┐                       ┌──────────────────┐
  │   International   │                       │     Mergers      │
  │  Trade Conditions│                       └──────────────────┘
  └──────────────────┘
                    ┌─────────────────────────┐
                    │      Transportation      │
                    │        Conditions        │
                    └─────────────────────────┘
```

Supply markets are also influenced by many indirect factors. One of these factors is the transportation system. Good systems can cause distant sources to be easily accessible, whereas a poor transportation system can cause even close sources with good prices to be expensive and time-consuming to acquire from. Company mergers among suppliers can geatly affect supply. Though this activity is watched by domestic antitrust groups, it can have profound influence in the market. Labor relations, and the potential threats of disruption, affect supply market prices. Even labor relations at foreign sources that are not acquired from can affect the pricing and demand configuration of the domestic source. General economic conditions affect pricing, vendor delivery performance, and the degree of research and development practiced by vendors. Still further influences are government legislation and regulations, the effects of which can immediately be seen in environmental and safety areas. Finally, government fiscal, monetary, and other financial management policies affect supply markets. More pervasively, inflation, as it is caused by these actions, greatly affects supply markets.

Active, strategic orientations are necessary today and in the future by purchasing management. Purchasing is part of the strategic makeup of the firm, and it must apply the same concepts to assure optimum quality, low final costs, and adequate supplies for the firm. Supply markets are complex. These markets require active attention and strategic positioning by buyers. This chapter presents many of the key roles purchasing plays in addition to buying, including scrap and surplus goods management, purchasing in uncertain supply and inflation economies, the management of goods in short supply, and the development of information systems for daily operations and to detect research needs in the firm.

Scrap/Surplus Goods Management

One important facet of commodity management is the control and disposition of scrap and surplus goods. Scrap goods, waste products, and surplus items are almost unavoidable in production and distribution operations. In many firms, one department is assigned the task of maintaining control over these goods while some disposition can be determined for them. This task often falls to purchasing or materials management, for lack of any other place to assign it.

This section is devoted to asset and commodity strategies that include control and disposition of these goods. First, each group of goods in this realm is defined. Sources are then explored in order to give insights into how such goods might be controlled and minimized, and finally, channels of disposition are presented and explored. The concept of recycling is also presented. Lastly, a method of capital goods disposal, as practiced by a major chemical firm, is presented.

The issue of excess goods not immediately needed by the firm requires definition of the general groupings of such goods. *Scrap* is the remaining portion of a material that is not needed after the required portions are used in production. An example might be circles of tinplate that are used in making canning tops and bottoms. There is a certain amount of scrap that will naturally result from cutting circles from square or rectangular sheets of tinplate. There is simply no way of avoiding this type of scrap; firms can only minimize it. Scrap also exists when goods that are no longer usable are recycled. Again, this is not seen as undesirable; in fact, recycling can be seen as positive recapturing of value out of old goods. *Waste* arises from inefficient production or loss and damage in logistics operations. Poorly controlled production machinery causing output that cannot be sold or recycled is an example. Similarly, rough handling in warehouses can cause wasteful damage. *Surplus goods* are those goods that are in excess of regular requirements. These goods can be excess raw materials, goods in production, finished items, or idle capital goods. Scrap, waste and surplus goods are each caused by different reasons, and each requires different corrective approaches and different methods of disposition.

Sources of Scrap and Waste

Scrap and waste occur from a variety of sources. By understanding each source, different reduction tactics can be applied.

Surplus Purchases

Quantities acquired in excess of those needed in production or sales arise for several reasons. Production or sales may be less than previously expected. Such surpluses are not the fault of the buyer, if he or she originally made purchases according to plan. Goods acquired in a forward buy situation that are not now needed by the firm are another example of surplus purchases. Originally this might have been a good purchase decision but the result might be lost value to the firm. These surplus goods represent a higher than necessary inventory cost, but unless they deteriorate, they are often flexible for use in future production.

Overruns in Production

Overruns are generally finished or work-in-process units that occur when production operates for a full shift or other optimal production period without regard to the specific quantity planned or needed for sales and distribution. Such practices can also cause a greater than planned quantity to be drawn from raw materials. This illustrates why cycle counting is often necessary. Production overages are often disposed of through normal sales and distribution channels of the firm.

Obsolete or Deteriorated Inventory

In the raw material realm, obsolete goods are those that have become old or have deteriorated in physical value in some way. This situation can develop through age, careless handling or control in storage, or sudden shifts in production and sales needs. Obsolescence can occur through poor storage stewardship as well as through loose coordination between sales, production, and purchasing. Disposal is often the task of the purchasing department.

Production Scrap

Production scrap is a normal by-product of production technology. Examples are trimmings, ends of coils of sheeting, the leavings of stampings, metal shavings, and spent chemicals. These items are not necessarily an economic waste. They are unavoidable. The key to watch here is that such scrap does not become excessive or that production unduly inflates the scrap factor when calculating the amount of raw material necessary to produce a given quantity of finished goods. Scrap items are often amenable to a routine system of recycling or sale through scrap channels.

Production Waste

Production waste is usually finished or part-finished goods that are not of sufficient quality to sell, nor are they in a form that is recyclable as raw material scrap. An example might be poor quality units that come off a production line at the start of a run before the system is finely tuned and adjusted. Production waste can also be goods that are beyond acceptable quality limits which are discovered during production. The problem with this form of waste is that such items are often difficult to use or recycle. In Chapter 15, ways in waste factors can be minimized, are discussed. Again, the task of disposing of such goods is often the responsibility of purchasing.

Materials from Reworked and Returned Goods

Reworks are goods that have been returned from customers in order to correct defects or other problems. Reworks tend to be fairly new goods; the parts and scrap items removed from reworked units sometimes can be corrected and reused on other new goods. This situation often represents an inventory problem over which there is little single control in the firm. Such inventories can often grow unless monitoring and reduction efforts are applied.

By-Products

Many chemical processes create by-products when producing other primary goods. This joint production situation causes secondary goods to be produced that are unavoidable. This form of "excess" is often disposed of through the basic sales and marketing activity of a firm.

Natural Pollution

Natural pollution is a form of scrap and waste in that it is created when the firm produces its primary goods. Natural pollution can be in the form of noise, air-borne particles, odors, run-offs, and heat. Some air-borne particles can be recycled into salable products, and heat can be recovered for reuse elsewhere in the plant. Such recycling activities can be the responsibility of engineering, production, and sometimes marketing.

Returned Old Goods

Some industries are able to obtain goods back from the market that can be reused. One example is glass from the bottling industry. Another is telephones and other communications equipment which contain copper and other key metals that can be recycled back into new production or sold in general markets.

The various forms of scrap and waste stem from specific activities. Some forms are unavoidable, some are due to poor control over production, purchasing, and marketing activities. Each type is presented separately here because different remedies and control approaches are necessary in each area.

Alternative Channels of Disposal and Use

There are many ways in which scrap and surplus goods can be disposed of by a firm. One way is reclamation for use in production. A second is for use elsewhere in the firm as-is. And, selling to another firm as-is is still another way of ridding the firm of resources that are not required. Returning goods and items to vendors is another alternative. Materials that are not of adequate quality, can be disposed of in this way and some purchase arrangements include provisions for the return of unused goods for redisposition by the vendor. Scrap dealers represent a sales channel for goods that are not needed or are in scrap and waste form. Especially with metals, batteries, paper, cloth, and wood chips. Brokers are still another disposal channel. Brokers are intermediaries who do not take possession of the scrap goods, but rather arrange sales to other firms needing them. The sale of excess items to employees is often an outlet used by firms that produce consumer goods. This outlet is frequently used with excess production run items. Donation of excess goods to institutions is another avenue of goods disposal. And, finally, discarding or destroying goods is another disposal method.

Hazardous goods disposal has become a critical problem since the early 1970s. The Environmental Protection Agency has jurisdication over pollution as well as the terms of the Resource Conservation and Recovery Act. The terms of this act call for careful transportation and disposal of all hazardous waste products. This expensive problem has resulted in the development of broker or clearinghouse organizations that attempt to find firms that can use the waste products of other firms.

Each of these disposal methods should be viewed as a business decision. Scrap, waste, excess or unwanted materials can be disposed of in a number of ways. Some represent pure cost elements that are viewed as factors to be minimized. Others can be a source of revenue which can offset the cost of the excess resource expense.

Recycling is the active processing or disposing of scrap, waste, and excess goods in place of treating them as industrial refuse for "throwaway" disposal. There are several factors that will favor one of the positive avenues of disposal versus treating them as refuse. A prime factor favoring recycling is the cost of disposal as refuse. For example, there are now penalties for pollution caused by disposal of refuse goods. The more costly these penalties become, the more favored some of these recycling and positive disposal forms will become. The high price of virgin metal versus scrap also favors recycling.

On the other hand, there are factors that can hinder recycling as well. One factor is the cost of transportation, handling, and storage of these materials prior to transforming them into usable goods. Transportation rates on scrap metals have long been fairly comparable with those of virgin metals. This fact has had a hindering effect upon recycling activities and often has led to recycling taking place only at or near the source of the scrap and the point of next use. The capital cost of the equipment needed to recycle goods as well as the labor and energy required are another cost hindrance. In many instances, these factors along with the cyclical nature of scrap markets have caused marginal financial returns on investment in these ventures.

Scrap and other excess materials in basic forms are subject to varying degrees of value. Scrap price markets fluctuate in response to the price of the virgin materials, the cost of recycling and transporting them, as well as the supply and demand situation for both virgin and scrap goods. A manufacturer with a large stockpile of scrap goods will view them in different ways from the standpoint of opportunity costs. In one way, scrap goods are costless because they represent past production expense outlays. In another setting, such goods represent an opportunity cost in the form of storage space taken up and related expenses. In still another way, these stockpiles can be seen as costing the firm cash and related investment earnings that could be gained if the goods were sold as scrap. And, finally, scrap goods can be seen as an opportunity for production materials or salable goods. The urgency applied in disposing of such goods will depend upon these factors as well as the firm's need for cash or its desire to tighten controls over all resources.

Recapturing Value from Surplus Capital Goods

Capital equipment represents another opportunity and disposal situation for purchasing and materials managers. Capital equipment consists of machinery and other long-term assets that the firm uses in operations. It is common for such assets to become surplus as plants replace equipment with newer, improved, or altogether different items. This surplus equipment is often still in usable condition. Disposal of these items can be considered as investment cost recovery.[1]

Surplus capital goods represent opportunity in many ways. They still can be used in their present form by the firm, or they can be sold for cash. Disposed capital goods also reduce the firm's asset base, which has beneficial financial return on investment impacts. Further, an efficient system of disposal will reduce the chance that company managers will continue to use old capital equipment merely because the effort of disposition is more than the continued maintenance cost of keeping and using such equipment. Such practices will eventually cause a firm to operate with relatively older equipment and a more expensive capital asset base.

American Cynamid Co. has a comprehensive system for disposing of surplus goods. Each facility having idle capital goods in the corporate system notifies a central investment recovery office at the corporate headquarters. The investment recovery office then publishes and distributes a listing of all surplus goods throughout the corporation. Items most typically included are motors, automotive equipment, tanks, instruments, and office equipment. This listing includes the item, location, condition, terms of transfer, and where it can be inspected. If there are no interested buyers within the firm, the coordinator then publishes a list for outside distribution. This distribution consists of direct mail to various brokers, dealers, and other firms. If goods are still not sold through these channels, then they are scrapped for their metal and parts, if any. One person is in charge of this system. It is both an investment reallocation and recovery system that can be seen as a profit entity for the firm.

Management of Critical Commodities

Real and potential shortages of minerals and other goods is a problem that historically has hit buyers in times of war. In 1973, however, many shortages arose in the world in the wake of the OPEC oil price increases. Many firms were unable to acquire goods that previously were easy to obtain. The shock of this situation was accompanied by a realization in the U.S. of several key factors relating to minerals and other commodities. First, there was a relatively nonexistent stockpile of critical minerals in the U.S. What stockpile existed had been sold by the government during fiscal crises in the 1960s. Second, there was no minerals policy in the U.S. government with regard to such factors as long range need, sources of supply, and maintaining links to assure adequate supplies from overseas, etc. And, third, a treaty regarding mining in the oceans was being negotiated worldwide, and its outcome was unfavorable for economic mining.

Table 13–1 highlights the amount of minerals that the U.S. must obtain from overseas. It points to the fact that many source areas pose potential disruptions to the supply lines for these goods.

During the 1970s the U.S. increased its dependence upon foreign sources for many of the key minerals needed to operate its economy. Supply disruption from many of these sources can arise from political problems, shipping breakdowns, East-West influences, and other tensions. Many of the sources in the U.S. have closed or cut back production due to depletion of raw commodities, the high cost of labor or uneconomic capital equipment, and stronger operating requirements imposed by the Occupational Safety Hazards Administration and the Environmental Protection Agency. The problems of supply do not stem from actual physical shortages on the earth. They relate to the actual mining, shipping to the processor, and the physical capacity of the mines and processors.[2]

Shortages no doubt will appear on the market in ways that will pose problems for buyers in the years to come. This condition calls for a long-

☐ **TABLE 13-1.** *U.S. Purchases of Key Minerals from Overseas*

Mineral	% Acquired 1971	Abroad 1979	Primary Foreign Source
Bauxite	92%	93%	Jamaica, Guinea, Suriname
Chromium	89%	90%	South Africa, Philippines Suriname
Cobolt	75%	90%	Zaire, Zambia, Finland
Diamonds	100%	100%	South Africa, Zaire, Botswana
Gold	48%	56%	Canada, Soviet Union, South Africa
Manganese	96%	98%	Gabon, Brazil, Australia
Mercury	42%	62%	Algeria, Spain, Italy
Nickel	66%	77%	Canada, Norway, New Caladonia
Platinum	75%	89%	South Africa, Soviet Union, Canada
Potash	45%	77%	Canada, Isreal
Silver	34%	45%	Canada, Mexico, Peru
Tin	64%	81%	Malaysia, Thailand, Indonesia
Zinc	45%	62%	Canada, Honduras, Mexico

run strategy by a firm that will require such goods. Similarly, buyers will often have to use a series of short-run tactics to assure a supply of needed minerals and other shortage commodities in problem times.

Long-Run Mineral and Commodity Strategy

A strategy for maintaining a supply of products subject to shortages or disruption includes annual procurement planning, integration with customers and vendors, long-range planning of material requirement strategies, and broader minerals management input to business planning.[3] Annual procurement planning often is nonexistent, since many buying departments are not provided long-range forecasts of the firm's activities, or the firms and the departments do not perceive the need for long-range planning. Annual procurement planning can highlight commodities facing potential shortage and allow "forward building" of inventories. Such planning also permits the use of hedging, a practice often not allowed by corporate boards. The annual planning process starts with the overall corporate production and sales plans. Attention is placed upon critical commodities in a materials forecast from this end-product forecast.

Interaction between customers and vendors will bring to light future sales needs as well as the ability of vendors to supply the firm. It is necessary to analyze the vendor's ability to supply goods in the long term rather than for each specific order. Vendor capacities as well as product plans are central to this analysis. The firm's own backlogs and those of vendors, stated in terms of production run schedules rather than aggregated dollar amounts, will show the extent and nature of customer-firm-vendor timing flows. This information might be analyzed through simulation or merely by close cooperation and communication.

Long-range planning focuses the two previous informational processes into in-depth minerals needs and possible problem areas. At this point, problem commodities and minerals will be highlighted either in the form of true shortages or merely vendor bottleneck shortages. Key data to be gathered are: percent of the final good value represented by the critical material(s), percent of the firm's total purchases, commonality of the critical material to the firm's other products, substitutability potential, and margins obtained on each of the end products requiring the critical materials.

Further analysis should then include:

1. Identification of primary and alternate suppliers of the minerals.
2. Projected availability of supplies to these suppliers.
3. The profitability of selling to one particular firm rather than to other customers by the vendors.
4. Likely cost trends in the material industry, probable impacts from energy, capital, and political events.
5. Likelihood of capacity expansion in these vendor industries as well as productivity improvements.
6. The availability and likelihood of substitute raw materials becoming available in the industry.[4]

A major approach to assuring future material supply is backward integration into the vendor industry. By acquiring a firm that is a source of the material needed, a company can then favor material supply to itself from this captive vendor. There are some cautions to this approach, and these include avoiding acquiring a product source that might not be needed in the future, and the commitment of capital to an area that might not produce an adequate return.

A final long-range planning factor calls for the active input of purchasing in the firm's product planning processes. Some large firms have personnel monitor long-range future supply markets with an eye toward alerting the firm to potential problems on the horizon. This information is part of the considerations needed in future product planning and even product line trimming.

Micro-Tactics to Provide Product Supply

The previous discussion was oriented toward long-range positioning of the firm in the supply market. Prior to a pending supply problem period or during it, there are several approaches that can be used by buyers to acquire needed materials. One of these is to contract for a percent of the buyer's total requirements. That is, rather than settle for being allocated a fixed tonnage amount from a vendor, such contracts might require a percentage of the vendor's own supply. Another is to contract for a definite fixed quantity at a fixed price that is favorable to the vendor. Some firms have contracted with vendors for fixed percentages of the buyer firm's requirements. This means that Vendor A will supply forty percent of whatever the firm requires, Vendor B will supply thirty-five percent, etc. This assumes that the vendor industry is in a position to physically supply the goods, and that it is not dependent upon allocations from its own supply sector. Escalator agreements are useful in maintaining vendor interest in honoring purchase orders and contracts. Such agreements protect the vendor in the event of increases in alternate world price shifts. Gentlemen's agreements are common between firms and suppliers as well. And, incentive contracts are a supply method that are useful when the buying firm can pass along the higher cost features of the vendor incentive factors.[5]

Information—The Key to Effective Purchasing Management

There are three primary areas of information needed for developing effective purchasing strategy for the future. These areas are 1) monitoring, detecting, and acting upon areas of purchasing research need, 2) developing and maintaining an effective information system, and 3) directing attention to areas that are often administrative "gaps" in the firm.

Purchasing Research Needs

Harold E. Fearon has presented a list of factors that point to the need for research in purchasing. Each factor might not exist in every firm, but the list does highlight the need for research into specific areas.[6]

Value

Research is suggested or necessary if a firm is paying high amounts for an item or material. Value is a relative concept that includes comparisons of like components or materials from other sources or used in other applications. This factor becomes obvious when prices on certain goods climb higher than other products in similar product groupings over past periods. The element of price can either be current or projected.

Product Profitability

An unprofitable product is an indicator that purchasing research might be required in order to reduce costs or improve salability of the product.

Price/Cost Characteristics

Many factors exist in this area. One is high unit cost. A high unit cost is an obvious target for purchasing research, since a savings in this area will have a high impact upon total cost reduction for the entire product. Another research indicator is infrequent price changes. Most commodities undergo price fluctuations and inflation. If no price changes have been made for a purchased product, this is an indication that the vendor has a very high markup in the product or the firm has attained productivity savings that have shielded it from the need to increase prices. In any event, this indicates a wide production-cost-to-sales-price margin. Still another indicator of the need for purchasing research is frequent or seasonal price changes. The possibility of events existing that lead to predictable price changes arises. Buyers can avoid these price changes through such tactics as forward buying, bulk purchasing, and other cost savings approaches.

Availability

Negative factors in this realm are the existence of a limited number of suppliers and limited material. The buying firm is in a vulnerable position here, since most of the buy-sell power is with the seller. On the positive side, the availability factor points to some positive reasons for research: 1) new suppliers coming onto the market with new, similar, or divergent forms of supply, 2) the possibility of imports or buying from afar, and 3) the possibility of making a product rather than merely purchasing it.

Quality

Any time there are specification or quality problems with procured goods there is the potential for positive results from purchasing research. The same applies to a quality problem on the firm's own production lines. Perhaps another material or component might solve a quality problem inherent in the machinery or manual processes. Another component might be less prone to damage or allow rougher handling during production, packaging, and distribution.

Data Flows

Information internal to a firm that is late, costly, or inaccurate is a sign of the need for purchasing research. Any area for which information is not available represents an investigative opportunity that might lead to reduced costs or improved quality. Information that is costly to obtain is often not sought for that reason alone. The possibility exists that this area might contain some savings opportunities. The assumption here is that information not available might in all likelihood provide avenues for cost savings and quality improvement. Finally, research is necessary when a buyer does not have sufficient time during his or her normal day to investigate analytical work. In this situation, the line work of buying, expediting, etc. consume all the buyer's time, with little or none left for positive research.

Research of Areas Often Overlooked

Purchasing is charged with the task of acquiring goods and services for the firm. This includes raw materials, finished goods for resale, MRO items, capital goods, or various services. However, still many other items are required by the firm that are not the responsibility of any particular department for monitoring and analyzing. By viewing many of these purchases in their entirety the firm can save costs and improve services.

Electricity and other energy sources are not always controlled by any one central department in a firm nor are they considered as a cost-reduction element. Quite often these energy expenses, which are incurred by the firm for plant and office buildings, are not subject to analysis except through lighting and specific machinery studies. The economics of electricity generation today tends to favor smaller facilities in comparison to the past. By analyzing total site electricity consumption, other energy management and alternatives might become possible.

Communication systems is another area that is not researched in its entirety by any one party in the firm. New forms of telephone options and other communication devices are now available and these new developments open the way for cost reductions not previously possible.

Copying and printing services and equipment are other cost areas that are simply overhead expenses to each plant or facility. Considered together, these services might be obtained through larger-based leases, purchases, or contracts.

Car rentals, hotels, and even travel expenses are incurred by persons at nearly every separate facility and level in a firm. In many instances, the collective buying power of the firm can be used to negotiate favorable prices or service relationships with these suppliers. This is often accomplished by obtaining a corporate account number with car rental firms or hotels that entitles the user to a discount. This buying power can also be used for favored reservations systems or simpler billing processes that avoid normal credit card fees.

Conclusion

This chapter presented three key strategy areas worthy of attention by purchasing, i.e. scrap, surplus goods management, critical commodities management, and information management. These categories are major areas that can save a firm expenses or improve the quality and availability of goods and services. However, this group of topics is by no means all-inclusive. The most critical element to effective purchasing management is to be open to any area posing a threat to the firm's strategic mission or profitability and to direct research attention to that area for possible correction or alternative action.

FOOTNOTES

1. Thomas F. Dillon, "Finding New Markets for Surplus Equipment," *Purchasing*, 23 October 1980, p. 73.
2. "We're Not Running Out—Just Short," *Purchasing*, 10 April 1980, p. 67.
3. John J. Piepgras, "How to Live with a Shortage Economy," *Business Horizons* (June 1975), p. 75.
4. Ibid.
5. "Long-Term Emphasis Will be on Supply and Quality," *Purchasing*, 29 January 1981, p. 109.
6. Harold Fearon, presentation at Physical Distribution and Materials Management Executive Program, The Pennsylvania State University, February 1981.

SOURCES FOR FURTHER READING

Aggarwal, Sumer C. "Management of Material Shortages." *Guide to Purchasing* (Oradell, NJ: National Association of Purchasing Management, 1982).
Langley, C. John Jr., and Morice, William D. "Strategies for Logistics Management: Reactions to a Changing Environment." *Journal of Business Logistics* 3:1–19.
Bird, Monroe Murphy, and Clopton, Stephen W. "A New Look at Scrap Management." *Journal of Purchasing and Materials Management* 13 (1977): 26.
Matwiejczyk, Thomas. "Aircraft Maintenance Parts Clearinghouses." Monograph, The Pennsylvania State University, University Park, PA 1983.
Temple, Barker & Sloane, Inc. *Transportation Strategies for the Eighties.* Oak Brook, IL: National Council of Physical Distribution Management, 1982.
"Make Purchasing an Information Center." *Purchasing*, 4 September 1980, p. 77.

QUESTIONS FOR REVIEW

1. What are the various forces that act upon the total supply situation for any one firm?

2. How might a labor or supply situation at a vendor that the firm does *not* use affect the firm's supply situation?

3. Are the concepts and approaches used in foreign buying any different than those in domestic buying? If so, why? If not, why not?

4. How might the firm's competitors affect the supply market for the firm?

5. Why does scrap and surplus goods management have to be directed in many distinct areas?

6. What are some of the ways in which purchasing can act to reduce scrap and surplus goods from occurring in the firm?

7. Are there any alternative methods of capital goods disposal other than the ones mentioned in this chapter?

8. What factors have made scrap/waste and even capital goods disposal more difficult in recent years?

9. Why should the firm adopt a long-range, critical materials policy?

10. Is the U.S. too highly dependent upon foreign sources for its critical materials?

11. What are some of the actions purchasing can take in face of materials shortages?

12. How can purchasing become a key information center for the firm?

III

PURCHASING AND THE LOGISTICS OF MATERIALS MANAGEMENT

Purchasing is an integral component of all the inbound logistics functions required to bring goods and services into a firm. It cannot be separated from the other activities used to acquire and place goods at their points of production, resale, or consumption. These other activities include handling, storage, stock identification, inventory control, production scheduling, and inbound system design. Including purchasing, these activities are referred to generally as materials management.

A study on productivity conducted by the A. T. Kearney Company in 1979 revealed that logistics costs in the U.S. economy approximated $680 billion in 1979. This figure is made up of $300 billion in freight transportation costs, $180 billion in warehousing costs, $170 billion for other inventory holding costs, and $30 billion in logistics administration costs. The $680 billion figure represents twenty-three percent of the gross national product of the United States.

The A. T. Kearney study estimated that a conservative $40 billion could be saved through improved logistics functions. Purchasing is central to this problem in that it is the buyer using "dollar votes" in the economy for one product over another, one acquisition system or method over another, or one logistics service entity over another.

Purchasing acquires selling firms' goods and distribution services. It often is difficult to separate a selling firm's distribution services from the buying firm's materials management system. The informed and productive purchasing and materials manager of today and the future must consider the physical logistics flow activities of inbound goods along with price, quality, and the make-up of the goods themselves.

This section consists of four chapters. Chapter 14 presents an overview of materials management and introduces the role of inventories. Inventory control concepts and methods are the subject of Chapter 15. The objectives and constraints posed by production are presented in Chapter 16. And, finally, Chapter 17 presents many of the operational factors related to the efficient holding and handling of goods.

14

CHAPTER OBJECTIVES

After reading this chapter you should:

- Understand the impact of inventories and materials management upon the firm.

- Appreciate the strategic and operating roles of materials management.

- Understand the primary approaches used in materials management.

- Be able to assess the basic roles and uses of inventories.

Materials Management and Inventory Decisions

Introduction

Materials management is the planning and control of all inbound product flows into the firm. It includes purchasing, raw material inventory control, stores, inbound transportation, and production scheduling. Until recent years materials management has been overlooked as an area of efficiency improvement and overall financial gain for the firm. Today, it is the target of attention by production, purchasing, logistics and corporate planners and consultants.

Purchasing is directly involved in the trend toward integrated materials management. Buyers initiate the movement of goods into a firm for use by production and other departments. The purchase timing, cost, and specific product chosen all impact the performance of this inbound system.

What Is Materials Management?

Materials management includes all the control flow and physical goods flow activities in a firm up to and often through the production process. However, no two firms practice materials management in exactly the same manner.

The reporting lines and organizational placement of the individual materials management components vary from firm to firm. In some firms purchasing reports to a materials manager; in other firms, equal purchasing and materials management peers report to production. Some firms include transportation and warehousing in the outbound distribution department, and a small but growing number of firms combine materials management with distribution for a fully integrated logistics organization.

Materials management is a new area for purchasing and firms. The combination of purchasing decision making with that of production, distribution, marketing, and finance brings the entire firm's resources into focus. Purchasing decisions cannot be made independently of the rest of the firm, nor can other department's decisions unilaterally be foisted upon purchasing where they might result in higher costs. This chapter explores many of the emerging materials management elements that are causing an increasing integration of purchasing with other areas in a firm.

The Firm's Planning Cycle

Materials management is a critical part of the planning and operating cycle activities of a firm. The following subactivities in the overall planning process require specific purchasing and materials management input.

- Long-range plan—Purchasing and materials management resources, processes, and capacities (actual and desired).
- Corporate plan—Sources as well as material availability, quality, and cost (now and future).
- Operating Plan—General timing requirements of goods for production market plan.
- Production—Provide goods and services when required.
- Materials Management and Distribution Plans—Plan for above production needs, anticipate and advise if possible disruptions foreseen, coordinate with firm's own and vendors' distribution activities, and maintain contact with vendors.

Purchasing and materials management provide periodic planning and continuous operating input to the four activities listed. In more and more firms, the task of production scheduling is being shifted to either materials management, distribution, or both. This shifting is made in recognition of the fact that purchasing-materials management-distribution timing and quantity economies are greater than those typically accruing to production alone. Kodak, for example, has integrated the function of production scheduling within distribution so that purchasing, inventory, and warehousing costs can be balanced with production and marketing timing and quantity considerations.

Financial Impact of Materials Management Role with Inventories

Materials management has stewardship responsibilities over inbound inventories. Inventories, in turn, have a major impact upon the overall financial performance of a firm. The double digit cost of capital experience at the beginning of the 1980s and the memory of product shortages and profit problems in the 1970s has led top management to direct attention to these areas. Inventories represent cash that could be used elsewhere by top management. In fact, excessive inventories have been the reason for some firms' failing. In any case, it is imperative for the purchasing and materials manager to understand the overall role of the inventories he/she is responsible for within the firm. More and more firms are integrating inbound inventory investment, placement, and positioning into the entire strategic decision process.

A sample company's financial statements are shown in Exhibit 14–1. Included are the income statement and balance sheet. On this general level, inventories appear as a component of the cost of goods sold and within the asset holdings of the firm. Stockholders and lenders evaluate the profitability and health of the firm based upon these two reports.

■ **EXHIBIT 14-1.** *Financial Statements of JJC Corporation*

JJC Corp.
Income Statement 198x

Sales		$1,000,000

Less costs —

cost of goods sold:

beg. inventories	$200,000	
total purchases	650,000	
goods available	850,000	
end inventory	(250,000)	
cost of goods sold		(600,000)

Gross margin	$400,000
Operating expenses	(300,000)
Net income before taxes	100,000
Taxes	(40,000)
Net income after taxes	$ 60,000

Balance Sheet
As of December 31, 198x

Assets —		Liabilities & Equities —	
Cash	$50,000	Payables	$75,000
Receivables	200,000	Long-term debt	1,000,000
Inventories	250,000	Stock	50,000
Plant/equip.	1,500,000	Retained earnings	875,000
	$2,000,000		$2,000,000

The income statement shows the results of sales and expenses for the year. It presents the total purchases and usually inbound freight costs for the year. Expenses for holding inventories, such as warehousing, handling, etc., are often found in "operating expenses." The top management of many firms attempts to report low inventory dollar values at year end so that reported profits are low for taxation purposes. This practice assists in cash retention in the firm. During the 1970s many firms switched to LIFO inventory valuation in order to achieve this end.

This is also the reason for year-end inventory liquidation efforts, including sales, promotions, and the write-off or write-down of excess, older or damaged goods and obsolete parts. Thus, what might be a good purchase timing decision during the year may run counter to the wishes of top management and the company treasurer near year end.

On the surface, the income statement shows inventories as a major overall profitability component of the firm. In the JJC Corp., every $1 of sales results in a $.40 margin to cover operating expenses and taxes. These figures are of value when comparing year-to-year trends or looking at similar products sold by competitors.

The balance sheet is a statement of corporate position on a given day. It shows the inventory holding of the firm at the end of the year. In this example twelve and one-half percent of all assets are represented by inventories, which are clearly assets that could otherwise be converted to less risky and more liquid receivables or cash.

The income statement and balance sheet together can be used to show other elements of inventory in the organization, including 1) Return on Sales—One measure of the firm often sought by analysts is profit in relation to sales. This ratio is net income after taxes divided by total sales. In the sample in Exhibit 14–1 it is $60,000/$1,000,000 or six percent. This figure is greatly impacted by beginning and ending inventories, purchase timing, and the expenses related to holding inventories. Reduction in purchase prices has a multiplier effect here as was shown in Chapter 1.

2) Return on Equity—Return on equity is profit divided by common stock and retained earnings. This figure is $60,000/$925,000 or 6.5 percent for JJC Corp. It is a measure of how well the owners' investment in the firm is performing for them. Obviously, profit, as it is calculated by using purchases and inventories, is a factor in this measure.

3) Return on Assets—A measure of how well the assets of a firm are being utilized is indicated by the return on assets. This figure is determined by dividing net profit by total assets. In Exhibit 14–1 it is $60,000/$2,000,000 or three percent. Every $1 reduction in assets will serve to increase this measure.

4) Working Capital—Working capital is the residual when all short-term liabilities are subtracted from short-term assets. Within this context, short term is usually about thirty days. In the JJC Corp. example, this is cash plus receivables plus inventories less accounts payables, or $500,00 less $75,000, or $425,000. This is a healthy position.

5) Acid Test—The acid test is current assets without inventories less current liabilities. The argument for this measure is that inventories might not be easily liquidated within the short term. In the JJC Corp. this is $200,000 + $50,000 less $75,000 or $175,000. Within this measure, financial personnel and top managers would prefer the firm's resources in cash rather than inventories. Many firms look healthy from a working capital standpoint but cannot pay bills from an acid test position.

6) Days Inventory on Hand—Days inventory on hand is a rough measure of how many days of sales can be covered by the inventory on hand.

This figure is found by dividing sales by 365 to determine a daily sales average. This average is then divided into the inventory balance. In the example in Exhibit 14–1 this is $1,000,000/365 which is $2,740 per day; $250,000/2,740 is 91 days. This measure is of value when comparing competing firms within some industries. The lower the figure the more favorable the firm's position is viewed, unless it is too low and an increase in sales is anticipated.

7) Inventory Turnover—Inventory turnover is determined by dividing sales for the period by the average inventory. In the JJC Corp., this is $1,000,000/250,000 or 4.00 times. This figure is an efficiency measure of asset turnover. Again, industry comparisons are necessary.

The measures described here are keenly watched by top management and financial personnel. Generally speaking, a reduced level of inventory or inventory values is sought for favorable result in these measures. Each factor must be weighed by purchasing and materials manager in day-to-day operations and overall planning. Several of these factors are pertinent for analysis as we enter the mid-1980s.

First, as the entire firm's logistics system is analyzed in the context of Exhibit 14–1, it is still apparent that inventories are not the responsibility of one operating person. Inventories are generally fragmented between purchasing, materials management (when these are separate), production, and distribution. Thus, total inventory control is often spread among many departments. This situation can cause unforeseen shortages or an unmanaged increase of inventories. Often, the inventory flow records of these departments do not correspond to each other. Until there is singular control over goods throughout the firm, there will tend to be problems in controlling this fluid asset.

Purchase and selling terms can have a key direct financial impact upon the firm. Goods purchased FOB receiving plant will reduce the overall holding of inventories by the amount of days in transit, versus those purchased FOB vendor's plant and sold FOB selling destination. While this action might have a favorable impact upon the reporting of the inventory position, it might represent a loss of transportation savings opportunities, especially on the inbound side. Clearly, this is a factor ripe for analysis in the 1980s as the importance of transportation increases for purchasing managers.

The make-or-buy decision plays a major role in inventory decision. The "make" alternative usually requires a larger overall investment in goods unless equipment is already on-hand. This cost and its resulting impact on the financial measures of the firm must become part of the make-or-buy equation.

Vendor performance and lead-time experience come into play here as well. Shipments from a great distance or from unreliable sources require a safety stock or lead-time inventory holdings. Such actions impact detrimentally upon inventory measures. This is particularly a problem with imported goods, which often must be paid for at the exporting port.

Consignment purchasing is a favorable alternative when inventory financial impacts are involved. Consignment purchasing makes goods available without having them "on the books" until actually used. Goods are physically available without lead time and payment for the subsequent sale might actually be received prior to payment to the vendor. Of course, the liability for payment for the total lot of goods must also be considered.

The financial aspects of inventories as they affect the overall firm are important considerations for top management. Corporate policy dealing with inventories will no doubt play more of a hand in the future. The purchasing and materials manager must understand these concerns as they relate to day-to-day acquisition and supply management tasks.

Materials Management Objectives

The objectives of materials management embody those for purchasing presented in Section I, including lowest final cost, optimum quality, assurance of supply, and lowest possible administrative costs to the firm. Brought down to an operating level, specific materials management objectives exist.

Minimized Inventory Investment

Inventories represent cash and other liquid assets that were converted into physical product form having less flexibility and greater risk than cash, marketable securities, or credit power (through increases in accounts payables or other short term debt). Firms continually seek to reduce inventories because they are seen as one of the cheapest forms of financing available to the firm. That is, cash released from reduced inventories is less expensive to obtain than that available by borrowing.

Inventories are also the subject of reduction efforts because they are a critical variable in the firm's return on investment. The example in Table 14–1, using abbreviated financial statements of two hypothetical firms, will illustrate the general impact of inventories upon the firm.

Firms A and B have equal sales, but Firm A has a very efficient materials and distribution management system that keeps its inventories very low. Firm B, on the other hand, has a higher inventory level. This phenomenon will tend to produce some distinctive differences between the two firms that are both overtly and covertly noted in financial records. On the surface, however, both sales and the reported cost of goods sold of both firms are the same.

The first difference between the Firm A and B is that the inventory turnover (inventory on hand divided into the cost of goods sold) is higher in A (5 times) than B (1.2 times). Second, Firm A requires less warehouse space for inventory than Firm B. This is disguised in less fixed plant and facilities assets ($1,500 versus $1,575). Third, Firm A can finance its assets out of short-term cash flow while Firm B must often borrow funds in order to cover its inventory purchases and holdings. This situation will be reflected in higher interest expenses. Fourth, Firm A's profit is higher due to lower interest charges and operating expenses of a smaller warehouse and inventory system. Fifth, Firm A will

☐ **TABLE 14–1.** *Impact of Inventories Upon the Firm*

Financial Components	Firm A	Firm B
Balance Sheet		
Cash/securities	$350	$300
Inventories	100	400
Other assets	1550	1575
Total assets	2000	2275
Income statement:		
Revernues	$1200	$1200
Cost of goods sold	(500)	(500)
Operating expenses	(250)	(300)
Profit after tax & interest	225	175
Cost of goods sold:		
Begin. inventory	$100	$400
Add purchases	500	500
Total goods available	600	900
Less: end inventory	(100)	(400)
cost of goods sold	$500	$500

experience less risk in inventory holding because there is always less inventory on hand that can become damaged or obsolete. And sixth, Firm A has a higher return on investment ratio (profit divided by assets), 11.25 percent versus Firm B with 7.7 percent. This occurs from the double impact of higher profits in the numerator and lower assets in the denominator. While this example was both hypothetical and simplified, the impacts shown are real inside the firm, and they illustrate the reason why minimized inventory investment is one fo the major goals of top, middle, and lower management.

Maximum Inventory Availability

The second major materials management goal is to maximize the availability of inventory for production, consumption, or resale.

This goal appears to be at the opposite end of the spectrum from minimum inventory investment, but it is crucial to the task of materials management, which is: provide all goods to the firms that are economically feasible while minimizing the funds required for doing so. This goal demands that material inventory be tightly controlled.

Firms that fall short of maximum inventory availability will often experience production downtime penalties, stockouts, and an overall loss of production and marketing productivity.

Minimized Logistics System Costs

This objective requires economical systems for storage, handling, information, communications, and management. This factor is found within the costs of purchased goods, work-in-process inventories, and the various costs for logistics activities that are usually reported in the category of operating costs in the income statement.

The Strategic Role of Materials Management

Strategy and its importance for the firm were discussed in Chapter 1. On a materials management and production level, strategy encompasses some specific factors, including[1]

1. Capacity—this factor includes physical system capacity and timing potential for handling and processing goods. Some firms actively build capacity in anticipation of product or industry growth.

2. Facilities—Production assets, handling entities, and purchasing-/materials management system plants, equipment, record, and communication systems all comprise this facet of strategy. Some firms have strategically placed themselves in the marketplace by utilizing their own freight brokerage operation rather than calling one when shipments are needed inbound. By keeping close links with the market in this manner, the firm can take advantage of spot opportunities when they arise.

3. Vertical Integration—This form of strategic placement entails ownership or control of entities supplying the production and materials management system and generally includes private trucking operations that can provide cost and/or service advantages. In the extreme form, vertical integration can be noted with chemical and fertilizer companies that also own pipelines and tank facilities, or the ownership of the Bessemer and Lake Erie Railroad by U.S. Steel Corporation.

4. Production Technologies—Production technologies include the processes, machinery, formulas, etc. that enable the firm to produce a distinctive product either physically or cost-wise. In the materials management realm, this can include the method employed to maintain tight inventories or the system of maintaining a standardized raw product with final production upon demand. One South American processor obtained an edge on competition by developing a long-term storage system for tomato paste. Previously, the firm would have to rush multistage operations from raw tomato to ketchup, soup, etc. A year's market mix would have to be projected at the beginning of the six-week peak tomato season in March. Forecasting errors would result in some stockouts and other products in excess by November and December. The firm developed a sanitary storage medium for all output from a single stage, making the raw tomato into a standard paste. Any specific tomato-based product could then be made from the paste. This production-materials management advantage enabled the firm to reduce the need for future production assets while it cut production scheduling problems and increased subsequent marketplace customer service.

5. Quality—This strategic advantage is pervasive from sourcing to handling/storage/inspection all the way through production. Quality is an attribute that exists in materials, design, or manufacturing processes. Adherence to high quality output requires a commitment of the entire firm. In many firms, however, quality assurance is left to the operational level where short-term cost targets can eclipse attention to product quality.

6. People Talent—People talent is another important strategic advantage that a firm can possess. This advantage ranges from management persons having special talents to production workers particularly adept at detailed assembly, or working with colors or tastes. In materials management, this can include persons who are able to very efficiently schedule production, negotiate, or conduct low-cost value analyses upon components and processes.

7. Alternative Recognition—This strategic advantage is more of a state of mind or an open process in a firm. It is the recognition that physical product handling poses trade-off ranges and decisions in plant and equipment, production planning and control, labor and staffing, and organization and management. Rather than strive for "the one way" of organizing and operating a system, this strategic advantage requires a management perception to problems and opportunities, the possible need for changes and adaptations, and the ability to change or accept alternatives when desirable. Again, alternative recognition is a corporate frame of mind that encourages new input rather than becoming entrenched with fixed methods.[2]

The growth of distribution and materials management has brought an increased awareness of alternative recognition to many firms. There are many combinations of transportation-warehousing alternatives available. Many firms may use just one form while others may use one form for small lot sales and another form for large lot distribution. That is, there is no "one way" of distributing. Purchasing personnel are now finding alternative methods of transporting goods inbound from different vendors. One method might be appropriate one time and yet another mode, at a different cost, would be best the next time.

The objectives of materials management are supportive of those of purchasing and the firm as a whole. The key in any one firm is to integrate the individual departmental goals into the overall corporate and marketing goals. Further, the firm must continually check for possible conflicts in both the objectives and the operational practices used by each department in carrying their individual goals out.

Historical Development of Materials Management

Materials management has not always received the attention it is today. Though these activities were always a part of purchasing and manufacturing, materials management as a discipline is a relatively new phenomenon that has grown since the 1950s. Following is a brief discussion about past practices and the trends that have caused materials management to become widely recognized.

Traditional organizational structures often had purchasing and manufacturing at an arm's length from each other. Purchasing had the goal of minimum material cost, and production was often evaluated on minimum unit cost obtained through long production runs. Even when purchasing was within manufacturing common emphasis was to supply the production line in ways that optimized purchasing's own operating conveniences and unit costs. Production scheduling was generally contained within manufacturing, and inventories acted as a buffer or reserve so that the operating necessities and conveniences of production could be maintained.

By the 1950s, several factors led to changes in this organizational approach. One factor was product proliferation. The growth in marketing, market segmentation, and an emphasis upon competition caused a growth in the number of separate products most firms produced and sold. This growth complicated the purchasing, manufacturing, and production scheduling tasks. These tasks became particularly problematic when the practice of infrequent long production runs of each product caused delays and stockouts in the delivery of specific products to customers. In this situation, marketing became a department in conflict with production scheduling. Product proliferation also led to large increases in inventory held within the firm.

Vertical integration was another factor that often caused firms to tighten the purchasing-manufacturing processes into what we today refer to as materials management. To achieve vertical integration it is necessary to coordinate the activities of interconnected plants. Production runs, transportation, and work-in-process inventories must be coordinated in order to prevent problems and to optimize any economies sought in such arrangements.

Lead time problems are another factor contributing to the evaluation of materials management. The need to maximize inventory availability in face of uncertain vendor delivery and/or in-transit transportation service requires a close link between purchasing and production scheduling. This problem often grows when procuring internationally or from sources distant from plants. Deteriorated rail service in the Northeast states during the 1970s caused problems for many firms when in-transit time on the Penn Central Railroad both lengthened and become erratic on many lines.

The development of the logistics concept greatly shaped materials management. This concept is recognition that trade-off relationships exist between interfacing functions. Further, whenever trade-offs exist, there are opportunities for total cost and service savings for the entire firm. Thus, many firms recognized that a unit cost increase from a shortened production run might have increased purchase order costs, but the firm saved a greater amount in inventory and warehousing. This is only one example of such coordination which suboptimizes each of the major functions for the good of both and the firm.

Many management science techniques, including the use of the computer in production scheduling evolved during this period. These techniques presented new opportunities for analysis and cost/service improvements in the materials management area. The advent of materials requirements planning (MRP) is one such tool that has had a great impact.

Product shortages in the mid-1970s forced firms to link marketing, production, and purchasing in a way that more closely coordinated what was marketed in the best possible production schedule with what component products were available. Some firms made major organizational and coordination changes during this time that resulted in more formalized management entities.

Finally, recognition of the high cost of inventories in the late 1970s and early 1980s has led most firms to seek ways of reducing inventories without penalizing major economies in purchasing, production, and marketing. Inventory investment minimization, while maximizing its availability, requires centralized interdepartmental coordination in materials management.

Materials management literature cites many examples of how specific firms adopted the materials management concept. Each company was shaped by specific events, impacts, and the personalities of those involved. All or most examples point to one or more of the factors highlighted in this chapter. Examinations of firms will also reveal that no two firms are exactly alike in organization, function, or reporting lines of materials management. Boeing, for example, has a much more refined system than does a food processing plant that receives its vegetable supply only once yearly. Each firm has specific products, vendor/supply configurations, manufacturing arrangements, time constraints, personnel talents, and information systems that all come into play with exactly how a materials management system will evolve.

Alternative Approaches to Materials Management

Literature in the 1980s contains much contrasting information on various approaches used in materials management. In particular, the various approaches are often labeled as the U.S., Japanese, U.S.-"just in time," and European approaches. Each approach will be presented and contrasted here to provide insights into how firms can structurally and procedurally address purchasing and production objectives.

Common, Traditional U.S. Approach

The U.S. has enjoyed extensive production capacity, labor goals, resource availability, and mass markets. Automation and large productive processes were economical because of large markets.

The quest for minimum manufacturing unit costs in many firms has lead them to optimize production lot sizes. Optimum run lot sizes are a function of balanced set-up costs, variable unit costs, and the scheduled needs of various products produced on each production line. Transportation vehicle sizes also come into play here, too, as rail car, truck, and container capacities enter into the inbound and outbound lot size equation. In the U.S., these capacities are quite large as railroad and highway size and weight limitations are larger in comparison to many other nations of the world. Further, transportation economics generally favor larger vehicles and single handlings of many shipments at once resulting in the form of lower unit carrier prices.

Inventory is used to buffer transportation, production, distribution, and sales when flow rates, availability, or demands are at different rates from each other. Purchasing usually has many materials sources available throughout the country, which requires selection monitoring and expediting efforts. The situation is intensified with the great product variety that is created and expected in our economy. Consequently, U.S. firms have emphasized materials delivery systems.

Many industries, and the automobile industry in particular, have recently been highlighted for quality problems. Quality and its control often are elements that are generally defined by top management but left to lower management levels for follow through and administration. In an effort to reduce unit production costs, line managers often opt for less inspection and the use of less than target quality components in order to avoid scrap, waste, return costs, or production inconvenience. Thus, quality is often treated as a trade-off against purchasing and/or production unit cost. Quality frequently suffers because worker task assignment is often defined in very specialized terms either through the nature of line automation, labor skill rules, job descriptions, or both. This phenomenon creates repetitive and often boring jobs. It can prevent the worker from relating to the overall output of the line and the products of the firm as a whole. Here, too, lax attitude of commitment to the firm, its systems, and the quality of its products can become endemic.[3]

Japanese Approach

Vendor supply lines, transportation systems, production scheduling, and quality control are approached differently in many Japanese firms.

Large Japanese firms will often procure from small vendors that are in close proximity to their plant. This action minimizes lead time problems and often takes place several times a day, and in some instances a vendor's truck and driver are always at the firm's inbound dock. The driver acts as a production inventory monitor, supplier, and legal party in the purchase of goods. This minimizes inbound inventory for the manufacturer to such an extent that it is nearly nonexistent. Vendors are informed weeks and months in advance of production schedules.

Work-in-process and production activities are often "pulled through" the system according to the firm's sales and delivery requirements. The "pulling" approach is often organized around a system of KANBAN tickets that travel with small lots of goods through various production stages and are posted where all workers can see them. Workers may then relate subsequent production needs with what they are currently producing. This approach often permits a smoother, less hectic production rate than when machinery and manufacturing are running at maximum pace. Observers of Japanese factories note that their high productivity is not necessarily attained through faster work activity. The pull-through system helps pace multiple production stages so there is little or no work-in-process inventory.[4] In fact, safety stocks are regarded as a form of organizational waste.

Inventories are further minimized through simplification of production set-up and changeover processes. Product variety is less than that found in the U.S., and this factor reduces the production lot problem somewhat. But, of most importance, is the drive to reduce production changeover efforts to an absolute minimum. This process is analyzed and implemented as an on-going, all-employee effort. This factor, combined with the almost real-time vendor delivery requirement, reduces the need to optimize production unit costs with run sizes that pay off any high changeover costs.

Quality and its control receives more pervasive attention in Japan that it does in the U.S. Quality problems are minimized in many ways. First quality assurance often involves everyone in the firm from top management down to the individual worker. Production line employees are rewarded for detecting quality problems. A poor quality component is viewed as an opportunity to correct an inherent problem. Correction efforts involve workers who are familiar with the goods and processes, engineers, top management, and the vendors. Firms often hold seminars with vendor's workers to stress quality and how it might be improved. Quality is looked at in a global manner in addition to design and defective parts. It is viewed as a whole concept that includes delivery and inventory problems, communications and anything relating to operations as well. Thus, the materials management process is an attribute of quality. Emphasis upon quality is viewed by many observers as sometimes excessive to the point of being uneconomic, but this is a judgment that is best made in light of market success.

Decision making tends to come from the bottom up in Japanese organizations, which rely highly upon consensus decisions. Production, quality, and other problems are approached with the worker's input along with others in the organization who might be involved or can contribute. This is in contrast to some production settings in Western firms where employee input is minimized; instead, problems are approached by middle management information specialists, and/or consultants.

The human resource system must also be included in this contrast of production and materials management. The Japanese culture is very much a part of this analysis. Lifetime employment with one firm is the norm. Inherent to this is a concept of employee trust in the organization. This trust extends to the fact that the employee will not be laid off or have his/her job abolished in slow periods, nor will a suggested improvement in a process eliminate one's employment. Instead of individuals being recognized for periodic improvements, whole teams are involved through consensus decision making. Each employee is generally attuned to the success, operations, and directors of the firm of suborganization. The team concept also extends to worker flexibility. It is common for a production worker to be rotated through many jobs and tasks. This diminishes the boredom problem associated with repetitive work activities; it enhances flexibility and the ability to detect improvement opportunities; it leads to a team performance goal rather than just that of an individual; and it reduces worker assignment constraints that are common in many Western firms. These factors all led to a sympathy for and a smoother operation of the entire organization. It reduces the situation in which one department strives to maximize its goals to the detriment of others.

These phenomena of Japanese production approaches appear distant from pure materials management concepts, but they do all relate, and they can be of benefit for other firms to analyze. Inventory risk is one factor that is often overlooked, however, in the literature highlighting the benefits of the Japanese systems. The firms observed and reported on merely shift much of the risk of inventory uncertainty from the major manufacturer to the smaller, dependent vendor. The risk is not removed from that economy and society, it is largely shifted. Close communications and links that include informing vendors of the firm's planning horizons go far in reducing much of that total risk. This is a practice that has only of late come to Western purchasing operations.

U.S. "Just-In-Time" Approach

Several firms in the U.S., automobile firms in particular, have long scheduled inbound materials flows along what is called a "just-in-time" approach. Similar to the Japanese vendor supply practice mentioned above, this system coordinates production plans with vendor production and transportation deliveries so that goods can be removed from a rail car or truck and immediately be placed on the production line. Close links with carriers in planning, scheduling, and shipment monitoring are all necessary for this approach.

It is not difficult to visualize the need for this "just-in-time" approach. All the components of a car individually take up many times the cubic footage of storage space that the completed vehicle does. Tremendously large component storage facilities, inventory investment, and multiple handling systems would otherwise be required. Problems arise, however, when delivery delays occur or incorrect or low quality components arrive. Production downtime or alternative scheduling costs can be excessive, since there is little or no inventory reserve.

European Approach

European firms have approached production operations in a different light. World War II left the continent with scarce or nonexistent production facilities and with a small, young labor pool. Further, each of the countries was fragmented into relatively small economies having limited resource and outlet markets. Emphasis tended toward optimal utilization of the plant's capital, goods, labor, and invested capital. Rather than mass production, job shop situations were common. Purchasing lead times were uncertain, so inventories were subordinated to promote efficient production scheduling and capacity utilization.

The emergence of the Common Market has opened both resource and sales markets. Capital costs are recognized more as a part of inventory holdings, and capacity is not the problem it once was. Observers note a convergence of European and American materials planning and re-source management.[5]

Each of the four materials management systems has positive features. Though the Japanese KANBAN system is receiving wide publicity in the 1980s, it has not been universally successful there. Additionally, there are differing environmental factors in each place that affect the system's success. Japan has almost no natural resources and must obtain them from afar. Europe is a fragmented area that is becoming unified through the Common Market and the ease in international product movement. All nations experience high energy and capital costs. Capital costs will cause the drive for reduced inventories to be purchased further.

The efficient use of inventory by large firms in the U.S., Europe, and Japan can be noted in a productivity measure composed of the annual cost of goods sold divided by inventory. During the 1970s Japan's measure was 5.7, the U.S. 4.1, and Europe 3.7 times.[6] Again, the practice of forcing inventory risk onto small, and possibly unreporting vendors might be the reason for such a high Japanese inventory turnover figure. This figure would no doubt be higher if inventory in the total economy was considered. Be that as it may, there is no doubt room for adopting some of the Japanese people management and production flow concepts in the U.S.

Inventories in the Firm

Inventories exist in six basic forms: 1) raw materials and components; 2) work-in-process goods; 3) finished goods; 4) idle capital goods; 5) repair, maintenance and supply goods; and 6) scrap and waste. Each of these categories serves a different purpose in the firm, and the control, stewardship, and disposition can differ for each. Most inventories are physical assets that purchasing personnel acquire by converting financial resources that the firm could use elsewhere. Therefore, a careful balance must be made between the cost of having goods on hand when desired versus the cost and opportunities of not having them available.

Purchasing plays a key role in inventory reduction and can be one of the primary goals for the department. This is frequently necessary in times of high capital costs, particularly when these costs are higher than the inflation rate in the economy. Materials requirement planning and production scheduling systems that minimize the firm's total logistics costs call for tight inventory management decisions by purchasing personnel.

Why Have Inventories?

Inventories represent stores of physical resources that are held prior to, in between, and after production processes. In merchandising settings, inventories are stores of goods awaiting outbound movement to customers. In each setting, the reason for having an inventory is either 1) because the costs of inventories are less than the penalty cost the firm would incur without them or 2) the cost of the inventory is less than the profit gained through the convenience of having them. There are many specific reasons for developing inventories many of which are presented in the following.

On the outbound side, inventories are held at certain spots as a customer service advantage. Goods produced in Chicago but sold to someone in New York would endure a two or three day order cycle time. By storing goods at a second location in or near New York, cycle time can be reduced to one day. This advantage often results in a stronger sales position for the selling firm, since it represents a quick replenishment time for the buyer.

Inventories located near a market can also reduce order cycle time variability for customers. The farther goods must be shipped, the greater potential there is for uncertainty in transit time. Goods located closer to the buyer will generally endure less of this uncertainty. The buyer, then, does not have to build inventories to cover the chance of stockout. These two reasons are major elements considered by outbound distribution and marketing management of most firms. Purchasing and materials management persons necessarily see the results of these distribution strategies through vendor performance. Close warehousing or consignment are two ways in which a distant vendor can equalize or gain an advantage over other vendors.

Inventories within the firm exist to cover transportation uncertainties. Transcontinental rail movements can have a variability of many days. Import movements can vary by weeks from the target arrival dates. Problems in routing, documentation processing, and border clearance all contribute to this uncertainty. Thus, it may be cheaper for the firm to order goods far in advance of the needed date and hold them in storage when they arrive early. The inventory holding cost might only be fifty dollars per day as compared to a production downtime or customer misdelivery cost of much more.

Inventories also exist from differences in flow rates and available quantities within the entire logistics system. The materials requirements planning (MRP) examples in Chapter 16 shows how some quantities of goods were needed in the production run but available inbound lot sizes were different. Some goods had to be accumulated for production. Further, many are left over after production runs. For example, the firm's optimum marketing-distribution-production quantity might require 32,000 cu. ft. of a certain product. Yet, the vendor's shipping method by rail box car might be optimal with 40,000 cu. ft. inbound lots. Thus, on excess of 8,000 cu. ft. will accumulate with purchase and production run lots one through four. The fifth run will not require a purchase, since the 32,000 cu. ft. needed for it will now be in inventory. Another example of different flow quantities and rates arises when goods are only available in discrete lots yet production needs require large quantities for a continuous run of several weeks in duration. Here there is no alternative but to accumulate goods for the one run.

Pending price increases represent an opportunity for evaluating forward purchase of goods in advance of their normal acquisition date. In this instance, the cost of holding goods for the period is less than the increment of price increase.

Periods of product shortages give rise to inventory accumulation when the firm has an opportunity to acquire goods. This can represent a major competitive advantage when one firm has a source for goods, and its competition cannot acquire them.

Many firms will purposely maintain inventories as a hedge against sudden or unexpected increases in demand. This was a successful strategy in one chemical firm that observed the merging of one of its competitors into a conglomerate. One of the shakeout changes that took place within the merged firm was the discontinuance of a product line. This caused many of these sales to divert over to first firm. This is also a common reason for coal inventories in utility firms. A colder than normal winter creates the need for more coal consumption. Since orders for more coal might take weeks to cycle, a good level of inventory on hand can reduce the need for rush orders.

Disruptions from vendor strikes, plant shutdowns, and acts of God are threatening events that often cause purchasing firms to build inventories. Increases in sales and shipments are a common phenomenon that occurs prior to the steel industry labor negotiations every few years. Purchasing firms want to be able to continue their production, sales, and honoring of contracts through possible strike periods.

Finally, production overruns, scrap, waste, and byproduct creation is another reason for material inventories. In many instances these are unavoidable. In others, they arise from lack of adequate control. Be that as it may, these reasons are often why materials management and production area inventories exist and must necessarily be managed by the purchasing and materials manager.

Conclusion

Inventories, then, are found in the firm from a mix of reasons that range from profit potential, to cost savings, to cost minimization in comparison to other alternatives, from unavoidable sources, and from inadequate control.

The following three chapters present the rudiments of materials management. This includes inventory control, production-materials scheduling, and the physical management of goods in the firm. Purchasing in the past often could overlook these three areas. The integration of purchasing into production scheduling, materials management, and in some instances the entire logistics management of the firm necessitates an expansive view into the subjects of this section.

SOURCES FOR FURTHER READING

Epstein, Morris. "You Can Make Stockless Purchasing Work!" *Purchasing World*, April 1983, p. 50.

Farmer, David. "Why Materials Management?" *International Journal of Physical Distribution & Materials Management* 8 (1977).

Hoeffer, El. "GM Tries Just-in-Time American Style." *Purchasing*, 19 August 1982, p. 67.

Miller, Jeffrey G., and Gilmour, Peter. "Materials Managers: Who Needs Them?" *Harvard Business Review*, 57 July–August 1979, p. 143.

Teplitz, Charles J. "Manufacturers Shift the Inventory Carrying Function." *Industrial Marketing Management* 11 (1982): 225.

Wheelwright, Steven C. "Japan—Where Operations Really Are Strategic." *Harvard Business Review* 59, July–August 1981, p. 67.

QUESTIONS FOR REVIEW

1. Is materials management a new concept? Why or why not?

2. Is the concept of materials management a mere duplication or renaming of many of the activities traditionally performed by purchasing? Why or why not?

3. How does inventory impact upon the firm's financial performance?

4. Why is inventory reduction a financially desirable goal of top management?

5. What are the goals of materials management? Are these any different than what individual departmental goals of purchasing and production have been traditionally?

6. How does materials management fit into the corporate strategy of the firm? Is it any different than the role of purchasing in the same strategy?

7. Compare and contrast the U.S., Japanese, U.S. "Just-in-Time," and European approaches to materials management.

8. Why are purchasing and materials management intricately tied together?

9. Why do firms hold inventories?

10. Why is inventory management a difficult area to assign responsibilities and measure performance?

11. Why did the trend toward materials management accelerate during the 1970s?

12. Is materials management a concept for large firms only? Why or why not?

Problem 14-1

Refer to the data provided in Problem 1-1 in Chapter 1.

Questions:

1. *What is the company's asset turnover?*
2. *What is the inventory turnover?*
3. *Assume that the company will have sales of $20,000 in the next month. What is the current inventory-to-sales ratio?*

15

CHAPTER OBJECTIVES

After reading this chapter you should:

■ Appreciate the need for inventory control.

■ Understand the costs of inventories.

■ Understand the basic purpose and nature of the primary inventory control approaches.

■ Understand the basics of physical control of inventories.

Inventory Control Decisions

Introduction

Inventories are the goods acquired, used, manufactured, and sold by a firm. There are many forms of inventories, and since they represent a major portion of the firm's resources, they require ever constant watch and control. This chapter presents the key analytical and operational facets of inventories as they support the production and materials requirements planning aspects of purchasing and materials management.

Approaches to Inventory Control

Why the Need for Control?

Inventories are difficult assets to control because they are movable and because they are subject to decisions made by many persons including vendors and customers. Control is needed for such basic reasons as maximum profit, market saturation, minimized cost, stockout avoidance, maximized return on assets, lessened risk, and many more.

Inventories tend to increase on the inbound side of the firm for many reasons. Closer examination of these reasons leads the materials manager to specific areas of control over inventory. One reason for excess inventories is improper lot size. This means that the quantity ordered and received is not coordinated with production or sales needs. A second reason is that transportation rate breaks or large lot price discounts are inducements for many purchasing managers to buy lots larger than those currently needed. These cost-cutting opportunities can reflect beneficially on the purchasing budget, but they can balloon inventories or give rise to higher, often unmeasured, inventory costs elsewhere in the firm. Third, forward buying in a hedge or speculation move in a period of price increases or product shortage can cause inventory buildups that are excessive when prices stabilize or decline or the shortage disappears.

Excess inventories can occur for several reasons on the negative side. Erratic vendor order cycle time or inbound carrier service will often cause managers to increase the planned order lead times for purchasing. Then, whenever inbound replenishment service is anything less than this long, pessimistic time, an excess inventory holding will result. In many industries the need for product availability requires basing orders on the worst-case order cycle time. Failure to deexpedite orders also results in uncontrolled inventory build-ups. When the production run for Week three is slid to Week five, but the purchasing department does not inform the vendors of the additional time now allowed, goods will come in earlier than actually needed, will tie up company funds longer than necessary, may aggravate inbound warehousing space needs, and, might cause the firm and vendor to miss a less costly transportation move from consolidation opportunities.

Deflated production yield factors are another cause of inbound inventories increasing. Production yields are the units of output obtained from each unit on input. For example, a production department standard for stampings is stated as thirty stampings per single sheet of metal. It might be physically possible to yield thirty two out of each batch. But, when the standard is stated as thirty there is a comfortable margin for production managers to fall back upon in the event that less-than-efficient shifts and runs are used. Over a period of time a well-run production process will meet and beat this established standard of thirty units, which is a positive result for that department. Less sheets will be needed over the long run, and the inbound sheet inventory will increase. Thus, unless there is a close physical monitoring of inventories, they will increase until the excess is found by surprise at a later date. All through this period the firm's inventory costs and tied up cash will increase.

Another major reason often cited for increased inbound inventories is inflated production scrap yields. This is the ratio of final waste divided by total required input. If a run of extruded plastic sheeting requires a five percent loss through waste to set it up, but actual waste is only three percent, an average will occur in final units, or less raw pellets will be processed when the final finished units are processed. In either event, the raw material, finished goods inventory, or both will be higher than planned.

Lastly, incorrect repair and maintenance unit usage in comparison to projected needs will cause stockouts in some areas and oversupplies in others. Such problems are very difficult to project accurately, but these inventories can tend to build unnecessarily unless monitored and managed. For example, an airline maintenance manager originally projects the need for a part and places a large supply at each station, regional airport maintenance centers, and at the headquarters base. The actual need might be less than that projected or the system might gain by having the part stored regionally rather than locally. Unless deprioritized to fewer regional centers, large stocks of these parts can be left in the system beyond their shelf lives or way past the discontinuance of the plane model in the fleet. The situations described are eight major reasons often cited by materials managers as causing inventory inflation, and these are fruitful areas for inventory reduction or control monitoring.

What Is Control?

"Control" has many meanings within the context of inventories. It can mean having enough in order to avoid stockouts, or reduce the number of stockout situations to a minimum. It might mean never exceeding a certain quantity. What it does mean is having enough, but not too much. While this only loosely defines control, it points to the fact that inventory control, per se, can have different meanings, and the need for control can vary from time to time. Strictly speaking, inventory control is the system of monitoring inventory levels for the purpose of detecting the need for replenishment, determining the quantity to be ordered, and physically managing and maintaining security over them.

Approach for Inventory Control

The proper levels, quantities, and points in time for reordering or replenishing inventories are primarily defined by the objective(s) placed upon the organization by top management. Corporate strategies may range from product implementation support, to supply development during growth, to tight resource management, and eventually to asset minimization as is explained in the product life-cycle discussion in Chapter 18. Thus, overall strategic objectives and goals for products must first be defined by top management.

Once the strategic role of inventories is defined, a schedule and master plan should be developed with production as outlined in Chapter 16. This schedule must also include a cash expenditure forecast and a budget with finance personnel, as well as logistics planning with transportation and warehousing. A well-timed buy at one point by the purchasing department might only be bottlenecked in transportation or require more costly overflow storage at a public warehouse.

The next step in inventory control is to stratify the entire inventory line. This is usually accomplished through "ABC" analysis. Since it is often not physically possible to monitor all inventory items on a perpetual basis, ABC analysis provides a way of categorizing items in terms of the most important ones, the least critical ones, and those in between. This determination is useful in resale settings where thousands of line items are handled. ABC analysis is conducted so that the most important items (the "A" goods) receive a high degree of attention and control applied to them, the medium group ("B" goods) have a lesser degree applied, and the least important goods (the "C" goods) have minimal cost controls imposed upon them. Such separation permits those responsible for the total inventory to focus time and efforts of control in the most efficient means possible.

ABC stratification can be made according to unit purchase price, volume in units, total dollar requirement, or penalty costs if stocked out. Assume, for example, that total dollar requirement is the method of selection. Table 15–1 presents a list of goods involved. This list is small for illustration purposes, but it serves as an example for larger lists. One airline maintenance materials director reevaluates over 300,000 items yearly according to hourly stockout costs and dollar investment. This information is requested from his data system on a quarterly basis. The key is to determine the total dollar requirement, in this case, for each item. A table is then constructed starting with the item requiring the largest amount first and others following in descending order. The cumulative percentage of the entire 100 percent of total dollar require-

☐ **TABLE 15-1.** *Illustration of "ABC" Analysis of Inventory Flow Data*
Basic data:

Product ID	Annual Volume	Unit Value ($)
83K	370	$ 20
42K1	24	180
27B	90	1
14C	200	40
4C	125	25
32R	160	100
92A	19	5
66F	35	40
49M	100	1
18D	80	20
22T	70	22

Placed into an "ABC" Context:

Item	Volume ($)	% Volume	Cumul. $	Cumul %
32R	16,000	36.64%	$16,000	36.64%
14C	8,000	18.32	24,000	54.96%
83K	7,400	16.94	31,400	71.90
42K1	4,320	9.90	35,720	81.80
4C	3,125	7.15	38,845	88.95
18D	1,600	3.67	40,445	92.62
22T	1,540	3.52	41,985	96.14
66F	1,400	3.21	43,385	99.35
49M	100	.23	43,485	99.58
92A	95	.21	43,580	99.79
27B	90	.21	43,670	100.00

ment is then shown alongside of each item. A phenomenon is reflected in a graph that corresponds to each item, and this shows that only two of the stock items comprise about 55 percent of the percent of the total 100 percent requirement. On the other hand, the last five items comprise only 3.86 percent of the total.

In Table 15–1 the first group of materials comprise highly important items. These would be called the "A" items and would possibly require on-line, computerized, perpetual inventory control and coordination between all sites stocking that item. On the other hand, the last five "C" items might only require a weekly check or a system of replenishment that is triggered when the next to the last unit is removed from the bin. This is a common system in greeting card and book stores. The "B" items would have a system of moderate control and expense applied.

The exact determination of where the A/B and B/C cuts are made can be largely judgmental. This determination might require some adjustments especially if a product family consists of five "A" items and one "C" item. It might be wise for the "C" item to be included in the high control group. Similarly, future projections of increases or declines should also be used judgmentally in this cut-off process.

The next stage in the inventory control process is to determine proper lot sizes and lead times for each item. Lot sizes are initially defined by sales, production, and MRP systems. At this stage it is necessary to analyze lot sizes within the contexts of ideal inventory model and realistic transportation systems analysis. Such analysis will point toward optimum lot sizes given various factors such as holding costs, lead time variability, carrier equipment capacity, etc. Some of these tools are presented later in this chapter. Quite often lot sizes require readjustment for production and MRP quantities.

Up to this point, the "how much to order" and "when to order" decision rules have been defined. It is now necessary to implement monitoring systems that will actually show the level of inventory on hand at any one time. This subject is discussed later in the chapter.

Several perspectives are appropriate at this point with regard to inventory control. One is that if a firm is never out of stock of an item, then there might be excessive inventories of it. Rarely does an item deserve one hundred percent fulfillment. This information should be used as a starting point to determine whether it is feasible to reduce the levels held. Of course, this requires a balance of stockout costs. Another opportunity for change arises when frequent orders from suppliers occur. This might mean that volume discounts, transportation rate savings, handling or order processing economies might be overlooked. Finally, if allowable storage space is expanded within a warehouse or plant setting, inventory will grow to fill it. These are simple, perhaps primitive, indicators that are often valuable in directing attention to some immediate areas of inventory cost reduction.

Stockouts—A Primary Inventory Element

Stockouts exist whenever goods are not on hand when needed. When this occurs in production settings, schedules must be pushed back because some planned-for goods are not on hand. In resale merchandising settings, customer orders cannot be satisfied because there are no units of the item available to fulfill the order. Stockouts occur for any number of reasons.

Some root causes for stockouts are: 1) Longer than planned for inbound transportation times. Winter weather disruptions or routings via unreliable carriers will often be cited as reasons. 2) Incorrect lead times. The MRP-inventory system might release orders with four week lead times yet vendors might be recently providing a deteriorated lead time of six weeks. Constant monitoring of this crucial materials management element is required between the firm and its sources. Failure of the inventory system to detect a critical reorder point in quantity on-hand or point-in-time can cause stockouts. Pickers and record controllers might not find the desired goods due to either of these reasons. This problem can carry an added cost of misusing goods where not desired, especially in the case of similar appearing parts or electrical components. 3) Finally, stockouts can arise if the vendor is slow or stocked out.

The cost of stockouts is an area to be minimized, but it is a difficult element to measure with analytical inventory tools. One stockout cost is production downtime and/or rescheduling. Another cost arises when an inferior substitute part is used that later causes quality problems for customers. In a resale setting, stockout costs might be the cost of back-ordering, reshipping costs often at smaller quantity or expedited carrier service rates, and the cost of the lost cash flow opportunity during the delayed period. Another stockout cost configuration occurs when the customer orders a substitute product providing a lower profit to the firm. This shift can occur for one instance or become a permanent shift. A further stockout cost arises when the sale is lost to a competitor. And, finally a stockout might frustrate the customer and cause him/her to cease buying from the firm.

Firms can reduce the incidence of stockouts through higher inventory holdings and the stocking of goods closer to the user. Faster and more reliable transportation can reduce stockouts as well. This reliability factor is often cited as more important to the consumer than average transit time or use of a cheaper carrier. Obtaining a more reliable vendor is a major tactic in stockout reduction. Faster need detection and order processing within the buying firm can also reduce this problem. And, often overlooked, is faster receiving, stocking, and recording practices for inbound goods.

Many of these stockout reduction approaches can be fruitful with modest expense and effort. In a great many situations, however, stocking more inventory is the selected alternative to reducing this problem or to expand the operating convenience of production and marketing departments. Until recently these stockout reduction approaches were not weighed against the cost of providing the desired level of inventory. Yet, this is a major cost in the firm.

Holding Costs—The Other Key Element of Inventories

The cost of holding inventories is an important item of information in the firm. It can be used to determine the desirability of a certain stockout acceptance point. For example, if $100,000 stockout costs are reduced inventories at a total holding cost of $25,000, the firm stands to gain an advantage. The cost of inventory is a valuable tool with which to evaluate decisions related to new products, production run lots, purchase quantities, value analysis, "make-or-buy" decisions, transportation alternatives, product substitution and standardization, line trimming, and buy-direct versus through-distribution options. The cost of inventory is an item of information that is utilized analytically in both absolute dollar and percentage-of-unit value contexts.[1]

The stockout versus cost-of-inventory example serves to illustrate how one decision might be made using inventory holding cost. In this instance, a penalty cost was reduced by using an increase in holding costs of a smaller absolute amount. The basic approach usually consists of balancing an increase or decrease in the cost of one function against a decrease or increase in holding costs.

The cost of inventory for any given decision consists of the total relevant space, capital risk, and related system function costs. The analytical process requires determination of total inventory holding costs prior to a proposal decision versus what the total holding costs would be without the decision in place. The difference between the two is the total dollar inventory holding cost impact of the decision.

Space Costs

One major, identifiable, inventory holding cost is that of the space that it occupies. This includes only those additional heat, light, power, rent, depreciation, and insurance costs and taxes that are incurred or available by the firm as a result of the decision in question. In some instances this cost will be zero as in the case of a company warehouse that is now only part full, and the inventory in question will occupy some of that empty capacity. In this situation there is no additional space cost outlay for the firm. However, if the firm's warehouse is full and the goods in question are placed in space the firm must rent, then these rental payments are a relevant space cost. Also, if the goods in question are stored in the plant facility but force other goods to an outside rental facility, then the rent cost for the second goods must be included in the analysis. If the goods in question are already in a rented facility, then whatever increase or decrease in rental and handling fees that result with the decision become part of the analysis. Again, only those reduced or additional cash outlays that occur as a result of the decision in question are to be tallied for this analysis.

Capital Costs

This component is a measure of the value of funds tied up in the changed, higher, or lower inventory. For example, if the current level averages $1,000,000 in value throughout the year, the new level will be $600,000, and the firm's cost of capital is 18 percent, then the released cost of the capital component will be $400,000 x 18 percent which is ($72,000). If the decision is to require a $1,500,000 level, then this cost component will equal $500,000 x 18 percent which is $90,000.

Some firms view various inventories and decisions in differing ways, and the cost of capital component is treated accordingly. For example, if goods in the firm's normal line of activity are being analyzed, the firm's cost of capital is an appropriate percentage rate to use. If an expansion is being considered, such as a new market entry, then a slightly higher rate might be required by finance management. If a new product line or new venture is being considered, then an even higher rate might be required. These higher rate alternatives account for the increased risk involved in the decision.

Risk Costs

This category includes many elements. First some obsolescence costs might be possible with the decision. This can occur if some goods remain unsold or become technically inferior to newer ones as time progresses. This is common with seasonal or food goods where there is an identifiable penalty from lost use or resale value on goods remaining too long on the shelves. This is admittedly a difficult cost figure to obtain, but historical records and sound forecasting can help in this analysis. Many department store chains assess a budgetary penalty against the ordering department for any obsolescence in excess of certain amounts. This tends to force managers requesting the inventory to more closely monitor and conservatively project demand.

Deterioration is another risk cost to consider in holding-cost analysis. This is seen when goods become worth less through physical degeneration such as loss of freshness, taste, or color or strength. Again, this is a major factor in food where shelf lives are critical with produce, soups, and beer. It is also a factor in chemicals and textiles. The larger the lot sizes, the longer the stock might be held on hand, and the greater probability of deterioration.

Product loss and damage is another risk cost associated with holding costs. Product loss can occur through theft, pilferage and general lack of physical stewardship. Damage can occur at any movement and stocking point in a logistics system. Examples are rough handling, water or other environmental damage, or breakage by impact by materials-handling units that must travel past goods in a warehouse. In many settings, logistics analysis has shown loss and damage to occur in a certain percentage of all units moved through various systems. Deviations from these "average" percentages can occur, however, from switching to other forms of transportation altogether. Larger lot sizes also can result in higher than normal damage percentages when goods are shipped and stored in stacks of three or four pallet loads at a time rather than the original two-stack high lots. This was the experience with one paper goods firm. Normal damage averaged one percent of all orders. When stacked in higher weight loads in high cube rail cars, the pallet loads on the first tier experienced over five percent damage for the added stack weight. This is one example of how a total dollar value of damage can be attributed to, in this case, a different inbound shipping method.

Related System Costs

Other inventory system costs relate to alternative procurement-distribution decisions that impact upon the rest of the firm in production, finance, and even marketing. A new source, transportation method, or inventory decision might require lot sizes that alter product run quantities. If the decision causes smaller production runs, a higher manufacturing unit cost may result. If longer runs are permitted, a lower unit cost will in all likelihood result. This advantage is obtained by spreading the initial set-up costs over more units so that each unit shares a lesser cost than in smaller runs. In both these settings, the total dollar impact of higher or lower production costs must be included in the cost of the inventory decision.

The inventory cost component associated with vendors having different minimum order quantities or payment terms is a part of this total equation as well. A firm that can purchase small weekly requirements yet have 30-day payment terms has the advantage of acquiring, manufacturing, and possibly selling and receiving payment for the item before the vendor must be paid for the component. A larger lot that represents three month's supply requires payment for the goods prior to manufacturing and eventual sale. This second alternative represents a very real dollar cash-flow cost.

The four cost areas discussed here are the major components of holding inventories; i.e. the relevant costs of space, capital, risk, and related system costs. Relevant costs are the cash costs that will change as a result of handling and holding inventories under one system versus another. The resulting cost or cost savings can then be used in a cost-benefit context against revenues, projected stockouts, capital investment expenditures, etc.

Inventory Control—Quantitative Approaches

Inventory models are a part of the science of inventory control. Inventory models are mathematical tools that determine lot sizes and provide some indication of when to reorder. These models also serve three other very important purposes which are often overlooked. First, they provide an ideal answer that can be used as a benchmark to compare actual operations. Second, they are very useful in sensitivity analyses. And, third, the process of reducing the firm's costs and flow activities into a simplified inventory model often helps the manager/analyst visualize and understand the working interrelationships in the inventory area. The specific answer obtained from a quantitative inventory tool is often an ideal that is difficult to use in practice. But the process of modeling is useful in providing perspectives about the present system in relation to possible improvement opportunities.

Several quantitative tools are available, and they are relatively simple to use. But, their simplicity is also the cause of several inherent drawbacks. Table 15–2 presents six of the most common quantitative inventory tools. These range from the one-time purchase situation, which is common with seasonal or single purchase settings, to handling situations of uncertain demand and supply times.

Nonquantitative Approaches to Inventory Control

Quantitative inventory tools provide lot size quantities and indicate when to order. They represent "ideal" quantities that must be further analyzed in light of operational realities. A further factor in inventory control is the use of nonquantitative decision rules which are often at play in firms and agencies. These arise from physical factors or overriding financial considerations.

Size of Transportation Vehicle

Firms often order, sell, or ship quantities that fully utilize rail cars, trucks or air/sea containers. The private truck EOQ formula might result in shipments using eighty percent of a trailer. Though holding costs might cause this "ideal" quantity to result, the underutilization of a vehicle that charges a flat fee per run will often force one hundred percent truck capacity quantities. Moving twenty percent of "air" is a more visible cost penalty, than the suboptimization of holding costs, which are usually not tangibily reported in budget data streams.

☐ **TABLE 15-2.** *Summary of Primary Quantitative Inventory Tools*

Tool	Basic Concept	Key Points
Single Order Tool	Finds optimum order quantity given probabilities of making certain sales levels	Finds highest profit or lowest loss quantity to order. Good in one-time purchases when exact need or demand is unknown but some history information is available. Weakness is need for probability estimates.
Economic Order Quantity	Finds order quantity that represents lowest cost of total order costs and total holding costs over a period $$EOQ = \sqrt{\dfrac{2(\text{Annual Demand})(\text{Order Cost})}{2(\text{Value})(\text{Holding Cost \%})}}$$	Uses annual demand, order cost, holding cost, and product value. Simple to compute and use. Key application is when demand is independent (not for company's own production operations which are known and planned). Weaknesses from assumptions of certain demand, certain lead time, constant holding and order costs.
Price or Rate Break EOQ	An EOQ approach that also considers varying price breaks. Finds optimum quantity considering order and holding costs in light of price breaks $$EOQ = \sqrt{\dfrac{2(\text{Annual Demand})(\text{Order Cost})}{(\text{Value} + \text{Unit Freight Rate})(\text{Holding Cost \%})}}$$	Same as regular EOQ.
Private or Contract Truck EOQ	An EOQ approach that considers a single cost per inbound truck move in which freight is single charge regardless of quantity in shipment. $$EOQ = \sqrt{\dfrac{2(\text{Annual Demand})(\text{Order Cost} + \text{Truck Run Cost})}{(\text{Value})(\text{Holding Cost \%})}}$$	Same as above.
Uncertain Demand Tool	Uses past history or expected probabilities to compute optimum quantity to purchase in face of uncertain demand	Aids in reducing stockouts in situations of uncertain demand for goods. Determines quantity to acquire so as to meet expected demand. Weakness is assumption of demand probabilities.
Uncertain Supply Tool	Determines quantity to acquire in face of uncertain supply times as well as uncertain demand	Requires means of both supply times and demand as well as standard deviations of both.

Beginning-of-Period Purchasing by Public Agency Purchasing Managers

Western accounting systems for federal, state, local, and not-for-profit organizations generally do not utilize the concept of depreciation and capital costs. Budgetarily, then, holding costs are not considered or a reported factor in these organizations. This often causes procurement managers in these situations to purchase a single-lot quantity of goods at the beginning of the budget period. The rationale for this is that the advantage of volume buying and the holding constant on purchase price for the period outweighs any holding costs. Thus, a $1,200 typewriter purchased October 1 and held for requisition until next September, when the price then might be $1,300, will appear as a $100 savings for the organization when the unit is set into operation later in the year. This system places a great demand on the purchasing and warehouse systems in the beginning of the period.

Real money costs and the drive for effective public organization performance evaluation systems are diminishing the use of this approach. The federal Office of Management and Budget and various state liquor control boards are beginning to assess capital use charges upon operational units, which might reduce this practice in the future.

Purchase at the End of a Budget Period

Public agency and private firm budgeting systems tend to encourge the full use or draw-down of budget allotments by the end of each period. The tendency for this practice is created by the individual manager's real or imaginary fear that the unused portion will be an amount of budget allotment reduction in the next period. Consequently, there is often a rush to purchase or spend at the end of the period, even if the goods or services are not ideally required at that time. This, too, can create excessive inventories.

Allocation Purchasing

In periods of commodity shortages, suppliers' allocations among customers will often cause some purchasers to obtain more goods than needed. A case in point is exemplified by one East Coast plastics processor who was informed that he had a one hundred percent allocation based upon the previous years' purchases from its major source. The processor knew that his young competitors were allowed only seventy percent of their last years' tonnage allocation. During the tight period the firm only needed about ninety percent of the last year's tonnage, but it continued to purchase the full one hundred percent. This action was taken for two reasons. One, to build a safety inventory in the event a large increase in stock was needed in the future; and two, the firm would able to sell whatever it did not need to a few of its competitors at a high markup. This is one example of some of the distortions that can take place with allocation schemes.

Speculation or Hedging

Many times firms will ignore the normal MRP or other inventory re-order decision rules in order to take advantage of forward buying price or speculation resale opportunities. This is particularly prevalent in raw commodity industries such as minerals and coffee.

Inventory Reduction Edicts

Inventory reduction is a common pronouncement made by top management and financial personnel to the rest of the firm. Such reductions, made in the interest of freeing up funds for other uses, usually are in the form of X percent reduction of raw materials and finished goods. These edicts often force purchasing, materials, and distribution managers to subvert the normal inventory ordering and holding systems.

Inventory reductions in and of themselves are well intentioned but often ill resulting unless they are accompanied by entire production, distribution, marketing, and customer service shifts. Otherwise, the firm incurs smaller lot purchases or more premium deliveries at higher transportation rates, and the same occurs on the outbound side to customers. Thus, the apparent cost advantages sought through stock reduction can often be reduced or eliminated by unmeasured cost increases in transportation or production shifts.

Nonquantitative inventory control rules are prevalent in day-to-day operations. These inventory control rules are not necessarily to be viewed in a totally negative light as practices to be avoided. Rather, these decisions provide benefits to either the entire firm or to one or more departments within it. The key for purchasing and materials managers is to evaluate these nonquantitative tools and their resulting benefits against the costs and benefits of the cost, profit, or service-optimized MRP or quantitatively based inventory control process. In this way the full cost or benefit of the imposed nonquantitative decision can be fully evaluated.

Physical Control and Security of Inventories

The physical control of inventories consists of decisions and processes related to: 1) the method of inventory recordkeeping, 2) the methods of stock layout and control keeping, and 3) the process of inventory reconciliation. These three measures represent the follow-through and operational necessity of inventory management that begins with forecasting and production plans all the way to the handling of goods to production or customers.

Inventory Records

Two basic approaches exist for physical stock recordkeeping; these are perpetual inventories and bin-resource systems.

The perpetual system keeps track of the number of units on hand at all times. Exhibit 15–1 shows an example of one form of this system. It

■ EXHIBIT 15-1. *Full-Status Perpetual Record System*

Item #:	M913		Source:	DELAO SUPPLY			Lot Size:	500	Reorder Point:	50
Description:	Q-FUSE						Usage Rate:	VARIES	Unit cost:	$9.17
Location:	K-9-4		Lead time:	3-4 wks						

			Assignment				Stock			
Line	Date	Requisition/ Order	On-order	Outbound Assignment	Line Ref.	In	Out	On-hand Balance	Free Balance
1	1/2	RECONCILIATION	500 R19275	50 M942				60	10
2	1/3	R19275			1	500		560	510
3	1/5	N-07		75				560	435
4	1/7	M942			1		50	510	435
5	1/10	R19275			3		75	435	435
6									
7									
•									
•									

■ **EXHIBIT 15-2.** *Simple Perpetual Record System*

| Item | R-293 | | | Lot Size: | | 300 |

Item   R-293   Lot Size: 300

Description: ANGLE FASTENER   Usage rate: 230/MO

Source: HOUTS or GEN. PROD'S INC.   Order point   40

Lead time: 4 DAYS   Unit cost: $1.22

Storage Location: L - 2 - 7

Line	Date	Order or Requisition No.	Received in	Withdrawn	Balance on hand
1	1/2	RN002	300		335
2	1/4	F019		20	315
3	1/5	F037		15	300
4	1/7	F069		10	290
5	1/9	F111		18	272
6					
•					
•					
•					

shows each in and out movement with the corresponding requisition or order numbers as well as the balance on hand. The perpetual inventory record in Exhibit 15–2, shows the in, out, and balance statuses as well as what has been ordered or requisitioned but not yet placed into stock or not yet pulled from stock.

This simple system is useful when there is very little time lag between reorder points and receipt on the one hand, and orders from the customer and outbound pick and ship on the other hand. The key element here for manufacturing settings is that the on-hand balance be equal to or greater than the required number of units for production in any future time periods less than the lead time. In the ideal, stockless MRP system in which reorder quantities can equal production lot requirements, there should in theory, be a zero on-hand balance for any items whose planned production requirement date is farther ahead than the lead time.

The full status perpetual system shows more information. This system shows forthcoming inbound moves as well as goods earmarked for outbound move but still on the shelves. The free balance is those goods on the shelf that are available for sale or transfer. This system is useful when a time lag exists between customer ordering, picking and shipping/transfer or when the replenishment lead times exceed several production runs. It is also useful when there is a lag in time between the firm physically taking possession of the goods and the point in time when they are available for use by the manager responsible for the records. Such is the case with inbound private trucking, inter-plant, and work-in-process moves. This system is a bit cumbersome to use because it requires two entries for each in and out move. In Exhibit 15–2, orders M942 and N07 are entered when received and when shipped. The key here is to compare the free balance against the lot size and lead time in order to cut new replenishment orders. An advantage of this system is that the outstanding inbound and outbound assignments can be analyzed for transportation consolidation opportunities with other shipments. One eastern consumer goods manufacturer uses a daily computer printout of goods assigned in order to construct full trucks and rail car consolidated shipments to customers in close proximity to each other. If any are in the system more than five days, they are shipped direct in small lots.

The bin reserve system is the second basic approach to inventory recordkeeping. This system is useful for low usage items. These are goods that represent small inventory investments or low daily or weekly usage rates. In essence, these are goods that should not have the high degree of labor cost control applied to them.

The bin-reserve system requires segregating the stock of goods into two lots. The reserve lot consists of the quantity of goods that will be expected to be used during the lead time period. The active goods are all those above that quantity. A simple example shows how this system can work. A distributor buys an electrical connector in 10,000 unit lots consisting of 10 boxes of 1,000 each. He estimates that about one thousand are sold each month and the lead time is thirty days. In the bin, a tag is attached to the tenth box on the bottom of the stack. When the ninth box is emptied and discarded, the tag and tenth box are then exposed. The tag then "travels" to purchasing in order to place another lot order for 10,000 connectors. The reserve quantity hopefully will be sufficient during the lead time period. As long as usage rates and lead times are stable, no problems should arise. Periodic checking during slack times should take place to determine if usage rates are increasing or decreasing and whether lead time is changing as well.

The selection of either the perpetual or periodic system depends upon usage rates and inventory investments. Generally, perpetual records are called for in MRP-linked systems and for all high volume goods. It is a labor-intensive system that necessitates tight control procedures. The bin-reserve system uses the actual material as a control and count medium. While it is less costly to administer, it has the drawback of the firm not knowing at any time exactly what is in possession unless a physical count is taken.

Physical Inventory Security

A proper, secure inventory system is one in which access to the goods is limited, and direct control is assigned to persons who are responsible for it. The system should then be laid out for the most convenient method of control by these persons.

The first concern requires the physical isolation of goods. This includes keeping goods in separate rooms from the rest of the receiving, production, and shipping operations. The only persons that should be allowed to store, shift, or remove goods from the shelves are those who have responsibility for them. This means that access should be restricted and check-in and out systems should be formalized. Salesmen and engineers should not be allowed to remove samples, nor should they be allowed to put them back. This is why well-run libraries have signs posted stating that only the staff may reshelve books. Goods may look alike but have one serial number difference. The stock person is aware of this and can be held accountable for accuracy in this area.

Goods layout is another concern. Goods can be stored at random wherever there is empty space or they can be grouped into families. The random system has the advantage of greater overall storage space utilization and flexibility, but it requires that computer or labor-intensive perpetual locator systems be employed. Of major consideration here is that goods be related properly. The family approach has goods grouped in logical sections according to type of product, vendor, customer, or production bill of material lots. This system is easier to memorize and can lead to better stock rotation. However, if the goods in the facility vary in usage, mix, or have wide seasonality, less than optimal space utilization can result.

Dead stock is another physical goods control consideration. Some system of periodic checking and reporting should be used at the stockroom level for goods experiencing no movement. These reports should go to purchasing, higher materials management, production, engineering, and possibly marketing. Such goods might have slipped from the higher inventory system of the firm or are no longer needed. Reported in an exceptions-like manner as this will highlight them for use, scrap, disposal, or alternative application elsewhere in the firm.

Conclusion

Inventory control is a vast and multi-faceted subject that encompasses a firm's moving and changing assets. It entails an overall view that begins with needs forecasting, system capacity balancing, determination of purchase timing and quantities, and dealing with interruptive factors all the way down to the physical monitoring and security. Because inventories have a large and increasing financial impact upon the firm, efforts are continually being made to reduce inventory costs while maintaining or increasing their availability.

Inventory management must be closely linked between the final users or customers, the firm, and sources or vendors. This includes timing, notifying the interfacing parties, and sometimes making long-term commitments and planning horizons. Informing vendors of company forecasts, blanket orders, consignment systems, and seeking sources with adequate supplies are ways of avoiding inventory build-up within the firm.

Management attention to this area will no doubt be fine-tuned by assigning responsibility for inventories and applying performance evaluation measures against them. Inventory is a fluid asset that passes through the hands of transportation, purchasing, materials management, production, distribution, and sometimes marketing personnel. Singular, overall control is difficult in this set up. The number of parties involved is being reduced gradually through organizational changes. Performance evaluations can be implemented through many measurement forms. One evaluation is simply a flat maximum inventory dollar level. Another might be inventory turnover as measured by total inventory movement during a period divided by the average inventory held during that time. This provides unit turnover measure. Still another might be the total value of item markup or margin during a period divided by the average stock value. This provides a dollar productivity of the goods involved. To be sure, no one measure is singularly valid for performance evaluation and decision making. Each provides one facet of activity. Others will no doubt be implemented and refined as this asset experiences changing organizational control systems.

No one inventory control system is proper in all settings nor should all goods in one setting necessarily deserve the same form of control. Each firm, situation, and movement setting calls for differing control approaches. The key throughout this entire area, however, is to continually review forecasts, plans, and expectations, and use these as input to the subsequent, more detailed, control processes.

FOOTNOTE

1. Douglas M. Lambert and James R. Stock, *Strategic Physical Distribution Management* (Homewood, IL: Richard D. Irwin, 1982), Chapters 7 and 8.

SOURCES FOR FURTHER READING

Lambert, Douglas M., and Stock, James R. *Strategic Physical Distribution Management.* Homewood, IL: Richard D. Irwin, 1982, Chapter 7.

Buchan, Joseph, and Koenigsberg, Ernest. *Scientific Inventory Management.* Englewood Cliffs, NJ: Prentice-Hall, 1963.

Purchasing. Boston: Cahners Publications. Semi-monthly publication.

Fetter, Robert B., and Dalleck, Winston C. *Decision Models for Inventory Managment.* Homewood, IL: Richard D. Irwin, 1961.

QUESTIONS FOR REVIEW

1. What is meant by the term "inventory control?"

2. What is a good general approach to use in controlling inventories?

3. What are the various types of stockouts?

4. Against what trade-off factor should the cost of stockouts be considered?

5. What is the nature of space costs in inventory control settings?

6. What is an appropriate rate to apply for the capital cost component of inventory costs?

7. What general uses are there for quantitative inventory models?

8. What are the basic trade-off elements in the EOQ?

9. How should the decision relating to the nonquantitative inventory tools be placed in proper perspective?

10. What are the relative merits of the bin-reserve method of inventory control?

11. Compare and contrast the simple inventory record approach with the full status perpetual record approach.

12. In the future, inventory management might be in control of one person or department. What appropriate performance evaluation measures might be used?

Problem 15-1

A purchasing analyst has collected the following information about the eight basic products used by the firm in production.

Product Code	Number of Units	Unit Cost
M4	10,000	$ 1.37
P1	4,250	32.11
E7	22,700	.33
M2	125,000	2.18
P5	1,300	43.74
E8	280	11.65
T1	7,900	2.36
T2	12,930	5.12

Question:
Sort this data into an "ABC" array. At what points would you make the breaks between the three groups? Why?

A company has the following records about a certain raw material held in inventory.

Inbound receipts:

July 3	140 units
August 8	300 units
September 13	280 units
October 19	70 units

Requisitions:

July 15	200 units
August 1	125 units
August 20	180 units
September 4	100 units
September 27	250 units
October 20	125 units

Units on-hand as of July 1: 192 units

Question:

Develop a running inventory record of this product from July 1 to October 20.

16

CHAPTER OBJECTIVES

After reading this chapter you should:

- Understand the basic objectives of materials flow management.

- Appreciate the impacts caused in the firm from various production scheduling approaches.

- Be able to use materials requirements planning (MRP) as a purchasing tool.

- Possess skills for primary project control management.

Production-Materials Management Decisions

Introduction

Materials management is the primary function providing goods to manufacturing for production. In traditional settings, production requirements were known, and purchasing had the task of obtaining goods for the convenience of production. Manufacturing requirements then defined all other processes, timings, and actions in interfacing inbound and outbound areas. This dominant position of production has gradually been reevaluated by most firms, and a different approach is often employed today.

If functions are organized separately and production is allowed to dominate decision making in interfacing departments, many distortions tend to occur in the firm. The lowest production unit cost is, of course, a primary goal of manufacturing, and this necessitates that high inventories be held on each end of the production line. Inventories become a buffer between purchasing and manufacturing, acting to insulate each function from the other in the attainment of their respective goals. Often neither function effectively manages the level of inventories for the benefit of the firm as a whole. Purchase timing might not necessarily be synchronous with that of production. And, the seeking of lowest prices by purchasing might cause quality problems for production and that extend into marketing and product service. It is important, therefore, that a close link exist between purchasing and manufacturing.

A balance of price, unit cost, quality, availability, production process scheduling, and inventory level costs is necessary. It makes little sense for purchasing to attain a purchase price savings of $.00135 per unit if production experiences an increase in unit costs of $.007 due to an increase in waste with every twentieth unit being defective. Likewise, it makes little economic sense for production to seek long runs of three month's supply of product thereby saving $2500 in two monthly set-up processes when the additional inventory investment is obtained with borrowed funds costing $8000 per month in interest charges. Problems such as these are largely taken into account when firms link purchasing and manufacturing organizationally, with strong reporting lines and/or effective management information systems between them.

This chapter presents the production-materials management link with an eye toward joint objectives, the various orientations of production, and traditional approaches employed in the manufacturing scheduling task. Also discussed are materials requirements planning, (MRP) a materials management contract tool, as well as distribution requirements planning, and construction logistics, and the timing and sequencing problems these methods present for purchasing.

Specific Materials Management Goals

Several objectives relating to materials management were presented in Chapter 14. This chapter addresses three of those objectives that directly relate to production and the supply of goods.

Maximum Protection Against Uncertainty

This maximum protection objective seeks to buffer the overall system from costly, unexpected events such as supply failure, sudden production line changes, or major shifts in the marketplace. A materials management system must be able to adapt to these types of changes and permit the system to continue with a minimum of disruption.

Optimal Purchase Timing

Optimal purchase timing seeks to balance supply availability with production and market needs in such a way as to maintain maximum inventory supply at the least feasible total cost.

Balanced Production Operations

A uniform and consistent production operation that maximizes the utilization of labor and capital is sought here, and this system is illustrated in Exhibit 16-1. This exhibit illustrates one scheduled operation that incurs heavy overtime and congestion costs in some weeks while operating at less than full capacity in others (weeks 3 and 7). In the underutilized weeks, many labor and machinery costs are still incurred but each week has less than the full production potential to match against these costs. The relatively balanced operation shown in Exhibit 16-1b has less of the peak and valley problem and a more full and uniform use of production capacity.

Attaining these materials management goals requires a balancing of the constraints of varying supply lead times and differing production orientations and scheduling approaches. Simple, reliable, and credible information links are necessary in order to attain these goals.

Production Orientations

Production operations can be classified into four distinct groups. Each group requires different approaches for expediting the flow of goods leading to production lines.[1]

■ **EXHIBIT 16-1.** *Production Operations and Capacity*

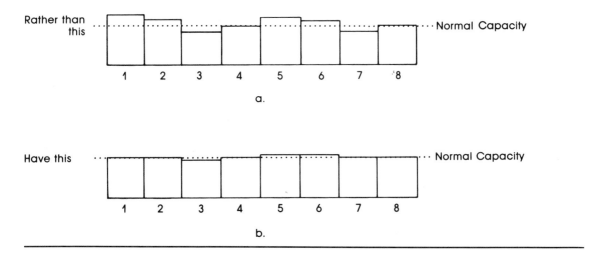

Continuous, Produce to Stock System

This production process is found in many food, fertilizer, and appliance industries, as well as many industries that supply wholesalers and distributors. In continuous production, technology exists in such a way that products are made on large-unit-run production lines or in bulk liquid or similar process settings. Changes in demand can be addressed by altering the rate of production or by employing fewer or more workers on production lines. Inventories are generally relatively simple to administer since standardized products are being produced for shipment according to predictable shipment schedules.

Continuous, Produce to Order System

This production and distribution approach uses a continuous production line that has products moving directly from the line to customers according to orders already received. This type of operation is generally not as standardized as the continuous, produce to stock system. Textiles, cable, and many plastic operations are typical of this system. In this approach, production must be more responsive than in the former system, and specific input components are often needed for particular orders. Purchasing is concerned with the quantities and flow rates of the standardized items, as well as with having the special goods on hand for specific orders.

Intermittent, to Stock System

This production technology takes place in discrete lots, batches, or even in single units. This system also must match the available production flow rate as closely as possible to that of the wholesaler's or distributor's demand or the firm's own distribution center's requirements. Inventory of finished goods is a key cushion here that somewhat insulates production from daily market demands. Much of the attention, then, can be directed toward balancing production and purchasing concerns.

Intermittent, to Order System

This batch-like production system is found in machine tool, specialized construction equipment, and building and construction settings. A long tie between the market, production, and purchasing is necessary. Completion date requirements are constantly eyed as targets for a coordinated production and purchasing link. In repetitive batch operations, purchasing attempts to develop a supply as near real-time as possible in order to eliminate inbound materials or reduce them as low as possible while still obtaining them when needed for order entry and production start-up.

These four basic conditions establish distinct operating links between marketing, production, and purchasing. Inventory plays different roles in each system, and the type of information link required is very often defined by this condition as well.

Approaches to Production Scheduling

Many techniques are used by production managers to schedule manufacturing activities. It is important that purchasing be aware of the technique used as well as the material needs for each run or batch. A discussion of many of the common approaches is presented here along with some of the important impacts these schemes can have upon purchasing.

First Come, First Serve

This scheduling rule produces goods for customer orders according to the sequence in which orders were originally received by the firm. This system is fair from a customer order cycle standpoint, and it is a relatively easy system for purchasing. Since the specific production schedule is defined by the sequence of orders on file, both production and purchasing rely upon the same information source for their timing. Problems can arise when there is little or no inventory for certain items, and the vendor lead time for replenishment is longer than the production backlog.

Customer Priority

This approach is used in conjunction with another discussed here, except that any order from a specific customer receives priority by moving to the front of the backlog list and production schedule. This system is often necessary in the marketing relationship with major customers. It can cause suboptimization of production labor and capacity when short notice, priority-related schedule shifts are made. It causes particular problems for purchasing and materials management as well. This system forces the use of two provisioning approaches in the purchasing and inventory task: one for the normal, planned production schedule and another with a larger built-in safety stock requirement. The priority order will not wait for vendor supply lead time because it is one of the next production runs to be processed. Therefore, a supply of those items that are normally required for the prime customer's items will have to be held in stock. If all goods are standardized, this problem is minimized, but the more distinctive the special customer's orders become, the more problematic the raw material inventory task becomes. This priority system is also costly from the standpoint that it causes nonpriority raw materials to be held longer than the time minimally required due to their being delayed because of the priority run. Thus, normal goods incur higher inventory costs, and the firm suffers cash flow loss from having received and paid for goods earlier than necessary.

Longest Run Possible

This scheduling rule is often found in firms in which production has total authority over manufacturing scheduling, extensive set-up costs and efforts are involved, and there it has little or no responsibility for pre- or postproduction inventories. By making runs as long as possible, set-up costs are spread over many units thereby making unit production costs as low as possible. Further, labor and machinery capacity is utilized at a high rate throughout the long run. But, while this approach can provide cost benefits to production, it can cause higher costs and problems elsewhere.

One problem with this approach is that customer orders might be held for long periods so that a single, long run can be made. This can result in erratic customer order cycle times. Another difficulty is that a small run might conceivably be put off indefinitely; sometimes the "backlog" is finally cleared up only in an economic downturn. Further, the inventory needed for items in small runs might be sitting on shelves during this period of unknown lengths. If purchasing operates separately from production, purchasing can subvert this system by not allowing certain items to accumulate for large runs. However, purchasing might not have an incentive to act in this way if it can reduce its unit cost through large purchases, if it is not aware of the specific nature of orders and the production backlog, or if there is little or no reward from becoming involved in the issue. The problems arising from application of this tool has led many firms to remove the specific production scheduling tasks from manufacturing. In these other settings, scheduling is either in materials management, distribution or by a joint committee involving all the parties.

Longest Cycle Work

This approach often is employed with the assumption that the larger the work task, the greater profit from the output. This system is often applied in construction contracting and machine tooling operations. Here, the motive is increasing profit by involving many tasks, much labor, and high use of capital assets. The larger the job, the more total profit potential. Problems from purchasing and materials management standpoints are similar to those of the longest production run.

Shortest Operating Time

This approach attempts to move a majority of jobs through a production system in the least total time. It entails assigning the job requiring the least time on machinery first, with others following in ascending order. It is often used when production is evaluated in terms of number of jobs completed in a time. This system is useful if all jobs can be completed within a day, a week, or within the planning horizon of vendor lead times. It can create problems, however, if all jobs cannot be serviced, and some are continually held over into subsequent periods. This can be the case with very long runs. Inventory items required for these long runs can be held for an extended time awaiting production.

Fewest Remaining Operations

This approach is helpful in working off a large backlog or work-in-process inventory. It requires that all jobs be analyzed in terms of how many remaining steps are required on each; work is then assigned first to those needing the fewest operations. Here, too, the problems of some runs never being processed or backlogged for long periods can result. The inventory problems found in the shortest operating time approach are also common here.

Minimized Inventory

This approach places primary emphasis upon inventory holdings, and production optimization can become secondary. It is not recommended unless close purchasing-production coordination exists. Approaches to this minimum inventory investment goal are successful if production is planned in advance, and purchasing is directly tied to this schedule. This approach is the heart of materials requirements planning (MRP), which is discussed later in this chapter.

Minimum Slack Time

This tool schedules those jobs having the least amount of slack time first with others following. Slack time is determined by due date minus days required to set up and process. This approach is fairly successful in meeting due dates. However, due dates must be assigned on a fair basis, such as first come-first serve. Priority assignment can cause scheduling problems, missed dates, and increases in stock holdings.

Critical Ratio

This approach is similar to minimum slack time. The critical ratio is the number of days to the due date divided by the required set-up and processing time. It has the same basic features as minimum slack time.

Maximum Delay

This is an override-type approach that causes a job to become a top priority when it has been backlogged or delayed a certain length of time. This rule will cause raw materials for the run in question to finally be consumed by the maximum date. "Run-around" priority rescheduling from applying this rule will cause delays in others and in increase in inventory due to other jobs being pushed back.

Most of the approaches discussed incur inventory holding costs in excess of the absolute minimum that would exist in a totally certain environment. Cost impacts become more of a problem as each production run becomes different from the others in terms of specialized raw material components. The problems cited with these approaches to production scheduling impact from purchasing through to distribution and marketing. The production scheduling function should be integrated with the overall planning and operating system of the firm.

Toward Integrated Production—Materials Management: Materials Requirements Planning (MRP)

The overall planning and management cycle of the firm presented in Chapter 2 shows the planning and operating cycle beginning with market analysis and finally refined to specific operating processes. The operating aspects are: market timing, distribution positioning, manufacturing activites, and purchase timing. Market timing usually is stated in general terms with target dates and spans listed in months, thirteen four-week "months" or quarters. These requirements set the stage for aggregate production planning, and act as the starting point for specific production and materials flow and purchasing scheduling. What follows is a discussion of a highly successful approach called materials requirements planning (MRP) and its closed-loop planning and control cycle.

MRP is a simple tool that plans for and controls the flow of materials up to the production line in an efficient manner. It integrates the constraints of customer demand with those of production flow and capacities. MRP is flexible in that it provides for feedback and periodic updating and change. MRP accepts change; it is not destroyed by it.

The Closed-Loop Process

MRP is at the heart of a closed-loop process that begins with overall production plans and ends with initiating orders to vendors and the receipt of those goods. Exhibit 16-2 illustrates this closed-loop process.

The process starts with an aggregate plan for production over a period of time. This plan is refined into specific production runs, or master production schedules. These runs dictate inventory replenishment and vendor order placement in an MRP-type approach that is presented in detail later. With the closed-loop process, production, inventory, and ordering/lead time configurations are analyzed in terms of capcity capa-

■ **EXHIBIT 16-2.** *MRP in Closed Loop Production—Materials Management Planning and Control*

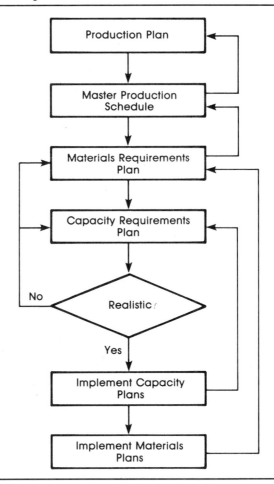

bilities. If capacity is exceeded, then MRP timing and possibly the master production schedule and the overall production plan must be changed. Feedback and analysis continues until a realistic plan is determined. Once this final plan is selected, then a specific capacity and materials requirements plan are established. The MRP system is able to adopt to changes because scheduling or capacity problems can be handled by readjusting interfacing activities rather than becoming problems when they are later detected.

MRP Constructs

Materials requirements planning consists of three basic constraints: 1) the master production plan, 2) inventory management, and 3) the bill of materials. The master production plan is developed in tandom with the system capabilities defined in the closed-loop approach. Various aggregate planning approaches can be used, and these are the subject of production and operations management texts. Suffice to say, within the realm of purchasing and materials management, it is the final schedule resulting from the planning process that purchasing and materials managers should analyze and provide refinement suggestions for efficiency improvement possibilities. Positive suggestions can usually be made when specific day-to-day production scheduling is made by using one of the micro-dispatching rules presented in the previous section. In the final analysis, the established master production schedule sets target dates for purchasing and materials management to order and schedule the delivery of goods to the production line.

Inventory control and monitoring is the next MRP construct. Ideally little or no inventory should be on hand. Production runs are known in advance and should be supported by inbound inventory schedules using these run dates as targets. Raw and work-in-process materials should only exist if production, transportation, or purchasing flow rates or economic quantities differ. Exhibit 16-3 illustrates the ideal inventory situation in which production will run on days 4, 9 and 14. An MRP system does not operate with common reorder points for inventory replenishment in uncertain situations. Instead, vendor orders are based upon future production dates and required lead times. This approach attempts to eliminate stock rather than develop a safety stock.

Cycle counting is the second aspect to inventory in an MRP setting. This practice consists of continuous counting of goods on hand and performing a reconciliation with the stock records. While it might be impossible to perform this task on all goods during, say, every week of the year, it can be accomplished on a rotating basis during a slow period during each week. Several advantages accrue to the firm using cycle counting. One, stock is constantly checked. This prevents some goods from becoming lost or obsolete, a situation that can easily occur when goods are only checked annually. Two, if problems exist in the actual stock-to-record information system, a cycle count system will detect these inequities so that attention can be directed toward solving them. Three, record inaccuracies can be detected early thus preventing major production problems later when part of an expected lot is found not to be on hand. Four, cycle counting can be used to reduce some of the inconvenience of annual accounting/inventory reconciliations. These audits can consume several days and require a shut-down of an entire stock

■ **EXHIBIT 16-3.** *Inbound Inventory Holdings—Raw Materials.*

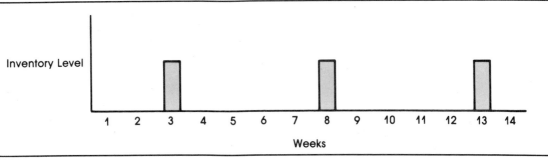

center. Implementation of a cycle counting system with personnel from accounting can go for in reducing this overhead cost. Cycle counting can be performed 1) upon key items on a constant basis, 2) on moderately active items every few weeks, and 3) on low volume goods every month or quarter. In any event, this process brings a discipline to the firm that improves accuracy of inventory records and reduces the incidence of unknown stockouts prior to production operations.

The third MRP construct is the bill of material. The bill of material is a schematic listing of all components necessary in the production of the firm's final product(s) along with the sequence of production. Exhibit 16-4 shows the bill of materials for an electrical product that is often installed on large farm harvesting machinery. This chart shows that the final item is assembled from three subcomponents—a frame, motor, and mechanism. The frame is first assembled in a prior production operation within the firm. It consists of a front, back, and four other plain panels and fasteners that are purchased from outside vendors. The motor is purchased from another vendor. The mechanism is assembled from two items, one a subassembly and the other a purchased switch. The subassembly is made in the firm from fasteners, wires, and a con-

■ **EXHIBIT 16-4.** *Bill of Materials Chart*

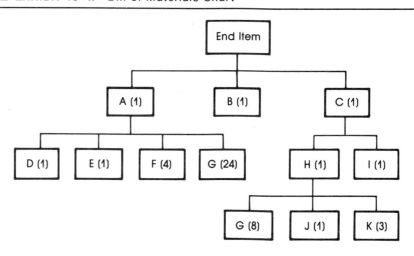

Item	Description	Vendor/Source
A	Frame	Production line: Bldg. 3, Line 7
B	Motor	Vendor 1
C	Mechanism	Production line: Bldg. 3, Line 5
D	Front panel (frame)	Vendor 2
E	Back panel (frame)	Vendor 2
F	Top, bottom, sides (panel)	Vendor 2
G	Fasteners	Vendor 3
H	Subassembly	Production line: Bldg. 3, Line 6
I	Switch	Vendor 4
J	Meter	Vendor 1
K	Wires, #10	Vendor 5

necter. Thus, there are four levels to this process requiring four production steps in the firm.

Two key components of the bill of material are yield and scrap factors. Yield factor is a standard number of output items produced from a set, batch, or bulk quantity of input items. Or, put another way, it is the standard number of input items required to make a stated number of output items. For example, if twenty-four ounces of an ingredient are necessary to produce one final unit, then that is the yield factor. Scrap yields refer to known and tolerated waste that results from a production activity. The stamping of circles for can tops and bottoms is made from square and rectangular tinplate. Scrap is inevitable in this function. Production convenience and sloppiness can cause the production yields to decrease and become new normal standards. Unduly slack scrap and yield factors increase raw material needs as well as work-in-process holdings and scrap. Careful auditing and an attention to technical operations is necessary to prevent or reduce this phenomenon. The bill of materials shows the items, quantities, and steps required in this entire process. In the example in Exhibit 16-4, items B and J can be purchased from the same vendor as also items D, E, and F. Item G, fasteners, is needed at two distinct steps in this final item (in items A and H).

The MRP Approach

Application of MRP using the electronic assistor example is implemented with a master production schedule for the final product. Exhibit 16-5 shows this schedule for this product. Production is planned for 500 units each in week 12.

This schedule and the bill of materials are then used to create target dates for receiving all required items from vendors. Exhibit 16-6 shows the weekly periods in which goods must arrive for planned production and when orders will have to be released, given required lead times from vendors.

Items A, B, and C must be completed and available by the end of Week 11 so that final production can take place in Week 12. Items A and C are produced by in-house production, and Table 16-1 shows projected inventories. Item B is purchased with an eight-week lead time. Table 16-2 shows that the firm now has 100 of these units on hand. If 500 are needed in Week 11, then an order for 400 must be placed in Week 3 (eight weeks prior to Week 11). During Week 11, the 400 expected units will be added to the 100 on hand for a total of 500 units required for production. During and after Week 12, no units will be on hand, since they will have been integrated into the production of the final product. Items A and C show no previous inventory holdings in the actual form of these pro-

■ **EXHIBIT 16-5.** *Master Production Schedule Electronic Assitor Final Item*

Units												500	
Week	1	2	3	4	5	6	7	8	9	10	11	12	

■ **EXHIBIT 16-6.** *Required Delivery and Order Placement Times*

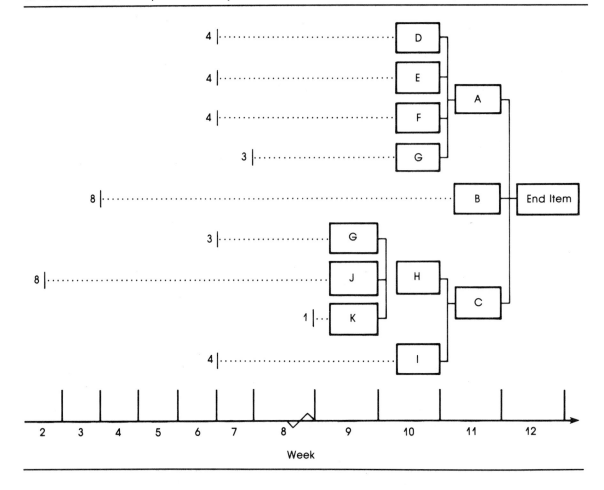

ducts, since they will be produced during Week 11 (see Table 16-1). In fact, a master production sheet will exist in the system for these and all other products that are produced in-house.

MRP Perspectives and Extensions

MRP is a simple scheduling device that can be created, updated, and revised without major complication occurring in the firm. Several facets related to MRP warrant further discussion.

Order Schedules

MRP simplifies the task of order scheduling in purchasing by highlighting the weeks in which orders should be transmitted to vendors. The key elements of this activity are the needed week of delivery and a reliable lead time. An improved or deteriorated lead time performance will directly impact upon an MRP system. It is critical that purchasing monitor lead times on both existing orders and with most vendors so that future orders might be placed within the proper time frame. Since MRP

☐ **TABLE 16-1.** *Items A and C MRP Sheet*

Item/Component: A = Frame   C = Mechanism

Order Quantity:

Lead Time:

	\multicolumn{12}{c}{Week}
	1	2	3	4	5	6	7	8	9	10	11	12
Gross Requirements											500 Each	
Scheduled Receipts											500	
On Hand											500	
Planned Order Releases												

☐ **TABLE 16-2.** *Item B MRP Sheet*

Item/Component: B = Motor

Order Quantity: Any Quantity

Lead Time: 8 weeks

		\multicolumn{12}{c}{Week}
		1	2	3	4	5	6	7	8	9	10	11	12
Gross Requirements	—	—	—	—	—	—	—	—	—	—	—	500	—
Scheduled Receipts	—	—	—	—	—	—	—	—	—	—	—	400	—
On Hand	100	100	100	100	100	100	100	100	100	100	100	500	—
Planned Order Releases	—	—	—	400	—	—	—	—	—	—	—	—	—

automatically schedules order placement based upon known lead times, it is critical that this information be accurate.

Tracing/Priority Control

Tracing is the task of monitoring orders outstanding with vendors to determine whether planned delivery dates will be met. This is a good practice if only to maintain confidence that receipts will meet production plans. Even if delivery dates slide anyway, it is better to be aware of the problem far enough in the future so that production schedules can be revised with minimum inconvenience and cost. The closer to actual planned production dates that changes and delays are imposed upon the system, the more cost impact they cause.

Expediting

Expediting is the process of speeding up delivery of inbound deliveries from vendors. An MRP system will show which orders will require expediting if production plans are advanced to a date earlier than originally established.

De-Expediting

Production plans can change in ways that delay planned manufacturing schedules. An MRP system is helpful in this setting for de-expediting, which is the act of allowing outstanding orders to be delivered later than originally planned. De-expediting has several benefits. One, it helps build credibility with a vendor regarding the firm's delivery dates, and makes production scheduling easier for the vendor.

A second benefit is that it makes expediting efforts at other times more creditable. De-expediting prevents inventory from being received earlier than necessary, reduces space costs, and inventory holding costs. Further, it is beneficial from a corporate cash flow standpoint, since goods are not received until needed, and they won't have to be paid for until after production. One expensive facet of inventory costs is the cash paid for goods held on shelves. De-expediting can reduce or avoid this situation.

Cash Flow Protection

MRP is useful in determining cash outflows and inflows. Cash payments can be projected by extending the firm's payment period from date of delivery. For example, if it is the firm's policy to pay bills on the fortieth day, then MRP-based delivery dates can be accumulated and sorted to determine cash needs forty days later. The system can also be used to estimate outbound shipments from actual production dates. This is an important element in billing and cash receipts from customers.

Vendor-Sorts

An MRP system can be adopted to present listings of vendors and their outstanding orders. Vendor-sorts over long periods of time for all production runs, and even plants, are valuable in determining the volume of business conducted with each supplier. This information is useful in negotiations in seeking price, service, or product design concessions. It can also be used to develop a vendor performance file with regard to delivery performance and product quality experience.

Vendor Locations/Transportation Consolidation

Another data sort listing that can be spun off an organized MRP system is vendor location and shipments by scheduled delivery dates. Two or more vendors located in the same area and shipping inbound in the same week might represent a simple, consolidated, low-cost inbound shipment. This information can help avoid two or more smaller shipments by each vendor.

Traffic Flow Projections

MRP-based data can be used to forecast inbound transportation movements. This information assists in planning cash outlays for freight expenses as well as scheduling equipment with carriers, planning unloading sequences, and scheduling manpower. Quite often, matched outbound moves of finished product can be made in the same emptied carrier. Similarly, two-way hauls in the firm's own private transportation equipment can be scheduled using inbound and outbound movement projections.

Warehouse Requirements

An MRP listing of scheduled arrivals can be a sound source for planning warehouse space needs. Stocking locations as well as unloading and flow-through sequences can then be planned. This listing assists firms in scheduling optimal manpower requirements. Large work crews in slow weeks and overtime situations for small crews in busy weeks can be reduced.

Verify Yield and Scrap Factors

The MRP system, assisted by cycle counting for both inbound goods and finished, postproduction goods, will go far in verifying production yield and scrap factors. If these two factors are overly inflated, build-ups of raw materials, work-in-process or finished goods will result and be detected through cycle counting. These variables can then be recomputed and adjusted within a refined bill of material.

Vendor Link

A few firms are experimenting with links between their master production schedules and individual item MRP sheets and those of vendors. This link assists vendors in planning their own scheduling of production and purchases. One ultimate benefit from this approach is increased vendor reliability, since he/she will have a longer and more certain sales horizon. A vendor-linked MRP system can reduce the time lag in learning about lead time slippages. Further a link such as this can assist both parties in reducing inventory costs, which might beneficially impact upon product costs and prices.

Release Time
An MRP system can simplify daily purchasing department activities. One survey shows the before and after MRP implementation impact upon purchasing.[2] Time spent in order processing, phone calls, and meetings remained the same. Expediting was greatly reduced, since a more stable production plan was in use. The released time resulted in production increases in time spent on de-expediting, negotiating, sales interviews, and other products information input, and cost reduction and value analysis.

Marketing Benefits
A closed-loop MRP system will alert the firm to problems in deliveries and production. Slippages in these areas can be detected early so that the company's customers can be informed. Here, too, a delay noted and communicated several weeks in advance is less costly for the recipient than one noted during the expected delivery week. This knowledge, though still negative in nature, can be a strategic advantage for the firm. As noted elsewhere, a known longer lead time is less of a problem than a shorter, uncertain one.

MRP II
In recent years an extension of MRP has been developed called MRP II. MRP II ties the basic MRP system into the business planning cycle of the firm, including cash budgeting, market planning, and new product implementation. This refinement, however, can only be brought into use once a solid acceptance of basic MRP exists.

Purchasing Input to MRP

MRP is highly production oriented, and it might appear that purchasing is adversely affected. This is not necessarily the case. Purchasing must be highly involved with MRP actively as well as defining and refining constraints upon the MRP system. Several points of necessary interaction are[3]

Lead Times
The MRP system needs accurate information about lead times for each product it will require. This necessitates a monitoring of the market for most probable vendor lead times, transportation problems, as well as supply problems by vendor.

Standard Units
Those in charge of the production planning system should be aware of the standard units of product available from vendors as well as the lead order quantity. The order quantity might be based upon vendor minimum order requirements and/or transportation economies. Deviation from standard packages, pallets, or containers might be possible but at cost penalties to the buying firm. For example, let's say 1,000 units are desired; but only 900 fit on a truckload, so the remaining 100 are split-

shipped by common carriers. This situation not only increases freight cost, but might also force receipt in two time periods as well.

Minimum Orders

Minimum orders are a result of firm's own ordering system, the vendor's marketing/production/accounting policy, and economic transportation movements. Knowledge of these constraints will avoid cost penalties in this realm. Some ways in which minimum orders can be handled are lengthened purchasing cycles so that more orders over a period are processed as one (often with split shipments) or by multiple product sourcing through a single vendor. Transportation minimums can be reduced or avoided through scheduling consolidation moves by using an inbound shippers' association. Options such as these are discussed in Chapter 10.

Volume Discounts

Just as cost/price penalties exist for small or odd lots in the system, so too price discounts for volume purchases and transportation moves should also be included. These discounts could include price breaks for goods as well as transportation rate breaks expressed in terms of the number of units rather than in the carriers' rate, which is usually expressed in per weight or cube contexts.

Substitutes

The bill of material, stated in terms of specific products, can become flexible if the supporting rates includes standard equivalents. Substitution is often possible with fasteners in which screws, nuts, bolts and adhesives can usually be replaced by close equivalents. Substitutes often simplify purchasing and production because one item in a large quantity is easier to manage than two items of lesser quantities.

Vendor Problems

Knowledge of vendor problems is a valuable input for purchasing, materials management, and production system. Vendor problems can range from supply disruptions and energy interruptions to labor difficulties, technical and/or quality problems, etc.

Price Hikes

Pending price hikes can be avoided by ordering greater quantities than normally purchased. This practice should be evaluated from production cost, scheduling, and cash flow viewpoints.

   Knowledge of all these factors is important for the smooth operation of a production-materials management-purchasing system. Purchasing is the firm's eyes to the inbound market. It must not only monitor conditions there, but it must inform the firm as to the changing conditions.

Distribution Requirements Planning (DRP)

Distribution Requirements Planning (DRP) is an extension of MRP into the outbound goods area. DRP is useful for purchasing nd materials managers in wholesaling operations; it provides a long-range planning horizon for manufacturing, purchasing, and materials managers, and it illustrates how the MRP approach can be employed in a channel situation.

DRP, like MRP, starts with the demand for products by a customer or the next stage in the channel. It then works backward using goods on hand, planned receipts, and planned order dates to establish a schedule. A DRP sheet is made for each final distribution center in the field. The centers supplying the required item to the field centers have consolidated sheets with forecasts summed from the field centers. The plant has a simple sheet created from the individual regional centers. Exhibit 16-7 illustrates the general relationship between the field centers, regional centers, and supplying plant. The ultimate product demand, forecasted by the various markets, serves to initiate demand from which on-hand stocks, planned receipts, and planned orders are generated. The planned orders become forecast demands at the regional centers. The stock on hand, planned receipts, and planned orders at these regional centers become production requirements at the plant.

■ **EXHIBIT 16-7.** *Distribution Requirements Planning Flow*

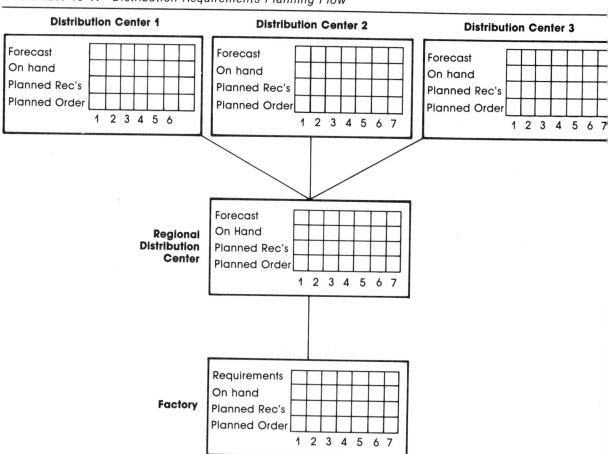

Materials Management in Projects and Construction

Many procurement endeavors involve acquiring goods and services and coordinating many activities toward the completion of a construction project. Construction situations are generally nonrepetitive in nature. Another characteristic is that construction tasks often depend upon the efforts or deliveries of good or services from many sources, some of which have completion or delivery lead times that are difficult to specifically forecast. Scheduling uncertainties such as weather often add further problems. Often, previously untried tasks are attempted which bring about learning curve difficulties. The goal at hand usually rests with a leader who must coordinate all activities in order to meet a target completion date. The specific task, then, is to determine the sequence of jobs and to monitor each one so that a delay in any one will not impact on or delay the target completion date.

Program Evaluation Review Technique, or PERT, is a useful tool to use in these contexts. With a complex project, it is important to determine the specific sequence of individual tasks that, if any one is delayed, would cause a slippage of the final target date. This sequence of tasks becomes the criteria for monitoring, and expediting activities. Other sequences might experience delays, but stock may exist along these alternative tasks that might not result in target date slippage.

An example project is shown in Exhibit 16-8. It is a small construction job that requires purchasing to coordinate engineering design, site preparation, requests for bids, and actual job management. The step by step sequence of tasks is shown in this exhibit. For example, steps A and B are in a sequence requiring a total of four days each. Step D follows Step C, and together they require a total of eleven days. This presents a slack on slippage capability at point 4 of 3 days in tasks A and B. Neither task H nor K may start before both B and D are complete. Likewise, D and E cannot start until C is complete. The relationships continue until step M, which is the final one, and this can only be completed once J and L are finished. Again, the critical sequence of tasks is that path from point 1 to 11 that cannot experience a delay in any intervening task

■ **EXHIBIT 16-8.** *Sample Construction Project*

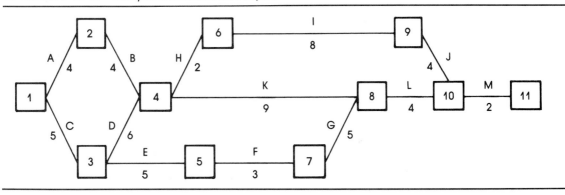

without causing a delay in the entire project. This route is known as the critical path.

The process used to determine which task sequence is the critical path is as follows. Exhibit 16-8 delineates the point, sequence, and time requirement for each task. Each task is laid out in a table with its time requirement. The major groups of information are then determined and these are as follows.

Earliest Start

This is the earliest point in time that a particular activity can begin. A and C can start at time O. On the other hand D and H cannot begin until C is completed. Likewise, H cannot start until *both* B and D are completed. The earliest point at which Step H can take place is in time period 11. Table 16-3 presents all these times.

Earliest Finish

This is the earliest time each activity can be completed.

Latest Finish and Start

It is now necessary to make a backward pass through the network in order to compute the latest finish and start times. The target date for the project is twenty-seven weeks away; that is also how long the longest sequence of activities happens to be. M cannot start until Week 25 and it takes two weeks to complete. Working backwards from M, we know that the latest M can start is at Week 25 and the latest it can finish is at Week 27. This time constraint can be stated as the equation $(LS) = (LF) - (Activity Time)$.

At Point 10 we are at the junction of activities J and L. The rule here is that the latest finish (LF) of both J and L is equal to the latest start (LS) of

☐ **TABLE 16-3.** *Sequence Schedule of Construction Project*

Activity	Length	Earliest Start (ES)	Latest Start (LS)	Earliest Finish (EF)	Latest Finish (LF)	Slack (LS-ES)	Critical Path
A	4	0	3	4	7	3	
B	4	4	7	8	11	3	
C	5	0	0	5	5	0	YES
D	6	5	5	11	11	0	YES
E	5	5	8	10	13	3	
F	3	10	13	13	16	3	
G	5	13	16	18	21	3	
H	2	11	11	13	13	0	YES
I	8	13	13	21	21	0	YES
J	4	21	21	25	25	0	YES
K	9	11	12	20	21	1	
L	4	20	21	21	25	4	
M	2	25	25	27	27	0	YES

any and all following activities. Both J and L, then, have a latest finish of Week 25. Latest start for J and L is Week 21. The latest finish (LF) for I is the last start for J, which is Week 21. The latest finish for H is the latest start for I, and its latest start is 21 less activity time of 8, or 13.

At Point 4 we are at a diverging-type junction with regard to activities H and K. Here, the rule is that the latest finish for both B and D is the earliest (ES) or latest start (LS) of the following activities H and K. This time element is 11.

Slack

We now need to know how much slippage can be tolerated in each activity along the route without causing a delay beyond the target date. This is called slack. It can be found by either of the following:

LF − EF = slack, or

LS − ES = slack

Critical Path

The critical sequence of activities during which no time delay can be allowed is the path along which the slack periods are zero. In this example, that is C-D-H-I-J-M. Steps A and/or B can delay up to three weeks. The sequence of E-F-G can experience a total delay of three weeks. K can slide by one week to a Week 10. And, L can be delayed by four weeks in its completion.

This tool targets the project and directs attention to the critical activities that must be closely monitored. Those permitting some slack can then be reanalyzed for cost reduction opportunities that might result from other ways of performing the tasks or by efficient dual or phased scheduling of manpower and equipment. The slack activities also require less tracing and expediting of lead times.

PERT and the critical path method can handle much more complicated projects. The tool can also be easily computerized. It can also be modified to account for the most probable, optimistic, and pessimistic activity times of each task.

Conclusion

Materials management is an all encompassing term that includes the planning and control of product flow into the firm through production processes. This chapter explored many of the decisions typically made in production, and it presented the spillover effect these decisions have on inventory and purchasing. Materials requirements planning (MRP) is a way of linking production and purchasing together in a way that creates greater flow certainty and minimizes inventories in ways not often possible with other approaches.

This chapter also presented a basic tool for organizing, monitoring, and controlling construction-type projects. The PERT tool highlighted areas of timing concern. Like MRP, PERT provides an early warning to problems that might result in missed production or completion dates.

FOOTNOTES

1. Elwood S. Buffa and William H. Taubert, *Production-Inventory Systems: Planning and Control.* (Homewood, IL: Richard D. Irwin, Inc., 1972), chapter 1.
2. Vinnie Chopra, "Productivity Improvement Through Closed Loop MRP," *Production & Inventory Management Review and APICS News,* April 1982, p. 50.
3. Somerby Dowst, "Production Control Needs Data From You," *Purchasing,* 11 June 1981, p. 145.

SOURCES FOR FURTHER READING

Orlicky, Joseph. *Material Requirements Planning—The New Way of Life in Production and Inventory Management.* New York: McGraw-Hill, 1975.

Carlson, John G., and Gilman, Richard. "Inventory Decision Systems: Cycle Counting," *Journal of Purchasing and Materials Management* 14 (1978): 21–25.

Morgan, James I. "Questions for Solving the Inventory Problem," *Harvard Business Review* 17, July-August, 1963.

Stenger, Alan, and Cavinato, Joseph L. "Adapting MRP to the Outbound Side—Distribution Requirements Planning," *Production and Inventory Management* 20 (1979): 1–13.

QUESTIONS FOR REVIEW

1. What are the primary functions of materials management?

2. What are some potential conflict areas between purchasing and manufacturing?

3. Distinguish the four basic types of manufacturing processes.

4. Describe at least five approaches to production scheduling, and mention a potential problem that might arise with each one.

5. What are the three basic elements of materials management planning?

6. "EOQ attempts to create safety stock while MRP tries to eliminate it." Evaluate this statement.

7. What are the purposes and uses of a bill of material?

8. Besides scheduling inbound orders, what other benefits does MRP provide purchasing?

9. Describe how DRP can be used. Where might it not be appropriate?

10. What inputs should purchasing provide to MRP?

11. What is the objective of PERT?

12. What is purchasing's role in a PERT-controlled situation?

Problem 16-1

A materials management analyst is working out the inventory and buying situation for a particular product over the next few months. The information on-hand is as follows:

400 units on-hand today
Production runs by the firm needing this product are every four weeks
(one just completed yesterday)
250 units needed in each production run
Lot sizes from vendors are 125 units each
Lead time from vendors is 5 weeks

Question:
Today is January 3. Create a table for the next 26 weeks similar to the inventory-pro-duction tables used in the MRP discussion. Show points in time at which orders must be placed and when the goods will be received.

A firm is installing a new piece of plant machinery. Several separate tasks will be needed which include site preparation, electrical line installation, plumbing line work, training, testing, etc. The following tasks are presented along with the time for each one and the preceeding task that must be completed before each one can begin.

Problem 16-2

Task	Time Needed	Required Prior Task
A	8	None
B	15	None
C	13	B
D	4	A
E	6	D
F	8	E
G	8	F
H	7	A
I	14	H
J	10	I
K	7	C, G, & J
L	4	C, G, & J
M	2	L
Completion		K & M

Questions:
1. Draw a CPM chart for this project.
2. What is the critical path for this work?

17

CHAPTER OBJECTIVES

After reading this chapter you should:

- Understand the primary importance of a sound receiving procedure.

- Appreciate the reasons for and management principles of warehousing.

- Understand key materials handling and packaging concepts.

- Appreciate the basic components of product coding systems.

Physical Components of Materials Management

Introduction

Purchasing is the key control system for sourcing and obtaining goods for use by a firm. Transportation and traffic management are involved in physically bringing these goods to the firm. The previous chapters in this Section dealt with inventory control, and the planning and control of materials in line with production scheduling. This chapter presents the functions and activities related to physically receiving goods and storing them for future use.

Purchasing and materials management usually are responsible for the physical receipt of goods as well as stewardship control over them. In the past, this area of the goods flow cycle was often neglected or considered low in importance. Product shortages, the high cost of money, and recognition of the total magnitude of inbound logistics has led most firms to tighten control in this area. Now, the actual responsibility for these areas can be found within the spheres of purchasing, materials management, production, or even distribution. In any instance, purchasing shares many key trade-offs with these physical components no matter who has direct control over them.

Close links and coordination are required so that lowest total cost to the firm is attained. Consider, for example, the overtime labor hours incurred by one firm when purchasing was not advised that its warehouse facilities had changed to stocking racks that were no longer compatible with the pallets being received under a long-term contract. Warehouse dock personnel had to double handle the goods from one pallet to another before the goods could be stored efficiently in their facility. It took several weeks for the vendor to react to the new system. A close link between purchasing and the warehouse would have avoided this problem and its resulting expense.

In another firm, a buyer noticed that the outbound distribution department was acquiring handling equipment for moving goods outbound to customers on slipsheets instead of on pallets. Further investigation revealed that the vendor had on extra charge of $11.00 per pallet lot for the inbound, palletized goods. A slipsheet, on the other hand, cost only $1.00. The buyer sought partial conversion of the inbound plant warehouse to slipsheet lifts trucks. Price changes were then negotiated with other vendors and inbound transportation firms.

Warehousing

The Forms and Types of Warehousing

Warehousing is performed for many reasons. The design, shape and operation of a warehouse is often highly dependent upon the purpose it is to serve. Different warehouse forms are examined here in terms of purpose or function and business form.

The function and purpose of different warehouses can vary from firm to firm and facility to facility. Each form is examined here from the perspective of the purchasing and materials manager.

Stock-spotting Warehouse

The stock-spotting warehouse is located near customers in order to provide a fast customer order cycle time. This warehouse exists as a sales and profit advantage to the seller. Vendor firms use stock-spotting warehouses to place inventories of goods or repair parts as close as practically possible to the customer. Rather than rely upon premium transportation, which might take two days from the factory to customer, a stock-spotting warehouse can hold the goods near the customer for fast delivery in a few hours or a day. Repair parts for copying equipment and computers are often distributed in this manner.

Breakbulk Warehouse

Breakbulk warehouses exist to save the selling firm, and possibly the purchaser, transportation costs between the source point and final destination. In many industries and markets the added expense of a warehouse near a market can be offset by considerable savings in transportation costs due to the lower unit cost of transportation for larger shipments. That is, a positive trade-off often exists in which increased warehouse expenses result in lower factory-to-customer transportation expenses. An example will illustrate. A factory-to-customer move requires a less-than-truckload freight charge of $7.12 per case. The manufacturer determines that a certain region (the Southeast, e.g.) produces sufficient sales to justify a warehouse. Now small lot purchases can be made with the following landed costs:

Plant to regional warehouse	
truckload freight	$4.80/case
warehousing	.15/case
local delivery charge	.25/case
TOTAL LANDED COST	$5.20
Savings over long distance less-than-truckload freight (7.12) =	$1.92/case

Of course, if the customer orders a full truckload quantity, it would probably be least costly to ship directly from the plant to the customer, since there are no transportation rate break economies for truckload into and out of the warehouse. The concept of a breakbulk warehouse usually includes some of the benefits of stock-spotting as well. While the motive for stock-spotting is improved customer order cycle time and the motive for breakbulk warehousing is freight cost savings, some interchangeable benefits are often experienced with each one.

Inbound Consolidation

This form of warehouse acts in reverse from a breakbulk facility. An inbound consolidation warehouse collects small-lot inbound goods from many vendors at a central point and ships them in bulk form over the long haul into the firm at a savings in transportation expenses. One department store on the East Coast has its Japanese vendors ship their small-lot shipments to one point in Kobe, Japan. Here the goods are loaded into full container lots and shipped to the firm's main facility in the U.S. This warehousing action avoids expensive, long-distance, small-lot freight moves. Many firms within the U.S. save transportation costs through inbound consolidation and full truckload shipments for distances as short as 400 miles. The purchaser is the one who directly establishes this form of warehouse.

Mixing Warehouse

A mixing warehouse is a combination of the breakbulk and inbound consolidation warehouses. Mixing warehouses are common in the food industry. Supermarket stores and chains often do not wish to purchase entire carloads or truckloads of the same item at one time. Instead, small mixed lots are common, since reduced inventory levels and fast turnover are sought-after goals in that industry. Packing firms, then, move full load shipments to central warehouses for long-term storage. A buyer on any one day, for example, may seek part loads of corn, peas, berries, or beans. If purchased direct from each packer, each purchase would require either many small-lot transportation moves or higher store inventories. The mixing warehouse, however, is central to many vendors and customers; it can serve as a breakbulk warehouse to the packer and as an inbound consolidator for the buyer. For example, on a full truckload from the mixing warehouse to the food store there could be as many as four part loads attaining the freight cost benefits of a full load. .

Exhibit 17–1 shows in schematic form how each of the above four warehouses function in product flow between the source and customer.

Warehousing is also used for many other reasons, which were cited in Chapter 14. The key point to keep in mind is that the specific need for holding the inventory in a warehouse should dictate the existence location, layout, and operation of the facility.

Efficient Storage Approaches

Over time some basic principles of efficient storage have been determined or discovered by managers and engineers. These principles should be viewed as general approaches for possible adaptation rather than hard and fast rules. They are as follows.

■ **EXHIBIT 17-1.**   *Flow Illustration of Four Basic Types of Warehouses*

a. Stock-Spotting Warehouse

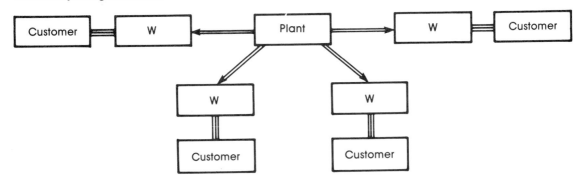

b. Break-Bulk Warehouse

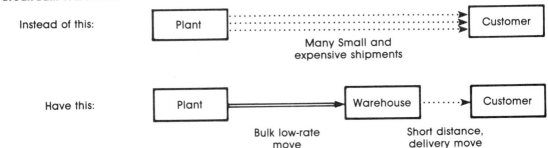

c. Inbound Consolidation

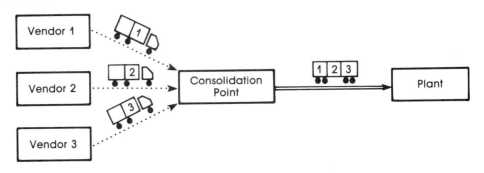

d. Mixing Warehouse

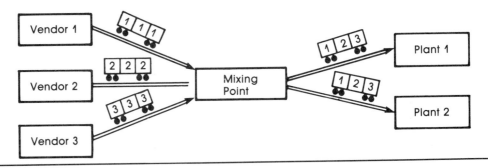

1) Concentrate goods in blocks. A block that is square or rectangular is more efficient to warehouse than one that is spread out or zig-zag shaped. The block permits easier counting and tracking of goods and does not waste space that other goods might require.

2) Use walls for the back-up of goods. Walls with adjacent aisles result in poorer overall facility storage efficiency compared to warehouses where goods are stored against walls. Against the wall storage is not always possible, and, in fact, it is generally not permitted in the case of food warehouses where many state laws require sanitary zones out from floor-wall seams.

3) Maximize density and access. This principle calls for storage in the most concentrated way possible while maintaining easy access for stocking and picking of the goods.

4) Use racks, shelves, and bins for short lots. Goods that are in very small lots or are odd shaped can be stored in bins, etc. This permits storage of many items, which would otherwise require much floor space, in as efficient a manner as possible.

5) Utilize height where feasible. Construction of warehouse horizontal square footage is generally more expensive than vertical height. In line with this, anytime goods can be stacked several tiers or pallets high, the less the unit warehouse cost will be.

6) Goods should not be locked in. All goods should be visible and accessible from the aisle or shelf front. That is, there should never be a unit of A stored behind a unit of B. To do so might result in overcounts of B and undercounts of A. It would also require a double handling of goods to access A.

7) Store goods according to popularity and cubic footage. An efficient warehouse layout takes into account the product characteristics of relative demand and required cubic footage. Generally, the more times a product is demanded for picking, the closer it should be stacked near the outbound door. Also, the smaller the total cubic footage required for storing a product, the closer it should be stored near the door in order to minimize handling costs. These two concepts can be combined into a tool called the cube-per-order index. This calls for dividing the total required cubic footage for storing an item by the number of times a day it must be accessed. Various goods are then arranged from the outbound door with low cube-per-order index numbers near the door and high ones toward the back of the warehouse. This tool will provide a low cost ratio when picking cost minimization is an objective. This concept is often modified, however, when it is desired to store all goods of a particular product family or manufacturer together. It often is suboptimized, too, when certain goods cannot be stored together, e.g. rubber and textiles, chemicals and food, and some different chemicals in the same room.

Alternatives to Warehousing

Perhaps the best way to attain the objectives of minimum warehouse investments and costs is to avoid or minimize the use or warehousing all together. Several possible practices should be kept in mind in routine operations as well as in periodic planning activities that can lead to such warehouse cost minimization. Some of these are:

1) Schedule production and purchasing in a tight manner. This idea was captured in the MRP discussion and basically requires delaying purchases to result in a near-zero inventory holding.

2) Utilize slow transportation when goods will not be needed immediately. Many times a fast or premium mode of transportation is used on inbound goods only to have them sit for several days or weeks prior to use. A slower form of transportation often allows a lower freight cost, and it acts as the warehouse while in-transit.

3) Buy rather than make. This option will often result in a lower total inventory and less required warehouse space than when the firm produces goods itself. When goods are bought rather than made in-house, no raw components or work-in-process items need to be warehoused. Only one stock-keeping unit is involved when goods are bought.

4) Use demurrage or detention in trade-off against warehousing. Some firms take possession of full carload or truckload quantities of purchases, store them, then retransport them to the final plant or use point. If the time between initial purchase and reshipping is not too long, it might be less costly to hold the goods on the freight vehicle and pay the carrier demurrage or detention than unload, store, and reload the goods. Here, the relative cost of detention/demurrage versus storage and handling will have to carefully be evaluated.

5) Use a close-by vendor warehouse. Tight scheduling and order processing and shipping links between the purchaser and vendor will often enable an inbound warehouse to be avoided. Instead, the vendor's facility is used as the storage point. This option requires close communication among the vendor, purchasing, and the manufacturing department.

It is often difficult to determine where warehouse costs end and handling costs begin. The two are intricately linked in operational and planning contents.

Materials Handling

Materials handling is short-distance transportation that on the inbound side usually takes place between a transportation vehicle and storage, from storage to production, or between different stages of production. Materials handling is often very repetitive and represents a large, but sometimes unnoticed, cost.

Objectives of Materials Handling

Materials handling should be operated in the most efficient manner consistent with investment cost and product characteristics. It is a cost function that should be minimized. One problem that often arises is that each product or handling situation could be achieved in a least-unit-cost manner by using different forms of equipment. Avoiding this problem often requires many different types of equipment and moving systems. The task for the materials manager is to find one system, or a few systems, that lead to the least total cost or least inefficient option(s) of all available. The purchasing and materials manager has an interest in materials handling from the standpoint of cost and handling efficiency to the production line.

Special Materials Handling Topics

Two key areas of cost and movement efficiency that concern the purchasing and materials management manager are unit-load programs and the pallet/slipsheet decision. Each method of movement can represent large inbound handling cost savings or inefficiencies if not properly utilized.

Unit-load programs are systems of handling two or more product units as one. It is the principle behind the shipping container, the grocery bag, and even the suitcase. The idea is that handling, lifting, and travel energies require lesser unit proportions as the number of units handled is increased. That is, moving ten units at once between a rail car and a warehouse storage spot requires less total time, manpower, and energy as two trips of five units each.

Unit-load systems include pallets, cartons, containers, baskets, movable hampers, and cages. Shrinkwrapping also is used which consists of tightly wrapped plastic sheeting around two or more units made into single handling units. If four boxes are wrapped into a single unit, a load of one hundred can be treated as only twenty-five handlings. Many obvious handling economies can be obtained through these systems. Usually these handling systems are developed by the outbound distribution managers of vendor companies and promoted by their salesman. But it is wise for the inbound purchasing and materials manager to critically analyze all benefits and costs related to these systems.

Unit-load benefits can be determined by comparing the total labor and machinery costs of handling units individually versus in fewer movements. But, the unit-load program costs and drawbacks must also be weighed against these savings. One possible cost is the empty return of a shipping container to the vendor. This can be reduced if roundtrips or reciprocal sales can be worked out. Another cost might be special handling machinery for just that vendor's load programs. Several vendors might ship goods on pallets that can be handled by the firm's forklift, but one vendor might ship goods that require a clamp handling lift truck, which can cost upwards to $25,000. Another drawback to unit-load systems is that goods might be unitized into specific quantities that are not always convenient lot sizes for the purchasing firm. Palletized goods might be in lots of 120 each, while the desired purchase and production quantities might be 300. In summary, the purchasing and materials manager must determine the economic worth of participating in a vendor's unit-load program.

Another unit-load issue is the pallet versus slipsheet decision. Pallets are sturdy wooden devices onto which goods are unitized, stored, and shipped. Slipsheets also can be used for this purpose but there are relative merits of each. Table 17-1 shows comparative benefits and drawbacks of each. Pallets can cost a vendor between $6.00 and $10.00, and

□ **TABLE 17-1.** *Comparison of Pallet Versus Slipsheet Advantages*

The Major Factors	Medium Favored Pallet	Slipsheet
Initial price		Y
Cost per trip:		
in exchange program	Y	
in in-plant system	Y	
in shipments without exchange		Y
Use of cube in carrier vehicle		Y
Repair cost		Y
Administration cost		Y
Weight		Y
Empty storage requirements		Y
Product damage	Y	
Resistence	Y	
Ventilation	Y	
High stacking requirement	Y	
Freight cost per vehicle		Y
Product characteristic:		
heavy	Y	Y
light		Y
odd shape	Y	
uniform shape		Y
Infestation		Y
Fire hazard storage		Y

□ Source: "Pallets vs. Slipsheet: The Great Controversy" *Modern Materials Handling*, June 1979, p.66.

the slipsheet ranges between $.50 and $1.75; these costs are built into the price of the purchased goods.

A further point to consider is that of returning or disposing of pallets or slipsheets. Some materials managers turn this into a benefit for the firm. Sometimes it can be more economical to acquire these pallets through inbound goods purchases than it would be to purchase them new from primary sources.

Materials Handling Efficiencies

Several principles or tips on handling exist, some of which are discussed here. All operations should be reviewed periodically with an eye toward these elements.

1) Move goods in a straight line whenever possible. Straight lines represent the minimum travel distance between two points and the least energy consumption in comparison to slowdowns, speedups, and friction wear experienced with curves and turns. They also minimize, somewhat, the chance of movement damage.

2) Utilize continuous flow. This means the use of nonstop uniform speed movements. Again, this represents minimized energy, friction, and damage possibilities. The economy of this principle can be noted on a broad scale in the lower-cost structure of nonstop airplane and rail movement.

3) Use gravity whenever possible. Gravity is a free form of energy. It can be used for short or intermediate distances (up to 200-300 feet) with conveyors and flow-through storage racks.

4) Maximize the number of units per handling operation. This is the principle of the unit-load concept.

5) Combine handling with another function. Counting, inspecting, sorting, and unwrapping are basic functions to the inbound goods flow process. Movement can be combined with one of these to reduce two separate steps into one.

6) Standardize handling systems. Uniform handling equipment and methods tend to minimize training, equipment investment, maintenance costs, and movement processes. The same applies to pallets, of which there are ten standard sizes, and slipsheets.

7) Eliminate handling if possible. Handling consumes manpower and machinery resources. Opportunities to eliminate handling should be investigated wherever possible. A feasible way is through direct inbound vehicle-to-stock point movement with tallying and inspection taking place on the vehicle or at the stocking point. This avoids the double handling associated with the vehicle-to-dock and subsequent dock-to-stocking point movement. Another method of handling reduction is timing inbound loads from vehicle to production line thus avoiding intermediate storage and multiple handling in a warehouse.

Other techniques of efficiency exist, and many are associated with particular handling equipment. The key is to develop an approach for periodically evaluating the handling methods employed with an eye for possible improvement. This area is often treated as a mundane, but necessary cost function that is ignored until a unit of handling machinery must be replaced. Many opportunities can be realized by closer attention to this area.

Packaging

The package is another major physical component of materials management, and it is one that is often overlooked by purchasing managers. Packages are generally created by the vendor, but purchasing and materials managers are the ones who ultimately pay for them, and they are the ones who experience many of the final benefits and drawbacks of their design. The critical facets of packaging of interest here are: 1) its basic types, 2) its roles or functions, and 3) its cost configuration to the user/buyer of the product.

Over three hundred forms of packaging materials and forms are in use today, and the list grows as advances in various materials and adhesives develop. But, all packages can be grouped into two basic forms as far as the purchasing manager is concerned. One is the marketing package and the other is the distribution package. The marketing package is one that directly encloses the product. This package is often designed to maximize point of display appeal and visibility of the product. The problem is that this package unit is usually small, and it is made of weak packaging materials such as cellophane. It cannot endure warehouse and transportation handling without some damage or loss.

The distribution package, on the other hand, is the one that encloses one or more marketing package units for movement outbound from the factory. Examples are cartons and cases. This package serves to protect goods from transit, handling, and storage damage. Another of its functions is that of providing identification for persons involved in movement and warehousing. These external packages contain product name, unit size, quantity of units, and often company codes for accounting and inventory purposes as well as key information as to temperature, humidity, or stocking constraints and handling requirements. Much of this information is printed on cases, but it is not necessary on individual consumer units. A final function of the industrial package is what is often referred to as mobility. That is, the outer carton, case, etc. permit storage, handling, and movement in ways not possible nor efficient with individual units. A case of ketchup bottles is a good example. Alone ketchup bottles are difficult to handle, and they are fragile. But, contained in cases of 24 units, they can be handled on pallet of upwards of 900 bottles at a time, and these can be stocked three or four pallets high. This unit-load economy further extends to loading and unloading forty-eight-foot-long trailers, which can be accomplished in less than thirty minutes rather than the day it would take for hand stocking.

The purchasing and materials manager's interest in the packages containing acquired products include their strengths and cost. Strength is a necessary attribute that protects the product through distribution to the purchasing firm and beyond. Package strength is necessary to protect the goods against the many handlings in warehousing and transportation. Carriers require certain minimum distribution package configurations, but attention to this area should not stop at the acceptance of these firms' standards. For one, damaged goods received at the dock entail claims, and possibly litigation with carriers, insurance companies, and warehousemen. Damaged goods also require extra effort in filing for returns and allowances and in processing them for return transportation or product segregation for disposal. Finally, damaged goods represent stockout possibilities and lost cash flow opportunities. Problems with transit damage might be attacked through packaging, switching to more careful carriers, or using other modes that require less handling or provide smoother movement (e.g., motor versus rail). Packaging will become more important as transportation deregulation reduces the carrier's legal obligation. Package strength has a trade-off relationship with the possibility of product damage. But, the cost of a strong package, vis-a-vis, a more economically priced one should be analyzed. It is more economical to use a $1.00 package on one million units that results in damage one-half of one percent of the time rather than a stronger $2.00 package that experience damage one-tenth of the time. Further, in past years stronger packages usually were metal ones. The extra strength came at an added package material cost as well as extra weight that increased freight charges assessed by the carrier in the movement of the product. Material innovations in plastics today can reduce the weight without sacrifices in strength.

Purchasing and materials managers are directly involved in packaging goods that their firms sell. Package materials are purchased, received, stored, and moved to production lines. These materials vary in market price and availability, and new forms are continually evolving. The key costs here are the costs of purchasing, freight, inventorying, and materials handling. Improvement potential often can be found by value-analysis processes or whenever a new material comes onto the market.

The package is a component often ignored in the total cost of landing and ultimately using a product. It is often designed and used in the same form throughout the entire life cycle of the good. Along with the facts of material cost, strength, loss and damage, and package weight as a freight cost element, the purchasing manager also can look to use of standardized packages, package waste disposal, storage and handling economies, or subsequent use and/or recycling of these materials. If the buying firm has engineering talent in the packaging area, the purchasing manager might beneficially use that talent in packaging analysis contexts with smaller vendors who do not have such talent.

Product Identification Codes

Product identification coding is another materials management feature that is gaining greater attention and use. It is the assignment of a number or other identification to each item or good the firm produces, sells, or purchases.

Firms find product coding useful for several reasons. One, product coding can simplify the tracking and control process. This reduces confusion that can arise with seemingly similar products or the same products of different sizes. Product coding is a common communication means. A distinct code for each good is especially necessary for items that look alike but are different in chemical or electrical capability. Two, product codes are adaptable to computer control and processing. A ten-digit code is easier to use than the entire product name, such as a chemical name that might consist of over thirty letters. Computers can handle digits as codes simpler than the alphameric name. Three, inventory control can be simplified by product codes. Codes can contain data about the vendor, lead time, handling and use requirements, or government hazardous or toxic labeling needs. Four, codes can include product family information that eases materials requirements planning for bill of material construction and control. Codes can also be extended to include vendor data for tracking experience in this realm. Fifth, codes are often needed for subsequent tracking of each specifically identified unit produced or handled by the firm. This is often a requirement for product recall purposes where individual components and/or production runs must be identifiable. Sixth, product codes enable automated tracking, sorting, and other handling functions as well as inventory tallying throughout a distribution network. Such systems are being implemented on industrywide basis in the grocery, liquor, and publishing sectors. And, seventh, product codes are often useful for identifying substitute components when the requested item is out of stock. This has been implemented in the auto parts and electronics industries, and can readily be observed in lawn mower repair shops where specific parts are identified, coded, and shown on exploded charts on microfiche. Cross references, substitute parts and often other manufacturers' parts are often shown as well. Such a system would be very difficult to implement without codes.

Codes exist in many forms, but all contain similar features, including reference or identification of the producing firm, product family, the specific product, and quantity or capacity. In a ten-digit code, these items might be treated in five or six digits with the remaining digits reserved for special attributes. For example, the Uniform Product Code, or UPC, was developed for use throughout the grocery industry. It is a barcode system that is readible by various scanners in factories, distribution centers, and at cash register checkouts. A sample is shown in Exhibit 17–2. The UPC system consists of two sets of five digits. The first set identifies the manufacturer while the second set indicates the specific contents of the package. It is only one of ten frequently used barcoding systems in vogue today.

This code system allows machine reading of the product in an accurate manner. Inventory clerks can use a small wand to read the code on the side of a bin then punch in the count of the item so that the item and count are quickly and accurately recorded. Improvement here is realized by speeded up processes, since the clerk does not have to manually record the item name or description. Further, accuracy is increased as well.

Code systems with accurate reading devices can be used in production settings as well. One code readible item can be attached to a unit going through production. This code can be read along the line so that special production requirements can be performed. This system is being used in some auto assembly plants today.

■ **EXHIBIT 17-2.** *Uniform Product Code*

Two other systems are in use in addition to the bar codes. One is an optical character recognition (OCR) system that can read letters and numbers. This system is now in common use in the retail garment industry. The other system uses human readible cards with magnetic strips that contain information about the product.

Materials managers should be heavily involved in the creation and maintenance of product code systems adopted by the firm. Several points should be kept in mind when adopting these systems, which are often in use for the long-term of the firm.

First, there should be some logic to the code such as in the UPC. This allows faster access, and memory of the general system. It will enhance the efficiency of use by those on the shop floor and in control positions. Secondly, the system should be designed with a very wide margin for future expansion. It is easier to modify an existing system for expansion than to create and replace one in future years. Product proliferation is inherent to industrialized nations, and product code systems should freely expand when new goods, materials, and products are developed and used. Thirdly, another point relating to future expansion capability in the actual code is that the capacity for expansion in all computer systems using the code must exist. Many mistakes have been made when firms developed, say, eight-digit codes, and only programmed eight-digit-wide fields into computer programs. By the time the firm sought to expand the code, program fields did not allow for this growth.

Codes and coding systems should also allow for cross-reference and substitute product identification. This point is of strategic importance as materials managers seek to reduce inventory needs through standardization and inventory system simplification. Finally, some effort should be made to relate the firm's code to those of vendors. This includes relating the product code to the firm's own outbound coding system, if one is in use by distribution personnel from the end of the production line outward to customers.

Product coding systems are a major element in the overall process of seeking closer control and coordination of the firm's resources. Many firms extend codes to capital goods and office equipment. The advantages of this approach are obvious. Code development and maintenance should be a part of the purchasing and materials managers' responsibilities; it should not be left to personnel in data processing alone. Code development is a key item that must involve all of the ultimate users.

Conclusion

The physical aspects of materials management include warehousing, materials handling, packaging and product identification. These logistics components can represent major costs in the entire inbound flow activities. These functions were traditionally separate from purchasing. But, in the recent evolution toward integrated materials management, they have become a part of the purchasing decision process and management responsibility.

SOURCES FOR FURTHER READING

Ackerman, Kenneth B. *Understanding Today's Distribution Center*. Washington: Traffic Service Corporation, 1983.

Apple, James M. *Material Handling Systems Design*. New York: Ronald Press, 1972.

_____. *Plant Layout and Material Handling*. New York: Wiley, 1977.

Falconer, Peter, and Drury, Jolyon. *Building and Planning for Industrial Storage and Distribution*. New York: Halsted Press, 1975.

Harrell, Gilbert. *Universal Product Code: Price Removal and Consumer Behavior in Supermarkets*. East Lansing, MI: Michigan State University, 1976.

Hicks, Lawrence. *The Universal Product Code*. New York: AMACOM, 1975.

Heoffer, El. "Bar codes: A Boon to Material Control," *Purchasing*, 9 September 1982, p. 10881.

Margulies, Walter P. *Packaging Power*. New York: World Publishing, 1970.

Sacharow, Stanley. *Handbook of Package Materials*. Westport, CT: Avi Publishing Co., 1976.

QUESTIONS FOR REVIEW

1. Why would the inbound logistics factors presented in this chapter be of importance to buyers today?

2. Why do firm's warehouse?

3. How do stock-spotting, breakbulk, inbound consolidation, and mixing warehouses benefit purchasing?

4. Cite three efficient storage techniques and state why they are good objectives to seek.

5. What is materials handling, and why do firms spend money in this area?

6. Why are some unit-load programs efficient? Is it possible that such a program might benefit the seller and not the buyer? If so, how?

7. Is it wise to always adopt a specific form of materials handling to every product? Why or why not?

8. What are the prime trade-offs between using pallets and slipsheets?

9. Discuss how three forms of materials handling efficiencies might save purchasing money?

10. What concerns should the purchasing manager have about packaging?

11. How do product identification code systems simplify the job of the materials manager?

12. What cautions would you put forth if your firm was considering an automated product identification system?

Problem 17-1   A buyer for a major manufacturing firm is examining the cost of inbound shipments from Europe. The product has been shipped by air, which takes two days. The inbound moves are from Germany, Netherlands, Belgium, and

Denmark. The rates from these countries to the main receiving plant average about $72.50 per package.

The buyer has been approached by a firm that is willing to set up a consolidation facility at a European port for the firm. The arrangements would entail consigning the goods from vendors to this site in Rotterdam. The land transportation would average about $17.25 per package. Storage and handling at the consolidation point would be about $4.50 per package. Full container volume loads via ocean carrier would be about $23.00 per package. And delivery at the Port of New York would be about $6.00 per package. The longer transit time (seven days) would incur an additional inventory cost of about $3.00. Documentation and customs is the same with each logistics system choice.

Questions:
1. *Is it worthwhile to use this alternative system?*
2. *What costs change in trade-off with each other?*

PART IV

SPECIAL TOPICS IN PURCHASING MANAGEMENT

Purchasing cannot be viewed purely in an isolated setting. It is very much a part of the overall system of the firm. Marketing is one of the major disciplines with which purchasing interfaces.

Purchasing and marketing interface in two ways. First, the marketing effort of the firm that is selling to a buyer. There are many facets of marketing that purchasing personnel must be aware of, if they are to effectively understand and function as consumers of marketed products and services. Second, purchasing personnel interface with marketing in their own firm. Marketing stimulates the demand for a firm's goods and often sets the prices and specifies the product design.

This section covers purchasing in settings other than manufacturing. Wholesaling, retailing, and government agency organizations perform purchasing tasks, yet the underlying objectives of these organizations are somewhat different than those in production settings. Marketing and purchasing activities in wholesale and retail firms are very closely linked. In public agencies, the purchasing task involves obtaining goods and services that seek to attain objectives other than market sales revenue. Be that as it may, purchasing in these agencies still operates under organizational objectives that shape daily operations.

This section delves into product decisions and what they demand of purchasing personnel in both the selling and buying organizations. Chapter 18 presents product management concepts that both directly and indirectly bear upon the purchasing function. Chapter 19 presents the theory and practice of pricing and how purchasing personnel can utilize these ideas to the best advantage of their organizations. The knowledgeable purchasing manager must be in tune with pricing behavior in the market in order to make sound daily decisions and conduct long-run planning. Chapter 20 covers the channels of distribution used by manufacturers to move products to ultimate users. Intermediate firms in the channel are examined along with their buying and selling needs. Finally, Chapter 20 also presents an overview of public agency purchasing practices and constraints.

18

INTRODUCTION

PRODUCT CYCLE

New Product Research and Planning
Product Life Cycle
Risks in New Product Development

MAINTENANCE, REPAIR, AND OPERATING SUPPLIES

STANDARDIZATION

CHAPTER OBJECTIVES

After reading this chapter you should:

- Understand how the product life cycle provides insights into appropriate purchasing strategies.

- Understand the basic processes for product introduction and phase-out.

- Be able to relate maintenance, repair, and operating supplies to the primary purchase processes.

- Understand how standardization is a key component in purchasing activities.

Product Management Decisions for Purchasing

Introduction

Product management encompasses a range of activities including the development, introduction, general manufacturing, support, and eventual phase-out of a product. It is an essential part of corporate strategy, since products are what the firm presents to the market in exchange for other resources.

This chapter explores three distinct facets of product management. First is the manufactured and marketed product from its conception to eventual phase-out. Products experience four basic stages, and each phase calls for different purchasing strategies. Maintenance, repair, and operating supplies, or MRO items, are another area of product management. These are supplies that are needed to operate the firm's basic operations. Many of the administrative facets of MRO management fall to purchasing. And, standardization is another product management activity that purchasing generally conducts for the purpose of cost reduction.

Product Cycle

The product cycle, or life cycle, is a series of phases that nearly every product passes through between conception and ultimate phase-out or elimination. It is pertinent for study because a different set of approaches and tools are often required for purchasing and marketing at each stage. Furthermore, marketing efforts by vendors will noticeably be different at each stage.

New Product Research and Planning

New product research is a basic part of a firm's survival. The reason is simple: existing products sold by the company will be obsolete someday due to improved competitive products or changes in buying preferences of the market. A 1980 survey by McGraw-Hill cites that $41.7 billion was spent that year by U.S. firms on research and development.

Research conducted by firms tends to fall into five distinct areas. First, is product research. This includes the development of new products. The 1980 survey indicated that new product research was the largest segment of all categories. Some responding firms in that survey expected one-third of their sales three years hence to be comprised of products not in existence in 1980. Product improvement was the second largest research area. These efforts are directed toward modifying mature products in order to reduce their cost of manufacturing and distribution or to enhance their competitiveness. A third major research area was new processes. This area was dominated by petroleum and chemical industries seeking ways to improve production processes. Energy research was the fourth major area studied. The improvement in energy efficiency in machinery and vehicles continues to be important in firms. New materials, designs, and approaches are continually being developed to improve energy efficiency of capital, durable, and consumable goods. And, fifth, research related to government regulation continues to be a major activity. The compliance of noneconomic regulations in transportation vehicles, toxic and hazardous materials, and environmental areas often forces research dollars into these areas before monies can be applied to the product and process areas.

Product development and improvement research is necessary and, in fact, critical for the long-run viability of a firm. In a competitive environment there is often a higher risk associated with not innovating than there is with trying new products, approaches, materials, and designs. But, the cost of product research is high, because 1) many researched product ideas are never launched into the market 2) many of those that do enter the market fail, and 3) product life spans are becoming shorter.

One research source presents what is called the "decay curve" of new product ideas. It shows that out of sixty new product ideas, only one reaches the market. Exhibit 18-1 shows how product ideas are dropped as they go through initial screening, business analysis, development, testing, and commercialization.

The same type of curve exists with industrial products as well as with consumer products. Purchasing managers are very much a part of the research process. As customers, they are often the source of many ideas that start out on the decay curve. These ideas may have come from their own marketing departments, from production or by value-analysis processes. Purchasing is often a part of testing as well. Feedback to the selling firm is very important in the final launching of the product.

Purchasing also gets involved in the new product idea generation process within its own firm. Purchasing's input with regard to material costs and supply availability greatly impacts upon the screening, business analysis, development, and testing stages of a new product. Firms that do not involve purchasing at this stage are limited by information in all phases of the process. Purchasing can advise of different design approaches based upon new or standardized components available on the market.

Purchasing can become involved in product development in a mixed sense as well. One eyeglass frame assembler presented his vendors with many ideas regarding a new material and potential process. None of the vendors proceeded past the business analysis stage of the idea. Instead, the assembler embarked upon research on his own, eventually manufactured the item, and became a dominant firm in this new area. The

■ **EXHIBIT 18-1.**   *Decay Curve of New Product Ideas*

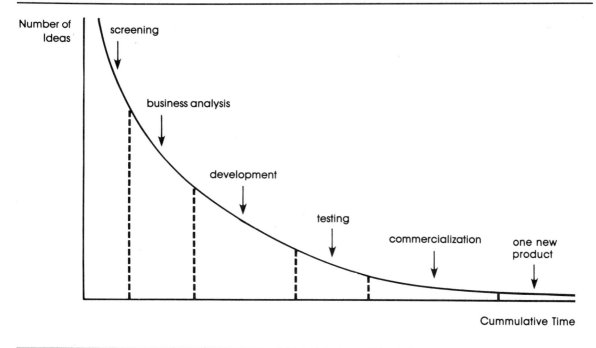

market potential for the new material was mistakenly underestimated by his vendors.

Risks in New Product Development

Risk is a key factor in the introduction of new products. It is the chance that the product will not be profitable. In specific form, risk can present problems in several definable areas that generally include the market, production technology and buying. Any one or more of these areas can present major problems in product management or cause the firm to scrap the new product idea altogether. Roger More presents an analysis of the key risk factors of product introduction.[1] These factors should be used as a checklist of areas to investigate when considering new products.

Technology
The technological features of the new product should be compared to the skills already present in the company. Specifically, the amount of experience in or perceived difficulty with developing both the technology and production processes should be evaluated. A low level of engineering and production talent in a company can blunt new product development.

Cost
The cost of developing the product, moving it through its testing and shakeout period, as well as the expenses of production when in full operation should be carefully evaluated.

Market/Competition

Careful attention should be paid to the time between introduction and obsolescence. If this time span is too short, the company will probably not recoup a total life profit or return. Some firms will avoid this product and direct attention to the next level of technology. Such was the case when Boeing leaped from piston-driven stratocruiser to the all-jet B-707, thus avoiding the turbo-props which enjoyed a marketplace advantage of less than five years.

Of further consideration in the competitive realm is the degree of patent protection for the new product, as well as the ability of competitors to quickly duplicate the item.

In the pure marketing realm, the skills of the sales and marketing force must be considered. Questions relating to similarities with current products, markets, and customers will arise. The new product might be so unique that it requires an entirely different marketing effort by the firm altogether. New approaches, new customers, and new promotional methods might be required. Further, customers might be forced into an area of greater risk as well.

Purchasing

Several key evaluative criteria enter here. Problems in purchasing are often cited as reason for dropping new product ideas. Low buyer purchase experience can be one problem. The new product might require purchasing skills not currently present in the department. Another problem is low buyer time commitment to becoming familiar with or handling the new product's components. A major buyer adaptation, or large learning curve hurdle for purchasing is another reason. These are real concerns of both top management and purchasing people. An objective skill's assessment of the department's systems and personnel capabilities will highlight any strengths or deficiencies. However, the purchasing manager might be reluctant to admit weaknesses, and they might not appear as a problem until actual operations begin.

The path from product idea to actual launching is an expensive one. Firms are concerned with market timing, short-run costs versus long-run benefits, and the movement into product, technology, market, and management structure areas that are hoped to be new strategic advantages over competitors. All these factors must be weighed against the risk of failure.

Product Life Cycle

The product life cycle is a series of phases or stages through which marketed products travel between product launching and the elimination decision. Exhibit 18–2 illustrates sales and profit experiences generlly found with this cycle. Most products can be categorized according to stages in this cycle.

Introductory Stage

During the introductory stage the product is launched onto the market. Consumers are not yet aware of the product, so marketing must often

■ **EXHIBIT 18-2.** *General Product Life Cycle*

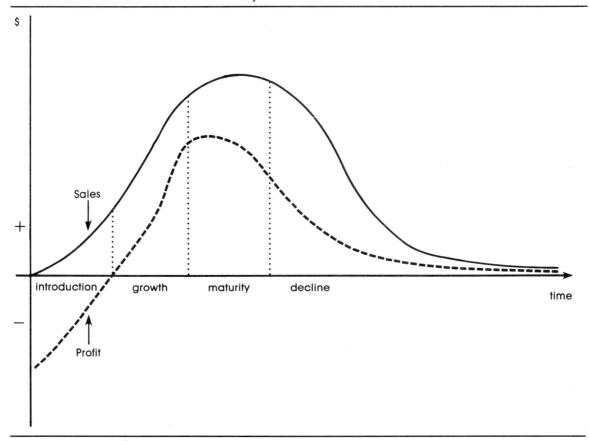

make "cold calls" on new and existing customers; middlemen must be encouraged to purchase and promote the product. The firm's distribution approach is that of "pushing" the product to the market. That is, inventories are placed in the field and in retail outlets without being "pulled" from orders made by these parties.

Buyers are often approached in the form of a sales call, and highly developed promotional literature is presented. The product is displayed and demonstrated at sales fairs and trade shows. In the pharmaceutical industry, salesmen will visit doctors and hospitals with drug samples and technical literature. This marketing and buyer acceptance process causes this stage to be characterized by slow sales growth and high initial expenses, which result in short-term net profit losses. Buyers are often involved in testing the new product in their own firm.

Purchasing in the selling firm is greatly involved during this stage of the product cycle. In spite of extensive research, design, and limited testing, product changes are still necessary once full-scale market distribution takes place and user experience is gained.It is necessary here for sales personnel to maintain close links with customers in the field so that product problems and changes necessary to correct or improve the item can be communicated back to production, product design personnel, and purchasing. Production must remain flexible in order to change methods, processes and/or make product design changes. Materials management should maintain low inventories at this stage because a product design change might cause one component to be eliminated and another one to be needed.

Purchasing must utilize a wide range of vendors, and small lot purchasing is common. Quick design changes might necessitate a fast change in vendors, or sudden alterations in the specifications desired. Vendors must be as flexible as the purchaser's own firm at this point. A good practice might be to use one or more vendors who are adept at making product design changes, even though they are not necessarily the same ones who would be best in stable, large-scale buying situations. For example, there are many small firms in the transformer industry whose strategic advantages are innovation and flexible technical and management skills, but they have limited production capabilities. These firms are valuable during the design and introduction stages, but they are not competitive nor are they desirous of competing against full-scale manufacturers in large-run settings.

It is not uncommon to tap the expertise of vendors in order to find ways of reducing costs or otherwise improving product design. This input often consists of material specifications, relaxation of tolerances, or standardizing individual components. Thus, in the introductory stage, a close-linked communication system is necessary all the way from the user-customer back through the production-engineering-purchasing areas to the suppliers.

Growth Stage

In this phase the product has gained market acceptance, and greater demand is now generated by an overall widening market. Sales increase as do profits. The product is often "pulled" from the market, and manufacturing sometimes cannot keep up with demand. Shortages appear since not all customers can be served. The product design is fairly solidified by now, and new competitors are beginning to enter the market with copied or similarly designed products.

Marketing activities are often increased during this stage. A common problem here is handling shortages that irritate the early buyer or loyal customer. Market allocation decisions are common. New applications for the product are being discovered, and this often leads to small sales surges and new marketing efforts. While sales increase, the entrance of competitors can often lead to a peaking in total profits toward the end of the growth stage.

Buyers often experience the problem of order delays at the beginning of this cycle stage. The buyer's own firm often switches to a new product only to experience supply problems with it. This is a penalty of sorts for being an early adapter or new user of an item. It is important here to establish a strong, long-term relationship with the vendor in order to be favorably treated during this stage.

The purchaser inside the firm selling the new product now must switch to new approaches. The tight system of low inventories and quick design changes is no longer necessary. The product will now only undergo minor design changes. Approaches called for now include seeking vendors with the ability to suddenly expand. The vendor who is at or near production capacity will not be able to expand without an expensive and time-consuming capital construction project. Larger lot sizes are appropriate here, since the company's marketing and production systems are having difficulty keeping up with demand. Fast order cycle time is sought, and premium forms of transportation are often used to speed up inbound supply.

Maturity Stage

During the maturity stage, the product is characterized by a slowing and eventual flattening of the growth rate. The leveled-off demand is due to all potential customers having been reached, with little new penetration into other areas that might result in major sales boosts. A cost-profit squeeze comes about here that often causes the firm to drop the product because the firm is either inefficient in manufacturing or does not possess the market strength to exercise market leadership in the future.

The impacts of product maturity and saturation upon marketing are great. Price cutting and discounting becomes common as firms seek to boost or maintain sales. Market share and sales increases are often only attainable by attacking competitors, since the entire market is no longer growing. Marketing seeks to regenerate the product by finding new uses and applications for it. Promotional efforts become intense as emphasis turns away from educating the market about the item to differentiating it from those sold by competitors. Sales efforts are often directed toward the ultimate buyer or user, thus bypassing intermediate customers. Attention is made to improving the firm's customer service performance to make it better than that of competitors.

The buyer of the product in this marketing phase will be affected by many of the changes taking place. In fact, market maturity might impact the buyer's firm before it is felt by the manufacturer. This is especially the case with retailers and wholesalers who are often first to notice a softening of the market. This can create a squeeze for these channel members if the manufacturer is still dictating terms that are appropriate only in the market pull area of the growth stage.

Buyers will notice or seek changes in their relationship with the vendor of a mature product. The products of the various vendors will tend to become homogeneous, and this will heighten the competitiveness of these goods. Liberal credit terms will be offered, as will cash discounts and discounting in general. Shifts in sales terms are often made from "FOB manufacturer, freight collect" to "FOB origin, freight paid by seller." Emphasis upon customer service is important in ways that include shorter order cycle time — making it more consistent, improving order fill accuracy, or making the process of purchasing simpler through computerization or vendor-controlled inventories. Relative bargaining strength shifts somewhat from seller to buyer during this stage.

The purchaser of the firm producing the now mature product also must switch tactical operations in much the same way as the marketing people in the firm. The slowing of sales causes revenues to flatten or fall, and in many instances some of the tolerated high-cost practices of the growth stage will continue until checked. Attention to costs now becomes great for this product line, since less control exists over revenues in the total profit equation. Cost reduction efforts usually become major tactical goals. Inventory reduction is an important means to this end. Since the maturity stage can be a relatively long, stable period, production, manufacturing and distribution economies often can be gained through long-run operating practices. Cost reduction through long-run buying practices can bring economies of scale to the vendors, and the certainty of operation can be translated into lower prices. Value analysis becomes important here through efforts to reduce product cost while maintaining its primary features and efficiency. Inbound logistics improvements are fruitful in the maturity stage through long-term transportation arrangements, implementation of order processing and inventory control techniques, as well as two-way, unit-load programs with pallets and containers.

Decline Stage

The fourth stage occurs when industrywide sales begin to decrease in response to other products taking over in the market. In this stage, new products are preferred to older ones, price competition can become severe among the remaining firms producing the older goods. Large scale production runs do not sufficiently lower costs to widen the spread between unit revenue and manufacturing expenses. Low margins and high inventories are often an indication of a problem product. From time to time one competitor or the other might drop out thereby leaving some additional market share to the remaining firms. In some industrial and consumer durable goods markets, the remaining demand is for replacement items only.

Marketing efforts for declining products become cash-contribution oriented. That is, the margin of sales over direct manufacturing and selling costs is the key indicator to watch. Long-run costs such as depreciation or unamortized research are not as relevant here as short-term cash spin-off. No capital investment is added now. Promotional efforts are re-aligned in order to maximize the total cash margin. Sales territories are changed, and some territorial markets are dropped altogether. In some instances, customers are warned of pending line discontinuances in the future.

Buyers of products in the decline stage must adopt a contingency approach. On the one hand, warnings of line dropping must be immediately passed on to production, engineering, and marketing. The firm's own use of the product should be evaluated at this time. If the firm continues to need the product, the buyer must then investigate several possible avenues of product supply assurance. One might be to line up other sources that are still in the market. Another approach is to make a long-run commitment with the original longstanding supplier. This might be accomplished through a long-term purchase agreement, or other seller cost-reduction means such as consignment purchasing or partial manufacturing with finishing in-house. One firm needing specialty gears actually purchased the old machinery from a vendor in order to continue producing the needed item in-house. These are just a few ways in which products can continue in supply in face of vendor line trimming.

The purchasing manager in the firm producing a declining product should be aware of when the product might be discontinued or eliminated by the firm. This warning should be passed on to vendors so they will not then be faced with a sudden cessation of sales.

Purchasing managers should be a part of the decision process to eliminate a product. As previously noted, declining products are often managed from a cash spin-off basis rather than from total reported accounting profit. The approach employed here is that of contribution margin analysis. Three products are shown in Table 18-1 that illustrate this approach. Product C is currently incurring a cash loss and should be eliminated. The total contribution margin of the firm would rise to $15,000 if C was eliminated, and the total profit of the firm would rise to $5,000.

Product B, however, is subject to question since its total profit is $0. It also appears to be a declining product, but the firm should not eliminate it at this point, unless it has another more productive use for the manufacturing capacity. While Product B does not produce a profit, it does contribute $5,000 of cash to the firm over and above its direct costs. If it was also eliminated, the firm would avoid $5,000 of direct expenses but lose $10,000 of revenue. The overhead would still remain. Thus, if available revenue is greater than available expenses, do not eliminate the product unless something else that is more profitable can be made in its place.

Scrap and surplus goods are another way in which purchasing is involved with declining and eliminating goods. When products are eliminated, the firm will usually have some old production machinery and left-over inventories. The profitable disposal of these items is usually the responsibility of purchasing. This topic is discussed in further detail in Chapter 19, Pricing Strategies.

Several concluding points can be addressed that have further bearing upon the development, production, and marketing of products in line with the cycle. First, product life cycles are unpredictable in terms of total length. But, they have tended to become shorter in the past several

☐ **TABLE 18-1.**   *Cash and Profit Analysis LuJa Products, Inc.*

Product	Revenue	– Direct Cash Expenses =	Contribution Margin	– Overhead =	Profit
A	$20,000	(10,000)	$10,000	($5,000)	$5,000
B	10,000	(5,000)	5,000	(5,000)	$0
C	5,000	(5,250)	(250)	(1,000)	(1,250)
	$35,000	$20,250	$14,750	$11,000	$3,750

decades. Second, the rate of technological innovation is increasing thus posing problems for product planning. Exhibit 18-3 shows a general trend that appears to exist for technological products. Once a basic technology is created, it tends to advance with larger and larger capabilities coming with each refinement. This was the case with transistors, computer capabilities, and data transmission. A problem arises for both the producer and user as to at what point to commit themselves to products or capital assets using a certain level of technology. Selection of one configuration can lock a firm into a commitment for several years, while competitors go after the next level.

Another relevant point with life cycles is that some products do not appear to have one. That is, some products appear to be in a perpetual state of maturity. This seems to be the case with some toothpastes, soups, cooking oils and, on the industrial side, some materials and fasteners (nuts, bolts, screws, etc.). But even here, a product cycle might be present with regard to foreign competing firms. While sales in the industry might be stable, low-cost foreign competitors might cause a domestic supplier's business to experience a decline stage.

Overall, the product life cycle is a useful guide in establishing the status and trend of products. It provides helpful insights into the managerial approaches that appear best for each stage. One large Fortune Top Ten firm actually identifies each one of its basic product lines within a context close to the stages of its life cycle. The company identifies and often transfers managers in purchasing, manufacturing, finance and marketing out of one product line and into another when the product advances to the next stage. This firm assigns management talent to

■ **EXHIBIT 18-3.** *Advances in Technology*

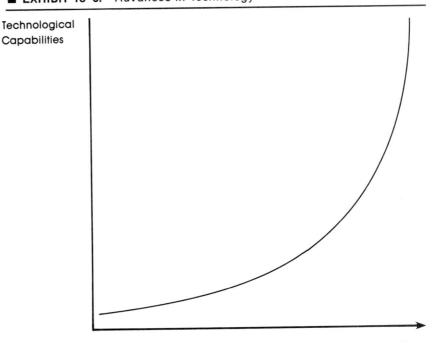

Technological
Capabilities

Time

those lines that require the managerial skills that each person appears to excel in. That is, the company feels that growth-minded marketing managers are perhaps misassigned in a declining product, and vice versa.

Maintenance, Repair, and Operating Supplies

All organizations, especially manufacturing firms, require quantities of maintenance, repair, and operating supplies. These items are often referred to as MRO items. MRO items are goods required by the firm to operate production and other machinery and equipment, but these items do not become part of the actual output of the firm. MRO items typically include oils, lubricants, belts, seals, hoses, couplings, pumps, valves, work clothing, drill bits, filters, bearings, and motors. Unlike raw materials and components that become part of the firm's salable output, the firm is the actual consumer of MRO items.

The principles of purchasing are the same for MRO items as they are for any other procured goods and services, but there are some additional MRO considerations that are becoming recognized more widely today than in the past. These considerations relate to the cost of MRO inventories versus the cost of production downtime, the benefits of standardization and systems contracting of MRO items, and the use of internal and external clearinghouses for MRO items.

Two diverse schools of thought exist with regard to MRO item acquisition and use. One theory assumes that most MRO item costs can be minimized by obtaining low cost products that can be easily replaced and disposed of when they fail or reach the end of their life on equipment. This approach consists of acquiring MRO items that are low in cost and often relatively low in quality. The rationale here is that item cost can be minimized as well as the cost of inventorying them. The other approach places a high value upon the cost of lost production, or production downtime, and seeks to maintain a minimum total cost between the cost of MRO items, their inventories, and the cost of production downtime when replacing units.

A general inverse trade-off relationship exists between MRO item quality and the number (frequency) of production downtime events necessary to replace MRO items and the associated lost production costs. This relationship is illustrated in Exhibit 18-4. With the use of low quality MRO items there is the likelihood of greater frequency of production stoppages to replace needed MRO items. As MRO item quality increases, the frequency and cost of production downtime tends to decrease. A direct relationship generally exists between MRO item quality and item purchase cost, as well as inventory holding cost. The total costs of these two factors are shown in a "U-shaped" total-cost curve. As the firm recognizes the increased costs of production stoppages (production downtime cost curve increases), then the firm will optimally seek higher MRO item quality (and cost). This point is illustrated by a shifting to the right to a new, low-cost optimum point of MRO item cost and production downtime cost.

■ **EXHIBIT 18-4.** *General Relationship Between MRO Quality and Production Costs*

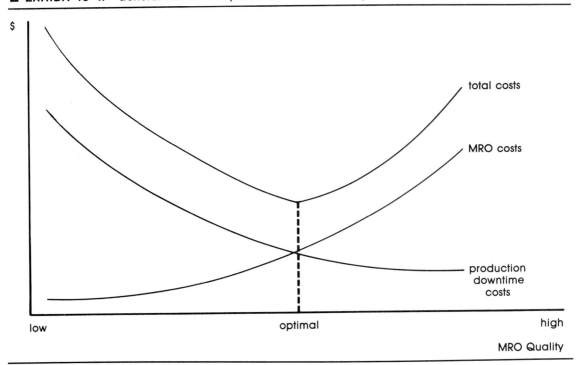

Standardization is another key facet of MRO item management. Standardization provides the benefits of fewer item stockkeeping units (SKU's), which leads to easier purchasing processes, a greater number of vendors who can participate, and a lower overall required inventory level. In some instances, standardization can lead to a fewer number of SKU's handled but a higher total number held on hand for better service performance. Thus, it is possible to decrease total inventory investment in MRO items while increasing the service level to plant and equipment items. Value analysis efforts directed toward MRO items can provide equal or greater cost benefits than those directed toward the firm's output products.

Standardization in the capital goods decision is one area in which purchasing can provide beneficial input. Though the actual choice of the brand and equipment is the prerogative of the user seeking the capital good, purchasing should review the list of brand candidates with an eye toward obtaining assets that will require MRO items already consistent with those used by the firm. This factor can then be evaluated by the user department, since maintenance, repair, and operating supplies will be paid for by that department for the duration of the capital asset. This is an important consideration for any equipment that is purchased in large numbers such as materials handling equipment, copying machines, trucks, motors, and pumps.

MRO purchasing is an area that lends itself to the adoption of systems contracting. MRO items tend to be required quickly upon discovery of need. This need exists with some degree of predictability over long periods of time but arises sporadically in the short term. The key trade-off is inventory holding versus the penalty costs of machinery downtime. MRO items tend to be available from a wide number of sources. The options available for purchasing processes are purchase order, competitive bidding, and systems contracting.

Purchase order methods of obtaining MRO items can result in many orders, much paperwork, and lengthy lead times between need discovery and goods receipt. The alternative is specific forecasting of need, larger purchase orders, and large inventory holdings. In the multi-plant setting, the need might arise to cross-haul parts from one plant having a supply of MRO items to that plant suddenly needing them. Competitive bidding can be used but this, too, requires specific identification of parts and quantities. Specific MRO need is somewhat unpredictable, and this can lead to shortages and overages at each demand location. The benefit of competitive bidding is the reduced administrative purchasing expense and the opportunity for lower prices. Systems contracting, on the other hand, has the benefit of lower price and reduced paperwork expense, as well as the benefit of not having to specifically identify the exact need for each item. Goods can be inventoried at a central vendor location for on-call demand by any of the firm's sites.

Clearinghouses are another opportunity area for MRO items, especially for high cost parts. Such a system is in use in the airline industry where downtime costs are high and large parts inventories can be prohibitively expensive at each maintenance site. Informal systems are sometimes used at airports when one airline maintenance manager requires a specific part on short notice, but would have to wait for several hours to obtain the part from his firm's central parts depot or the vendor. In this situation, a part might be obtained from another airline's maintenance manager at the same airport. The process then calls for the first manager to replace the part when his arrives. This practice has been in existence in areas where truck firm maintenance terminals are in close proximity and one firm experiences a stockout of a critical part that another nearby firm might have on-hand.

Systems such as these are informal, but they can conceivably be expanded into organized processes. For example, the Airline Inventory Redistribution System is a method whereby airlines having excess inventories of engine, equipment, and frame parts may enter a listing into a monthly report that is distributed to other subscribers to the system. The benefit is that parts can be obtained through transfer relatively quickly. The firm with the excess rids itself of extra inventory, and the firm in need obtains the goods sometimes faster than from vendors. This process could be expanded into other industries. The key, no doubt, would be for firms to be noncompeting, in order to avoid antitrust problems, and to be close in proximity, for ease of transfer.

Standardization

Standardization involves activities designed to bring about some degree of conformity of specifications in the firm. In its basic form, it is the combining of specifications of two or more items into utilizing one. Standardization is applied to materials, construction, methods of operation or practice, and performance specifications.

Standardization has many benefits, including cost reduction, easier repair ability, and the enhancement of greater supply competition. A simple example shows how standardization reduces costs through inventory reduction. Part A has a daily demand of about seven units, and Part B has a daily demand of ten units. Both are a supply component used on production machinery, and both parts are purchased from firms that provide thirty-day lead time in ordering. By modifying one machine so that it can use the other part, then only one part must be purchased. Now, only one bin is needed to store the units, less space is required, and only one part needs to be monitored through inventory control processes. The combination might also enable the firm to make a single larger purchase with a volume discount.

Standardization reduces costs and problems by having fewer items to control in production, lowering the possibility of obsolescence, increasing the flexibility in inventory use, lessening the chance for errors or misunderstandings in the requisition and purchase order process, as well as allowing volume buying benefits and simpler budgeting.

A standardization program is one of the staff activities that a purchasing department can initiate that will bring payoff benefits to a majority of the firm. Such programs entail a large amount of staff work, examination of products, meetings, some travel expense, and redesign work by other departments. Standardization benefits must overcome these initial costs. These benefits are usually pervasive throughout the firm.

Approaches to standardization include many separate areas of analysis. One approach is through review of specifications of like products. This approach will bring to light areas where some specifications might be relaxed or otherwise slightly modified in order to merge the need for two, three, or more separate items into one. One Middle Atlantic state's machine manufacturer noted that six different machine bolts and screws were used in production and an additional four were included on components purchased from vendors. Analysis indicated that the seven could be changed at only a slight cost to the vendor and the firm for a new total of three bolts and screws.

Another approach is to start with those items causing problems in the current system. Parts that are difficult to obtain or ones that are often production or repair stockouts provide a valuable starting point for standardization efforts. By attacking these parts first, the firm attains the benefits of standardization as well as reduces a problem area.

Another approach to standardization is to anticipate future problems in an area. This is particularly valuable in the product design process, especially when the firm is involved in new components, processes, and products. Many new products often are "overdesigned" with components and parts designed to fit in the best manner possible. This "overdesigning" can lead to two and three different items being used when slight tolerance modifications might reduce the number of items needed to one. It is in this design stage that purchasing can provide valuable input as a check-and-balance reviewer of designs for standardization purposes. It is much more difficult to change specifications once the product is being produced and marketed.

FOOTNOTES

1. "New Product Research Gains Despite Recession," *Purchasing*, 7 August 1980, p. 27.
2. Philip Kotler, *Marketing Management* (Englewood Cliffs, NJ: Prentice-Hall, Inc., 1967) p. 315.
3. *Management of New Products* (New York: Booz, Allen & Hamilton, Inc., 1965), p. 9.
4. Roger A. More, "Risk Factors in Accepted and Rejected New Industrial" Products, *Industrial Marketing Managment 11* (1982): 9–15.
5. Glenn R. Dundas and Kathleen A. Krentler, "Critical Path Method for Introducing an Industrial Product," *Industrial Marketing Management* 11 (1982): 126.

SOURCES FOR FURTHER READING

Fox, Harold W., and Rink, David R. "Coordination of Purchasing With Sales Trends." *Journal of Purchasing and Materials Management* 13: 10.
———."Purchasing's Role Across the Product Life Cycle." *Industrial Marketing Management* 7 (1978): 186.
Rink, David R., and Dodge, H. Robert, "Industrial Sales Emphasis Across the Life Cycle." *Industrial Marketing Management* 9 (1980): 305.
Souder, William E. "Effectiveness of Product Development Methods." *Industrial Marketing Management* 7 (1978): 299.
Yelle, Louis E. "Industrial Life Cycles and Learning Curves: Interaction of Marketing and Production." *Industrial Marketing Management* 9 (1980): 311.

QUESTIONS FOR REVIEW

1. What is the product life cycle?

2. Why do firms engage in product research?

3. What are the steps for moving a product from an idea through to full market introduction?

4. What risks are involved in developing and introducing a new product?

5. What are the four basic stages of the product life cycle?

6. In what stage(s) of the product life cycle would you say it is a) a sellers' markets and b) a buyers' markets?

7. What are the different roles throughout the product life cycle for the purchasing manager in the firm that is selling the item?

8. What are the different roles throughout the product life cycle for the purchasing manager who is buying the product in question?

9. Why is MRO management a study in product management, and why might the task of managing it fall to purchasing?

10. What is the basic trade-off in MRO with respect to MRO quality and production costs? How might this relationship have changed in recent times?

11. Why is standardization a strategic product management factor in the firm?

12. How might standardization provide benefits for the firm?

19

CHAPTER OBJECTIVES

After reading this chapter you should:

- Understand the basic approaches to pricing.

- Appreciate the need for different pricing policies throughout the product life cycle.

- Be able to evaluate discounting policies.

- Understand the rate of transportation in product pricing.

Pricing Strategies

Introduction

The role of price is one of the prime elements in the marketing mix. In an economic sense, price serves as an exchange of value and as an allocation medium in the distribution of goods. In a marketing sense, price is both a unit of resource measure as well as a constraint for various segments of the market. Purchasing sees prices on inbound goods, but this factor follows through as part of the total cost and profit of the firm.

This chapter presents prices from the standpoint of the marketing firm and discusses how pricing is part of corporate strategy. Chapter 4 differs from this chapter in that it approaches prices from the viewpoint of purchaser. It is concerned with simple cost analysis, target cost break-even analysis, methods of price publication, contracts, and several other special topics. Chapter 18 approaches pricing from the viewpoint of the selling firm. Here, too, concerns of the buyer are presented. These two chapters can be viewed individually and complementary.

This chapter presents a general approach to pricing, an overview of some economic basics to pricing, an evaluation of pricing throughout the product life cycle, as well as many special topics in the area.

Approaches to Pricing Decisions

A firm faces important pricing decisions at five primary times in a product's life. The first decision comes when the new product is being introduced. A decision relating price to the overall strategy the firm wishes to follow in marketing the product must be made. Other difficult decision points occur when price changes are initiated by the firm or when price changes must be made in response to a competitor's price change. Finally, the price charged for an item must continually be related to the prices of other goods in the product line. Marketing, accounting, and other managers must meet to determine the pricing decision at these five points.

Pricing decisions have several implications that must be considered. Many demand factors are entwined into this decision. 1) The elasticity of demand for the general product in the market as well as the demand for the firm's own specific item is a major consideration. 2) The change of competitive market entry is important. 3) Cost-related factors must be analyzed. And 4) How the purchase price of the product becomes a cost and margin potential for intermediate customers is a key cost factor. Still other considerations are the profit margin against cost increases for the firm itself, use of scarce commodities in the item, and the future costs of promoting the product, to name a few.[1]

Pricing goals relate directly to overall strategic goals of the firm, which typically are: maximization of profits, return on owners' capital and on total assets of the firm.[2] Typical short-term goals of pricing strategy include prempting the market with a low price to exclude competitors, reaping high profits in a temporary monopolistic market before competitors enter, and discouraging competitors and those set to encourage market expansion.[3]

Economic Basics of Pricing

The basic concepts pertaining to pricing include: full costs as they relate to price; elasticity of demand; and price discrimination in an economic sense.

Full Costs in Pricing

It is often said that to price below cost is sheer folly, but the exact cost first must be defined for this statement to hold true. Full cost is just one cost. It is the sum of the variable costs per unit plus a figure consisting of total fixed costs for the period divided by the number of expected units to be sold. For example, a company makes an item that costs $5.00 each in variable expenses, the total fixed costs for the shop are $50.00 per month, and the firm expects to produce twenty-five units each month. Full costs are

$$\$5.00 + \frac{\$50.00}{25}$$

or
$7.00 each

The above statement says that the firm must charge at least $7.00 for the item. But, if the first twenty-five units are already sold, and demand arises for another five units toward the end of a month, then the cost below which the company should not now sell is $5.00. Likewise, if product demand increases so that forty units becomes the new sales level, the full cost becomes $6.25 each.

Elasticity of Demand

Another key concept in pricing is elasticity of demand. Higher prices will generally result in fewer unit sales; conversely, lower prices will usually result in greater unit sales. The market for an item is said to be elastic if decreases in price actually cause total revenue to increase. Table 19-1 shows the price and demand data for a Product A, which has elastic demand. Decreases in price cause more units to be sold with resulting increases in revenue. On the other hand, Product B is said to be inelastic. Decreases in its price lead to greater sales but lower total rev-

☐ **TABLE 19.1.**   *Examples of Demand Elasticity*

Product A:

Elastic Situation

Price	Quantity Demanded	Total Revenue
$10	80	$ 800
9	90	810
8	120	960
7	150	1050
6	190	1140

Product B:

Inelastic Situation

Price	Quantity Demanded	Total Revenue
$10	42	$420
9	45	405
8	46	368
7	48	336
6	50	300

enues. The elastic Product A is very sensitive to price as far as revenue is concerned, while prices for Product B are the opposite.

In a realistic analysis, both of these products should have the variable costs of production subtracted from total revenues. The best price is usually the one producing the maximum contribution to overhead. If variable per-unit costs are $1 each, the highest contribution is achieved at a $6 price for Product A and a $10 price for Product B. The company would be earning less total contribution if the price for A was more or if the price for B was less. This simple analysis illustrates how a company might price according to product demand rather than on the basis of costs.

Economic Price Discrimination

Many products are produced by a firm in the same way but are sold to different customers at different prices. Electricity to homes, factories, and municipalities is one example. Phone rates to different classes of customers is another. And, transportation charges that are different for two separate commodity shipments while the cost of service is the same is another example. Lime is often sold to different markets at different prices. Even airlines exhibit this practice when a coach cabin might be filled with passengers each paying nearly a dozen different fares for the same trip. Some specialty products are manufactured on the same production line but sold to different classes of customers at different prices. Tubing to beer tap distributors and medical lab equipment suppliers might have different prices. These are examples of price discrimination in an economic sense. It exists when a similar costing service or product is charged differently, or when a different cost product or service is sold at the same price to two different markets.

Firms that are legally allowed to do so, practice price discrimination in order to maximize profits. For example, Table 19-2 presents the price and contribution margin (revenue less variable costs) for a single product in three separate submarkets. Each product unit costs $15 in variable costs, and the prorata share of fixed cost is another $15 for a total of $30.00. The maximum contribution of submarket G is attained when a $40 price is charged, submarket H at $30, and I at $20. Submarket G is priced $10 above the $30 full cost, H is at full cost, and I is $5 above variable cost but $10 below full cost. The total contribution is $2000 + $1200 + $300 or $3500. Submarket I represents a marginal cost of $15, and a marginal revenue of $20 per unit.

One criticism states that all product submarkets should be charged the same price. But, addition of the contribution margins for all three submarkets sold at the same price will yield total margins below the $3500 figure. So by charging all the same price, a lower total contribution is attained. Another criticism states that the "loss" on I must be made up on the "profits" of G. That is, there is a cross-subsidy taking place. This can be countered by pointing out that the firm is receiving a $300 contribution it would not otherwise have if submarket I did not exist. In fact, submarket I contributes some to the overhead of the firm. If submarket I did not exist, the full cost of G and H would be even higher. As long as submarket I produces some contribution to the firm, the company has excess capacity and no better alternative exists for that capacity, then the firm is better off keeping the product. Product I might also be a product submarket needed by some customers who also purchase a more profitable item in the entire line because the firm provides this other needed item.

Price discrimination in an economic sense is possible when various submarkets have different elasticities, when the firm experiences high common or joint costs as a proportion of the total costs, and the submarkets cannot legally or conveniently sell to each other. Transportation and utility laws have permitted this pricing approach to be used as long as the submarkets do not compete against each other. Thus, there is no competitive economic form. In product settings, price discrimination is technically not allowed unless the differences in costs are justified by cost differences such as volume or packaging. But even here, firms can produce primary products in sufficiently different ways to sell to entirely distinct industries at various prices.

The buyer who represents the inelastic submarket is at a disadvantage. The price-reducing alternatives available here include making the product instead of buying it, or switching to substitutes that are close and satisfy most of the need. It may be possible for the buyer to discover a lower-priced submarket item and purchase that specific item for use. In either case, it is worthwhile for the buyer in this situation to discover or develop substitute products or competitors to the firm exercising inelastic pricing.

☐ **TABLE 19-2.** *Price and Contribution Margin Situation For Three Products*

	Submarket Contribution Margin		
Price	**G**	**H**	**I**
$40	$2000	$1000	$0
35	1800	1100	0
30	1750	1200	200
25	1700	1150	250
20	1650	1100	300

On the other hand, the buyer of the low-priced elastic product often enjoys a price that is lower than manufacturer's full cost. But, this situation will usually prevail only as long as excess capacity exists in the selling firm, and the submarket earns a surplus of revenue over direct expenses. This is sometimes a product that will be produced for as long as the capital assets that are devoted to it function, or there is no better alternative for utilizing those assets. Thus, there is a future termination date for this product supply. A firm cannot justify reinvestment for a product that does not cover full costs. Possible courses of action here for the buyer include those tactics mentioned in Chapter 18 in dealing with the product life cycle. A product in this situation is akin to ones in the decline stage of the life cycle. It can be dangerous for the buyer to assume long-run availability of such products. Supplier plans should be closely monitored. Long lead time notice of termination is better than sudden stoppage or high price increases designed to discourage sales.

Pricing Throughout the Product Life Cycle

The product life cycle corresponds with most of the junctures of major price decisions. To the outside observer, prices and their changes can be used as an indicator of where the product is at in its life cycle.

Introductory Stage

During the introduction stage price of the product must be considered in a general way in the analyses leading up to its introduction. Commercial analysis, market testing, and the final "go/no-go" decision are all based upon an approximate sales price and expected volume. But, many things can change before actual product launching that will affect the final selected price.

Many good products fail due to improper timing, distribution, or pricing. Some key questions that act as a checklist for pricing considerations are presented by Oxenfeldt. These considerations are:[4]

1 Is it a new product or does it meet on existing need in a different way?
2 Does the product pose a large learning curve burden for the customer; if so, are the customers' perceived benefits from using the product great?

3 Is it a capital item or one involving routine expenditure?
4 Is the technology it is based upon still evolving or is it mature?
5 To what degree will buyers become dependent upon the firm for replacement, supporting supplies, etc.?
6 Is the producer protected against competition?

These considerations help build a picture as to 1) what degree price is or
is not important in the customer's purchase, 2) the posed threat of new
competition either copying or entering with an advanced technology
and 3) the profit risk to the firm.

Several basic points come into play here that help focus the final price
decision.[5] These points relate to flexibility, desirability of the product to
intermediate parties, and cost economies of production. One consideration is that a high initial price always leaves room for lowering it later.
The reverse is often impossible without loss of goodwill and market potential. Two, the greater the profit margin, the better the potential for
sales to wholesalers and retailers. Three, the larger the sales base, the
greater the possibility for production economies and low unit costs.

Firms generally adopt one of four pricing strategies when entering a
market, i.e. skimming, penetration, early cash recovery, or support of
product line. A skimming approach involves charging a high initial
price and gradually lowering it over the life of the product. The assumption here is that the early purchasers will tolerate the high price. This
policy is a form of economic price discrimination with different customers rather than geographically. New markets are sought that will
react to the lower prices. The price is gradually lowered as competition
enters, as the firm gains experience in the market for the item, and as
production economies bring lower unit costs. An initial high price
helps recover research and introduction costs early in the product's life.
The lowering of price also has some promotional appeal for sales forces
and as a threat against competition.

Skimming is generally possible when product demand is relatively inelastic at first, when there is a segment of customers who will buy at the
high price with other identifiable submarkets at lower prices, and when
actual production and marketing costs are not readily known at the
start.[6]

The buyer of such products faces a risk situation. Product benefits
must be carefully evaluated in relation to the high cost. The success or
failure of using or reselling the product must be carefully evaluated in
light of several questions. Does it represent a low risk competitive edge
that only the one firm can afford at the moment? Will it give the firm an
edge on the market. Will the initial high price leave the firm in a high
cost position later when new competitors are obtaining it at a lower
price?

Penetration is the second market price strategy. This strategy consists of entering the product into the market with a low price that will
remain unchanged through most of its life.[7] Penetration serves to create
and expand the new market quickly, and the product's low price will act
to hold off competition. This approach is appropriate where demand is

relatively elastic, competitors might come on the scene early, price distinctive submarkets do not appear to exist, and low unit-cost, large-scale production is possible from the start.[8] The quick market entry with a low price might establish the firm with brand loyalty and market share before competitors enter the market. Penetration pricing is not as common in industrial markets as is the skimming approach.

Early cash recovery is another pricing approach that is used in market entry. This pricing strategy attempts to gain a short-run increase in cash flow without regard to future ramifications. Firms that currently are in need of cash often take this approach. Unfortunately, outside observation of the price alone will not detect use of this tactic. This situation is one where the buyer should be as knowledgeable as possible about the vendor's financial position for the duration of the relationship.

Product line support is another market entry pricing approach. This strategy entails pricing the product in line with similar goods in the line. For example, if the item is a new die that is used on a machine sold by the firm, the new die will be priced similarly with existing ones. If the product has a different price and quality configuration in comparison to others on the market, then this will be a guide to either higher or lower prices. In still other settings a firm might initially provide the product as a loss leader in order to develop the repeat component sales necessary to operate the item. For buyers, this is an example of how life cycle costing applies when considering purchases of items that also require repeat component or material purchases from the same firm.

Growth Stage

During product and market growth, demand is being pulled from customers. The firm is often producing at a level that cannot keep up with demand. Competition often enters the market at this stage. Monroe presents three phenomena of this point.[9] One, the range of feasible prices that existed in the introductory stage will have been narrowed by the growth stage. Two, economies in production will have reduced unit costs by now. Three, fixed expenses in marketing and distribution will have increased by this stage due to the investment in manpower and facilities to support the higher product volume.

If competition is a factor during this stage, products on the market have a tendency toward standardization. Price becomes more of a purchase decision factor. In the price skimming strategy, price is gradually being lowered. If competition does not exist, through patent protection or sufficient product distinction, it might be possible to raise prices at this point, especially if a penetration price tactic was used originally. This has been the situation in many foreign automotive and machinery markets. Price increases might be possible here if sales are higher than planned, costs are higher than expected, and the factory cannot keep up with sales.[10] If skimming was the strategy used originally, then this situation might call for a postponement of price reductions.

If the vendor is in a seller's market situation, several price and sales-related tactics might be observed by buyers during this stage. These include dropping quantity or cash discounts, removing the ability of salesmen to negotiate and quote prices, and dropping marginal customers or territories by shifting these sales to higher volume distribution areas instead. Some cost-related strategies in this seller's situation might include dropping low margin items from the product line, increasing emphasis on cost-based pricing, delaying in making a specific price quote until the order is received or the item is shipped out, and increasing prices across the board on all products in response to company-wide cost increases.[11]

Product Maturity

The maturity stage is characterized by slowing sales growth, a saturation of the market, declining or flattened profits, and softness in the price situation. At this point replacement sales comprise a large part of the capital goods market. Price increases are difficult to implement; instead, price cut decisions begin to dominate pricing decision making. Value analysis becomes important in the effort to reduce costs in order to maintain a healthy contribution margin in face of price cuts.

Price cutting takes place temporarily or permanently. Firms are often "pushed" to reduce prices for such negative reasons as 1) a need to raise cash in the short term, 2) sales have fallen and a price cut might raise sales, or 3) the firm has experienced an unexpected cost increase. In this last reason, a price cut is used to stimulate a larger demand that will produce a greater contribution even with the cost increase. Price cuts made for these reasons often will be reversed once the prime problem reason is gone. If the price is not reversed, it can cause long-run problems for the firm and competitors.[12]

Price cuts of the "pull" type are most positively motivated, and these include reducing price to 1) tap a new submarket, 2) attack marginal competitors, 3) take advantage of new production or distribution cost economies, or 4) seek sales to higher quality distributors or other intermediate buyers.[13]

Firms initiating price reductions must consider how best to do so and what the impacts will be upon wholesalers and ultimate buyers. The price cut hopefully experiences a high degree of price elasticity. That is, if price is cut by ten percent, then the net increases in revenue and contribution should be greater than ten percent. If revenues do not increase, then the firm experiences a drop in revenue and would have been better off not cutting price. Price cuts should only be attempted after careful research into the possible reactions of customers. Reactions by price sensitive users will generally be positive. But, firms and customers that are quality sensitive might view the reduction as a quality drop as well. Wholesalers, having large inventories of the item will not view the cut kindly unless it is proven to them that the cut will stimulate a positive elasticity for them as well. It is important to prove this situation to them. Of course, wholesalers stand to gain all around, if the manufacturer initiates a retail price cut only out of his own margin of the sales price thereby leaving intact the absolute size of the distributor's margin. The producer who sells directly from his/her own private distribution system does not have to consider this factor. This is one advantage of having one's own complete distribution system.

Price cuts designed to meet competitor's reductions present another situation. The prime question is whether the price cut will affect the firm to a large degree, and whether it will be a new permanent price. If these two situations apper likely, then the firm can utilize a number of reaction tactics including meeting the price cut through "sales" prices that act to dilute the impact of the competitor's cut. Another approach is to increase advertising and other promotional efforts. Still another possibility is a modification of the product that achieves cost cuts as well as revamped packaging, advertising, and other image configurations. Finally the firm might drop the product at this point and seek other opportunities using the fixed assets and manpower.[14]

The buyer in this period of product maturity will begin to observe these temporary or permanent price cuts as well as boosts in promotional efforts by some firms. Products are fairly homogeneous at this stage of the life cycle, and competition begins to provide some cost reduction buying opportunities. It is at this point, however, that weak firms start cutting prices for survival. Weak or strong producers might begin dropping the product at this point. Care must be taken not to become too dependent upon a weak firm unless the product has very little distinctive features from firm to firm. Again, the buyer might be able to create his own purchase price cut through long-run contracts or other commitments with one or a few producers.

Decline Stage

In the decline stage, the product is often being superseded by others. Total industry sales are declining. Individual firms drop out either because the price is now too low even for long-run production economics, the market is too small, there are better alternatives for the production capacity, the profit is lower than that wished, or revenue is equal to or less than the out-of-pocket costs of producing and marketing the product.

Individual firms that stay in the market during the decline stage may experience temporary market strengthening because of others dropping out. There may even be an opportunity for price increases as the suppliers in the field drop faster than the demand. There are distributors in many fields that specialize in this type of business.

Selling firms must consider two things when dropping a product. The first is that the dropped product might harm sales from those customers who purchase other highly profitable products from the firm. Thus, the declining product might have some joint effect in linking the customer to other products. The second factor is that of opportunity for other products in the capacity now occupied by the declining product. If there are no alternatives and a positive cash flow is still occurring, then it will probably be decided to retain the product.

The pressure to drop a product might come from wholesalers. High investment in slow moving items is a condition wholesalers seek to avoid. The cash investment in inventories often is too great a risk. Even healthy wholesalers might wish to drop a product because it occupies space and preempts opportunities for other products in their line. In this case the producer might seek ultimate users and consumers for direct sales without wholesalers. The reduced cost and price cut possibility realized by avoiding the distributor might justify large lot purchases by ultimate users.

In the decline stage buyers who still wish to obtain the product will find decreasing promotional effort being placed upon it. The firm might have to special order the product or contract to purchase it from just one firm. The sourcing effort will increase in time and cost. This declining product situation can easily occur when a firm purchases a capital asset item late in its product life cycle. The problem of repair parts and other maintenance and replacement items will increase as time progresses and this is one of the key factors to consider in a capital purchase. Obtaining parts and maintenance is especially a problem in the acquisition of used machinery. The seller might be selling the machine due to the difficulty in obtaining support items for it.

Special Pricing Topics

Several specific topics relating to pricing are important to discuss. These topics are a direct part of marketing the firm's good, and they are very much a part of the purchasing decision.

Target Pricing

Target pricing is a cost-based concept of pricing that sets a certain rate of return as the primary objective. Product sales revenue must cover variable costs and committed fixed costs as a minimum in the long run. The firm also must earn a minimum profit return for the firm as a whole to remain viable in the long run. Return on assets is often the measure used to evaluate a firm's profitability. That is, a firm might be making a margin of profit over all costs, but the perspective as to the relative strength of that profit is provided by return on assets. A firm might make a profit and its return on assets might be four percent, but whether or not that is a good return depends upon the return of competitors.

Many firms attempt to establish a price that will provide a minimum or target rate of return. The formula for such a price is as follows.

$$\text{Price} = (\text{Unit Variable Costs} + \frac{\text{Required Fixed Costs}}{\text{Expected Volume}})$$

$$+ \text{Desired Rate of Return on Assets} \left(\frac{\text{Required Capital}}{\text{Expected Volume}}\right)$$

For example, a company knows that unit variable costs are $4.00, total committed fixed capital of the machinery used to make the item is $1,000,000, expected sales volume plans are for 50,000 units, and the firm seeks a 10 percent rate of return. This price computes to

$$\text{Price} = \$4.00 + (\frac{\$1,000,000}{50,000}) + .10\,(\frac{1,000,000}{50,000})$$

$$= 4.00 + 20.00 + 2.00$$

Price = $26.00.

Test: Sales @ $26.00
       Variable cost   = $1,300,000
       Contribution   =   (200,000)
       Fixed costs   = 1,100,000
       Residual   = 1,000,000
                    =   100,000

The residual of $100,000 is 10 percent of committed capital in fixed cost items.

The price is a minimum for rate of return purposes. It must be compared to demand possibilities for making a sales volume of 50,000 units at a price of $26.00. If this price is low then a higher profit and return will be made. If the price is too high, then lower prices and higher sales volumes will have to be attained to achieve the profit of $100,000, which is the ten percent return on capital investment.

A major drawback exists in this type of pricing in that it uses an expected volume term to set a price when in reality purchasers buy the quantities (volume) they do because of the price that is set. Again, the initial target price must be tempered by the market prices and realistic expectations of the sales force.

Purchasers are impacted by target pricing in several ways. First, is the target percent rate figure. Second, is the level of capital a company invests into making the product. Third, are the variable costs. And, fourth, is the rate of fixed investment write-down or depreciation. As time and sales progress there will be less book-value investment in the asset. Thus the second and third terms of the above target price formula will gradually become smaller. Over the course of a year, these terms can at times be nonexistent once the expected volume is surpassed. That is, if a purchaser seeks to purchase units 50,000 through 55,000 at the end of a fiscal year, neither the second nor third terms need to be in the price computation. The seller has already achieved fixed cost and capital return for that year. Sales practice distortions can take place here, too. If the expected volume is less than planned, a sales push at end of year might be conducted to achieve the target volume. But, this only serves to divert what would otherwise be sales at the beginning of next year. On the other hand, the sales department might already be over on its quotas, so it might then delay posting or shipping of some year end orders until the next period in order to start that year with a comfortable sales level.

Sales and Shipping Terms

Exactly where title passes and who shall pay the freight bill or file loss or damage claims against carriers has a large bearing upon the landed cost or price to the buyer. Ten basic terms of shipping can exist in domestic settings.

1. FOB Origin, Freight Prepaid. This term transfers goods to the buyer upon carrier pick up and loading. Freight is paid by the seller. The invoice for the goods may have the credit period begin at the moment of

carrier pick up. A loss and damage claim against the carrier should technically be made by the buyer, since the buyer owns the goods in transit. But, transportation regulations allow either party to make the claim. This ambiguity is of benefit when the seller has more clout with the carrier than the buyer.

2. FOB Origin, Freight Prepaid and Charged Back. This term is the same as the previous one except that the freight is initially paid by the seller but later collected from the buyer.

3. FOB Origin, Freight Collect. This term requires that the carrier send the freight bill to the buyer. Again, either party may file loss and damage claims.

4. FOB Origin, Freight Absorbed (Prepaid). This term has the seller paying the freight bill, and only invoicing the buyer for a portion of it. This is done to equalize the buyer's freight cost with that of a competing vendor.

5. FOB Origin, Freight Absorbed (Collect). The portion of the freight bill to be paid by the buyer is billed to the buyer by the carrier. The absorbed portion is billed by the carrier to the seller.

6. FOB Destination, Freight Prepaid. In this setting, goods technically belong to the seller until the buyer receives the goods and signs a carrier delivery receipt or accepts the goods after inspection. Either party may file a claim against the carrier. The free time for credit period computations usually begins upon receipt of the freight bill.

7. FOB Destination, Freight Prepaid and Charged Back. This term is the same as number 6, except the seller pays the freight bill and then collects this sum from the buyer.

8. FOB Destination, Freight Collect. The carrier bills the buyer for the freight.

9. FOB Destination, Freight Absorbed (Prepaid). Similar to number 4 for freight charges.

10. FOB Destination, Freight Absorbed (Collect). Similar to number 5 for freight charges.

Sellers can create great price increases or decreases by continuing with the posted product price but shifting the selling terms. The buyer's most favorable term is perhaps FOB Destination, Freight Prepaid. But an effective price increase can take place by shifting the term to FOB Destination, Absorbed or Collect, or even to FOB Origin, Collect. On chemicals, the freight cost for a tank car might be $5,000 and the transit time might be two weeks. In a seller's market, a $50,000 load might be payable by the buyer a week before it gets the product. Thus, the buyer must pay $55,000, receive the goods a week later, and fight a possible claim settlement with the carrier. Later, the market may soften and the terms might drop to FOB Destination, Freight prepaid. Here, the buyer will experience a lower cost since only the $50,000 goods invoice is payable after receipt of the goods.

Discounts

Discounts are stated price reductions based upon specific sales objectives.

1. Temporary Sales-Related Discounts. These discounts are designed as short-term reductions of the base price in order to meet a competitive situation, seek a higher short-term cash flow, or build market identity for a product. Such discounts are usually short term in nature, and the normal base price is still usually the one published.

2. Seasonal Discounts. Seasonal discounts are designed to either stimulate new off-season demand or divert demand away from the peak season. In the first setting, the discounted price is offered to a new submarket that is sensitive to the lower price. In the other setting, firms that normally purchase during the peak season are instead encouraged to purchase in the slack season.

For the buyer to react to this lower price, the discount must be at least equal to or greater than the cost of storage and capital opportunity loss for the period. For example, a firm is offered a discount price to purchase its normal July needs in April. The lot cost is $100,000 it costs $1,000 per month to store, and the firm normally borrows funds or can find opportunities to invest excess funds at 15 percent annual rate. The discount must be at least equal to three months at $1,000 each, plus $100,000 times 15 percent times 3/12 of the year, for a total of $6750. This can also be expressed as 6 3/4 percent discounts. The buyer must also consider that by July the price might be higher and that during the April-to-July period the product might deteriorate or become obsolete in comparison to newer items.

3. Cash discounts and credit terms. Cash discounts are used to induce buyers to pay cash immediately for purchases. Credit terms apply to the length of time buyers are permitted to take to pay for purchases and possibly take advantage of a discount for early payment. A buyer must be offered a discount that is, at minimum, equal to what his firm could earn with those funds if invested elsewhere.

Cash payment or early payment discounts are computed using the *time period* between which the cash or early payment could be made and the entire credit period ends and payment must be made. This would be thirty days if immediate cash payment is one option with thirty days on credit; or, it would be twenty days if ten days entitles a buyer a one-half percent discount with a new term of thirty days. Another consideration in this analysis is the company's cost of funds or opportunity rate of investments. This might be anywhere between twelve percent and twenty-five percent per annum. And, finally, the discount percent for cash or early payment is needed for this computation. The formula for determining whether or not to take such a discount follows.

$$\left(\frac{365}{\text{Time Period}} \right) \times (\text{Discount Rate}) \text{ versus } (\text{Cost of Funds or Opportunity})$$

If the left-hand terms (*Time Period* is equal to *Net Days* less *Discount Days*) are greater than the right-hand terms, then the purchaser should pay the bill during the cash or discount period. It is cheaper to use company funds for the remaining period rather than implicitly borrow them from the vendor. If, on the other hand, the left-side term is less than the right side, then the firm should delay paying the bill until the latest date. For example, a firm offers one-half percent, ten days, net thirty. If the buyer's company has a fifteen percent opportunity rate, then the analysis becomes

$$(\frac{365}{20})(.005) \text{ versus } (.15)$$

.09125 versus .15.

The vendor is implicitly lending the firm funds for twenty days (from day 10 to 30) at a rate of nine and one-eighth percent. This is less than the company's cost of funds. If, on the other hand, a vendor is willing to sell goods with a two percent discount for payment upon delivery, the analysis shows twenty-four percent versus fifteen percent. The buying firm would implicitly be paying twenty-four percent to hold cash for thirty days, if it did not take this discount opportunity.

Cash and credit discounts are highly dependent upon the vendor's and buyer's opportunity cost of funds as well as the prevailing interest rate on borrowed funds and investment market opportunities. The analysis must continually be evaluated in light of changing conditions. A vendor in a cash-short period would do well to offer a discount to vendors who would respond to a twelve percent effective rate if the vendor must borrow funds at twenty percent.

A problem exists here, however, when a firm offers an early payment discount, and buyers take the discount but use the entire credit period or longer. Here, the selling firm has little opportunity other than to discontinue the discount offering or raise its price to reflect the cash held by the vendor. Sellers will often consider the cost of funds in a thirty-day credit period. This will create an upward push in prices or hasten particular products toward elimination.

4. Cumulative Discounts. This form of discount comes into play once a certain minimum quantity has been purchased in a time period. The minimum usually is set at a level higher than most purchasers will buy in a single order. For example, most buyers purchase from a certain firm in 100 unit lots. The selling firm's regular price is $10 per unit, but it provides a discount of $2.00 on all cumulative purchases of over 1,000 in any calendar year.

Cumulative discounting is useful for a seller in a market in which many competitors exist, the product is homogeneous, and buyers purchase from two or more firms throughout the year. The cumulative discount minimum should be set by the marketer at a quantity level higher than most individual buyers normally purchase from the firm in a year, but below that which is the total level of their annual needs. This tool is designed to create brand loyalty habits. Buyers seeking cost reduction through this means must evaluate this benefit against the risk of concentrating to souring.

5. Noncumulative Discounts. Quantity price breaks are a common pricing device. Price breaks can be, say, $5.00 per unit, but all units are priced at $4.75 if 200 or more are purchased in each lot. The motive for this discounting practice generally is to achieve recovery of certain

minimum expenses in order processing and distribution with small lots; it provides for a passing along of some economies of distribution to the purchaser when he/she buys in large lots. The price break situation might also appear in transportation company pricing. Here, smaller shipments have higher rates than smaller ones.

The price and/or rate break situation requires analysis when normal purchase lots are at levels close to the break points. For example, a company offers a price of $8.00 per unit, but the price drops to $7.00 when purchased in lots of 100 or more. If a buyer has been purchasing in lots of 90, he/she has been wasting company funds. To illustrate: the buyer purchases 1400 units per year in lots of 90 for a total of 15.6 purchase lots and a cost of $11,200. If the lots were 100 each, there would be only 14 purchases and the total cost would be $9800. The regular price break occurs at 100 units, but it effectively occurs at a lower level. The purchase of 90 costs $720, while the purchase of 100 costs $700. The effective price break occurs at a level lower than the actual rate break and any quantities between the two costs more than those at the actual price break. The effective price break is found by the following:

$$\text{EFFECTIVE BREAK} = \frac{\text{Quantity Price} \times \text{Quantity Minimum}}{\text{NonQuantity Price}},$$

or in this situation,

$$= \frac{\$7.00 \times 100}{8.00}$$

$$= 87.5 \text{ units.}$$

A buyer will always save money when buying at least 100 units than it will when purchasing 88 through 99 units at a time. Of course, the additional inventory holding and warehousing costs have to be considered as well.

6. In-Excess Quantity Discount. This price break only applies on units above a certain minimum level in a single purchase. For example, the regular price might be $3.00 per unit but a price of $2.80 is charged for unit 100 and above when purchased with the first 99. This discount seeks to make buyers purchase more in each lot only when the seller experiences savings in large lots. For example, a seller determines that buyers normally purchase 600 units at a time. The seller must produce these in single shift 800-unit lots. Thus, 200 units are always carried over onto inventory for later sale. An in-excess price might be set for units 601 through 800 in order to induce buyers to purchase full-shift lot quantities.

These various types of discounts also come into play in transportation pricing. Cumulative discounts apply after certain minimum tonnages are shipped in a period, noncumulative price breaks apply between shipments of differing sizes, and in-excess rates are often used to entice shippers to use each rail car or truck more fully. Sellers can do well to utilize these discounts in their pricing and selling practices.

One specialty chemical manufacturer analyzes each order in its distribution department against shipment weight and carrier rate breaks.

The goods are sold to small firms on a FOB Origin, Freight Prepaid and Charged Back Basis. Each 100 pound drum costs $11.00 in freight cost, but when shipped in 20,000 lots the rate is $9.25 per drum. The firm's distribution analyst notices that a certain order is for 180 drums or 18,000 lbs. The applicable carrier charge for this shipment is $9.25 × 200/hundredweight, or $1,850.00. Thus, $1,850.00 is the charge for 180 drums and would also be the applicable charge for 200 drums. Thus, another 20 drums could be purchased and moved in this lot for no additional transportation charges. He calls the buyer and points this out. In fact, any lot purchase between (200 × $9.25) / $11.00, or 168 and 199 costs the same in freight charges as a 200 lot shipment. Over the course of a year, ten purchases of 180 units would cost $18,500, or $10.28 each, while nine purchase of 200 units would cost $16,650 or $9.25 each. This is a savings of ten percent in freight costs. In this situation a seller is using a carrier's pricing system to effectively create a discount in his/her own pricing to the buyer.

Geographic Pricing

Several approaches are used to handle the distance cost of transportation in pricing including uniform pricing, zone pricing, and freight absorption. The transportation element in the total landed cost of goods becomes larger with farther distances from the plant. This distance element poses a problem for firms that seek to have fairly equal prices at the retail or user-purchase level throughout the nation or a region. It is particularly a problem when national or regional advertising states a price or when the firm wants a common price identity among all customers. In this setting, goods moved to points farther from the plant will result in higher sales prices than those sold closer to the plant.

Uniform pricing is a system of charging the same FOB Destination, Freight Prepaid price to all customers throughout the nation. The seller charges one price to all customers, and it pays all freight charges. The charges to nearby customers are low, while farther ones are higher. The transportation cost element to all customers is averaged. This simple cost element is included within the total price for the product. In this manner, a product with a cost of $7.00 might be sold for $14.00 delivered to all buyers throughout the U.S. Close customers cost the seller $7.00 plus $1.00 freight while those far away cost the firm $7.00 plus $3.00 freight. All customers pay $14.00 regardless of location.

Uniform pricing achieves the goal of consistent pricing, and it minimizes the possibility of price competition between resellers. It has a drawback of being unfair to nearby customers while in effect subsidizing distant purchasers.

Zone pricing is the same approach applied on regional applications. That is, New England, Middle Atlantic, Southeast, Midwest, Mountain and Pacific regions might each have separate delivered prices. This approach is used when a national uniform price would result in too drastic a cross-subsidy of the transportation element in the final price. It also serves to equalize competing retailers or other resellers in an area. Some forms of zone pricing are based upon transportation company blanket rates that are equal rates from one origin point to entire regions.

Freight absorption is another method of geographic pricing that is linked to geographic settings. It is used when freight charges are directly borne by the buyer. A New York manufacturer might have a main competitor in St. Louis. West Coast customers might favor the St. Louis firm because the freight charges from New York are too high. The New York seller might counter this by paying for the freight charges between New York and St. Louis, with the customer paying the remaining freight charges. Freight absorption equalizes the firm with its competitors from a freight-cost standpoint.

Transportation Allowances

The Motor Carrier Act of 1980 amended the Revised Interstate Commerce Act with a section that allows sellers of food and grocery products using uniform zone pricing to provide allowances to buyers who pick up their purchases in their private trucks at the sellers shipping point. The law requires that such compensation shall be on a nondiscriminatory basis, and it cannot exceed what the actual costs to the seller would have been in making the delivery.

Pricing of Services

The pricing of services is seen as a difficult task by many. Services are often provided without tangible materials. Janitorial, maintenance, repair, and data processing are a few services that have little actual physical product provided with them.

The pricing of services is discussed by Gabor.[15] As with products, the pricing of services can be either cost or market based. Cost-based service prices are easily implemented in accounting and medical areas in which entry of supply is limited. The prime goal here is target profit pricing in which there is little price competition. Market pricing, on the other hand, will be made in line with the nature of customer demands. It may be value-based, in which the price is dependent upon the value gained by the customer. It may be competitive and price sensitive; firms may expand market share by lowering prices. And, market-oriented prices may be set according to the range of quality that is provided.

Pricing literature contains several observations about service pricings that are pertinent here.[16] One, prices can either be set and stated or negotiated. Two, the greater the material content in the service, the greater the tendency toward cost-based pricing. Three, the more standardized the service, the more competitive the pricing behavior among sellers. Cost will be the floor level. Four, the more unique the service, the greater the tendency for demand-based pricing. And, five, service quality is more variable than product quality. These features can be seen readily in carrier rates, but the principles also apply in other service areas.

Various service pricing tactics can also noted based upon observation of practice.[17] Loss leader pricing is one form. This is the practice of offering a low price to the first-time user with the hope of obtaining subsequent assignments. Offset pricing is another tactic; one that offers a low price on the basic item with much higher profit obtained on add-on and extra items. Guarantee pricing provides the assurance of a no-payment obligation if promised results were not attained from the work.

Service pricing can be administered in a number of ways. Time plus materials based upon actual work finished is one approach. This is an open-ended situation against the buyer in favor of the seller. Another is a fixed price approach for work that is set ahead of time. This fixed price places risk-of-sale costs onto the seller, since the fixed price is the table for the buyer. However, the buyer might still face a quality risk. Contracts for service provide minimum levels of periodic work or protection against repair and maintenance problems. Such contracts should be evaluated in light of the possibility that the firm might be able to perform these tasks itself at less cost.

Several other special topics relating to pricing strategy were presented in Chapters 4 and 18. These relate specifically to pricing in inflationary periods and in face of scarce materials.

Conclusion

The pricing approaches presented in this chapter relate to firms actually providing a service or producing a product. The concepts pertaining to markups in reselling firms are presented in Chapter 20.

Firms face the task of pricing products at several points in a product's life. Various factors taken into consideration include the customer's need or desire for the product, his/her ability to pay, relative bargaining skills of all buyers and sellers, the knowledge of buyers, competitors in the market, the relative strength of competitors, the ability or willingness of resellers to vertically integrate backward into producing or private branding the item, government influence, and the niche of the product in relation to other products.[18]

Pricing is not a simple mathematical science. It is a complex task that is perhaps best administered by persons having responsibility over all marketing aspects of the product, including product make-up, methods of distribution, and tactics for promotion. This is often referred to as brand management. Whether or not this responsibility rests with one person or many, the point is that pricing decisions cannot be made in a vacuum.

FOOTNOTES

1. Kent B. Monroe, *Pricing: Making Profitable Decisions* (New York: McGraw-Hill Book Co., 1979), pp. 11 – 14.
2. Andre Gabor, *Pricing* (London: Heinemann Educ. Books, 1977), chapter 3.
3. Lawrence Fisher, *Industrial Marketing* (Princeton, NJ: Brandon Systems Press, 1970), p. 202.
4. Alfred R. Oxenfeldt, *Pricing Strategies* (New York: Amacom, 1975), p. 177.
5. Ibid, p. 182.
6. Philip Kotler, *Marketing Management* (Englewood Cliffs, NJ: Prentice-Hall, 1967), p. 357.
7. Fisher, *Industrial Marketing*, p. 224.
8. Monroe, *Pricing: Making Profitable Decisions*, p. 131.
9. Ibid, p. 136.
10. Oxenfeldt, *Pricing Strategies*, p. 28.

11.   Monroe, *Pricing: Making Profitable Decisions*, p. 10.
12.   Oxenfeldt, *Pricing Strategies*, p. 224.
13.   Ibid.
14.   Kotler, *Marketing Management*, p. 379.
15.   Gabor, Pricing Strategies, chapter 10.
16.   R. E. Sibson, *"A Service" in Creative Pricing* (New York: American Marketing Association, 1968).
17.   Aubrey Wilson, *The Marketing of Professional Services* (London: McGraw-Hill Book Co., 1972).
18.   Oxenfeldt, *Pricing Strategies*, p. 243.

QUESTIONS FOR REVIEW

1. What is a price, and what is its purpose?

2. Should a product always be priced at or above full cost?

3. How does elasticity of demand cause firms to practice price discrimination in an economic sense?

4. What are the basic pricing practices found throughout the product life cycle?

5. Is target pricing a valid approach to setting a price?

6. How can price be affected by the sales and transportation terms?

7. What is the rationale behind a premium price during a season and a lower one in the off-season?

8. What basic approach should a buyer use when evaluating whether or not to forward buy in the off-season at a low price?

9. When should a firm take advantage of an early payment discount in the credit period?

10. How can weight breaks in transportation pricing be used to a buyer's advantage?

11. What objectives are sought when firms use zone pricing?

12. What are the basic principles of pricing for services?

Problem 19–1

Newtrends Trucklines charges your firm competitive rates that were developed through negotiations last year. The line approaches you again with the additional offer of a discount for paying the freight bill early instead of within the current thirty-day term. The truckline's offer is a one-half percent discount for payment within seven days or the net within thirty days. Your firm's current cost of capital is eleven percent.
Question:
Should you pay these bills in seven days? Why or why not?

Problem 19-2

A vendor approaches you with the request that your firm pay its bill for goods within fifteen days of receipt instead of the current forty-five days. It is willing to offer an early payment discount for this request. Your company's cost of capital is twelve percent.

Question:

What discount will have to be offered as a minimum in order for your firm to pay within fifteen days?

Problem 19-3

A company has a product that earns revenues of $100,000 per year. Direct variable expenses are $73,800 per year, and these include production labor, energy, materials, and machinery maintenance. Company overhead, depreciation on the machinery, and other fixed expenses total $42,000 per year.

Question:

1. *Why does the company keep the product in its line?*
2. *What might be done to bring the product into profitability?*
3. *What strategic alternatives does the firm have with respect to this product?*

20

CHAPTER OBJECTIVES

After reading this chapter you should:

- Understand the functions of intermediate buyers and sellers.

- Appreciate the purchasing and pricing roles of wholesalers and retailers.

- Understand the relationship between markup and inventory turnover.

- Understand public agency purchasing.

Purchasing in Resale Firms and Government Agencies

Introduction

Purchasing is a key part of nonmanufacturing and government agency organizations. Much of the discussion in this text up to this point has revolved around the purchasing and marketing aspects of production firms. As the American economy shifts more toward that of a service economy and away from its traditional dependence upon manufacturing and the "smokestack industries," increasing attention will be made to nonmanufacturing purchasing.

The first part of this chapter presents an overview of the channels of distribution. Wholesaling and retailing are covered along with specific product line and pricing aspects found in them. The second part of the chapter investigates public organization purchasing. Explored are the differences in for-profit purchasing, the various buying agencies in federal, state, and local governments, the centralized versus decentralized purchasing issue in agencies, and the legal processes that shape government buying.

Resale Firms

What Are Resale Firms?

Products move from a manufacturer to the final user in a number of ways. This flow can take place through a chain of middlemen—some who actually purchase goods for resale, some who merely act to facilitate the flow from one firm to another, and others who take legal possession of the goods and arrange sales and purchases between other firms.[1]

Channel firms perform valuable marketing and logistics functions. In some instances they are more efficient at the task of marketing and selling the product than the manufacturer. In other instances, they can reach broader or more extensive markets than the producer. In still other instances, channel firms hold inventories near the buyers in much the same way that a seller's distribution center would function. Here, customer service benefits are provided by the investment in inventory by the middlemen. It other ways middlemen act as full-line assortment sources for buyers. Exhibit 20-1 illustrates this concept. Rather than each producer reaching every customer, and vice versa, middlemen col-

■ **EXHIBIT 20-1.**   *The Economical Logistics Role of Middlemen*

Producer-Consumer Goods Flow Without Middlemen

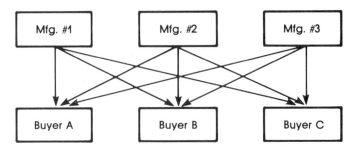

Nine combinations of goods flow

Producer-Consumer Goods Flow With Middlemen

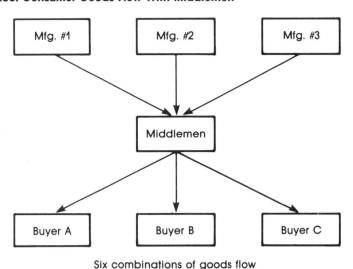

Six combinations of goods flow

lect goods from many sources and hold them for sale to many buyers. This system also is useful when the logistics economies of the producer do not correspond with those of the ultimate user. This can be seen in the simple example of milk. No one household can purchase a truckload quantity at one time. Yet, this is the most economical way for the producer to sell. Middlemen perform the role of breaking down larger quantities and making them available for purchase nearly everywhere.

Resale firms view a vendor's price in a somewhat different light than buyers of manufacturing firms do. This is generally due to the fact that the buying price directly affects the selling price. And, the purchase price is larger in proportion to the final selling price than in manufacturing settings. The price structure of a manufacturer is often stated in terms of a retail price less discounts that are granted to various middlemen who perform specific functions in production distribution. This enables a clear indication of the size of markup granted to the wholesalers, retailers, or other parties.

To illustrate, assume a product is sold on a retail basis for $20.00, and the manufacturer states a trade discount as 30–20–10–5. This can be interpreted as thirty percent for the retailer ($20.00 @ 30% = $6.00). That is, the retailer purchases the item for $14.00. The wholesaler receives the twenty percent as a basic markup ($14.00 @ 20% = $2.80). The base wholesaler price is $11.20. The wholesaler might also receive an additional ten percent for paying for the inbound freight rather than buying the goods on an FOB Wholesaler basis with the producer paying the freight. And, the last five percent might be an advertising allowance during a period of strong promotion. Each discount is taken sequentially. The wholesaler buying the product on these terms will pay $9.576 per unit.

Trade discounts are designed to accomplish many of the objectives indicated here. That is, trade discounts are structured to maintain a fairly consistent price system among wholesalers and retailers for specific functions performed by them. Factors to consider in the development of a price structure include providing adequate markup for the middlemen, allowing a margin roughly comparable to the value of the functions performed and providing one that is competitive in relation to other firms' products.

Pricing and Product Decisions of Resalers

Wholesalers and other middlemen are profit-minded firms that seek to maximize efficiency and obtain high returns. The behavioral aspects of managing a reselling organization are somewhat different than those found in manufacturing settings. An understanding of these differences is important for both the manufacturer who is trying to sell through and motivate these parties as well as the final purchaser who is seeking quality, cost, and supply assurance objectives for his/her own firm.

Price and Cost Considerations of Middlemen

Middlemen earn their revenues and profit by turning over inventory that is bought from one source and sold to others. In the example in the previous discussion, the wholesaler's basic purchase cost was $11.20 and sales price was $14.00. The markup was $2.80. This markup, or gross margin represents key cost and revenue figures for the firm. In this example a cost of $11.20 and sales price of $14.00 resulted in a markup of twenty-five percent. The cost of inventory, operating, and marketing products must all come out of the wholesaler's markup.

The markup or margin of one product must necessarily relate to others in the entire line handled by the wholesaler. Markups of competing products will be compared, and the product offering the greatest total revenue will be the one selected or emphasized. Thus, on an immediate basis, manufacturers must carefully develop the trade discounts in line with the markup objectives of middlemen.[2]

Markup is linked to turnover of the product as well. If a product is purchased for $11.20, is held for one year, and the company's cost of capital or opportunity rate is fifteen percent, then the wholesaler has a vested capital cost in the product of an additional ($11.20 @ 15%) $1.68 by year end. The cost of space (heat, light, power, taxes, depreciation of the building, storage bays, etc.) that holds each unit of inventory might cost $1.00 per year. By the end of a year, the firm now has $13.88 invested in the one item. If sold at this point, the net margin is only $.12. However, if the company turns the product over every six months (one is bought in January and sold by June with second one bought in July and sold by December), then both of these share the total capital and space costs. The $1.68 and $1.00 are divided in half and apportioned to each unit for a per unit allocation of $1.34 each. Now the company margin is $1.46 for each. If turnover takes place ten times a year, then the $2.68 is spread over ten units that move through each storage space. In this instance, the per-unit allocation of capital and space cost is $.268, and the margin to the firm is $2.53 each.

Turnover is a very important factor in the resale firm's selection of goods to handle as well as in deciding their price. A low turnover item will cause the firm to experience a low profit unless its margin is very high. On the other hand, the firm can profitably sell at a low margin if the sales volume and inventory turnover are very high. This concept can be seen in retail settings where low inventory stores with high sales can offer lower prices than some department stores with lesser unit sales and higher prices. Yet, both of these stores might end up with the same total profit at the end of the year.

The relationship between markup percent and turnover can be seen in Exhibit 20-2. This illustration shows that markups should be in inverse relationship with turnover. Again, a low markup can be tolerated if the wholesaler can move many units of the item through his/her facility in a year. Or, as shown, a ten percent markup item that turns over about twenty-five times per year will result in the same total margin to the wholesaler as a fifty percent markup item that turns over only five times per year.

Freight costs and allowances are another concern of wholesalers. Back to our earlier example, freight can be paid by the manufacturer, or the wholesaler can pay it and receive a discount of ten percent off of $11.20, or $1.12 per unit. The wholesaler must evaluate whether or not the manufacturer-arranged freight is less costly than arranging it himself/herself. Options here include picking up the goods in the wholesaler's own trucks or using a carrier that has rates lower than $1.12 per unit.

Freight allowances have become a new concern in the food and grocery industry since 1980. The Motor Carrier Act of 1980 contained a provision that is now found in the Revised Interstate Commerce Act. The new section permits firms selling food and grocery products on a uniform, zone-delivered price basis to grant allowances or compensate buyers for performing the transportation task in their own private vehicles. Section 10732 of the Revised Interstate Commerce Act states that such allowances may be used if they are offered on a nondiscriminatory basis to all buyers who ask, and if the amount of the allowance does not exceed the actual costs to the seller of delivering the goods to the buyer.[3]

■ **EXHIBIT 20-2.** *The Relationship Between Markup and Turnover*

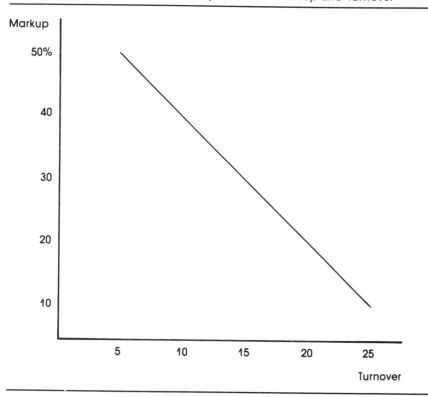

The freight allowance practice can be seen in the following example. A manufacturer of canned food is located in Ohio. It sells products to all buyers in a four-state area at a price of $9.00 per case. The cost of the product is $5.00, profit is $2.00, and the average freight cost to all customers in the region is $2.00 for a total of $9.00. The average freight cost is a composite of shipping to all customers in the area. This might range from a low of $.20 per case to those nearby to a high of $3.00 to those far away, but the overall average freight cost is $2.00. One customer requests to pick up goods in his own truck. The seller would normally pay $1.00 per case to deliver to that buyer. The allowance, then, is $1.00 for a total purchase price of $8.00 per case.

Problems can arise in this area, due to the multiplicity of transportation prices that are possible between two points. A motor carrier class rate might be $2.00, an exceptions rate $1.80, and a commodity rate $1.10. Railroad rates might range from $1.90 to $1.05. And, the seller's own private truck might cost $1.00 to operate between the two points. Within the letter of the law, the actual cost of delivery to the seller is the proper amount to grant as a freight allowance. If the seller would normally have used his own private truck, then the $1.00 is the appropriate allowance. If a motor commodity rate is the normal shipping process, then the allowance could be $1.10 for a price of $7.90. A problem arises here when the farthest buyer begins to pick up freight. The overall average cost of delivering to all of the remaining customers then drops. This causes the amount of cost built into the price for average freight to continually change.

Advertising is another allowance often granted in the trade discount. In our first example this was five percent or $.504 per unit purchased. This is an allowance the manufacturer hopes the wholesaler will use to acquire advertising services in the area. These allowances can be for all or a part of the advertising. Quite often the manufacturer will provide camera-ready copy of advertisements that can be placed in local media with little effort by the wholesaler.

Wholesaler Product-Line Decisions

Middlemen must decide which products or lines to handle as well as which ones to spend marketing effort upon. The bottom line decision is made in favor of those product lines that promise the greatest amount of total profit to the firm. In actual practice, this is generally an equation of maximum revenue minus cost of goods purchased, and is often referred to as "contribution margin." The contribution margin is that amount remaining after direct goods purchases and sales cover operating expenses, taxes, and profit.[4]

The decision process for product lines requires having discount and markup information. Assume, again, that the wholesaler can buy a product for $11.20 and sell it at a markup of $2.80 for a total price of $14.00. This is a markup of twenty-five percent. Three other manufacturers also approach the wholesaler to carry their product lines. The wholesaler, of course, wishes to select the one that will provide the greatest total contribution margin. Each of the options can be compared using the following formula:

Contribution Margin = (Turnover) (Average Inventory) (Markup in $)

The products are different in price and supply availabilities. The wholesaler estimates turnover and average inventory levels and combines these with the dollar markup on each. This information is shown in Table 20–1 for the four products.

The final decision does not necessarily relate to the total revenue, but rather total contribution margin is the key decision factor. As Tabel 20-1 shows, a lower turnover of a high markup item can provide a higher total contribution margin than a lower inventory item with higher turnover but lower markup.

□ **TABLE 20-1.** *Impacts of Turnover, Inventory Level, and Mark Up Upon Financial Results*

Product	Turnover	Average Inventory	Markup in $	Conbrib. Margin
A:	2	750	$1.60	$2,400
B:	4	500	1.10	2,200
C:	5	250	2.50	2,500
D:	1	1000	2.80	2,800

Wholesaler Performance Measures

Wholesalers and other middlemen also look to cost-as-a-percent of total sales as an indicator of performance for both product lines and firms as a whole. This figure is determined by dividing purchase cost plus inbound freight by total sales. For example, purchases and freight might amount to seventy-two percent of total sales. This means that the remaining twenty-eight percent must cover operating expenses, taxes, and profit. This measure is a grand average of all markups and the revenue receipts of the firm. It is closely watched by firm managers, because the financial health of the company is dependent upon this spread.

Inventory turnover is another performance indicator that is closely watched by distributor firms. This concept was mentioned previously, but when viewed from the vantage "point" of the entire firm, another application generally is more appropriate. In our example, an inventory turnover of two times per year means that goods are generally bought every six months and that each lot is depleted before another is purchased. Thus, each spot on the shelf is occupied by two units of an item during the year. This turnover measure is the best possible one to obtain. However, when a firm is handling over 3,000 stockkeeping units, it is nearly impossible to track individual turnover information on each one. Besides, some products might turnover fifty times per year while others might actually turn over less than once. Turnover of all products in an aggregate sense is what is of interest here.

Various concepts of turnover are presented here as illustrated by Alan Silver. A distributor has total sales of $4,000,000 and a purchase-cost-to-sales performance of seventy-five percent. Different turnover rates may be computed as follows.

1) Turnover Using Sales Prices. This rate is computed by dividing total annual sales by the inventory on hand. If the inventory is $600,000 and sales are $4 milllion, then the overall turnover is 6.6 times.

2) Turnover Using Cost of Goods. This turnover figure is obtained by dividing the $600,000 inventory into the total purchase cost and inbound freight expenses. Thus, $3 million divided by $600,000 is 5.0 times.

3) Turnover of Warehouse Sales at Cost. This measure excludes all those sales that were shipped by the distributor's vendor direct to its customers. In the example, only $2,264,000 in sales were made from the warehouse itself. With a total inventory of $600,000, the turnover rate of products actually handled in the facility is 3.6 times.

4) Turnover of Warehouse Stock Items at Cost. This figure includes only those goods that are continuously held as part of the product line in the warehouse. It excludes special orders and odd, one-time purchases for particular customers. It also excludes special orders by customers that actually go through the warehouse instead of being shipped direct to the customer. In the example developed by Silver, these total $1,964,000 in cost. At $600,000 in inventory, the turnover rate is 3.3 times. This rate is the main one used for products held on hand in the wholesaler's regular line of business. Thus, what might appear as a fair-

ly healthy high turnover for the firm actually diminishes when only the primary stock is examined.

5) Warehouse Special Orders at Cost. This financial measure consists of only those goods special ordered for customers and moved through the warehouse. The appropriate inventory to use here is the average of such special order inventories. In the example, $498,000 of special order sales is divided by $40,000 of inventory for a turnover rate of 12.5 times.

These five inventory turnover concepts are financial in that they measure sales or purchase costs against inventory cost levels. They are aggregated figures of all products and are different from the turnover concept presented earlier in which the physical flow of inventory was used. It is important whenever using inventory turnover rates that they be measured in a consistent manner and compared against those that were determined in the same way.

Middlemen use other criteria when evaluating product line handling decisions including product characteristics, packaging, merchandising support, advertising, compatibility with other products, the manufacturer's reputation, and logistics considerations.[6] Others consider how the product will fit into the firm's present line of operations. Is it in a new direction that will require new marketing efforts? Does it fill a gap in the present line of offerings? Is it a lesser-priced item that eventual buyers will switch to? What obligations will be imposed by the manufacturer when carrying this line?

Wholesaling Trends

This sector of the economy is a necessary one for many manufacturers and ultimate buyers. Wholesaling fulfills roles and functions in ways that were briefly described earlier. It is important for both buyers and sellers to examine the trends taking place in this field.

Uniform coding is gaining a foothold in the wholesaling area. Universal product number systems are currently in use in electircal and plumbing product areas, and they are coming into use in industrial commodities as well. The National Association of Wholesalers in 1972 established a committee called the Distribution Code Institute to create a voluntary numbering system. The way the system works is that each manufacturer is assigned a six-digit vendor code. The producer then assigns a five-digit code to each product. The key benefit of such a system is realized with the use of computers. Codes can be handled with ease on a computer, whereas names and descriptions can be cumbersome. Computer codes can be easily priced, cross-referenced, and tied into billing systems. Further, direct buyer to wholesaler computer order processing systems can be built easily around such codes.

The wholesaling industry is undergoing structural change. Factors contributing to the changes are the costs of marketing and logistics as well as the cost of capital in inventory. Surveys indicate that the number of distributors is shrinking. Where there were 7,600 industrial distributors in 1970, by 1975 this number diminished to 6,500. However, growth in large chain distributors is occurring. Firms like W. W. Grainger, Curtis Noll, and Motion Industries are examples of the multi-million dollar sales distributors in various fields. These distribution chains possess economies of logistics in the form of large scale purchasing, transportation, and warehousing capabilities, and these attributes enable the large firms to take over many of the distribution services from manufacturers. Producer sales to a smaller number of larger firms such as these distributors reduces the manufacturer's marketing costs as well as the costs of distribution. This trend is seen by some industry observers as leading to the large wholesalers supplying subsequent buyers and smaller regional distributors. The smaller distributor may, in fact, get caught in a squeeze with large distributors on one hand and direct sales from producers to final buyers on the other.[7]

Internal changes are taking place within industrial distributors. A report by *Purchasing Magazine* in 1981 indicated that the number of different products sold by distributors is decreasing. For example, medium-sized distributors with sales between $2.5 and $7.5 million decreased the number of items handled from 6,177 to 5,964 between 1978 and 1981. This is a significant shift in a period of only three years. The number of suppliers that these same firms purchased from dropped from an average of 43 to 38. further, the number of inside salesmen used dropped from an average of 5.7 to 4.9, and outside salesmen were reduced from 7.3 to 6.1. Coinciding with these trends is a move away from general-line wholesaling toward more specialization in product lines. Distributor-supplied computer order processing links allow reductions in marketing calls and expensive person-to-person sales activities.[8]

Public Sector Purchasing

Public sector purchasing refers to the acquisition of products and services for government agencies on the federal, state, county, and municipality levels. It is a distinct topic within the subject of supply and purchasing because environmental constraints in the public arena cause purchasing to be conducted differently in some ways than it is in for-profit firms. The same principles relating to quality and assurance of supply have long been the guiding practices of public purchasing managers. The treatment of cost, however, has been handled differently in public areas as distinguished from private organizations. But, even this area is slowly shifting toward a convergence with private practices.

Introduction to Public Purchasing

Public sector purchasing appears to be different as compared to private firm's purchasing activities in many ways. For one, the public agency's purchasing manager generally acquires only supplies, maintenance parts, and services. Few products are bought by any public agency that are reworked, handled, undergo manufacturing, and then resold. For the most part, the agency itself is the final consumer of the goods and services it purchases.

Another apparent difference in the two purchasing practices is that the accounting methods under which public and private purchasing managers operate are vastly different. The private purchasing manager usually operates within a production plan and budget that continually evolve. Though there are yearly and quarterly budgetary periods, the purchasing activity for production and other goods appears to be a continuum throughout long time spans. The yearly budget appropriation in a public agency is more clearly defined, which can result in purchasing activity being held off for coming new budget periods, or increasing toward the end of a budget period in order to completely use the funds allocated.

The cost of funds creates a vastly different set of practices between public and private purchasing counterparts. In the private firm, if a purchasing manager acquires goods in January to be used in April, his/her finance manager generally will apply a cost-of-money penalty against the funds tied up in the goods. For example, if the goods cost $100,000, and the company's cost of capital in that period was fifteen percent, then the charged use of the funds might be $100,000 times .15 times 3/12, or $3750. This is the amount of money that could be earned during this period if the money was invested in liquid securities rather than in goods. The cost of capital, then, is a factor that is considered in the purchase timing of most private firms.

In a public agency setting, however, the cost of funds generally is not considered in purchasing financial management. This is a feature common to accounting systems in most public settings. The opportunity cost of funds and depreciation in fixed assets is not an item of accounting. This will often result in an agency purchasing manager ordering an item at the beginning of a budgetary period in a quantity that will last the entire period. It can also lead purchasing managers to spend funds at the end of a budget period on large quantities of goods that are offered at good prices. A problem with this practice is that the goods might become obsolete a short time later. Storage cost is minimal, because there is no charge for depreciation or capital invested in the structure that houses the goods.

Another difference between the two sectors of purchasing is the source of authority under which both purchasing managers operate. In the private firm, the purchasing manager is ultimately responsible to top management. In the public setting, purchasing authority is created by law, and responsibility is to the legislative body that created and oversees the agency. The private purchasing manager must seek permission to extend his actual authority to purchase extraordinary items from top management. In the public sector, the purchasing manager seeks counsel from the agency's legal office and, if need be, they both approach the legislative body for changes.[9]

Budgetary limitations are also different in the two settings. While the private firm's purchasing manager might seek funds to take advantage of spot price shifts in the market, the public purchasing manager usually will not possess such flexibility. This makes long-term planning a crucial process in public agencies.

External pressures are perhaps greater in public agency purchasing than in private settings. Public purchasing managers will often come under pressure to acquire goods from vendors who are linked to firms in the political system.

Information is more freely available in public agencies than it is in private firms. While competing vendors might never know the prices offered by others in a private setting, almost all the actions, purchase prices, etc. are public knowledge in a public agency. This is a disadvantage for public purchasing managers because they cannot play one vendor off against another. Both vendors know what the other has bid and what the agency is paying. Further, because there is often pressure in public settings to exercise equity in buying from the entire market, vendors know that if they do not obtain the business this time they probably will the next. Therefore, there is often little reason to be extremely price conscious or offer special low price deals.[10]

Purchasing Bodies

Federal Government

Several major agencies on the federal level are involved in purchasing. The federal government spends over $125 billion per year on goods and services, and it provides nearly $80 billion to state and local bodies for assistance in their purchasing. The major agencies that purchase goods are the Department of Defense, General Services Administration, Department of Agriculture, Agency for International Development (AID) and nearly all agencies when acquiring contract research.

The Department of Defense is governed by the legislative mandate that is contained in Title 10 of the United States Code. Specific provisions are found in Title 10 of the Code of Federal Regulations. The Army, Navy, and Air Force purchase goods and services themselves, and items of a mutual nature are handled through the Defense Supply Agency. The Marines are part of the purchasing and logistics arm of the Navy, and the Coast Guard is part of the Department of Transportation. A form of pooled purchasing is handled through the Defense Supply Agency for goods that are used by all service branches.

The General Services Administration is responsible for nonmilitary purchasing of goods and supplies, and it oversees the federal government's holding of buildings, automotive fleets, communications services, etc. The Federal Supply Service (FSS) is the primary subagency with GSA that purchases a bulk of the products and services acquired by GSA each year. The FSS performs this task through three primary purchasing procedures. One is federal supply schedule contracts. This system includes a list of low-price vendors as determined by the FSS. This list is then distributed to each and every agency requiring the basic goods included in such contracts. Office supplies, vehicle parts, etc. are the basic items included in this process. Each agency then draws upon these contracts. Another purchasing method is nonstock purchasing. Many items are not kept in stock by FSS, nor are they handled through the schedule contracts. The nonstock system will accumulate the needs of many agencies for the same basic item, and it will then acquire the item in large lot quantities at favorable prices. Stock items is a third method of federal procurement. This system consists of purchasing, provisioning, and distributing critical goods to all agencies.[11]

The Department of Agriculture purchases large quantities of food and farm-related items each year. These items are not purchased for the agency's own use, but rather they are acquired as part of farm price support programs and U.S. foreign aid. Public Law 480 is the law that enables the Department of Agriculture to purchase surplus goods on commodity markets in the U.S. and distribute them overseas through relief agencies of religious organizations as well as through CARE, the UN, and the State Department's Agency for International Development.

The Agency for International Development (AID) is an arm of the State Department that is involved with the U.S. foreign aid program. This agency will often contract for goods to be acquired in the U.S. and sent overseas to countries that are receiving such assistance. AID will acquire small items such as forklifts to be used at a foreign port, or it will contract for an entire fertilizer plant to be acquired in the U.S. and built in an African nation. AID is the funding agency that solicits bids for such contracts, but GSA is often the agency that carries out the contract provisions.

The Department of Transportation (DOT) is also involved in purchasing, though it is not a major consumer of the items discussed here. It provides assistance to state and local bodies for rapid transit and highway projects. The DOT is heavily involved in specifying the contents and nature of the buses, subway cars, highway designs etc. that are parts of these grants. DOT also administers the shipbuilding subsidy program of the Maritime Administration. In this context, it has a large input to the design of the ships that private American steamship firms are building under the subsidy program. The Navy also stipulates certain military features that are to be built into commercial ships in the event that they might be used in time of war. The agencies concerned with providing grants to communities for sewer, school, and water facilities also stipulate the specification in the construction of these assets. So, while the agencies do not perform the purchasing, they do impact upon the purchasing decisions made by others.

The Office of Federal Procurement Policy (OFPP) within the Office of Management and Budget oversees the purchasing activities of federal agencies. Its role is to make the processes used by agencies consistent, and to assure that duplication is eliminated or reduced wherever possible.[12] The General Accounting Office (GAO) is the specific auditing agency that examines records of each agency. GAO acts as a watchdog to monitor goods purchasing and all other procedural practices.

State and Local Purchasing

Centralized purchasing is a common practice on the state level. States also heavily utilize open-ended contracts for acquisition of materials and supplies. These contracts typically are for common items required throughout the state by many separate agencies. Janitorial supplies, auto parts, and office items are examples. The contracts often include provision for local placement of the items by the contractor. Thus, the state gains the benefits of bulk purchasing, but it does not get involved with large scale distribution of these items to local offices and other facilities.

In county and municipality settings, purchasing concerns revolve around several main concepts. One, centralized purchasing is common within a city or town. That is, purchasing for each office or agency within the community is centralized through one office. This enables uniformity and economies of larger scale buying. The pros and cons of centralized versus decentralized purchasing are discussed later. Another feature found in local purchasing is pooling arrangements with other communities or buying through the larger county or state systems. This is common practice in many states. Another element of local concern is accountability in the purchasing function. Competitive bidding and objectivity in this process comes under frequent examination in local settings. Opportunities to favor certain local firms, especially construction companies for building and road work, are a point of criticism often found on the local level.

The role of negotiation and competitive bidding in state and local purchasing was the subject of a study sponsored by the Department of Justice, law Enforcement Assistance Administration, in 1974. The report was prepared by the National Association of State Purchasing Officials and a major accounting firm to cover the subject of public purchasing practices. It set forth suggestions for setting clear specifications in bid processes and their evaluation. Another Department of Justice grant was awarded to the American Bar Association in 1975 to delve into the subject of municipal level laws and regulations in purchasing. This document is known as the Model Procurement Code. It proposes odd systems and procedures for public purchasing "bodies." In many instances, government bodies needed to revise their entire sets of laws and regulations to conform to this new suggested set of practices. The Model Procurement Code includes separate sections for purchasing organization, contract formation, specifications, use of engineering and other professional services, cost concepts, supply management, ethics and other topics.[13]

Public Purchasing Issues

Cooperative or Pooled Purchasing

Many communities and counties will group purchases together in order to gain the advantage of lower cost, larger lot purchasing. This is conducted either by jointly establishing a single fund and purchase contract with a vendor, or it is accomplished by one of the bodies obtaining the goods then splitting them up upon delivery. Pooled purchasing provides the advantages of lower prices, higher quality, access to more vendors who wish to sell only in larger quantities, increased vendor competition, standardization of items purchased, and lower total administrative effort by all buying bodies. Drawbacks to pooled purchasing include the added effort by the buying office performing the service for others and often a longer lead time in obtaining the goods.[14]

Pooled purchasing is common among municipalities for capital equipment and road supplies, and in school districts and hospitals. Bus purchases by local rapid transit agencies is also becoming a common, pooled purchase practice.

Centralized Versus Decentralized Public Purchasing

Most states have a centralized purchasing body that is established to obtain the benefits of centralized buying. The advantages of this approach include 1) volume prices, 2) standardization of items needed by the entire system, 3) reduction in the need for high cost rush orders since a central inventory point often will be able to provide the item(s), 4) uniformity in purchasing processes that leads to a lower overall total administrative cost, 5) consistency in specification and bidding processes that foster objectivity in the purchasing process, 6) reduced sales expenses by suppliers who deal with only one major buying group rather than many small ones, and 7) centralized scrap, surplus, and waste disposal economies.

Disadvantages of centralized public purchasing include the longer lead time required by many individual sites when seeking the goods. But, this is often avoided with centralization, if central purchasing has a plentiful supply of items in storage that the subagency would often have to purchase on its own. Another drawback to centralization is the need for special items at many local sites. Centralization often forces standardized items onto smaller agencies or jurisdictions. There might be real needs for the nonstandard items at these locations. It is difficult in many centralized arrangements to depart from the uniform standard.[15]

Special Requirements in Public Purchasing

Many special laws and regulations are found in public purchasing in addition to the above Model Procurement Code. Some of the major regulations follow.

1) The Buy American Act provides for favoritism toward domestic firms in federal purchases as long as the American firms' prices are within six percent of those of foreign vendors. If a domestic vendor is in an area specified by the Department of Labor as a surplus labor area, the price difference can be as great as twelve percent. This factor generally causes conflicts between the purchasing agencies and the Department of Labor, which oversees this law. The purchasing or specifying agency wishes to minimize its budgetary expenses within its appropriations, and often does not appreciate being forced to buy from a higher cost domestic vendor. This problem has arisen in rapid transit equipment purchases. The Department of Transportation often pays eighty percent of the capital cost of new equipment, with the local community paying the remaining twenty percent. Both the DOT and the city desire low cost bidders no matter where they are located, and they do not wish to be forced to buy from one specific firm just because it is a domestic one.

2) The American cargo preference law requires that any federal, state, or local shipping or passenger-paid or sponsored movement overseas be

at least fifty percent in American flag airlines or steamships. This includes purchases from abroad. The problem here is that often the American flag carrier is either not convenient to use or has higher rates or fares.

3) Small business preference is another factor included in federal laws. Public Law 87-305 passed in 1961 states that a fair proportion of purchases made with public funds should be awarded to small firms. Small firms are those independently owned and operated and having a sales revenue of under certain amounts, depending upon the industry. This preference is to extend to the subcontracting work by major firms obtaining large contracts from the government.

4) Minority firm preferences are also within the realm of public purchasing. Included in various federal and state laws are statements designed to encourage purchases where possible from firms owned and operated by minorities. Many purchase contracts and bid specifications include provisions for this.

5) Prison-made goods are often an item of purchasing preference required in public buying. This requirement is made to provide for reduction or minimization of the prison system costs. In many states, food items are provided for state agencies by the prison system.

6) Local preference laws exist in many state and local purchasing regulations. These are similar to the Buy American Act, but they require a preference for local firms as long as their bid prices are within a certain percent of those of competing vendors. These laws are designed to keep monies circulating in local areas and boost local economies. But, these preferences often force purchasing decisions in the direction of noncompetitive firms.

7) The Prompt Payment Act now requires federal agencies to pay vendors within thirty days, plus a fifteen-day grace period, or else pay an interest penalty. The interest penalty is established by the Department of Treasury. This law was passed because payments to many firms were held up months and in some cases years. The effect over the long run was for firms to pad their costs to account for the slow payment or to not even bid on government work at all. In the end, the agencies suffer from higher prices or fewer interested vendors. The Prompt Payment Act should reduce some of these tendencies.

Public agency and institutional purchasing involves the same evaluative criteria and basic approaches as private firm buying. Differences lie in the agency's closer attention to centralization and standardization, as well as the mandate to conform to purchasing authority in the form of law and regulation rather than top management. Public purchasing is more open to outside scrutiny, and it is less flexible than private purchasing. The differences relating to budgetary and inventory costing have caused buying practices that appear noneconomic. Many states are beginning to remedy this by building costs of capital into purchasing systems. The Pennsylvania Liquor Control Board is an example. Over the years, some goods were bought in large lots only to sit on shelves for long periods. Now a cost of inventory is imposed upon buyers and inventory managers. In other agencies a cost of building use is beginning to be included in budgets to force agency tenants to behave in ways that account for the cost and opportunity values of the fixed assets.

Conclusion

This chapter presented two special areas of purchasing management. The first involved buying in resale firms in which the product acquired is in the same basic form as what the firm will then sell. Buying here is more closely linked to the final marketing effort of the firm than in manufacturing operations.

Public organization purchasing is another special area in the buying field. Purchasing activities here tend to be more in the open under the view of the public and the vendors themselves, and the budgetary and other processes tend to be different from those in private firm contexts.

FOOTNOTES

1. Thedore N. Beckman and William R. Davidson, *Marketing* (New York: Ronald Press, 1967), chapter 12.
2. J. Taylor Sims, J. Robert Foster, and Arch G. Woodside, *Marketing Channels* (New York: Harper & Row, 1977), chapter 13.
3. Title 49, United States Code, Section 10732, Food and Grocery Transportation.
4. Sims, Foster and Woodside, *Marketing Channels*, p. 154.
5. Alan Silver, "The Trouble With Stock Turns," Industrial Distribution, May 1979.
6. Donald G. Hileman and Leonard A. Rosen, "Deliberations of a Chain Store Buying Committee," *Journal of Marketing* 25 (January 1961); 52-55.
7. Ronald D. Michman, "Trends Affecting Industrial Distribution," *Industrial Marketing Management* 9 (1980): 213–216.
8. "The Pressure Is On To Do More With Less," *Purchasing,* 24 September 1981, p. 52.
9. Andre Gabor, *Pricing* (London: Heinemann Educ. Books, 1977), p. 61.
10. Warren Blanding, *Blanding's Practical Physical Distribution* (Washington: Traffic Service Corp., 1977), p. 8–22.
11. Gabor, *Pricing,* p. 151.
12. "What Buyers Want from Distributors," *Purchasing,* September 24, 1981, p. 57.
13. Michiel R. Leenders, Harold E. Fearon, and Wilbur B. England, *Purchasing and Materials Management* (Homewood, IL: Richard D. Irwin, 1980), p. 476.
14. Solon A. Bennett, ed., "Public Purchasing," *Aljian's Purchasing Handbook* (New York: McGraw-Hill Book Co., 1982), p. 20–42.
15. Ibid., p. 20–7.

SOURCES FOR FURTHER READING

Fisher, Lawrence. *Industrial Marketing.* Princeton, NJ: Brandon Systems Press, 1970.
Hutt, Michael D., Speh, Thomas W. *Industrial Marketing Management.* Chicago: Dryden Press, 1981.
McCarthy, E. Jerome. *Basic Marketing: A Managerial Approach.* Homewood, IL: Richard D. Irwin, 1975.
Office of General Counsel, General Accounting Office, *Government Contract Principles.* Washington: U.S. Government Printing Office, 1978.
Oxenfeldt, Alfred R. *Pricing Strategies.* New York: Amacom, 1975.
Page, Harry Robert. *Public Purchasing and Materials Management.* Lexington, MA: D. C. Heath, 1981.
Sibley, Stanley D., and Teas, R. Kenneth. "The Manufacturer's Agent in Industrial Distribution, *Industrial Marketing Management* 8 (1979): 286.
Stern, Louis W., and El-Ansary, Adel I. *Marketing Channels.* Englewood Cliffs, NJ: Prentice-Hall, Inc. 1977, chapter 3.
Swan, Captain Cathy. *Readings in Federal Acquisition Management.* (Lexington, MA: Ginn Custom Publishing, 1980.

QUESTIONS FOR REVIEW

1. What is meant by the term "channel of distribution?"

2. What economies can middlemen provide for producer and ultimate buyer?

3. Explain the trade discount system in laymen's terms.

4. How is the buyer for a resale firm more directly involved in the sale aspects of the product than buyers in manufacturing firms?

5. Are the basic buying considerations different for a buyer in a wholesaler than one in a manufacturing firm? Why or why not?

6. What must the wholesaler cover in the product markup?

7. How does turnover relate to markup?

8. What is contribution margin? How does it play in the decision by a wholesaler to carry certain product lines?

9. Compare and contrast the various ways of evaluating the sales and inventory management of a wholesaler.

10. How is public agency purchasing different form that in private firms?

11. What are the pros and cons of cooperative purchasing?

12. What special laws and policies must public agency buyers consider in their purchasing activities?

Problem 20-1

A store buyer is presented a price by a manufacturer that is $35.00 less fifteen percent, ten percent, twelve percent.

Questions:
1. What is the amount of the discount?
2. What is the final price to be paid?
3. What is the final purchase price as a percent of the base price?

Problem 20-2

A retailer is considering four different product lines from competing manufacturers. There is very little difference in the quality of the items and the final customer preferences for them. The main differences lie in the markups available, the quantity of inventory that must be bought each time from the various vendors, and the potential product turnover for each. This information is as follows.

Product	Markup	Avg. Inventory	Turnover
A	$3.00	200	6
B	6.25	200	3
C	5.00	400	2
D	3.50	50	10

Question:
Which one of these is best to carry?

V

DESIGNS FOR THE FUTURE

Purchasing is undergoing dramatic change and evolution. Supply problems of the 1970s, price instability, transportation changes, emergence of materials management, a management view that the firm is an integrated whole, and the efficiency of information and communications all bring changes to buyers, managers, and directors of purchasing.

Sections I through IV of this book presented the current and evolving state of the art in purchasing. These pertain to current and evolving ways of managing the same basic functions, integration with marketing and materials management, and adaptation of new or increased emphasis upon elements now seen as essential in purchasing management.

Effective purchasing organization is presented in this section of the book. It includes reporting lines, organizational issues, performance measures and auditing the function, the development of people and their skills, and how the future emphasis of the firm will further shape purchasing design and activity.

The future of purchasing will depend upon both environmental forces and active approaches taken by managers and top managements. Long-run supply in the future will not be as stable as in past decades; firms are becoming more flexible and adaptive. These forces require tighter integration of purchasing into the strategic development, long-run planning, and daily operations of the entire, integrated firm.

21

CHAPTER OBJECTIVES

After reading this chapter you should

- Understand the basic organizational structure of a purchasing organization.

- Understand the key issues behind the centralization versus decentralization issue.

- Appreciate the need for various organizational forms of the purchasing function in different settings.

- Understand the basic issues in developing purchasing professionals.

Effective Purchasing Organizations

Introduction

An organization is a body of people with tools designed to accomplish some purpose. It is a system that is charged by management or some other authority to carry out some stated activity or function. If an organization is operated and organized efficiently, it will experience revenues and profits as a reward to itself and its owners. An organization is created and shaped to enable persons and activities to function effectively.

Purchasing is one organized function within a firm. Its primary charge from management is to obtain optimum quality goods at the lowest final cost and maintain an assurance of supply. Many other objectives and activities support these three primary roles. The purchasing department is staffed, and work flows are designed to meet and satisfy these ends.

The Reporting Lines of Purchasing

An initial approach to the topic of purchasing organization is to view to whom it reports within most firms. This indicates the lines of authority, responsibility, and reporting. A survey conducted by *Purchasing* magazine in 1980 highlighted the then-current status of purchasing reporting lines. The results of this survey are shown in Table 21-1.

Purchasing appears to report to a fairly high level in the firm. At the highest level, eleven percent of the persons responding to the survey indicated an immediate link with the president or chairman of the firm. This indicates that the purchasing manager is probably at the vice-presidential level. At the second level, forty-nine percent report to a vice-president or executive vice-president. And, the remaining forty percent report to directors or plant managers. In summary, a total of twenty-eight percent are shown to report to the head of the firm or the executive vice-president. This indicates a fairly high placement of purchasing within the firm.

The use of titles within purchasing is relatively consistent. At the entry level, the title of assistant buyer is fairly common. This is the initial area of assignment for persons in training and with limited authority. Buyer is generally a higher title that often carries with it authority to

☐ **TABLE 21-1.** *Where Purchasing Reports*

I. Highest Level—	
President or Chairman	11%
II. Vice-Presidential Level—	
Executive Vice-President or Gen. Manager	17%
VP Manufacturing or Operations	12%
VP of Purchasing or Materials	6%
VP or Finance or Controller	5%
Other VP	8%
VP of Engineering	1%
III. Manager Level	
Director of Materials	15%
Plant or Works Manager	12%
Director/Manager of Manufacturing/Oper's	7%
Other	5%

commit the firm to larger sums and control wider ranges of activity. Though these titles are seemingly simple verbs that indicate one key activity, the job is generally wider in scope. A large degree of analytical work, negotiation, and even some supervisory responsibilities are found at these levels. Thus, the term buyer is perhaps limiting in today's scheme of activity.

The purchasing manager or director is usually a higher, or the highest, title found in the department. This is often the title for the head of the department. Within this context, the manager or director does little actual buying, but rather is involved in establishing goals, plans, and policies for the rest of the department. There might be many persons with the title of director or manager. In these situations, the managers might be responsible for the activity of buyers who operate within product spheres, or for certain plants.

The title of vice-president is also common in the field. There is no specific rule as to when it is used, but a general tendency exists for the use of this title in three situations. The vice-president title is generally found in larger firms; that is, the size of the organization, total dollar sum of purchases, numbers of employees, etc. all create a tendency for this activity to be headed by an individual of vice-presidential status. Another general tendency exists for this practice when the raw material expenditures are high in relation to the total sales of the firm. This would indicate the greater importance of purchasing decisions to the total expenditures of the firm. And, in still another way, firms will often require a person in this area to have a vice-presidential title if they are empowered to commit the firm to large sums. In this manner, some corporate charters and organizational policies require top officer approval when committing the firm to large sums. This is often a common situation in purchasing, and it is generally simpler for this approval to be made by the department head with this title.

Centralization Versus Decentralization Issue

Purchasing may be organized at one central location in a firm, or it may be situated at each and every production or major user site. The centralization versus decentralization issue is not clear cut either way. There are advantages and disadvantages to each. Further, there are other forms of organization, since these are not mutually exclusive.

Centralization

This form of organization consists of purchasing activities located at one site within the firm. Though there may be many plants and user sites throughout the entire system, centralization exists when all purchasing activity is concentrated at one place, usually the corporate headquarters. There appears to be a tendency toward centralization by U.S. firms in the 1970s and 1980s. The many advantages of centralization are presented as follows.

Purchasing economy through buying strength is attained when all or most of the firm's purchasing is concentrated in one buying group. This single group is able to buy in larger quantities and negotiate from a greater position of relative strength than would individual plant sites requiring smaller quantities. There is often a price advantage gained when buying through competitive bidding or negotiation. Generally speaking, however, the prime advantage is attained when there is a commonality of products required by each site, and there are economies in purchasing larger single lots for individual distribution to each location. This, of course, requires a high degree of product standardization among the separate locations.

Negotiation expertise is frequently cited as a reason for centralizing purchasing activity. This step is usually taken for price advantages, but it is also used to secure supplies or obtain quality or other concessions that smaller, individual buying locations would not otherwise be able to obtain. Further, negotiating is a skill that is often developed through experience. This experience is not always attainable at individual sites where buyers must spread their time and effort over many other daily activities.

Staff expertise is also developed to a higher degree when purchasing has a strong central group. Purchasing a specific item might be a part-time requirement for dispersed buyers, but it can often be the major responsibility of one person who can become an expert on that material when purchasing is centralized. A central group can also apply research to areas that would otherwise be overlooked or not feasible for study at individual locations. A problem that costs each site about $1,000 per year might not be analyzed and solved by each site nor would it be noticed by any one person. In a centralized organization, the $1,000-per-plant problem might total to over $100,000 per year for the entire firm. In centralized purchasing the problem would more likely be addressed and solved.

Centralized purchasing is also necessary when needed products are available only from fluctuating markets, or through national or international sources. In these situations, it is often best to consolidate the firm's requirements and apply the expertise of a central group. Some firms have a policy of conducting all hedging and commodity market buying at one place rather than from individual plants. Other firms have a policy of handling international purchases at a central location as well. The higher level of international buying transaction costs and the problems often encountered in monitoring and processing these orders makes it beneficial to concentrate this effort.

Centralized buying also has the advantage of eliminating duplication of effort. Where ten persons might be handling purchasing at ten individual sites, centralization would require fewer numbers of persons. Where each of ten buyers would be purchasing paperclips with ten orders, ten checks, ten mailings, etc., the purchase can be accomplished by simpler requisition processes and one order form one site to the vendor.

Record reduction is possible when pruchasing is centralized. Information pertaining to vendors used, files, etc.,is combined at one site rather than having it spread about separate locations. Like the personnel economies, there are also advantages to centralized recordkeeping.

Centralization provides a higher degree of control over the entire buying process in comparison to that found in scattered situations. This control extends to good vendor selection, product monitoring for standardization and value-analysis opportunities, and financial and inventory control. Again, this control also provides the benefit of detecting problem areas not always noticeable or of concern at individual sites.

Decentralization

Many factors favor decentralization, which is the practice of each plant having a purchasing operation. One of the main reasons for this practice exists when each plant has separate and distinct product needs. In this situation, little commonality in products exists between the various plants and there is little opportunity for standardization of goods. Few or no economies would be gained by centralized purchasing. In fact, added administrative time would be necessary for transmitting requisitions to the central office for processing. Also, added transportation expense might be involved if the goods are delivered to the main headquarters and forwarded to the plant.

Special plant needs is another reason why decentralized purchasing often exists. Special engineering, inventory, and coordination needs between the production line and the vendors might only be met when purchasing is at the individual plant. This includes such factors as close links with local vendors, and the need to tightly control the inbound flow of goods with production needs. This is especially true when one plant is producing a product in its growth stage. Special orders, changes in product design, and a fast-paced search for and coordination with an increasing number of suppliers is needed at this point. Heavy engineering involvement in the selection of goods for use in production will require a close communication between production, engineering, and purchasing. This would not always be possible or efficient if purchasing was centralized.

Plant autonomy is also cited as a reason for decentralized purchasing. In this setting, individual plant and/or product-line profitability is more easily determined when all necessary functions are performed at and are on the budget of the individual plant. When a function like purchasing is performed centrally, then a question arises as to how to allocate many of the overhead costs of the central purchasing unit to each and every plant. This problem is avoided when each plant has a purchasing operation under the authority and responsibility of the plant manager. This point is mentioned when firms view each plant as an entity that can or might be sold as a separate business. It is a common rationale used with plants and product lines owned by conglomerates.

The long-run trend appears to be pointing toward centralized purchasing. The ease of data transmission and computer-linked operations enables firms to exercise central control over many of its dispersed operations, and purchasing is just one of these. The need to reduce inventory investment in firms, tighten cash management operations, and utilize buying clout in commodity short periods tends to favor centralized buying. Data transmission links enable a single plant to inform a central office of the need for goods instantaneously, while in the past several days were required for a requisition to travel through the mails. Orders can be combined with other orders and purchased in a single consolidated move with split deliveries being made from the vendor to each plant. This is just one example of how centralized purchasing can take place.

Other Forms of Departmentalization

Purchasing operations can also be organized around other forms of departmentalization rather than merely the centralized versus decentralized forms. Common variations are by product, territory, or function. Buyers and managers are organized in order to attain the advantages of specialization, which are expertise and economy of operation. Product specialization leads to a buyer becoming knowledgeable about a certain material market. Insights into future problems and opportunities will be noted and used to the firm's best advantage. Some firms will functionalize people according to basic product areas, such as raw materials, capital goods, MRO items, etc. Territorial functionalization is often used in order to attain some of the advantages of centralized purchasing while maintaining a regional proximity to the vendor. Some large firms will maintain regional buying offices that serve many plants in a certain geographic area.

Specialization is also possible through function, and this refers to the practice of assigning certain tasks to specific persons. Examples are that some persons will perform strictly buying activities, others will perform only follow-up, and still others will be responsible for inbound verifications and voucher handling. While any form of specialization will lead to some economies, there is a danger of creating skills that are too specific in persons who are difficult to transfer at later points in time. Moderate specialization with periodic rotation will minimize this problem while creating rounded individual skills.

Some hybrid arrangements exist other than pure centralized and decentralized organizations. One such form is referred to as "lead division purchasing." With this system one division performs its own buying rather than use the services of a centralized group. It is an exception found when one plant has major engineering or special product needs different from those of the other plants.

Another variant is a two-tiered system in which each plant has a purchasing operation reporting to the plant manager, but there is also a central group. The central group will procure standard items such as energy, office products, and basic chemicals. These are fairly standardized products that can be purchased with some economy in consolidated quantities. The central group might also handle the processes necessary for import buying. Similarly, central purchasing often has staff personnel who monitor and report any trends in various commodity areas. In this way, a central expertise is maintained with advisory but no line responsibility. In still another context, the two-tiered system might exist with a central staff group to handle pooled or cooperative purchasing for the plants when there are common needs. Automotive equipment is a common example here. MRO items and the disposition of scrap and waste are other examples.

Multi-plant firms almost never have either purely centralized or decentralized purchasing. Typically, some blend of the two systems exists. While there might be a fairly strong centralized group, there will still be many needs for individual plants to purchase some items direct. On the other hand, even in a decentralized setting, there is often reason for some centralized purchasing. One major U.S. firm that is an advocate of decentralized operations recently analyzed and centrally acquired mini-computers for most of its facilities.

Purchasing: Is It Line or Staff?

The distinction between line and staff depends upon the role a function plays within the entire organization. Line activities directly serve the purpose of the firm. Traditional examples are production and sales. Staff activities, on the other hand, support the primary purpose or provide a service to one or more of the line functions. Purchasing has long been considered by management observers as being a staff function within the corporate organization. In this capacity, it serves to acquire goods needed by the production operation. Thus, while production provided form utility functions in creating the goods, purchasing was seen as being supportive to that end.

In wholesaling and retailing settings, however, purchasing is a line function. The primary activity in this type of firm is to obtain goods that will sell in their present form. The only changes made to the product by the firm are perhaps labeling, sorting, grading, tagging, etc. The act of buying in these settings is often done by the same person responsible for the sale of the goods. In this instance, buying has long been recognized as a line activity.

Purchasing also performs a staff role in the functions of value analysis, purchase timing analysis, material specification analysis, standardization efforts, and the development of new transportation options, etc. While these functions do not become part of the actual output of the firm, they do support its cost reduction and quality enhancement requirements.

Within purchasing several line and staff activities can be distinguished. Order processing and buying are key line tasks, which are followed by tracing, expediting, and general order follow-up activities. Voucher preparation and inventory control, while part of the purchasing function, are also seen in this light. On the other hand, staff activities in purchasing do not directly involve daily ordering and inbound goods movement. Some of these include value analysis, buying department policy formulation, employee skill development, and standardization and specification simplification analysis.

The clear distinction between the line versus staff role within the overall organization is blurring as new situations evolve. Purchasing is becoming less and less of a requisition handling and order processing activity; rather it is playing major roles today in production timing, product input, quality, and cash management decisions. As firms adapt to more integrative approaches, emphasis shifts away from the traditional specialization of hierarchical departments such as production, marketing, and finance. Emphasis is placed more upon tight coordination and control of the firm's entire assets in order to succeed in any manner or opportunity that is feasible. Assets include cash, all financial resources, inventories, plants and equipment, skills, information, and products. The firm begins to view itself as a horizontal flow of information and products that are acquired, converted, managed, and moved toward markets. Any activity along this physical or information flow is primary to the purpose of the firm. In this context, purchasing is one of the key line logistics activities needed in this new role of tight coordination.

Ethics and Good Business Practice in Purchasing

One of the first things noticed by new buyers is how they are befriended by a great number of persons, mainly salesmen from vendor firms. This situation often gives rise to problems later for the buyer, if he/she is not careful in the approaches used in relationships with vendors. Many of the key problems often faced by individuals and their employing firms are captured in a series of ethical practices. The National Association of Purchasing Management codified many of these into its Code of Ethics. These statements and other good business practices are covered as follows.

1) Interests of the firm are foremost in all dealings. The firm is the buyer's employer. The relationship of the buyer and manager to the organization is that of agent and principal. This calls for loyalty in deal-

ings between the agent and third parties or vendors and carriers. This concept implicitly indicates that personal gain from vendors in the form of "commissions," gifts, etc. cloud the objectivity necessary in making the best decision for the firm.

2) Buy without preference or prejudice. All vendors, their quality, and price should be considered without unduly favoring some firms or avoiding consideration of others. This again calls for objectivity and open-mindedness in vendor selection. Another point to avoid is conflict of interest where the buyer might have a financial or other personal interest in one vendor.

3) Seek maximum value in purchases. This statement reinforces the overall objective of obtaining the maximum value or the stated quality attributes at the minimum price to the firm.

4) Maintain a sound policy with regard to gifts and employee purchases. Gifts, entertainment, or other favors from vendors are commonplace. Many firms adopt policies with regard to these that tend to view such practices negatively. The cost of any gift is a marketing expense to the vendor that must be recaptured through higher prices to the employing firm. Some firms allow such gifts as long as they do not have any personal value; advertising items such as pens, calendars, paper, etc. fall into this category. Similarly, performing purchasing services for employees is a problem point often raised in firms. While this practice might improve morale by obtaining goods for employees or executives at less than retail price, this can backfire in many ways. For one, it consumes time and effort in the department. For another, there is the problem of how to handle defective goods. This can have a negative impact upon the public relations image of the department within the firm. Overall, these problems are best avoided by prohibiting such practice.

5) Strive for knowledge about materials, processes, and practical methods. This is a reminder to continually inquire into new facets of the needs of the firm. It is also a statement that the buyer should not merely process requisitions and purchase orders, but that positive proactive steps should be taken as well.

6) Be receptive to competent counsel from colleagues. This canon is a similar reminder to be open to new ideas and anything that might improve one's performance for their own development and for the furtherance of the goals of their employer.

7) Counsel and assist other buyers. This is a professional calling to be open in imparting ideas and assisting others in the purchasing area. The hallmark of a professional is to leave his/her chosen field in better condition than when he/she entered it. This means seeking improvements, aiding others, etc.

8) Avoid sharp practice. Sharp practices include misrepresentations in order to gain unfair advantage over a vendor. Similarly, it can mean misleading a vendor in order to induce him/her into providing or performing something. This type of behavior will only come full circle back to the firm in the form of the vendor not wishing to deal with them in the future. Or, worse yet, the vendor might seek like advantage in return.

9) Subscribe to honesty and truth in dealings. This is similar to the sharp practice point, but it also applies in many settings where misrepresentation is not the intended goal of the buyer. Honesty and truth will go far in building and maintaining the integrity of the buyer. It will in turn benefit him or her in the future with like actions from vendors.

10) Respect obligations. Obligations range from meeting appointments with vendors set up well in advance to following through on a verbal understanding with action.

11) Provide prompt and courteous reception to vendors. A vendor's time is often as valuable as that of the buyer on an hourly basis. In some cases it can be more valuable when travel, lodging, and other sales expenses are involved. This canon calls for the prompt reception of salesmen when they call within appointments or when it is not inconvenient for the buyer. This can be a problem when salesmen do not arrange advance appointments and drop in without notice. There is often a violation of this canon in reverse.

The Development of Purchasing Professionals

Another major area that contributes to an effective purchasing organization is the development and management of purchasing professionals. There are several facets to this management task, which includes sourcing of persons, their development versus training, and mobility issues.

Sources of Personnel for Purchasing

Personnel entering the purchasing field have traditionally come from the local area with high school backgrounds. Like those entering the job market in other fields such as banking, the primary entry level activities in purchasing have been clerical in nature. A long-standing practice has been to rotate first level persons through such tasks as follow-up, clerical processing, or basic analysis before promoting them to actual buying activities. This overall practice is slowly giving way to the practice of hiring college-trained personnel with technical or business backgrounds.

College-trained persons entering purchasing are being sought more today due to the technical, logistical, and financial demands of the field. Many firms hire engineers for purchasing so that they can technically perform buying and analytical work on a comparable plane with user departments and vendors. Similarly, purchasing involves large commitments of funds and the use of transportation, warehousing, inventories, and other logistical components. The field is becoming more integrated with production and other functions in the firm. Many of the routine clerical tasks of the past are now in management information system form, thereby enabling purchasing persons to devote more time and effort to positive analytical work. This overall trend will no doubt continue into the future as human resource managers and top management recognize more and more the need for management talent in the purchasing area.

Training and Development of People in Purchasing

Purchasing, like any other field, is changing continually. No longer can a person come into the field with a sound background and expect to function well for an entire career. Changes in a firm's products, their design, the use of computers, and the more integrated nature of purchasing with other functions all call for continual upgrading of personnel skills in the field.

Training is one basic way of building the skills of purchasing people. This is a task-oriented approach with specific skills in mind. Examples are concepts in law, new techniques in information systems, new transportation opportunities, and any other specific knowledge area. It is important for buyers and managers alike to keep abreast of new events and trends in the field. Training is active education in these new areas. It usually consists of attending short seminars, using in-house programs, or other task-oriented programs. It can consist of evening college courses in purchasing or related fields. Some firms use the certification in the National Association of Purchasing Managment as a training medium. The benefit of this is that there is a directed program of study in all phases of purchasing, and there is a tangible measure of attainment through the testing and career evaluation system of the NAPM. Training can also be very informal through a concerted effort of reading many of the field's magazines, journals, and training devices like the NAPM's PAL series.

Development, on the other hand, is the rounded development of the person's management abilities. As one moves to higher positions of responsibility, the specific buying tasks of purchasing involve less of the person's time. Instead, general management skills such as personnel motivation, development, and assignment become more important. Similarly, financial activities through budgeting and planning are encountered more. Further, integrated activities with other departments including planning of the firm's overall direction are necessary. These elements of a manager's background are not training oriented. Instead, they are part of a person's development of management tools and approaches. Personal development is often attained through seeking advanced college degrees or attending executive management programs away from the office.

Personnel Issues in Purchasing

Three key issues exist in the purchasing field today with regard to purchasing professionals. These relate to generalization versus specialization, rotation within purchasing versus other departments, and whether the purchasing person has a career after purchasing.

Generalization Versus Specialization

This is a general management issue that has relevance in purchasing. The question refers to whether purchasing persons should be rotated through many functions, commodity responsibilities, and even locations in order to become familiar with many purchasing situations. On the other hand, persons might remain in relatively narrow areas in order to specialize and hopefully become very efficient at them. The trade-offs with generalization are usually greater movement and training costs as well as the problem of persons not always being efficient at their tasks until they have performed them for some time. The benefits accrued are that persons might transfer knowledge from one area to another that would otherwise not have occurred. Similarly, this expands the breadth of total skills in an entire department, since the situation of only one or a few persons being knowledgeable about specific areas will not exist.

Specialization often provides efficiency of operation. Less effort is expended in moving persons from one job location to another and training them in the new areas. On the other hand, people are less willing today to remain in one spot or one functional area even if their compensation is continually increased. Boredom and the idea of personal career stimulation often makes specialization an option of lesser desirability.

Rotation Versus Career Paths in Purchasing

Another question that arises with greater frequency today than in the past is whether to plan career paths solely within purchasing or to purposely rotate people through other departments of the firm. The common phenomenon in the past was for many people to experience their careers only through various activities within purchasing. The one key aspiration was often to seek the top purchasing position. This practice contains all the specialization benefits noted above.

The rotation alternative is similar to the generalization issue discussed above, except it includes people being rotated through positions in many departments of the firm. It might consist of a person starting in purchasing and progressing to another spot in that department. The next assignment for that person might be in production scheduling, traffic, or marketing. Similarly, people from engineering might be rotated through purchasing as well as persons from production, traffic, finance, or any other department. The drawbacks of the rotation alternative are the mobility and training costs incurred. Further, it might take many months for a new person to be able to function with efficiency in his/her new post. On the other hand, the benefits include the firm experiencing a cross-fertilization of ideas from persons being shifted from one function to the other. Someone from engineering might be able to apply a technique from that area to a problem in purchasing. Similarly, someone from purchasing might be able to improve upon something in production or finance. Another benefit is the familiarization with persons throughout the firm. The rotation practice causes people from all departments to interact with others. This has an effect of breaking down some of the communication barriers between departments which can arise when this practice is not followed.

Where Is Today's Purchasing Person Going?

People are less likely to obtain a job today and remain in that function or firm for the rest of their careers. The two preceding issues presented points that have caused firms to provide generalized experience within a department as well as rotate people through other departments in their careers. In many firms this is done merely to provide some career stimulation to people, even if upward postitions are not plentiful or available. The career path practice of providing only upward positions for people in purchasing might diminish in future years as it is diminishing today in traffic management, distribution, and even production. This will pose a challenge for purchasing as well as the human resource function of firms. Questions will arise as to what paths are appropriate for people who have started in purchasing. Similarly, not many top purchasing managers have progressed into other positions except to become the head of other firm's purchasing departments. The trend toward an integrated materials management function poses an opportunity for purchasing people. This opens the way for movement into materials management and distribution. On a combined basis, these functions often include such other areas as transportation, warehousing, inventory control, production scheduling, packaging, forecasting, materials handling, customer service management, and order processing.

Conclusion

An effective purchasing organization can only be defined once its purpose, goals, and objectives are defined. Further, all the informational tools available must support these roles and complement the motivation they are seeking to create. These then become included within the performance measurement and decision-making information systems used in the firm. In summary, the form of an organization and its supporting information systems must follow from the functions they are to perform.

Key issues facing purchasing in the 1980s include the transfer pricing of its activities as well as integrating information sytems with the rest of the firm. The costs of capital and energy cannot tolerate the comfortable "cushions" of large inventories at the beginning of production and on the outbound side. Nor can the firm use premium transportation to make up for service failures or lax planning. The entire firm is gradually shifting toward an integrated whole with all components that deal with the physical flow and control flow being tightly linked together. Information is that linking mechanism. Another trend in the field is the changing nature of people and how they regard their careers. This has broad implications for purchasing as it deals with questions of specialization, job rotation, and integrated career goals and paths involving other functions.

SOURCES FOR FURTHER READING

Brown Arthur W. "Technical Support for Procurement." *Journal of Purchasing and Materials Management*, 12 (1976): 8.
Corey, E. Raymond, "Should Companies Centralize Procurement?" *Harvard Business Review*, 56 (November-December 1978): 102.
Dowst, Somerby, "Profile of a Purchasing Pro" *Purchasing*, 29 April, 1982, p. 48.
     "When Should Buyers Pick Up the Tab?" *Purchasing*, 16 April 1981, p. 97.
     "Xerox Centralizes Buys for Cost Fight." *Purchasing*, 7 October 1982, p. 56.

Dubinsky, Alan J., and Gwin, John M. "Business Ethics: Buyers and Sellers." *Journal of Purchasing and Materials Management,* 17 (1981): 9.

Giunipero, Larry C. "Entry Level Purchasing—Demand and Requirements. *Journal of Purchasing and Materials Management* 18 (1982): 10.

Temin, Thomas R. "Purchasing at Uniroyal Takes new Approach." *Purchasing,* 7 October 1982, p. 61.

Woodside, Arch G., and Samuel, David M. "Observations of Centralized Corporate Procurement." *Industrial Marketing Management* 10 (1981): 191.

QUESTIONS FOR REVIEW

1. Why does purchasing report fairly high in an organization?

2. Does a title always indicate the specific responsibilities and functions of a purchasing person? Why or why not?

3. What arguments can be made for centralized purchasing?

4. Why do some firms practice decentralized purchasing even if the economics of purchasing point to the centralized form?

5. For what reasons are there mixes or hybrid organizations that are neither centralized nor decentralized?

6. Is purchasing a line or staff function? Why is there a tendency to see it more as a line function today?

7. Why is objectivity a key requirement in purchasing?

8. How do personal purchases create a purchasing conflict?

9. Can a buyer be objective if he or she owns stock in a vendor company?

10. Why is there more of an emphasis upon college-trained persons for entry level purchasing persons today?

11. Should purchasing persons be specialists or generalists?

12. State the pro and con arguments for developing and maintaining a specialty career only within purchasing?

22

CHAPTER OBJECTIVES

After reading this chapter you should:

- Understand the basic need for performance measurement in purchasing and materials management.

- Be able to utilize the various tools in purchasing activity and cost measurement.

- Appreciate the role of budgeting in purchasing.

- Understand the need for periodic audits of a purchasing organization.

Measuring Purchasing Performance

Introduction

Purchasing performance is approached and measured in many ways. This chapter explores the individual measures that can be used to determine different facets of buyers' and departmental performance. Examined first are ways in which materials managers are generally measured for performance results. This discussion is followed by reviews of some specific measures that are used to evaluate purchasing activity and individual performance. Basic concepts of budgeting in the purchasing function are presented along with a review of management information systems needed to perform this activity properly. Finally, how other interfacing departments of the firm view purchasing performance is covered.

Concerns of Materials Management

Two contemporary topics concern the current materials manager. These topics are: 1) the establishment of managerial performance measures, and 2) the use of the quality circles.

Performance Measurement

The materials manager must seek operational procedures to determine measurement objectives. To bring these objectives into further focus for day-to-day use, various measures are used. Table 22-1 presents some of the objectives used by materials managers as discovered by a recent survey.

Materials management in many cases includes purchasing. For this reason several traditional purchasing measures are included. In other settings, purchasing and materials managers are equal peers, reporting to manufacturing or another executive level. Organizational relationships are not all uniform, and they are still evolving.

Materials management performance measurement is highly internal in nature. The immediate downstream customer of this function is either production or merchandising. Deliveries, stockouts, and subsequent product unit costs are highly dependent upon the skills of the materials manager. Many trade-offs must be balanced here, some that are direct and others that are inverse. The minimization of one measure,

□ **TABLE 22–1.** *Evaluation of Materials Managers*

Measure	Percent of Materials Managers Reporting This Measure for Evaluation
Inventory levels	87%
On-time deliveries	80
Stockouts	71
Purchased materials cost	69
Transportation cost	53
Ware house cost	29
Customer complaints	27
Profitablility	20
Other	16
Manufacturing cost	7

□ *Source*: Somerby Dowst, "Financial Rewards Keep Savings Coming," *Purchasing*, 23 October 1980, p. 78A7.

such as cost, might come only at the expense of another measure, such as stockouts. Performance and productivity measurement technology has not yet broken the barrier of multiple objectives. Complicating this are costs that are reported in accounting data streams that lead directly to the top of the firm. This information weakness often forces individual managers to optimize short-term costs in lieu of other measures which are not always emphasized as strongly. Much more behavioral, costing and information reporting research is needed before major advances are made in this area.

Quality Control Circles

Much has been printed in recent years about the advent of quality control circles. The materials and purchasing manager is at the heart of this phenomenon. The idea of quality circles is to seek improvements from a broad range of people in the firm in order to build quality into a product and thereby greatly reduce postproduction inspection.

A quality control circle is a continuous group in the workplace composed of volunteers ranging from workers, supervisors, and engineers to staff personnel. "Unrecognized" quality or productivity problems are brought to the attention of the group. Through broad representation and input, problems can be attacked that heretofore were known by or were limited to a small number of persons in one function.

In Japan, there are national competitions among groups. These competitions are seen as a way of developing the talents of persons involved in them. They can be successful in resolving some problems that are rarely approached because they fall in a managerial no-man's land where no one manager would see a personal gain for solving it.

Quality circles are a primary opportunity area for purchasing and materials management problems. This approach can be used to resolve some of the multiple objectives problems discussed in the previous sections as well as being a primary input to value analysis (see Chapter 12).

It is a key communication and problem-solving approach that can bridge marketing, production, and purchasing.

Measures of Purchasing Performance

There is no one measurement that captures the entire nature of either individual or departmental performance. Each specific measure provides insights into one or a limited number of actual performance attributes. The most common measurements fall into four basic groups: 1) activity, 2) cost, 3) efficiency, and 4) impact upon other areas. These are presented along with an analysis of what each seeks to determine and how they affect behavior in the buying area.

Activity measures capture features of actual tasks used in purchasing. Major ones in this area are as follows.

1. Number of purchase orders per period. This measure indicates how many actual orders were placed in a given time period. In one way it is a measure of how fast buyers were able to process orders. In this manner, it is a measure of individual and collective work activity. One problem with this approach is that it can appear that efficiency is dropping if several large capital projects consume much of the department's time during a period. Further, in a season when overall purchasing activity drops back, this measure can be interpreted by some as a drop in departmental efficiency. Or taken to an extreme, buyers can split requisitions into two or more orders to appear efficient with this single measure.
2. Dollars committed per purchase order. This measure presents the average dollar amount per purchase order. A low average dollar per order measure points to possible need to examine the system for consolidation opportunities. This measure can be used in conjunction with the previous one as a check against the practice of writing too many orders in order to boost the number-of-orders productivity measure.
3. Stratification of purchase order dollar quantities. This is a more detailed breakdown of the previous measure. An example might be as follows:

Dollar Amount of PO	Number of PO's
Up to $50	307
$50–$500	273
$500–$1,000	198
$1,000–$10,000	94
$10,000 and up	15
Total	887

This shows exactly the dollar amount groupings of the individual purchase orders.

4. Number of blanket orders or systems contracts per period. This measure indicates how many contracts or arrangements have been initiated or are in force during a month, quarter, half-year, or year. This measure is usually one that is to be maximized. An arrangement of this sort can be used to reduce many of the less than $500 orders shown in the breakdown of purchase activity in Item 3.
5. Number of orders/requisitions placed against contracts. Long-term contracts and systems contracts generally contain provisions for individual orders or requisitions to be placed against them. A measure of the number of these individual orders indicates the degree to which they are being used or are avoiding the need for regular purchase orders.
6. Percentage of requisitions processed in various time periods. This is a measure of administrative lead time, or the time taken by the department to process requisitions into actual orders transmitted to vendors. This can be stated as a single average of, say, 1.52 days, or it can be presented in a grouped form as follows.

Days	Number of Orders Processed
1	37
2	12
3	9
	58

Weighted average = 1.52 days

This measure directs attention toward the two or three day orders. It might show that only certain buyers were the problem, or it might show that these were very difficult orders to process. Care should be taken in this type of measure to not include capital acquisition orders. These are large, one-time orders which often take many weeks. Inclusion of one or a few of these in this measurement would unduly skew the perceived performance of the entire department.

7. Percent of orders issued without firm prices. Many orders must be placed without a firm price known at the time. While this is often necessary from an expediency standpoint, it leaves the firm open to unknown price obligations. Some purchasing managers view this practice as being sloppy; that is, buyers might do this to simplify or speed up the order process for them. On the whole, this measure should be minimized. It can also be shown in terms of total dollars of commitment issued without known price rather than number or percent of total orders.
8. Percent of overdue orders. The number of late orders indicates vendor performance failure or poor time estimating and follow-up activities on the part of the buyer. Knowing that this is a measure of their individual performance, buyers will tend to minimize this experience.

Cost measures attempt to capture other facets of performance. These measures relate to the actual expenditures and the management of the firm's financial resources under purchasing's control.

1. Actual-to-budget expenditures. Budgets are established in advance of each period. They consist of expected or target expenditure levels for purchasing and all other departments. A comparison of actual expenditures against the budgeted amounts shows either a) below or better performance, b) on target performance, or c) higher or worse performance. The differences between actual and budgeted amounts are called variances. Actual-to-budget expenditure performance cannot be viewed in terms of dollar amounts alone. As Exhibit 22-1 shows, a cost overrun must be considered in light of the actual quantities or volumes of purchases. That is, the cost "overrun" might be from price increases, larger than expected quantities purchased, or a combination of price and quantity increases. A budget variance showing a cost overrun is not fair to the buyer if the total cost increase was due to higher than planned sales and production needs.

2. Standard-to-target prices. This measure illustrates only the price experience in the previous concept. Some firms develop reports on every product with regard to budgeted or standard price versus actual price paid during the period. In periods of changing prices, the actual price is often either an average or the last price paid. While the absolute amounts of many of these prices is informative in and of themselves, it is often useful to translate these price differences into indices similar to the approaches presented in the index section of this chapter. These indices show the relative or percent change in prices. This is valuable when comparing a $1.00 price increase in two products. Product A might have changed from $100 to $101, which is

■ **EXHIBIT 22-1.** *Illustration of Budget-to-Actual Cost Performance*

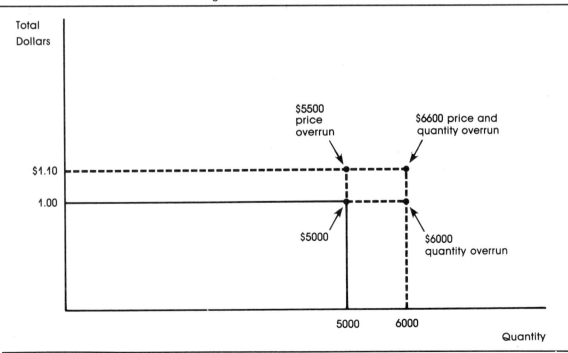

only a one percent increase, whereas with Product B a similar increase from $4 to $5 represents a twenty-five percent increase.

3. Purchasing outlays to revenue dollars. The total purchase costs of goods acquired for production and reselling are often compared to the total revenue of the firm. In Chapter 1 it was shown how this averages about fifty-seven percent for all firms, but it is higher for petroleum and chemicals and lower for instruments, etc. This percent figure can be perceived as one that the purchasing manager should minimize. However, this figure will drop in periods of purchase material stability while the firm enjoys a seller's market for its own goods. On the other hand, this measure can present the purchasing manager in a bad light if he or she bought at the same prices from one year to the next, but in the second year sales of the firm dropped.

4. Administrative expense to firm revenues or purchase outlays. This measure can be captured and reported in either way. The basic concept is to report the administrative expense of the purchasing department in relation to either the firm's revenues or the total dollar expenditures for raw materials. Perhaps the more stable measure is that of the firm's revenue. This might not fluctuate as widely as purchase outlays from one year to the next.

5. Dollars committed (outstanding and past). Another key measure useful in purchasing management is the sum of total dollars currently outstanding in the form of purchase orders, orders received but not yet paid for, and total payments made to date. It shows the status of the entire budget expenditure authorization for the period.

6. Negotiated savings. Some firms measure the amount of savings that have resulted from negotiations. This can be measured by the difference between a predetermined regular price, or budgeted standard price, and the final price actually negotiated for particular goods. Though this appears to provide an objective for purchasing managers to maximize, this measure is subject to manipulation by inflating the base or initial price. It might even be an unrealistic one. The final negotiated price is then a figure that is much lower than the initial one. A variant of this approach is to compare only currently negotiated prices over previous year actual prices paid. This serves to reduce the ability to unduly inflate the initial price figure.

7. Savings from forward buying. This measure is the difference between the expected prices for goods and the amount paid by exercising forward buying options. Forward buying savings arise from buying in larger than normal lot sizes or buying earlier than planned. Though this measure is worthwhile for buyers to maximize, it does not relate all the other costs resulting in the firm from the forward buy. These costs are: increased capital tied up, inventory costs, warehousing costs, and increased obsolescence.

8. Scrap and waste proceeds. Purchasing becomes a disposition and sales activity with regard to scrap and waste. Some firms apply a measure of the amount of dollars obtained from the sales or transferring of scrap and waste goods. This seeks to have purchasing managers maximize their efforts in this regard. This figure will naturally

depend not only upon the abilities of the purchasing manager in charge of this activity, but it will also fluctuate with the amount of the firm's scrap and waste as well as the markets for these resources.

Efficiency is another area of purchasing that is evaluated through different measures. These measures attempt to present insights into how well the overall purchasing activity is performing. Some of these measures are as follows.

1. Material quality. This measure can be reported in any number of ways. It might be the total amount of production problems resulting from poor quality items acquired, or it might be a percentage of product failures on the production line or items returned from customers. Or, still, it can be the number or percent of units rejected from use on production.
2. Value-analysis efforts. The savings or other improvements obtained through value-analysis efforts might be reported periodically to top management. In this realm, the report might show total effort expended or effort expended and savings or improvements attained. By showing savings or improvements, problems might arise as to which department is to obtain credit for each and every change. This measure is perhaps best reported by the entire team involved with the effort. On the other hand, if it was just reported in terms of purchasing department time and effort expended in value-analysis projects alone, it might be perceived that only efforts are being expended without corresponding benefits being received by the department.
3. Standardization savings. This activity often results in savings from reduced inventories, simplified purchasing, volume purchasing economies, shifts to blanket ordering from the requisition-purchase order process, etc. These efforts and savings are subject to the same reporting problems as value analysis.
4. Service performance to the firm. The percentage of all orders that were received on time in terms of the promised date given by user departments on requisition acknowledgements is another measure often captured and reported as part of departmental performance. This measure might only induce purchasing to unduly pad the lead time promised user departments.

Impacts upon other departments resulting from purchasing practices or failures are often measured and reported as departmental performance items. There is one primary measure found in this area and it is as follows.

1. Number of production schedule shifts caused by nonavailability of goods. This measure reports the number of late deliveries or poor timing performance of purchasing as reflected in changes in production schedules from goods not being on-hand when needed. Some firms go so far as to quantify these negative impacts in terms of dol-

lar penalties through higher unit production costs, lost opportunity of machinery and manpower, etc. For this type of system to be objective, purchasing must be a part of the scheduling process in the first place. The penalty costs must also be verifiable and relate directly to the late deliveries.

Performance measures can be developed and reported for just about any specific activity or function. Each one has a strength that others do not possess. Performance measures tend to be behavior modifiers. When a person knows that his or her superior is using a certain measure for evaluation purposes, he/she will tend to maximize performance within it. Problems will often arise when only one or a few of these measures are used. Persons will tend to optimize their performance within these measures alone and minimize with regard to overall impacts elsewhere. A classic example of this occurred in the 1950s with the Russian farm development programs. Tractor operators were measured on the number of acres plowed per day. As a result, the government was able to show how plowed acreage increased dramatically from one year to the next. But, this was accomplished on many farms by setting the plow to two inch depths instead of the original ten to twelve inch settings. Similarly, many manufacturing people in the U.S. can cite examples of how output is maximized to the detriment of quality.

Performance measures should be balanced and congruent with the overall objectives sought by the department and the firm as a whole. It makes little sense to have the purchasing department seek only minimized purchase price only to cause poor quality materials to be bought that serve to increase costs in other departments and eventually reduce the overall sales revenue of the firm. This congruency concept requires the use of multiple measures and objectives. Trade-off situations arise here because the measures and objectives of other departments must be considered.

A final problem with having some of the above measures and objectives imposed upon specific department managers is that the results of some of these processes do not get captured in the firm's accounting system. Value analysis and standardization efforts and benefits are two key examples. These processes will cost the purchasing department money in the form of manpower, travel, staff analysis, etc. On the other hand, many of the benefits derived from them are inventory reductions, simplification in order processes, and many other tangibles and intangibles not always captured in the accounting or budgetary systems. That is, many costs for these efforts are reported, but the benefits are "soft" and not always obvious in the prime measurement systems. This phenomenon can discourage participation or efforts in some of these areas.

Budgeting for Purchasing

Budgeting is a major administrative activity of top purchasing managers. The purchasing budget is an important one, since a very large part of the firm's total cash outlays is for the acquisition of raw materials. The budget is the prime financial communications medium within firms. It is used to direct managerial activity, measure actual performance against planned performance, and promote communication and coordination throughout the firm.

Purchasing plays a major role in the overall master budget of a firm. Exhibit 22-2 shows prime components of the firm's master budget. This budget is initiated or stems from a sales budget that sets the stage for all the other activities of the firm. The current ending inventory can be used against sales, with production being needed to produce the remaining demanded units throughout the period. The production budget defines the amounts of materials, labor, and factory overhead needed during the coming period. The purchasing department is mainly concerned with the materials budget.

The materials budget is derived from the statement of finished goods units that production will be producing during the period. Purchasing must then work back through bills of materials in order to determine the exact amount of specific goods that will be required in the period. A key data requirement here is the timing of the needed goods. Ideally, basic production information will provide purchasing with indications of when the various goods will be needed. Purchasing may then consolidate the bills of materials to determine the consolidated needs for all goods. That is, a certain fastener might be needed on Products A, H, M and Y. This recasts all the finished goods requirements into grouped raw material requirements so that bulk purchase opportunities, negotiating potential, and quantity-price information may be developed.

Purchasing must then predict or project the prices or total cash requirements for these material purchases. This task is performed in one of two basic ways. First is the aggregated method, which starts with a total finished goods requirement and an estimate of materials price changes from the last period to the next. In this setting, an aggregate cost of each unit is projected using last year's information and an estimate of total cost change since then. The estimate might consist of, say, a seven percent increase in all prices of all components needed for a product. This is used to project the cash requirement for the coming year. The other method attempts to project cash requirements through estimates of prices on all individual components. Each finished good item is "built up" with individual parts prices. This method is more detailed and requires more time and effort, but it is more accurate. The index number techniques presented in Chapter 6 are frequently used to determine the extent of cost increases from past periods and to project future ones for coming periods.

Purchasing is involved in this process in several ways. First is the preparation of the budget for materials and the cash outlays that will be needed for them. This is the primary budget. Second, purchasing administrative expenses are generally included within the firm's overall administrative expense budget. In purchasing, about three-quarters of this total administrative expense is for departmental wages and salaries. This is often followed by fringes, travel, data and communications, and miscellaneous expenses. These administrative expenses are generally

■ **EXHIBIT 22-2.** *A Master Budget*

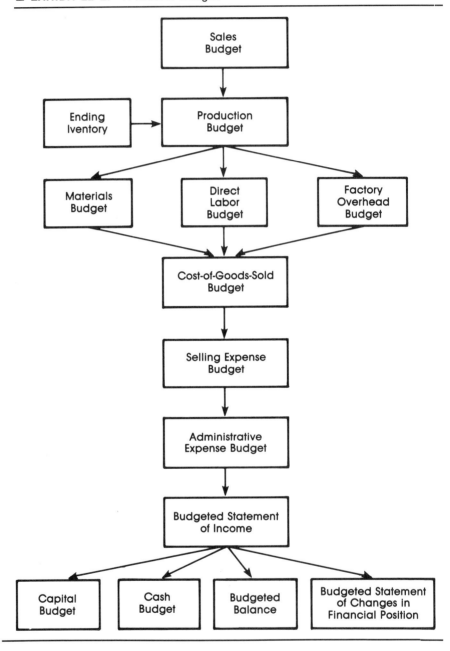

fixed, with travel and communications (phone) being two that can vary somewhat throughout the year.

A third way in which purchasing affects this process is through the cash budget. The timing of purchases and the financial commitments made in long-term arrangements directly impacts upon the firm's cash budget. Fourth is the capital budget. The prices that will be paid and the timing of acquisitions in this area are largely affected by decisions made in purchasing. Often, purchasing will be asked for estimates of capital goods costs at the beginning of the period so that various departments may make up their budgets for capital acquisitions. Thus, purchasing provides preliminary input to other departments' budgets. The actual prices later paid by purchasing will then be reflected back into these individual departmental budgets. Fifth, purchasing affects the production budget through MRO acquisitions. Sixth is input to the initial sales budget. Purchasing might be aware of pending price or commodity supply problems that would affect the final goods price or quantity the firm could supply to the market. This is basic information that should be provided to those who prepare the initial sales budget, since this is what drives the creation of the other ones.

Purchasing is primarily responsible for the direct materials budget throughout the period. Variances might be created through differences in price, volumes, or combinations of these. The final internal impacts of these variances will vary depending upon the structure of responsibility established by the firm. This is largely dependent upon the transfer price mechanism and any productivity measures used to supplement the behavior of this and any interfacing departments.

Index Numbers: Tools for Budgeting and Forecasting

Forecasts provide some direction for the different departments in the firm for future operational decisions. Budgeting is one of the basic managerial functions in each department. The forecast often serves to define the budgets for future periods, and each department is often asked for some input of future costs and activities so that the overall business firm budget may be prepared.

Index numbers are useful tools to apply in this budgeting process. This mathematical body of knowledge assists purchasing managers in explaining the general events in past periods and helps simplify the dollar requirement projections necessary in upcoming budgeting processes.

Cost Changes in Raw Materials

One use of index numbers is to determine the relative change in raw material prices. For example, a buyer is analyzing a material that currently costs $2.09 per unit. In 1983 the price was $1.97 and in 1982 it was $1.80 when it was first purchased by the firm. The simple index number to explain this price trend changes the absolute prices into relative figures through the following approach.

$$\frac{\text{Current Price}}{\text{Base Period Price}} \times 100 = \text{Year Index Number}$$

The following table shows how the total $.29 price increase appears in a relative sense.

Year	Price	Index
1982	$1.80	100
1983	1.97	109
1984	2.09	116

Another way of explaining the $.29 increase is to state that since the base year the price has risen sixteen percent. Another product with a different base price but with a $.29 price increase over the three-year period would be either higher or lower in percentage price increase. This tool will highlight which products are experiencing price increases of greater relative degrees than others. It reduces actual price changes into percent changes.

Price Change Analysis With Differing Product Mix

Another use of index numbers can be used to illustrate the total cost effect of raw material price increases and changes in material mix over a period of time. To illustrate, a product requires four raw material items that have changed in mix since 1978. The following table illustrates this analysis.

Item	1978 Price	1983 Price	'83 Quant.	'78 Price @ '78 Quant.	'83 Price @ '83 Quant.
A	$ .10	$ .18	20 lbs.	$ 2.00	$ 3.60
B	6.00	15.00	1 lb.	6.00	15.00
C	.75	1.00	3 lbs.	2.25	3.00
D	.40	1.35	5 lbs.	2.00	6.75
				12.25	28.35

$$\text{Index} = \frac{\$28.35}{12.15} \times 100 = 231.4$$

The individual item indices were 180, 250, 133, and 338, but the combined total based upon the quantities used in 1983 is 231.4. The total provides insights into the price increases on raw materials for the entire product. The individual ones point to those items that perhaps should come under closer analysis for reduction in use or replacement. That is, items B and D are the two that cause the entire index to climb the most. This type of analysis also highlights which elements or raw materials might be first reviewed for value-analysis study.

Comparison of Specific Item to General Price Index

Another useful analytical tool is an index number comparing the price changes in a specific product to those in the general product category. For example, a buyer notes that the specific commodity he/she buys has an index number in 1983 of 188.2 from a base of 100 in 1977. The overall price index for all products in that same vendor industry climbed to 234.8. A comparison index can be determined using the following formula.

Comparative Price Change
= Index of Special Commodity × 100

Index of All in Same Group

$$= (188.2/234.8) \times 100$$
$$= 80.2$$

This example shows how the price of the specific item in the general product line has climbed at a rate lower than that of the entire group. This might pose a danger to buyers in future periods. Products experiencing price changes similar to this might eventually be dropped by some vendors in order to make way for newer products with greater market strength.

On the other hand, if the index was greater than 100 then a buyer's attention is directed toward those products that should undergo substitution, replacement, or value-analysis study. It also points to the few products in an entire range that will require close scrutiny for price control through negotiation, etc.

This tool is useful in comparing an index of a specific commodity against general price level trends. The series of yearly indices then shows how the price level might have changed in a constant dollar context without inflation effects.

Purchasing Power Index

Another way of relating price changes to the purchasing budget process is by determining the relative buying power of dollars today in comparison to a past period. For example, a product has a current price index of 118 in comparison to 1977 of 100. This can be shown another way in terms of how much the buying power of the firm has dropped during this same period with respect to this commodity. It is done with the following formula.

$$\text{Purchasing Power Index} = \frac{\text{Index of Specific Commodity}}{\text{Index of All in Same Group}} \times 100$$
$$= (100/118) \times 100$$
$$= 84.7$$

This shows that the firm's purchasing power is only about eighty-five percent of what it was in the base year with respect to the commodity in question. This tool is sort of a reverse way of viewing the first index presented. The list of products to study is highlighted according to those that are the lowest on the list.

Purchasing Management Information Systems

Organizations communicate and function on the basis of information. It is the prime medium by which different groups and departments react, function, and proact. Data is the lowest denominator of information. It is the measure, notation, observation, or other item that records something. Information is data put into a useful context for decision making or action. Data and information are dealt with in three basic ways in purchasing. First is forms, which are the basic data documents of purchasing. Forms are used for a variety of purposes in the operation and control activities of the department. Second is reports, which are summary documents indicating the need for possible corrective action or for compilation of routine activity statistics. Third is management information systems, which are any information compilation, treatment, and reporting processes designed for specific objectives.

Forms constitute the basic information needs of a purchasing operation. They serve a variety of purposes, some of which are: to report or inform, request, record, instruct, follow-up, authorize, cancel, order, apply, acknowledge, estimate, route, schedule, and claim. Many forms are used in purchasing. It is good practice to conduct audits upon forms with an eye toward simplifying, eliminating, or removing problems that arise with them. Some functional considerations about forms are: 1) they should follow the flow and sequence of the work involved, and 2) they should be designed with the information needed in mind and how to achieve the desired action by the target persons to whom it is sent, the method of identifying the form, and the copies and distribution of each one.

Reports needed and used in purchasing revolve around the monitoring of order progress, the triggering of action at needed points in time, and the capturing of buyer performance and activity. Some common reporting systems are discussed as follows.

Open Order Status

Order status is often reported in detail for each order as well as in summary form. Open orders are those that are currently outstanding with the goods expected to arrive sometime in the future. The open order status detail acts as a "tickler" device to prompt follow-up communication with vendors to assure the goods will be received at an expected time.

Buyer's Activity

A summary is made of all the activities of each buyer. This includes orders placed, order cycle time performance of vendors selected, price variances, exceptions items, and any other information needed to capture the full realm of buyer activity.

Vendor Delivery Rating

The vendor delivery rating is valuable for the future selection of vendors. The data captured for this report system includes vendor name, plant, product, quantities ordered, prices paid versus expected, quality, order cycle times, order-to-receipt time performance, and any knowledge relating to other plants of the firm buying from each vendor. This is the key system for noting the quality of each vendor. It is useful in the vendor selection decision.

Commodity Report

This report can be captured in simple form with regard to the basic commodities or products purchased. It contains much of the same information as the vendor rating system, except it is referenced by commodity. The prime information generally included here is commodity, vendors, price history, supply problems (if any), and notes on pending problems or expected changes.

Vendor Sortation for Entire Firm

Some multi-plant and decentralized firms make periodic information sortings by vendor. This report gives a listing by vendor of commodities purchased, general experience with them, total dollars or units involved, and any other information deemed important to the firm. The value of this sortation is to highlight those vendors that the firm might have greater buying power with than originally thought by each separate buyer or plant. The collective volume of business given to a vendor can provide negotiating potential or increased strength to specific buyers at different sites. One major diversified firm found that up to the point in time of conducting this type of informational sort, two of its plants were actually competing against each other for capacity on one vendor's production line but neither was aware of it.

Management information system (MIS) is a term that applies to any data and information collection, processing, and reporting system. It is often used in computerized settings, though this is not a requirement for a management information system to exist. The basic tenant of MIS is that the prime objective of information needs to be defined by each department and activity center. The form of the entire information system then follows from the functions required. This frequently requires an entire audit of the firm's information and control flow processes. Many of the above forms and reports are potentially convertible to computer memory and transmission. Wherever there are repetitive data handlings, complex serial numbers that can be misread, or voluminous files, there is the potential for streamlining the information into computerized memory. It is common to have follow-up reports printed from a computer one or two days prior to the actual planned date of follow-up. Similarly, a purchase order can be entered into a file system with all the vendor, product, price, etc. information only to be sorted out at a later point in time.

Measuring Purchasing Impacts Upon the Rest of the Firm

Purchasing activities also impact upon other departments in the firm. Consequently, these other departments are in a position to evaluate purchasing activity. In fact, many of purchasing's impacts upon other departments are sometimes a part of the formal evaluation criteria of purchasing performance. An examination of some of these interfacing impacts and measures is presented here within the contexts of the departments affected by purchasing decisions.

Accounting

Accounting is concerned with cash management. Of concern here are purchasing's expenditures in total as well as the timing of the cash flow. Purchasing's annual budget is segregated into monthly, quarterly, or other period segments, and is often stated in terms of either order placements, goods receipts, or cash disbursement commitments. The cash commitments are the dates accounting will have to disburse funds. These commitments are for each order or for periodic payments on long-term contracts. Accounting must be aware of these commitments in order to take advantage of payment discounts and meet obligations as well as to optimally manage the firm's funds within light of cash investment opportunities. The firm can often lend funds overnight, or for just a few days, over periods of several weeks or longer. The key is to maintain as low a cash balance as possible in order to earn interest while not penalizing the firm's credit standing.

Finance

The finance department is concerned with purchasing actions that impact upon the financial position of the firm. Key factors looked at here are the investment in inventories, and the impact inventories have upon the working capital of the firm. (Key financial indicators were presented in Chapter 1.)Forward buying will often cause inventories to increase while creating the need to disburse funds earlier than normal. Forward buying can cause a form of investment of company funds. The benefit of this decision can only be made in light of other investment opportunities for the same cash.

Materials Management and Production

Materials management and production are concerned with inventory availability and the cost of the goods. While the finance department might not look favorably upon a forward buy decision, production often welcomes it because it boosts the availability of inventory while reducing the transferred price for the goods. Thus, a forward buy can reduce the final goods price for production. Here, two different departments will regard the same decision by purchasing in a different light. Another factor of concern here is product quality. Quality pertains to the ease of using the material or parts on the production line without breakage, waste, or scrap.

Transportation

Inbound traffic management looks to purchasing to inform it of the timing, quantities, and inbound origins of product flow. Traffic can often match up outbound movements with inbound moves and thus efficiently take advantage of roundtrip moves. Similarly, traffic needs to schedule inbound unloading dock space and personnel. It is necessary to optimally utilize daily worker abilities without undue surprises that result in overtime or payment for hours in which there is no work.

Marketing

Marketing looks to purchasing decisions as they affect the product quality, aesthetics, or any factor relating to materials that is a concern of customers.

User Departments

Requisitioners of goods look to purchasing for a variety of factors that include quality, landed cost to the user (transferred price), timing, arrival when planned, any deviations from the original request or acknowledgement, the percent of the time that purchasing reliably obtains the goods when desired, and information assistance and cooperation. User departments are the customers of purchasing. Every action or inaction by purchasing impacts upon its customer service and "public relations image" with these other departments of the firm.

Audit of Purchasing Activities of the Firm

Accountants and other top management personnel will often conduct examinations or audits of each department. In the accounting cycle processes, audits of inventories have been commonplace for many decades. The rationale behind this action is twofold: one, to reconcile the physical count of inventories with ledger amounts, and two, to examine the process, controls, and accountability for them. Purchasing often undergoes management audits to affirm good control practices or detect areas where various practice might be loose and possibly create problems for the firm. The primary goals of auditors are to determine that sound practices are followed, to ascertain that these practices and policies are adhered to, and to prove that purchases are being made in light of the primary interests of the firm.[1]

Areas of concern to auditors are many. One of the key initial areas of examination is the purchasing charter. This is the statement that top management made to purchasing to specify its responsibilities and authorities. These charters pertain to buying limits, commodity areas, purchases that require multiple or committee authorization, budgetary authority that permits hiring with or without other departmental authorization, international sourcing ability, or any other management mandate. Many firms grow in volume and personnel without ever considering the need for such a document. The charter is important, if for no other reason than to clearly provide the head of purchasing with actual authority to legally commit the firm to its normal purchase activity obligations.

The existence of a policy manual is another area of examination by auditors. Policy manuals are useful for several reasons. For one, policy manuals outline the various activities involved in the department. A typical manual starts with primary definitions of terms, roles of various forms, and what and when different functions are to take place. Policy manuals are also useful in delineating responsibilities and authorities. Specific signing limits might be indicated according to job title. Job classifications and descriptions of duties are often included in them. Policy manuals are also useful in defining relationships with other departments. This can range from the processes to be followed when requisitioning something from purchasing to the role of purchases for employees, as well as back-door selling practices (discussed later in this chapter). Manuals also define procedures and act both as training devices as well as references for questions anyone might have with regard to the processes to be followed in routine or problem purchase situations.

Signing authorities are another facet of auditing. These are the dollar limits each person or persons with specific job titles have the authority to obligate the firm to on their own. This is generally a relatively low dollar amount per purchase order for assistant buyers, with increasing amounts for higher job titles. Further, the ability to create and sign contracts and blanket orders is found with higher positions. There might be a limit for any one person in the department whereby one or more signatures from top management might be necessary for very large single transactions. Capital asset acquisitions are an example. Some firms require the department seeking the asset to sign for any capital item over a certain dollar amount along with a capital asset committee authorization.

Requisition authority from each user department is often examined in audits. This authority prevents anyone in the firm from acquiring goods or services through purchasing. It is common practice for each department head to sign a requisition with perhaps a finance officer of the entire department to cosign it as well. This is done for accountability purposes as well as to keep track of departmental budget amounts.

Vendor selection is another item of examination in an audit. What is sought here is a procedure or process that, if followed, will assure objectivity in vendor selection. This practice prevents undue preference or prejudice in the selection of sources for the firm. Problem examples might be vendors whose owners are related to top purchasing personnel or firms in which the purchasing officer has a large ownership of stock, etc. This area is also reviewed to make sure that a few vendors are not always selected without periodically analyzing others on the market.

Document control is carefully examined in an audit. This is performed by tracing the flow of all documents involved from the original requisition through to the final invoice payment to a vendor. Of concern here is the potential problem of goods being diverted to unauthorized areas, changes being made in the order without authorizations, overpayments without authorization, and any possible taking of product or payment of funds to persons or firms not entitled to receive them.

Separation of authority is a key element of proper resource control. It prevents the ability to divert funds or goods through the proper legal channels of the firm. In purchasing a separation is desired between purchasing, receiving and inspection, and accounts payables. Separation of authority tends to assure that goods ordered are received and properly paid for.

The auditing process will look into some seemingly unorthodox areas as well. One area noted is whether records are accessible or not. Another is whether there are few or no shifts in vendors. A further negative signal to auditors is when persons in purchasing rarely take vacations or sick days and put in many long hours. Further, buyers or purchasing managers living beyond their apparent means is another item of examination. While no one of these factors is a problem in and of itself, collectively they point to the possible situation of a purchasing person using his or her authority and position to further their own personal ends to the detriment of the company.

Auditors will begin their examination with a review of the purchasing charter and policy manual. The manual should be a form of administrative regulations that follow from the charter. Of concern here is whether the manual is up to date and followed. Sample requisitions and orders will be traced to assure that a sound practice is being followed and is the same as defined in the manual. Questions will arise if a manual does not exist or if it is out of date, even if the office is functioning efficiently and without potential problem areas.

Audits are a good practice for purchasing to conduct internally before an outside auditing team reviews the operation. Audits will uncover loose areas and highlight situations that have changed due to persons who tend to define or change the roles of their jobs on a daily basis. Such situations are common since jobs will often change because of the persons who occupy them. An internal audit will also increase the credibility of the purchasing manager in the external auditing process.

A major subject in the examination of an entire purchasing activity is what is referred to as "back-door selling." This is the practice of vendor salesmen calling upon user departments and encouraging them to specify their firm's products in requisitions sent to purchasing for ordering. There are often good reasons for this practice. For example, the user department knows what brand or item is best in application, or emergency orders might be made direct from the user department to the specific vendor in order to save time. This practice can become excessive and lead to many small orders at high total cost to the firm, result in nonoptimal products for various tasks, and create a problem of nonstandardization throughout the firm. Further, bulk purchase economies through blanket orders or consolidated orders are reduced when too many back-door purchases are made.

Purchasing managers can reduce the incidence of back-door selling through careful examination of the entire purchasing process and the service the department is providing users in the firm. Factors that can go far in reducing this practice are to improve the service activity and image of purchasing to other departments. This includes communicating the benefits of using purchasing rather than simply direct ordering or tight specification of product. Providing fast and easy-to-use service to various departments will encourage the use of purchasing rather than avoid it. Technical assistance is another form of purchasing service that can be provided to user departments. Finding quality goods equal to or better than those already used by user departments will build the product sourcing credibility of purchasing. Assistance in emergency situations will also build a reliance upon the department. All these factors tend to provide quality service and build an impression by other departments that purchasing is a well-run and a valuable service to them. Back-door selling and buying cannot be prevented by the purchasing department, but the incentives encouraging it can be reduced through proper management.

Conclusion

The management of purchasing means the directing of a system of resources and people. It further includes integrating the activities and plans of this system into those of the overall firm. This chapter presented key measures that are important to purchasing as well as others in the firm. These measures are becoming more important within the contexts of management information and budgeting systems that are evolving. A crucial aspect of purchasing management is to examine it from time to time from the point of view that the rest of the firm sees.

FOOTNOTE

1. Richard F. Verville, "Prepare for an Audit with These Checklists," *Purchasing*, 21 August 1980, p. 67.

SOURCES FOR FURTHER READING

Cavinato, Joseph L., *Finance for Transportation and Distribution Manager*. Washington, D.C.: Traffic Service Corp., 1977, chapter 8.

Croell, Richard C. "Measuring Purchasing Effectiveness."*Journal of Purchasing and Materials Management* 13 (1977): 3.

Monczka, Robert M.; Carter, Phillip L.; and Hoagland, John H. *Purchasing Performance: Measurement and Control*. East Lansing, MI: Michigan State University, 1979.

Paperman, Jacob B., and Shell, Richard L. "The Accounting Approach to Performance Measurement." *Journal of Purchasing and Materials Management* 13 (1977): 24.

Wight, Oliver W. "Making Performance Measures Work." *Purchasing*, 5 November 1981, p. 49.

"GTE Uses Benchmarking To Measure Purchasing." *Purchasing*, 31 March 1983, p. 21.

"Management Adopts New Yardstick to Rate Buying." *Purchasing*, 11 June 1981, p. 14.

QUESTIONS FOR REVIEW

1. Do the concerns of materials managers parallel those of purchasing personnel? Why or why not?

2. Is there *one* measure that can be used to indicate the nature of purchasing performance? If so, what is it?

3. What are the key features of the measures included in the areas of activity versus cost? Do any of these conflict with each other?

4. Are "the number of orders per period" or "number of contracts per period" good measures in and of themselves? Why or why not?

5. Why is an actual-to-cost budget comparison on a total dollar basis not always a valid one? Can you suggest a better or modified one?

6. Present and analyze two purchasing performance measures that indicate activity within the department. How might two of these conflict in what they report?

7. Negotiated savings measures are good in most settings. Can you think of situations in which this measure is not necessarily a valid one?

8. Why is savings from forward buying a one-sided measure?

9. In what ways does purchasing provide input to the overall corporate budgeting process?

10. How can index numbers be used to assist in both the budgeting process as well as evaluating performance after-the-fact against the original budget?

11. What key management information system components are needed in purchasing?

12. What is the purpose of a departmental audit? Is it purely to determine what people have done wrong in their positions during the past? Why or why not?

Problem 22-1

A firm produces three products using ten raw material components. The head of purchasing is concerned about price increases with most of these raw materials. There is limited analytical time to spend on research, because the department is understaffed and is rushed in its day-to-day activities. The purchasing head feels that not all of the products can be studied for alternative sourcing, substitution, negotiation, etc. Instead, he seeks a priority listing of those three or four products that should be analyzed immediately.

The following tables show each of the four products with the latest three year prices charged by the firm as well as the raw materials and the prices paid by the firm for the last two years.

PRODUCT A Sales Prices	1982	1983	1984
	$10.25	$10.22	$10.15

Costs per input unit		
Raw material	1983	1984
1	$1.20	$1.15
2	.87	1.03
3	.15	.32
4	1.00	1.02
Total	3.22	3.52

PRODUCT B Sales Prices	1982	1983	1984
	$8.79	$9.82	$10.83

Costs per input unit		
Raw material	1983	1984
3	$.15	$.32
5	$2.04	2.60
6	.47	.44

7	.65	.90
8	1.15	1.18
Total	4.46	5.44

PRODUCT C **Sales Prices**	**1982**	**1983**	**1984**
	$6.02	$6.01	$6.04

Costs per input unit

Raw material	1983	1984
2	$.87	$1.03
9	$1.63	$1.14
10	$1.47	$1.82
Total	$3.97	$3.99

Questions:
1. *Which three or four raw materials do you think are most critical to study first?*
2. *Explain the approach you used in analyzing the above data in order to arrive at the three or four raw materials for further study.*

Problem 22–2

A buyer is examining the department's budget against its actual buying for a particular product during the year. The budget stated 100,000 units at a unit cost of $16.00. The actual expenditures were $1,800,000 for 105,000 units.

Question:
How should this actual performance be explained in comparison to the budgeted amount?

INTRODUCTION

INTEGRATION: KEY ROLES FOR PURCHASING IN THE FUTURE

Top Management
Marketing
Finance
Distribution and Logistics
Manufacturing

RESOURCES FOR THE FUTURE

PURCHASING AND MATERIALS MANAGEMENT IN THE FUTURE

MATERIALS MANAGEMENT AND THE ORGANIZATION'S STRATEGY

CHAPTER OBJECTIVES

After reading this chapter you should:

- Understand the viewpoints of top management and other disciplines interfacing with purchasing.

- Appreciate the roles of energy, capital, labor, and information in shaping the firm of tomorrow.

- Be able to relate the evolving integrated role of purchasing.

- Understand the skills required to oversee materials management.

The Future of
Purchasing

Introduction

Purchasing will continue to evolve at an increasing pace in the 1980s and 1990s. This change bodes positive things for persons in purchasing as well as the firm in general.

Many of the current trends will continue to play roles in purchasing in the future. The trend toward noneconomic regulations as they affect workplace safety and environment as influenced by the Occupational Safety and Hazards Administration and the Environmental Protection Agency will greatly affect purchasing. Another is continued search for sources in international areas. Trade is both easier and less costly than in past decades. And, still another gradual trend in the field is the adoption of the metric systems, which will affect capital purchases, training, product planning, and MRO purchasing. Lastly, the computer will play even greater roles in purchasing. It will continue to evolve as a data-handling and retrieval center, and it will gradually evolve into an integrated, corporate control resource. And, no doubt it will expand to greater links between customers and vendors.

"Integration" is perhaps the one single factor that will affect purchasing the most in the next decade. Integration means closer decision-making links with the rest of the firm as well as interfacing firms. The positive gains to be attained from closely integrated planning and operations with the rest of the firm range from reduced inventories, increased productivity and profitability, to effective strategic planning and management for the firm as a whole. This action is being forced by the concept that purchasing can no longer be insulated from production and the rest of the firm by large inbound inventories that permit "decoupled" decision making between buying and production. Production itself is being integrated into other decision spheres of the firm, and it naturally follows that purchasing will do so as well.

The role of the buyer and purchasing manager is shifting from that of being a transmitter of need between an in-firm user and an outside source to that of being a creative innovator and manager of inbound resource movement. It is a function that is becoming more line oriented, providing more input than before into the product planning processes.

Purchasing has been indentified as one of the top twelve career areas for the 1980s in a survey published by *Business Week*.[1] This was based upon salaries in various corporate career areas as well as the future outlook for different occupations as identified by the U.S. Government.[2] The field is changing, but not with more of the past methods, procedures and types of job activities. The demands upon purchasing in the future will be greatly different than they were in even the recent past.

Integration—Key Roles For Purchasing In The Future

Fluid marketplaces that cause supply uncertainties, shorter product life cycles, expensive capital, and changing transportation services are major environmental forces affecting purchasing and the rest of the firm. All of these influences call for greater decision-making and performance evaluation ties with top management, marketing, finance, logistics and transportation, and manufacturing.

Top Management

Top management attention to purchasing has always been obvious because purchasing is one of the major expense lines in the firm's accounting records. In many instances, however, this attention decreases during the year once the budget is prepared for the next period. The viewpoints of chief executive officers contain key concepts for purchasing managers to continually check in their own operations and plans. A few of these elements are included in the following five questions which are logical for top management to ask of purchasing.[3]

1) *What are the price and supply histories of the firm's major purchase items, and what are their future prospects?* This loaded question comes from a strategic orientation as to where the firm's future resources will come from as well as how difficult or expensive it will be to obtain them. The question also inquires how well purchasing has done in managing the inbound flow of required goods in the past. It is a key question for the firm as a whole as well as the people managing the acquisition of material resources.

2) *Who are the firm's major sources, and how does purchasing evaluate their performance?* Knowing that the firm is dependent upon a relatively few key sources for materials and components, this question seeks assurance as to the stability, reliability, and maintenance of that flow. It also questions how well purchasing might keep close links with major vendors so there are few surprises in price or availability.

3) *What five current and future cost reduction projects are in the works in purchasing?* Cost reduction is always a quest in firms. This question seeks hard answers in terms of products, methods, etc. It also indicates whether purchasing is oriented toward some improvement planning in addition to the operations of solving daily problems.

4) *How is inventory and the inbound flow of material managed?* Inventories are fluid assets that represent investment risk. The well-managed firm today requires tight inventory management and control of material flow into, through, and out of the firm to customers. This question looks into how well purchasing is doing its part in this overall lo-

gistical mission. It requires close links and control over vendor movements and coordinated links with production and the firm's overall sales and production plans.

5) *What are the personnel and organizational profiles of purchasing?* The management of people in a system is the reason behind this question. Insights to be gained here pertain to salary scales, and training and development.

Marketing

The American economy appears to be shifting from heavy industries to high technology and service industries. This shift is causing many firms to move from basic commodities and other heavy "smokestack" product lines to other lines of business. A trend toward services being more dominant in the U.S. GNP has been taking place since the 1950s.

Further, product introduction is increasingly costly. Product research, development, and introduction involve high risks for firms. Products are experiencing shorter life cycles. Competition from other firms, countries, and evolving technologies force firms to alter products faster than in previous decades. Marketing has the task of selling goods to customers as well as interpreting marketplace conditions into strategic and tactical actions for the firm to implement. These greatly affect production and purchasing. Future communication links will no doubt be stronger between marketing and purchasing. The penalty for not progressing could be an inbound flow of goods that the firm can no longer use in its altered products, or the inability to quickly shift to new materials needed in new and changed products.

The methods of marketing noticed by vendors continuously changes. Person to person marketing is extremely expensive. The cost of inventories is high. Selling firms must evaluate their products, distribution methods, and approaches to selling in line with potential gains to be made. This situation causes many firms to become selective in their marketing efforts. Buyers can not assume that the entire range of products available on the market will be made known by the vendor visiting or promoting to them. Active investigation, travel, and visiting current and potential vendors will be a basic part of purchasing in the future.

Finance

Two major interactions take place between purchasing and finance/accounting. The first is during the establishment of annual or other period budgets for purchases and operation of the purchasing department. The second is through payment to vendors. This later area can have a major impact upon the prices the firm pays as well as the desire of vendors to sell to it. An example illustrates this problem point. During a period of high inflation and/or capital shortages, firms will often seek normal or early payment from customers only to delay payment to their own vendors. Vendors might experience a cash bind if they cannot pass on the same practice to their own vendors. Firms in need of early or normal payment will often offer early payment discounts. Many of their customers will still delay payment and take advantage of the discount in any event. Vendors have little choice in these situations except to raise their prices to account for the lost opportunity or cost of cash outstanding.

The above problem can place buyers in a bind between finance and vendors who complain, raise prices, or refuse to sell to the firm because the buyer's own finance department holds cash and delays payment. In this setting, the finance department might be earning monies in the money market with that cash only to incur hardships and higher costs in the purchasing of raw materials and components. Closer links between finance/accounting and purchasing, and illustrations of proof of price increases due to cash payment delay, etc. are necessary for purchasing and the firm as a whole to not be penalized by this financial practice.

Buyer awareness to company cash flow is an area of increasing concern in the future. The problem just cited is solved by some firms by having buyers evaluate 1) whether the firm should pay early and take the discount, 2) pay during the normal period, or 3) pay beyond the discount period with the discount without threat of vendor price increases. The buyer is the one person in the firm who should be most aware of the actions of the vendor. This calls for an awareness of the firm's own cash flow, cost of capital, cash investment opportunities, and the marketplace power the firm has with vendors. It also requires finance/accounting to follow the payment judgement decisions of buyers. This breaks from past practices in firms, but firms that have moved in this direction report good results.

Distribution and Logistics

Two key areas of attention in distribution and logistics will play greater roles in purchasing in the future. First is transportation and the effects of deregulation in that industry. These topics have been covered in greater detail in other chapters. They will of necessity be areas requiring greater coordination in the firm in the future.

Inventories and their costs are the second area of concern for the firm. Buyers often find that there are limits to vendor's delivery and order cycle time services. The issue revolves around purchasing seeking faster deliveries, while vendors are constrained by high transportation costs of accomplishing the same. Vendor stocking systems can be used as a means of shortening this cycle. There are several other options that should be explored, and each one requires a different level of investment and operating cost by both the buyer and vendor.

Each of the systems described in Table 23-1 incurs freight, warehousing, inventory and cash flow expenses for either the vendor or the buyer firm. In any event, these costs are being incurred by someone. The key is to determine which firm can provide the service at a lower cost than the other. Factors that enter into this equation are both firm's cost of capital, capital availability, and tax rates. Costs incurred by vendors only have to be passed along through fees or prices. Buyer firms eventually bear all costs of vendors. Firms are increasingly cooperating with innovative arrangements in order to reduce costs and increase productivity and profitability to both.

Manufacturing

A recent Delphi study conducted in the materials management area indicated that MRP will continue to increase in application and that purchasing will integrate further with manufacturing. This greater integration is seen as providing purchasing with more time for negotiations and positive research activities.[4] Some of this integrative initiative will

☐ **TABLE 23-1.** *Alternative Methods of Procurement with a Vendor*

Method	Vendor Cost	Buyer Costs
Direct plant buyer shipping	high transportation cost low warehousing cost chance of lost sales due to long order cycle	long lead time chance for stockout
Vendor distribution center intermediate to both plant and buyer (serve many customers	higher warehousing expenses lower transportation costs due to bulk shipments inbound to center and shorter small shipment to buyer lower lost sales	faster cycle time lower delivery costs
Vendor warehouse dedicated to buyer firm located close to buyer	increased warehouse expenses lower freight cost (same as above) problem of committing inventory to one buyer who might not buy all of it	extremely low cycle time costs might incur higher price for this advantage
Stockless vendor system (on site of buyer firm)	rent of space from buyer firm freight cost economy inbound, low or no delivery cost	no inventory cost cost of vendor inventory is passed on in price can receive rent for space
Consignment	no space cost freight same as stockless system	cost of space very good for cash flow problem of inventory obsolescense

be coming from manufacturing where an increasing trend is noted in firms sending manufacturing executives back for training and development in ways to adopt to technology and integrate production into the scheme of the firm. This is a decided shift away from regarding production purely as a manufacturing service fairly isolated from the marketing mission of the firm.[5]

Robotics will bring changes to purchasing as well. Robots are machines that can be programmed to handle many different tasks. Rather than use a machine designed for a single purpose, robots are general machines that can perform welding, assembling, packaging, or nearly any other task possible with special machinery or manpower. The key benefit to robotics is the consistency and precision that is possible. Many observers see robotics as becoming a major production resource in plants in the near future.[6] Robotics will enable firms to change production quickly, and even produce different products with little changeover time and effort. The implications for purchasing are that new materials, sources, and services might be demanded in short notice. No longer can the firm be expected to produce only Products A and B. With flexible production and innovative marketing and product development management, the firm will be able to move into new markets and products. This will require flexibility in purchasing.

Resources for the Future

Purchasing and the firm in general have a stake in the future trends of the major resources of the economy. These are energy, capital, and labor. Capital represents the cost of liquid and fixed asset opportunities and use, which also includes construction. Exhibit 23-1 presents inflation deflated price/cost data for energy, capital, and labor from the 1950s to the middle 1970s and out to the present time. The chart is centered on the 1973-75 period, but it has relevance for today and the future.[7]

This chart illustrates major driving forces in management decisions in the past as well as the future. In the period leading up to the 1970s, energy was declining in real costs relative to capital and labor. Firms recognizing this tended to switch to automation, increase warehousing, and use increasing amounts of transportation services. After the energy crunch of the 1970s, firms sought ways to minimize energy-intensive transportation through the use of warehousing located close to markets. This strategy minimized expensive transportation in a trade-off with capital. Increasing capital cost problems in the 1979-83 period forced many firms to evaluate warehousing and investments in inventories.

Looking to the future, energy will no doubt continue to be expensive in the long run. Capital will become a major problem as national currencies and governments incur capital crises in the 1980s. Labor will increase in real costs as a decreasing number of new labor force entrants appear due to the lower birth rate that started in the 1960s. A smaller labor force might have the effect of increasing labor-force strength through wages, unionization, etc.

■ **EXHIBIT 23-1.** *Real Costs of Energy Construction, Labor and Communications. (1972 Dollars)*

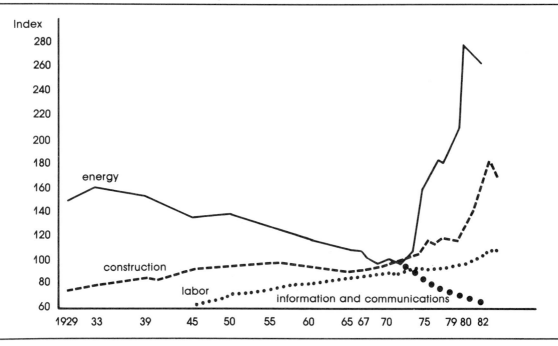

A positive sign on the horizon is the cost of information and communication. Computers and data transmission technology advances continue to unfold and bring quantum decreases in cost and increases in capabilities. Looking at this chart again, firms will seek ways of substituting information for transportation, inventories, and labor. Customer-firm communications will enable the firm to forward plan production and distribution in line with customer needs. This will further integrate the firm with its own vendors. Selling firms can use this advanced information to consolidate, forward buy with assurance, balance production operations, ship in least costly methods, and plan cash commitments optimally. All these techniques are possible through low-cost communications systems, and they all represent avoidance or reduction means for energy, capital, and labor costs. Computers will gradually eliminate or reduce order-by-order purchasing and the practice of not letting vendors know of future needs until right before they exist.

One example of information integration is being implemented in the food distribution field. The Grocery Manufacturers of America have embarked upon a project that includes communication links between manufacturers, brokers, warehouses, buyers, transportation companies, and bankers. Increasing sales at supermarkets can be monitored, and each member of the channel can see trends occurring before they appear as an order for immediate filling. This system also provides for cash transmittal from one party to the other thus eliminating cash floats and use of the mails. It is seen by observers as being adopted in the future as a long-range planning tool by each of the functionary parties in the channel of distribution.

Purchasing and Materials Management in the Future

The mineral and petroleum shortages of the 1970s brought closer management scrutiny to the area of product supply. Purchasing's role increased to that of being an active seeker of materials that in many cases were no longer in plentiful supply at reasonable prices. The firm was sometimes able to produce only what purchasing was able to acquire. In some instances, purchasing was the bottleneck constraint to the firm's operations and profitability.

The capital cost and supply crunch of the early 1980s caused a reverse tendency in the form of reduced inventories. High interest costs caused firms to reduce inventories and keep current assets in as liquid form as possible. In this mode, even closer integration was required between purchasing production, and the rest of the firm.

An integration movement has been taking place in U.S. firms that has combined outbound physical and control functions into what most firms refer to as physical distribution; the same phenomenon has been taking place on the inbound side and is known as materials management. These trends are noted in Exhibit 23-2. The inbound movement and control functions of purchasing, requirements planning, raw inventories, storage, handling, and forecasting have been gradually evolving into what is referred to mainly as materials management. This move occurred in recognition that perhaps the best way to bridge trade-off opportunities and conflicts is to provide information and organizationally combine the separate functions.

The question then arises as to who is selected to oversee the materials management activity, which includes purchasing in many firms. In some instances it is a purchasing manager. In other settings, this head comes from a background in production or engineering. In some other firms, this lead person rose through management information systems.

Materials management encompasses many distinct disciplines. Persons selected to manage this entire function must have certain skills that are necessary in integrative administration activities. These include, for one, an understanding of the basic economics of each discipline as well as the trade-offs that exist between materials management and the rest of the firm. Placement in this position does not necessarily indicate that this person possesses in-depth skills in purchasing or any of the other areas. Another key management requirement is the ability to manage people, including the ability to understand people problems, needs, desires, initiatives, and the ability to detect needs when they are not overtly signalled. It requires redirecting people in positive ways when they are askance of the firm's mission. And, it calls for the ability to integrate different people with the tasks at hand. Another key administrative quality is the ability to communicate. This includes both written and oral communications from one-on-one settings to speeches and presentations. Central to this is the ability to negotiate and persuade. These skills might seem far from the physical aspects of purchasing and

■ **EXHIBIT 23-2.** *Logistics Components*

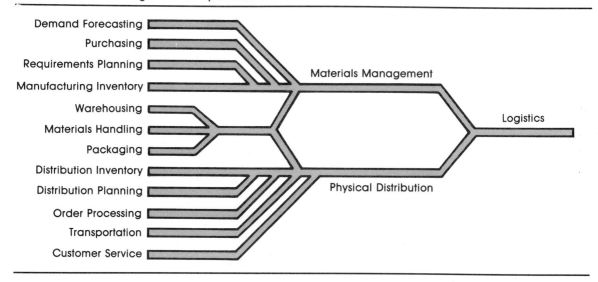

product control, but the farther up the administrative scale one observes, the less the actual discipline is noticed on a day-to-day basis.

Positive career strategies in purchasing and materials management should follow the lines of this integrative and administrative need. Personal skill development issues were presented in Chapter 21 that pointed to the need for exposure to all facets of purchasing, commodity flow and control, as well as other disciplines of the firm.

Materials Management and the Organization's Strategy

Purchasing is one of the key components in a firm or organization's strategy. Purchasing obtains the products needed for the firm to function as defined by its product or corporate strategy. In this capacity, it acquires goods and services that enable production to manufacture the goods product development and marketing have defined as satisfying customer needs.

In another way, purchasing plays an active role in the firm's strategy by maintaining close watch on future technological and supply market developments. In this capacity, purchasing is the eyes and ears on supply market developments and trends. Insights gained from these areas can be integrated "upstream" into product development and the planning of future product management decisions. These insights include both problem constraints on the horizon in supply and commodity markets as well as opportunities that the firm can seek in advance of competition and/or in anticipation of the market.

Conclusion

Purchasing and materials management are evolving into a system of inbound resource and people management. Less and less of the top job in purchasing is involved with the details of buying. The future promises to include more integration with the rest of the firm in addition to the spotlight that focuses upon purchasing when product supply markets are tight. Instead, purchasing will be more of a member of the strategic decision making of the firm. It will no longer be assumed that whatever the company wishes to produce that purchasing can buy the materials for it. Instead, what the firm wishes to produce will be determined in tandem with the supply opportunities and constraints as presented by purchasing. The firm of the future can not ignore purchasing as a key source of strategic input to its operations and planning.

FOOTNOTES

1. Steven S. Ross, "The 12 Top Money-Making Careers of the '80s," *Business Week*, 28 March 1983, supplement p. 7.
2. *Occupational Outlook Handbook*. (Washington, D.C.: U.S. Government Printing Office 1979).
3. "When Purchasing Talks With the CEO," *Purchasing*, 29 January 1981, p. 117.
4. P. George Benson, Arthur V. Hill, and Thomas R. Hoffman, "Manufacturing Systems of the Future—A Delphi Study," *Production and Inventory Management* 23 (Third Quarter 1982): 87.
5. Ross, "The 12 Top Money Making Careers of the '80s," *Business Week*, 28 March 1983, supplement p. 7.
6. Kenneth M. Jenkins and Alan R. Raedels, "The Robot Revolution: Strategic Considerations for Managers," *Production and Inventory Management* 23 (Third Quarter 1982): 107.
7. Presentation by Mr. Joel Wolff, Drake Sheahan Stewart Dougall, Inc., Madison, Wisconsin, July 1982.

QUESTIONS FOR REVIEW

1. What are the major trends that have recently evolved in purchasing, and which one will perhaps have the greatest long-run impact upon the field?

2. What are the major concerns of top management when viewing purchasing management?

3. How will purchasing and finance have a more obvious interfacing function in the future?

4. What is meant by: "The cost of capital, availability of it, and relative tax rates will govern economic logistics arrangements in procurement."?

5. How will trends affecting production impact upon purchasing in the future?

6. How have the relative costs of capital and labor changed from the past up to the 1970s? What had been the trend of energy in that time?

7. What major trade-off did many firms make during the 1950s and 1960s with the above trends?

8. What major cost problem will exist in the 1980s with regard to these three factors?

9. How might the cost of data and communications change the way firms procure and distribute goods?

10. How is purchasing evolving into the concept of materials management?

11. What management skills are best sought to manage the materials department of today and in the future?

12. Why is purchasing a part of the firm's overall strategy?

Appendix

MATRIX OF CASES AND CHAPTERS

Case	I	1	2	3	4	5	6	7	II	8	9	10	11	12	13	III	14	15	16	17	IV	18	19	20	V	21	22	23
Boaz Materials			X																								X	
Compass Point Enterpris.														X												X		
Corinthian Products		X	X														X											
Coyle Electronics				X			X																					
DLLP Chemicals						X								X														
EPO	X		X																							X	X	X	X
Five Points Mfg.	X			X	X	X	X																					
Fellowcraft Products										X			X	X						X								
Lion's Paw Mfg.			X																									X
Meridian Electronics										X		X						X				X						
On-The-Square Dept.										X		X																
Royal Electric					X									X			X											
TAA Mfg.	X				X	X	X							X														
Traveler Prod's.																			X	X								
Western Globe Ent.																									X	X	X	

CASE STUDY

Boaz Materials, Inc.

Dom Krumrine is vice-president of materials management for Boaz Materials, Inc. He was recently hired into this new post from the position of head of purchasing in another firm. The new post was created by a corporate reorganization of all inbound logistics functions that are now under an umbrella of what is called materials management.

Don's specialty has been the development of reporting systems both on and off the computer. He has keen insights into developing reporting systems for both performance evaluation as well as decision making. In his first week on the job, he interviewed each of the heads of the various functions that report to him. His first major task is to develop new and integrated reporting systems in Boaz.

Bob Pashek, inbound traffic manager, was the first to meet with Don. "Well, as you know, Don, my job has been to arrange and monitor inbound transportation flows. This job started years ago with just inbound receiving and inspection. It was little more than unloading, checking, and moving the stuff to storage. Ron Koot, the company's outbound traffic manager, started the firm's private truck fleet a few years ago, and he also got the company into some leased rail cars. That's where he and I do a lot of coordinating, since some of these moves are two-way; that is, his outbound moves sometimes are used on a backhaul to bring my stuff inbound.

"The way we've worked it here in the past few years is this. Any shipments he's got going outbound, he'll let me know about. I'll then ask the people in Purchasing what is coming in from some of those destinations or routes. If a match up can be made, then we do it. Otherwise, I keep close tabs with Jim Campbell in Purchasing to help him select carriers when vendors don't know what they are doing in the traffic area. Any transportation expenses our firm incurs inbound comes onto my budget, and it's a bear to handle. It's always over; yet, it's not poor management. Sometimes we need air freight when a vendor falls down on deliveries. I can show you dozens of examples in just the past month. Anyway," Bob concluded by putting out his cigarette, "my job has always been to minimize these inbound traffic costs."

Jim Campbell, head of Purchasing, was next that afternoon. "Don, we've always had a tight shop here. In fact, I've personally seen that no major problems surface to the rest of the firm from this sector. In fact, our people deserve more recognition than they've been getting. We work ourselves to the bone staying within budget, keeping the product coming, and now and then suggesting improvements in materials and products when we can get the time.

"What the current reporting systems don't show is what efforts we go to just to stay within the budget. Why, production is continually making purchasing order changes, they are great at back-door buying products we know we can do better on, and the specs they have worked into many of the products are absurd. Some of them are impossible to get vendors to adhere to. You know what some of these problems are like."

Don's appointment with Henry Karg was the next morning. He is head of raw material warehousing, and in this role he has responsibility for inventory stewardship. "Well, Mr. Krumrine, mine is a basic operation. I take the material that Bob Pashek has unloaded, and I store it in Building B. The high turnover production materials I keep near the factory side door. Many of the parts and supplies are in a shelf and bin area near the back. There are really few problems, except when the auditors come in once a year. They always find something out of wack, and that is a real witch-hunt to see who was at fault."

Don asked, "On these parts and supplies, how are they kept exactly?"

Henry's response was, "Well, there is a poster with each item's shelf and bin indicated. Whenever production needs new seals, say, for one of the main machines, usually Dennis Jaworski, he's the plant engineer, will come in and take them. Of course, he and anyone else is supposed to mark off what they've taken in the inventory ledger we keep near the door.

"But, getting back to my operation, I see it as keeping the place efficient and tidy. My boys don't goof around. You always see them working, and you can't find a neater and cleaner spot in the entire plant."

Don's job was to integrate these operations into the overall scheme of the firm as well as develop workable performance evaluation and information systems for each function reporting to him.

Case Question:

■ How would you go about this task? What elements would you include in this new system?

Compass Point Enterprises, Ltd.

Compass Point Enterprises is a multi-national manufacturing and engineering firm of construction machinery and specialty building products. It is based in the U.S. and traditionally earned most of its revenue in other nations. It has three primary sites in the U.S. with branches in France and Australia. The company is starting to bid on sales opportunities in some of the emerging third world nations.

Howell Cobb is director of Corporate Purchasing for the firm. In this role he coordinates the purchases of items needed by the three U.S. sites, and more recently he has taken on a coordinating role with purchases throughout the company.

On his first morning back from a business trip, Mr. Cobb received a call from Rick Randell, vice-president of worldwide sales. "Cobby, Randell here. How've you been. . . haven't seen you in a dog's age. Improve that golf swing yet? Hey, listen, the reason I'm calling is on this African job we just pulled together. We got the go-ahead from the ministry. It will be a $90 million job with most of the funds coming from the American aid agencies. The rest is from the country's own development ministry with funds they've got from other sources."

Cobb responded, "I heard about the proposal. I wish you guys would let us in Purchasing in on things before you go full blast to these outback places with some of these jobs.

Randell interrupted, "Yeah, well, you know how fast some of this stuff pops. Anyway this job calls for some different twists. We can tap our own company sources in Taiwan and our supply operation in Italy for a bulk of the work. Some of it you will no doubt arrange from stateside as well. But, they've thrown two clinkers at us, and the ball's in your lap, Cobby. Here it is: one, at least $10 million worth of goods of any kind must be bought and exported from that country before half of our job is done, and two, at least $2 million of local goods must be included in the work, you know, a regular local content requirement.

"The paperwork is coming over to your shop in a day or two. I thought I'd let you know before you read it cold. This one's real important. If we do a good job on this one, we've got more like it in the region and in Asia. I'll let you go; let's hit the course some time before the summer's gone."

Cobb assigned his assistant the task of working up an analysis of the country involved. Jim Barnhart sat across Howell's desk and summarized. "The country became independent from a major European power in the late 1960s. It has one port that can handle ships of up to 10,000 tons. That's not very big considering the size of regular liners and tramps today. We're going to have some problems getting our large equipment there. We'll probably have to trans-ship from Nigeria."

"The real problem, Mr. Cobb, is that the country produces so little we can use on the job or buy for use or sale elsewhere. It has a low grade but high cost tin mining operation, it also produces a little coffee, jute, some semitropical foods and herbs, and it has a very small manufacturing industry. Nothing much has developed since the colonial days. It seems that these countries had to import anything manufactured from the parent country, and once they became independent local industries were slow to develop."

"Thanks, Jimmy, I appreciate the information, as bleak as it is."

Howell sat in his office staring out the window while strumming his fingers on his desk trying to piece together how he would handle the purchase requirements for this job.

Case Question

■ What would you advise?

Corinthian Products, Inc.

The quarterly department heads planning meeting of Corinthian Products was just starting. Sitting around the table were Hugh McWorter, president, and the vice-presidents, Ken Greer, finance, Jim Gardner, marketing, Joe Nigh, purchasing, and Bill Olson, production.

Mr. McWorter opened the meeting by handing out some financial information, which is shown:

Company sales	$35.8 million
Net profit	1.7 million
Company cost of borrowing	13%

Balance Sheet ($ millions)

Assets:		Liabilities & Equities:	
cash	$ 3	accounts/notes payables	$ 3
securities	1	long term debt	5
acct. rec.	2	common stock	8
inventory	9	retained earnings	11
plant & equip	12		
Total	$27	Total	$27

"Gentlemen, inventories are thirty-three percent of total assets, and inventory turnover is only 4 times per year. Total assets to sales are only 1.32 times. This is poor in relation to our competitors, and we are being eaten alive with interest payments. We've got to convert some of our inventories to cash in order to work off our debt and present less of a risk to our lenders and owners. I don't need to tell you that we take a slow second to Fast Pace enterprises. Their new product line looks good and they are in better shape financially."

"The next exhibit is a listing I got from accounting on the latest inventory standing. It shows $1.5 million in raw materials, with $3.7 in work-in-process, $3.1 in finished goods, $.2 in supplies, and $.5 in obsolete items. We can't tolerate this. I know no one of us here is responsible for inventories as a whole. The buck actually stops at my desk. But, my charge to you today in the rest of your meeting is to reduce these inventories by at least one-third. We've got to run a tighter ship! I'm going to leave you with Ken Greer to iron out a plan to accomplish this."

"After the coffee break, Ken Greer called the meeting back together. "To fill you in on more of the details, the industry average of inventories to total assets is twenty percent. Take us out of those statistics and it is only eighteen percent. Further, the industry inventory turnover is between five and six times.

"Now if we reduce our inventories to $6 million, this will release $3 for debt reduction, which will save us $390,000 per year in interest payments. This has a more positive effect on our bottom line than an increase in sales of over $8 million."

Bill Olson spoke up from the production side. "These things look rough, but we're not running a sloppy operation. We've got some of the best production machinery in the industry. I ought to know. Let me tell you what I am up against, though. We've got a real problem of parts availability. Sometimes we have to buy supply parts when we can get them; and we buy two and three when we need only one that day because the cost of ordering is just as cheap for two as it is for one. Further, Purchasing has been getting us some stuff, that you have to admit Joe, is not always up to snuff. We're used to two to three percent defects. Over the past year they've been as high as seven to eight percent. I'll bet this report shows this garbage as raw materials or work-in-process goods.

"And, one last thing, is scheduling. I try to match up our manpower to our machines. That's the only way to get good productivity in an operation as ours. So, I've got to determine what jobs need to be done in line with the items we've got on-hand and with what job priorities have been set. One thing that destroys us in the shop is the need to continually stop one job and switch over to another because some customer comes down real hard on the marketing guys, and they, in turn, get on our backs. Why, I've got some jobs out there that are two months old that keep getting passed over because of all the rush jobs. I know I've talked to most of you individually about these problems, but I think we've got to air some of these problems once and for all."

Joe Nigh picked up the ball at that point. "Well, now that we're getting this all out on the table, let me get some things off my chest. First, some of the specifications we have to deal with haven't been the easiest in the world. Let me give you an example. The QE-L stamping, for instance. We can only get that from two sources, but if the tolerances on edgings and surface integrity are relaxed only slightly, we could open up and use about a dozen firms. The two we deal from now are real problems. I'll grant you that. Two, we've tried all we can with the erratic and long lead times. But, we are in an industry where our vendors have the same sort of job-shop scheduling problems as we have. There is little we can do other than work with long lead times ourselves in ordering from them and keep on their backs with almost weekly tracing. But, relaxing those specifications and cutting down on changed PO's will go far in getting rid of a lot of headaches."

Jim Gardner spoke up from the marketing side. "Well I don't know much about the inbound hassles you guys have, but the major complaint we hear from customers is that our stuff is slow and never on-time. Bill, I know I owe you a lot of favors, but if we weren't able to handle the rush jobs in your shop, we'd lose nearly half of our our accounts."

"I know this isn't the time to bring this up, but if we are to remain competitive on our stock product lines, we've got to set up a distribution warehouse on the West Coast. We just can't service orders in ten days from the plant. We've got to get some additional inventory out in the field in order to satisfy some of our orders in two to three days."

Case Question:

■ What would you recommend in this situation?

Coyle Electronics

John Coyle, III, is director of Purchasing for Coyle Electronics, a firm in the power transmission and household product industry. The firm does little manufacturing. It primarily acquires components from other firms, assembles them, markets them to dealers, and does some direct selling to final users. Examples of the product line are wire, junctions boxes, circuit breakers, terminals, and tools.

The firm uses a standard purchase order; it contains several "boiler-plate" elements that are printed on the back of the original PO that is sent to the vendor, and one copy that stays in the purchasing office.

John's concern is with one vendor, Ace Tools, Inc. Coyle Electronics has been buying from this supplier for nearly a decade, and its product quality, delivery, and other facors have always been acceptable until now. John has been aware of some minor problems, but he didn't think they were serious. This all came to a head when he received a call from Crystal Stover who is head of Production and Inspection.

"Hi John, Crystal here. Listen, on the latest shipment from Ace Tools we've got some problems. There have been some loose things around the edges with them over the past year, but this latest shipment takes the cake."

John replied, "Why, what's the problem?"

Crystal said, "Well, the main thing is that we're finding about a twelve percent defect rate on this latest shipment of units we buy from them to make splicers. We've lived with the two to three percent rate in the past, but this one is causing us to scrap an awful lot, and it will make us under count on this job to Nationwide Distributors. We don't like doing that even though they give us a five percent leeway up or down on delivery quantity from their specified purchase order quantity. And, Ace's shipments are always about fifteen percent either higher or lower than the quantity we requisition and you order from them."

He continued, "Further, Ace has been getting these shipments to us late. I'm just going to reject the next one that comes in over a week. That outfit thinks we can be abused. Now, Reliable Tools' shipments are OK, and the same with Jensen Fabricating, and the others. But, we've got to rattle the cage over at Ace or I'm going to ask that you not use them anymore. We've got one shipment that was due in here on the 4th, and here it is the 9th. I've gotten no word from your people nor Ace. The order just arrived about an hour ago. We opened one box and found about six percent defects in it. We even held the truck driver here while we did it. It's reloaded and on its way back to Ace. That company has cost us a lot of money already with shifted around production runs, wasted labor, scrap, and the use of premium transportation to keep *our* customers on schedule. Can we finally do something about this?"

John replied, "We'll handle it from this end. These guys know what we expect, and now we'll just have to put our foot down. Keep smiling."

John pulled the open order file for the current Ace order. The one purchase order Crystal was talking about was there. John felt bad about this one, since someone in his shop should have made a routine call to Ace during the job and once again the day before expected delivery. No one had done that according to the checklist that was attached to it.

John knew the purchase order terms that were printed on the form that Ace received and has been receiving for many years. John had wirtten them himself with someone over in the Legal Department back in 1971.

Turning over the copy of the order form that went to Ace, John looked at the boiler-plate terms once again. The terms he was most interested in are:

"4. Vendor to supply product in quantities specified on this order. Allowances are made for quantities of five percent plus or minus, but final acceptance of these are at the discretion of Coyle Electronics."

"7. *Delivery to be made on or before date specified on purchase order and confirmed by vendor in acknowledgement. Deliveries made past the confirmed date are subject to return to vendor at discretion of Coyle Electronics.*"

John also noticed a standard insert that is always typed in on the face of the purchase orders going to vendors: "Coyle Electronics reserves the right to reject lots that have sampled defects in excess of two and one-half percent."

Just then the phone rang. "John, Bill Hargraves here." John knew that this was Ace's executive vice-president, and one of the four owners of that company. "I just got a disturbing call from a, let me see, Crystal Stover in your production operation, I think. She says they are turning one of our jobs back to us."

John explained what happened, and he filled Bill in on the slowly growing problems that they've been having with Ace's deliveries.

"Well, John, that order cost us a lot of money in rush orders and production ourselves. It's a special job and all for you. In fact, it's got your customer's own name stamped all over every piece. In all candor, I don't think your people can just reject that lot."

To which John replied, "Yes, but the terms of the purchase order are clear. There are two printed terms and one inserted term that are clearly in violation of your own acknowledgement on this one."

Bill, containing frustration said, "Yes, but Coyle Electronics has overlooked minor problems like this in the past. I don't think you have a leg to stand on with this one."

Case Question:

■ What is your assessment of the situation?

DLLP Chemicals, Inc.

Roy Gearing is director of Distribution for DLLP Chemicals, a large chemical firm with its main operation located in Southeastern Ohio. Roy just received the following notice from the Great Eastern Railroad Co.

Great Eastern Railroad Co.

May 4, 198X
To: Governor of Ohio
      Ohio Department of Transportation
      Shippers and receivers on the Columbus-Ohio River Branch Division
Subject: Notice of Abandonment Application   May 31, 198X

Notice is hereby given according to the requirements of Sections 10901 through 10905 of Title 49, United States Code that applcation will be filed at the Interstate Commerce Commission on May 31, 198X to abandon what is known as the Columbus-Ohio River Branch Division. This application covers the track from mile 1.002 in the Columbus yards to the end of the line at mile 87.34.

Comments may be filed at the Interstate Commerce Commission within 55 days of notice of application filing as appearing in the *Federal Register.*

signed

Roy was surprised, since his firm ships nearly 2,000 cars per year to and from the DLLP plant, which is located about three quarters of the way down the line.

Chemical traffic is largely in bulk form with about half of the shipments being made in Great Eastern Cars and the remaining in tank and covered hopper cars owned or leased by DLLP.

Roy called in Bill Detrick, DLLP's traffic manager. Bill was promoted to traffic manager ten years ago after he led a series of successful negotiations with Great Eastern and other railroads to lower their rates so that DLLP could move its product at very low rates.

Bill said, "I just opened the mail myself, and there it was. Surprised the heck out of me! We give them a chunk of business each year. And, it's not all to and from this plant either. We've got six other sites located on their lines."

Roy interjected, "This is some note! You know we can't move the stuff in and out of this plant in anything but rail cars. The bulk nature of the goods, the size of the cars, and the economies of the rates just make truck or any other mode prohibitive. The rail rates are what makes us competitive in the East and South."

"The real bummer, Bill, is that our competitors have met our prices by locating smaller plants right next door to some of our customers. Though their prices are higher from the diseconomies of smaller plants, it all washes out when you consider our production economy with the delivery cost added in. If we have to go to truck, we'll be eaten alive. I don't need to tell you, Bill, that this plant is one-half of the corporate sales."

EPO, Inc.

EPO, Inc. is a multi-million dollar manufacturing, mining, and marketing firm. Its sales are about $1 billion per year, and this is as a result of a recent merger of Elite Consumer Products with Peterson-Oden Inc.

The former Elite Consumer Products lines consist of tobacco, liquor, lawn furniture, snack foods, and a franchise fast-food chain. This end of the firm has twenty plants with ten separate purchasing operations. A main purchasing group was located at the former corporate headquarters to handle companywide standardization studies, conduct large negotiations, perform international purchasing, and handle capital investment acquisitions for all plants. Each plant purchased its own materials and supplies needs. The Elite system employs about a thousand purchasing personnel.

The Peterson-Oden Company traditionally has been in the mining of minerals, manufacturing of paints and other coatings, and it operates a chemical firm and metal fabrication company. Its purchasing operations have been centralized for the past ten years. This seems to have worked well, since the operations have all been within about one hundred miles of the main headquarters.

Gene Stenger is the new Purchasing vice-president for EPO. He was director of Purchasing in the Peterson-Oden firm. At his semiannual review with Mr. Cyrus Peterson, president, he was told, "This is a big merger for us. We are doubling our sales with this move. Why, next year we probably will be listed on the New York Stock Exchange."

"Listen, Gene, I've picked you to head up all the purchasing operations because you've shown your stuff here for the past ten years. You know how to keep a hand on things in all our operations. There appears to be too many loose ends in the Elite side. There are people there with the same titles running all over the place."

Gene replied, "Yes, sir, but they are spread all over the country. Besides, they have vastly different operations. Tobacco is different than liquor, and they are both different than, say mining."

Mr. Peterson interrupted, "Yes, but I built this company believing that business principles are business principles. The concepts of one activity are the same as those in another. It's just that the products might be different, or you might call them different names. The important thing is not to be out of touch with all that is going on. You've got to maintain tight control, that's all there is to it."

Gene went back to his office realizing now more than ever that this acquisition is different than the others.

Case Question:

■ What would you suggest?

Five Points Mfg. Co.

Tom Miller is purchasing manager for Five Points Manufacturing, a metal fabricator that buys copper, aluminum, stampings, and polypropolene items. In the summer of 1982 the metals and plastic markets were severely depressed with prices being below break-even levels for many suppliers. Even polypropolene had dropped in price. This is something Tom has not seen since that product first became available around 1960.

The 1981-82 recession caused many of Tom's suppliers to offer extremely favorable concessions. These consisted of discounting off the posted price, vendor freight payment, sixty and seventy-day payment terms with discounts for paying within thirty days, and long-term fixed price contracts with small escalator terms.

One of Tom's metal suppliers, Vulcan Metals, offered a fixed price contract for certain minimum quarterly quantities for twenty-four months starting October 1, 1982. The contract only allowed for an energy cost escalator, which would translate into one-half percent price increases for every five percent energy cost increase to Vulcan. Tom held a meeting with other departments about the quarterly quantities required by the contract. All agreed that these were about half of the firm's normal need for the metal, and they felt that the contract was certainly favorable to Five Points. It was signed.

Through the winter and spring of 1983 the contracted metal deliveries were made with three weeks of order placement, and the price held stable. Natural gas prices rose fifteen percent in the summer of 1983 thereby causing the metal price to increase from \$.51/lb. to \$.5177/lb. This was not much of a concern to Tom, since spot prices for the metal had climbed to \$.60 and more.

During late summer and fall of 1983 Tom started to experience lengthening in order cycle times and poorer product quality. His order cycle time increased to over twelve weeks, and it was increasingly erratic in terms of actual delivery date compared to promised delivery date. Survey data in *Purchasing Purchasing World,* and the NAPM's *Report on Business* all indicated faster delivery times than Tom was experiencing. Generally delivery times were shown to be in the six to eight week range, while prices had firmed to around \$.64/lb. Phone calls to some of the other vendors indicated the same.

Tom called Gary Gittings, purchasing manager for ABC Manufacturing, another customer of Vulcan's across town. "Gary, Tom here. You did all right in last week's golf game. How's the family? Looking forward to our trip to the shore next month. Our wives and kids sure talk about it a lot. Listen, I meant to ask you this last week, but what kind of service are you getting from Vulcan? I'm running into a log-jam with them."

"Well, Tom, as you know we did not go with the twenty-four month contract they offered last year. We stuck it out and now we are getting what we can month-to-month. No complaints, however. Even with the price rise, deliveries are OK, and our marketing people tell us our own prices cover these increases. I'd say our deliveries are averaging about five weeks, and we're paying the prices you see in the trade publications."

Tom then called Jim Smyth, sales manager for Vulcan. "Jim, I'd appreciate some answers about our delivery and quality problems." He explained the erratic and long delivery, poor quality, and his recent checking around with other suppliers and buyers.

"Well, Tom, I'm sorry to hear about your problems with us. This sure is news to me. I'll look into it, but this is the first I've heard of our production and distribution people causing any kinds of problems as these."

Later that day Jim called Tom back. "Tom, I talked to our production, warehouse and traffic people. They claim that with the business pick up, they have experienced some problems on the line with handling and shipping congestion, but nothing major. We've got four of our five lines up, and they are pushing three shifts to get things out as it is. Let me know if there is anything specific I might be able to help you with on this, Tom."

Case Question:

■ What is your evaluation of the above situation, and what would you advise Tom to do?

Fellowcraft Products, Inc.

Al Tyworth is head of Purchasing for Fellowcraft Products, a metal mining and processing firm in the mountain states. He is reviewing a capital investment proposal one of the company's divisions is going to present at next week's equipment planning committee. At this committee meeting all the firm's capital investment ideas are reviewed and finally accepted or rejected.

Al is familiar with this investment proposal. He and his people were initially involved with it many months ago when they were asked to work up the preliminary cost data for the machinery. One of Al's assistants even traveled to several of the supplier firms to find out as much as they could about this line of machinery. The reason for the interest here is that the firm buy these machines frequently. A spot check of the current capital inventory shows that forty-two are in use, and they last about five years.

The current proposal Al is looking at is:

Item: Pulverizor
Requesting Plant: Green River, WY plant
Reason: Replacement with cost improvement
Rate of return: 33%, on first five years

Initial cost:	purchase cost	$ 92,000
	freight	8,000
	installation	17,000
	net	$125,000
	tax credit	(10,000)
	total	$115,000

New benefits:	labor savings	$25,000
	energy savings	15,000
	overhead reduction	5,000
	maintenance savings	5,000
	total	$50,000

Al is particularly concerned about this proposal because it is the first one of these routine replacements that is using a new type of machine. All indications are that routine replacements that will follow from the other plant locations will also adopt this model. Al dug out the files on this machine, reviewed them, and called Bill Jensen, the proposing plant manager at Green River.

"Bill, Al Tyworth here, Got a minute? I was going over this proposal you're going to present next week. All looks good from this end; you've got my signature on it. But, listen, I'd like to propose something extra on it.

"The main motor drive on the machine is of the traditional type. It is similar to what you've had on all the current ones. But, this vendor also has a motor drive that comes in complete module form. It costs an extra $5,000, but it saves about $1,000 more each year in operating costs. The main costs would be on this one machine. It will be used to train the maintenance people in the other plants as well. After this one, the additional investment costs will be about $500 per machine and the benefits will still be about $1,000 per year.

"But, it will take about six more months to get the new module system. The benefits accrue later in the form of having to only buy and stock the modules. We won't have to dicker around with individual belts, seals, drives, shafts, and motors. As you know these create all kinds of inventory, paperwork, and tracking problems."

Bill was not as enthusiastic as Al had hoped. "I see you're point, Al. I can see the merits of what you're talking about. But, I've got to think about it. I'll let you know in a day or so."

Lion's Paw Manufacturing

Jim Gray is the purchasing manager of Lion's Paw Manufacturing, a producer of chemicals, rubber goods, and other products used in high-adhesion and traction applications. The firm purchases relatively standardized goods from several larger firms located on the east coast. Lion's Paw had grown from a garage operation in the late 1940s to a $30 million dollar firm employing over 400 persons.

The company buys from about one hundred regular vendors, with raw materials coming from nearly twenty firms. Many of the orders are for small amounts of specialty chemicals that are blended and further processed into much larger amounts of output. While some inbound moves are bulk by rail, many are in small quantities such as four drums on a pallet.

Jim Gray has sought inbound transportation efficiencies in order to reduce lead times and cut transportation costs. This is particularly a problem with the smaller orders. In other areas, he has sought ways to reduce the time in which material need is detected in his firm, and orders are processed and transmitted to vendors.

One of the prime vendors has arranged a meeting with Jim and his assistant, Hank Fortman. The vendor is represented by Erik London, the salesman who normally calls on Jim, and the vendor's computer systems director, Joe Zyra. Jim did not know what the meeting was about nor that Joe Zyra, whom he had never met, was going to be there.

"Jim, Hank, glad to see you again. This is Joe Zyra our information system man at our corporate offices. I brought Joe along today so we could talk about some of the details of a new program we are starting with our prime customers. I think you'll see that this will greatly help you out in order placement and tracing. Joe, why don't you fill them in on some of the details."

"I'd be glad to, Erik. As you know we have a fully automated order tracing information system. Over the past few years we've taken your orders over the phone or those that come in by mail and entered them onto our Info-Chem System. This system contains all our customer information, credit history, billing, inventory status, and shipment data. It is used to create pick instructions in the warehouses and we tap into it to consolidate small shipments for transportation economies to customers in proximity to one and another."

"We'd like to make the system even more efficient for both you and us by offering to place one of our data terminals in your offices right here. The way it would work is that you could turn the system on at 8:00 a.m. and leave it on throughout the day. You've been averaging two orders per day and often have as many as ten or twelve orders outstanding with us. Our monthly bills often contain as many as fifty orders. And, of course, you probably give us at least one or two calls a day just to trace some of them. This system will cut much of the clerical hassle associated with order placement, tracing, and billing verification."

Joe continued, "Of course, only your firm's information will be accessible to you. You can query the system for an order of, say, Rub-Glide 33. It will tell you how long it will take to obtain delivery of four drums. If it is currently on hand at our Laurel, Maryland warehouse, it will tell you two days. If there is insufficient quantity there, it will tell you four days, which probably means that Laurel is stocked out and it will be delivered to you from Cleveland. So delivery time and freight charges can be determined by just hitting a few terminal keys. Tracing is done by just requesting an "Outstanding Order Status." It will show all your current orders by your PO number, our customer order, and the expected delivery dates per the standards our carriers have between our warehouses and your plant right here."

Erik added, "The system will be installed at our expense, and the open data transmission line is billed to us by the phone company, There is no expense to Lion's Paw."

Jim Gray said it looked interesting and would like a few days to think it over. It was something that the firm never had before, though Jim heard a few other buyers in the local purchasing association saying their firms now had terminals from vendors. He left it that they would call Erik in a day or two.

That afternoon Jim saw Hank in the hallway. "Jim, that proposal sure sounds good. It should cut some of our clerical effort around here. And immediate order status will make it easier for us to give answers to the guys over in production. For another, it enables us to determine order lead times without having to call and talk to someone when we are shopping around for the lowest price or fastest delivery that day."

"Hank, I'll grant you all that, but I've got some problems with it. I'm not so sure it would save us any time or effort. We can call our orders in by toll-free number and we get a telex confirmation by usually the same day. Tracing is easily done via phone. We usually don't have too much of a problem with billing errors with them, either.

"It sounds nice, but I've got a few nagging things in my mind as well. For one, our top brass will think just because we get a nice new terminal from them that we are committed to buy from them and that we lose some of our objectivity in playing them off against some of the other vendors. For another, I'm not so sure it will really cut any lead time. In fact, I'm worried about the production people coming in here, turning the thing on and making quick production schedule changes based on whatever deliveries are shown on that tube. In a way, it will take us out of the picture."

Case Question:

■ Is this a good proposal for Lion's Paw? Are the pros and cons valid? What other factors should be considered?

Meridian Electronics

Bill Gibson, purchasing agent for Meridian Electronics just got a call from Hal Kingsley, marketing representative of All-Region Motor Lines. "Bill, I've got an answer for you on the rate reduction request you made to us last week. Right now you are shipping about 650 units in less-than-truckload quantities, and the old tariff rate has been $1.18 per hundredweight or right on the nose of $4.00 per case. We are prepared to offer you a truckload rate of $2.63 for 1,200 units or a single charge of $2,367.00 from the West Coast to your plant. this is a reduction of about thirty-four percent over your present rate. That took some sharp pencil work on our part."

Bill said, "That sounds good, Hal. Let me kick it around a day or so, and get back to you."

Bill knew that 50,000 units of the product were shipped inbound each year. The unit value is eleven dollars, and total ordering costs are only ten dollars per order. The problem cost in the company is the twenty percent cost of inventory per annum.

The departmental analysis done last year indicated that on an EOQ basis, 577 units were optimal from order and holding cost standpoints. In order to take advantage of a break in the transportation rates, they ordered an additional 73 for a total of 650 for the four dollar per unit rate.

Bill started to analyze the new 1,200 unit proposal from the standpoints of the other departments in the company. For one, the purchasing budget would benefit in several respects, but he was unsure of the reactions from other departments.

Case Question:

■ Should Bill take advantage of the new rate?

On-the-Square Department Stores

On-the-Square Department Stores is a chain located in a major metropolitan area in the Midwest. Buyers from each of the seven stores place daily orders with King Housewares in Pennsylvania. Jeff Coppola, King's traffic manager, ships all orders on the day of receipt. Since less-than-truckload shipments to On-the-Square's receiving center cost eighteen dollars per case, Jeff attempted to consolidate these moves with others going to the same city or region. Rate and service information for all options Jeff uses are shown here.

Option	Cost to Customer	Delivery Time
1) Less-than-Truckload moves	$18.00 per case	3 days
2) Truckload	$10.00 per case	2 days
3) Consolidation with other shipments to same city with pool distribution firm making final delivery to each customer	$14.00 per case	2–6 days

4) Stop-off (consolidated shipment
with many stops enroute to other
customers) $15.00 per case   2–8 days

On-the-Square orders a total of about 200 cases per day. Less-than-truckload transportation cost is prohibitive. It is only used for rush orders just before Christmas and in the June wedding season. Jeff is never able to make a full truckload to the receiving center, since 900 cases are needed for this. His next option is to use consolidated moves to the same city (Option #3), and if this can not be done, he uses stop-offs (Option #4).

Jeff is now traveling to visit with On-the-Square buying people with a new option which he calls "hold and ship." With this Jeff will accept orders any day of the week, but will hold them and only ship to On-the-Square on Fridays.

Case Question:
■ Is this a good program for the buyers, Jeff, and King Housewares?

Royal Electric Co.

Royal Electric Co. is a large manufacturing company with its headquarters and main plant located near St. Louis. Like many other firms in the 1980s, it is seeking ways to boost productivity through tighter inventory control. In particular, a task force has been put together to develop ways of reducing the amount of inventories between the various production activities at its different plants.

John Mullen, director of production analysis, is heading up the study. He visited Dennis Jaworski, plant manager of the New Jersey facility, to seek ways of reducing the inventory levels of goods that are produced at the New Jersey plant then shipped to the Missouri plant for final production. "Dennis, I know we keep daily tabs on each other in terms of what you are making and what the main plant needs. In fact, marketing gives production a weekly demand listing, and the main finishing plant's needs are constructed from that, with initial production needs being distributed to the other plants like yours as well as some of the outside vendors."

"Well, as you know John, our job is to clear the floor of all jobs every Friday. I don't think we had work left over a weekend since the late 1970s. And our raw materials are supplied like clockwork from many of the vendors we have within a thirty mile radius of this plant. I'll tell you the culprit, though. And that is the rail service between my plant and the Missouri one.

Dennis continued, "As you know we've got a fleet of covered hopper rail cars for movements of semifinished product to the main plant. Let me grab a file here for you that might shed light on this. Here it is." Exhibit I shows transit time for one way moves between the two plants as provided by the rail companies connecting them.

Rail Transit Time—Royal Fleet (Plant II to Plant I)
Cars RMFX 0001 through RMFX 10

Days	% of Moves (198X)
6	0%
7	15
8	33
9	40
10	12

Dennis continued, "Look, John. Right here we've got an average of about nine days of inventory floating between the two plants. This alone represents about $800,000 worth of inventory that belongs to the company, but has no use of for over a week's time. In fact, we need ten cars to handle this flow, yet I bet we could get by with fewer of them if the transit time was better. That alone would save us about $600 per car per month plus maintenance costs for every one we could eliminate."

John returned to the main headquarters with a plan to meet with Nick Fucci, corporate traffic manager, to see what would be done about the slow and erratic rail transit situation. On his first morning back, he was called into Al Viceri's office who is vice president of production. "John, how's the inventory study coming? Find anything in New Jersey?"

"Yes, it appears that we might be able to do something about the interplant moves. If we can cut these down, we can eliminate some work-in-process inventories."

Al continued, "Well, I guess we also should bring into this work of yours at this point the idea of a materials requirements planning (MRP) link up between the plants. We've been kicking it around for quite sometime, and now Mr. Gordon, the president, wants us to go with it. Why don't you integrate the two studies, since both these efforts of yours are directed in the area of inventory reduction."

John Mullen was thinking about this conversation with some misgivings, but put them aside when he met with Nick Fucci, traffic manager later that morning. "John, I just got off the phone with Denny in New Jersey. He filled me in on what you are up to. You might not believe this, but the rail service we've been getting is actually good in comparison to what it was in the late 1970s. We keep in touch with the railroads, in particular this one, with a direct computer link up that tells us each midnight where every one of our shipments are in the rail network. If any get too far behind regular times, we give them a call and they expedite them."

"Nick, We've actually got to get better service from them. There is too much float and it is too costly for us to maintain ten cars in that service."

"I agree, John. In fact, I'm meeting with the New York and St. Louis Railroad people later this week in a rate negotiation on another move we make. I'll bring it up then."

Friday morning, Nick Fucci called John Mullen. "John, Nick here. The railroad people understood our concern, and I threatened them with taking the traffic away. In fact, I've got a bid sitting on my desk from Fast Lane Motor Carriers for a two-day transit, 35,000 pound moves, for $490 each between the two plants. That looks good in comparison to the $900 for 100,000 lb rail moves that also cost us $600 per month on car leases."

Over the next few weeks John was involved with the initial steps on the MRP implementation plan. He visited other plants with the idea, and he called upon several vendors with some purchasing people. In particular, he visited two East Coast vendors who supply the other half of the product flow to the main plant along with the company's own New Jersey plant. He came away from them wondering if the Royal's MRP system could really count upon these outside vendors for reliable deliveries.

He stopped in at the New Jersey plant before he caught a flight back to St. Louis. "John, we just worked up data on the rail move improvement Nick Fucci talked to the railroad about. Here are the latest three weeks of movements.

Rail Transit Time—Royal Fleet (Plant II to Plant I)
Cars RMFX 001 through RMFX 10
March 3 to 24, 198X

Days	% of Moves
6	10%
7	45
8	30
9	10
10	5

Case Question:

■ What should John do?

TAA Manufacturing

Frank Smith is head of Purchasing for TAA Manufacturing, a medium-size electric motor and other electric product producer. Frank has continually encouraged his buyers to seek "competition." That is, on all work done, his buyers have to report weekly how each one of them took steps to develop greater competition among the suppliers. This was typically accomplished though buyers encouraging vendors to consider jobs in areas peripheral to the ones currently being handled. In many instances a buyer, with Franks review and approval, would award work to new vendors or existing vendors with different work.

Al Forman, a buyer in the transformer line, came into Frank's office to show him the latest on negotiations with a small, untried vendor called Clarence Engineering. "Frank, as you know, this firm has never been used before by us. Their Dun & Bradstreet report is fine, it's in the file. I gave a call to Jim Bursome over at Concept Electronics. They use Clarence for some work, and he says they've been fine in their work."

Al continued, "The reason I homed in on Clarence is that they are in a slump right now like most everyone else. It looks as though they are working at less than full capacity. I visited them twice. Once with an appointment. Their shop appears to be in good order. The second time I gave no notice. Even then, their operation appears to have few loose ends. They've got a good plant manager there. In fact, I'll tell Bill Frederick over in Personnel to keep him in mind when we have a production slot opening up. He might want to look at him."

Frank said, "Let's see what you've got on Clarence."

"Well, here is the file on a preliminary negotiation I've had with them so far. From information I pieced together from the Dun & Bradstreet and other sources I came up with this." Al showed Frank the summary income statement for Clarence.

Clarence Engineering—First 9 Months 198X

	Basic Company	TAA Job
Sales	$2,375,000	?
Direct Costs	1,662,500	$502,500
Gross	$712,500	?
Overhead	385,000	115,575
Net Profit	$327,500	?

Al continued, "I constructed the direct costs for our job based upon their labor rates and a good idea of their production productivity. They stand out well in that area. The problem I'm having is with the $115,575 they claim they need for overhead. So far, we've both narrowed down on these two cost areas. They claim that their overhead is almost always billed at 23% of their direct expense costs. That's where the $115,575 figure comes from."

Frank added, "Isn't this the job in which we were going to supply some dies? In fact, weren't they going to be able to use the dies after our job for one year on other work?"

"That's right," Al mentioned. "These were the dies we obtained from Sutton Engineering about a year ago. We paid for the right to use these dies in our own shop. We either return them or pay for them outright at the end of the year."

Frank asked, "How's their quality capabilities?"

Al answered, "This job calls for tighter specs than they are used to. I tried to get a handle on their quality assurance program. They don't have a formal one."

Frank said, "Let me look over all that you've got."

Case Question:
- What would you do from here?

Traveler Products Inc.

Shirley Hendricks is Chief Executive Officer of a division of Traveler Products, a multi-million dollar conglomerate. The company produces goods in the areas of housing, truck trailers, electrical components, food, and other consumer products. She is currently examining the performance of one of the division's accessory product lines with Jim Kirkham, the chief of the arm of the firm that produces these as part of the housing division. This part of the firm produces eighteen primary products of which five accessory items are a sideline.

"Jim, as you know, I'm here to review the entire operation in line with overall corporate matters. This is not a witch-hunt to try to dig up problem areas or make anyone look bad. In fact, this division has been doing well over the past several years. I'm only here to review the product lines with an eye toward the overall firm's strategies with all of its products."

A summary income statement for the products is as follows:

$ (000's)

	A	B	C	D	E	Total
Revenue	$80	$75	$114	$62	$43	$374
Dir. Exp's	50	60	50	58	22	240
Margin	30	15	64	3	21	134
Overhead	?	?	?	?	?	70
Net	?	?	?	?	?	61

The line has products in the growth, mature and decline stages. The discussion between Shirley and Jim centered around marketing plans, pricing, capital investment, strategies, and profit performance.

"Well, Shirley, Product A's pricing position is strong. The product has been growing well since we brought it out three years ago. It fits in nicely with one of our main products, and we can sell it with little overhead effort and expense. It is an item that will grow, but we'll have to acquire robotics to increase its speed of production and enhance its quality tolerances. That investment will run about $125,000. We'll work up the papers on it and send them along to the equipment investment committee."

"Product B is doing fine. No problems there. It's been in the line for about five years. I see no major changes in it for the coming year."

"Product C is a mature product. There is some competition with this one. The margins just aren't as strong. I don't know if you remember this, but this was the one that we started the accessory line with six years ago. We have to do some advertising and now provide dealers with a few concessions here and there to keep an edge in the market with this."

Shirley responded, "I remember when this item had a markup three times over production costs. This was the one that gave us the idea to go with the line altogether."

Jim continued "Product D is the rough one. Competition is eating this one away. It is easy to copy; there is no patent on it. There are a lot of outfits producing it. Heck, it is being made locally in garages and sold to dealers by everyone. There is no pricing strength in it, but we've kept it on just to have a full line represented. About a third of the sales shown here are government sales on tight contract. The rest are sold on consignment in order to gain the sales. We do everything we can to keep the production costs to the bone on this one."

"Now, E is the bright star. This one just came on line a few months ago. We've got this one introduced nicely and the market is beginning to pull it. No problems here."

"By the way the sixth product is coming on line. I don't know where we have room to produce it, yet, unless the plant goes to two shifts on our other products. But, this one has been in design and field testing for about a year. Its introduction costs are well within budget. But, once it catches on we'll need another automated process machine to keep up with projected demand. That investment will be about $200,000. . . pretty much the same as with what we're using on the other products."

"Well, thanks for the overview on the product line, Jim. Let me take this summary, since it is not detailed within the overall division's financial reports. I'd like to look it over in line with what you've told me here."

Case Question:

■ What would you suggest to Shirley?

Western Globe Enterprises

Clark Meigs is the head buyer at the Lexington, Kentucky plant of Western Globe Enterprises. Clark has been with the company since he graduated from college in 1966. He started out in the engineering department as a quality control analyst, and he transferred to various positions in the firm including purchasing at the Lexington plant in 1979. He has held progressively higher positions in Western Globe's purchasing operations. Much of this upward movement is due to improvements he has made in buying operations as well as his negotiation abilities and a professional approach to supervision and employee development.

Clark has developed a close friendship with John Thomchick, Western Globe's vice-president of purchasing at corporate headquarters in Chicago. John was head of purchasing at the Lexington plant when Clark was transferred there. John and Clark worked well together, and it was John's recommendation that Clark get his post when John was promoted to the corporate head of purchasing.

Up until 1983 purchasing was centralized through the Chicago office. The different Western plants handled all their raw materials purchases through the Chicago office, if these materials were used at more than one plant. Further, capital acquisitions of more than $25,000 were handled in a direct link with the Chicago office. Exhibit I shows the general reporting lines used by Western up until 1983.

The links between corporate and the various plants were fairly direct. This included communications links, budgets, and even personnel review and promotions. Clark's own aspirations are to someday seek John's position at corporate purchasing when John retires in a few years.

In 1983, Western Globe decentralized most of its plants. In a major reorganization, the company placed every product line on a profit and loss setting. This meant that the Lexington plant

■ **EXHIBIT I.**   *Western Globe Enterprises—Corporate and Lexington*

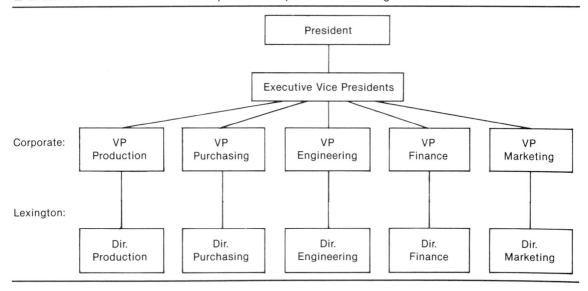

■ **EXHIBIT II.**   *Western Globe Enterprises—Corporate and Lexington*

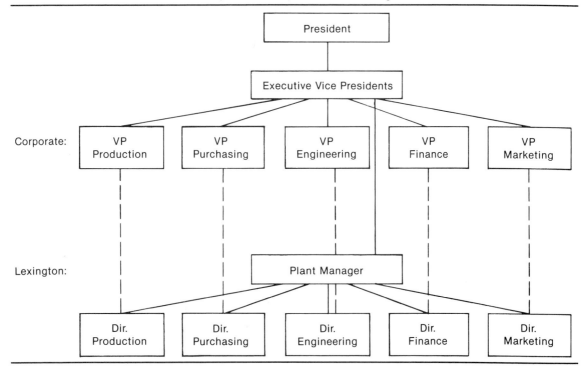

Index

†